DATE DUE

On Jameson

On Jameson

*From Postmodernism
to Globalization*

Edited by
Caren Irr
and
Ian Buchanan

STATE UNIVERSITY OF NEW YORK PRESS

Published by
State University of New York Press, Albany

For information, address State University of New York Press,
194 Washington Avenue, Suite 305, Albany, NY 12210-2384

Production by Michael Haggett
Marketing by Michael Campochiaro

Library of Congress Cataloging in Publication Data

On Jameson : from postmodernism to globalization / edited by Caren Irr and Ian
  Buchanan.
    p. cm.
  Includes bibliographical references and index.
  ISBN 0-7914-6591-8 (hardcover : alk. paper) — ISBN 0-7914-6592-6 (pbk. : alk.
  paper)
  1. Jameson, Fredric—Criticism and interpretation. I. Irr, Caren. II. Buchanan, Ian,
  1969–
  PN75.J3605   2005
  801'.95'092—dc22

                                                        2004030458

10 9 8 7 6 5 4 3 2 1

Contents

PART III.
TOWARD GLOBALIZATION

Introduction

Caren Irr and Ian Buchanan

To understand is to change, to go beyond oneself.
—Jean-Paul Sartre, Search for a Method

Globalization creates two major problems for the humanities today, each of which threatens the interlinked disciplines of literary study, philosophy, and history with obsolescence or—what amounts to the same thing—stasis. First, since the end of World War II and the weakening of the philosophical and political underpinnings of the European concept of humanity that followed the war, the humanistic disciplines appear to lack a distinctive object of study. Taking seriously, as one certainly must, the expansion of the category of the human to include not only the so-called civilized nations and people of the world but also those who seemed barbarous or primitive to the civilized has led to a situation in which all peoples, at least in principle, count as human. All are eligible for human rights, for example. This slow drive toward fulfillment of the universalist project of the Enlightenment has had a paradoxical effect for the humanities, however. Expanding the category of "the human" so that it more completely corresponds to the full range of human cultures suggests, on the one hand, a greater need for humanists as interpreters and analysts of culture. Yet, on the other hand, despite the arguably greater need for humanists with multilingual and cultural knowledge, in the context of the canon debate, for example, the expansion of the number and variety of objects of study has also (and perhaps rightly) been perceived as diminishing an earlier preservationist practice of the humanities. Multiplying the potential objects of study, on this account, effectively destroys the ideologically charged understanding of the humanistic disciplines as museums of genius, even though this destruction is and should not be total. The multiplication of objects of study in the humanities at present produces a lack of objects, because the task of attacking the old canonical practices must be ritually repeated. In the context of a global multiculturalism, humanists on both sides of the canon wars repeatedly exhume their antagonists in order to slay them over and over. The multiplication of objects of study in the humanities produces a necessary lack.

1

For related reasons, in many places, the humanities today are also characterized by a tremendous methodological diversity. This is in part the result of the fact that, with the postwar acceleration of global flows of communication and migrants, humanists now have much greater difficulty anchoring their projects in self-evidently national traditions. Limiting the set of objects with which one works by isolating a single national culture, and then further restricting inquiry to a single historical slice of the national tradition, increasingly seems to many students of culture an artificially narrow enterprise. Surely, if public discussion of globalization means anything, it means that we cannot simply assume the autonomy of distinct national cultures in the present—or in the recent and distant past. Yet, despite our ability to pose this methodological problem in the abstract, humanists have not attained the genuinely global perspective that would provide the necessary corrective. Under the influence of the new transdiscipline of Theory, many have examined cross-national themes—language or gender, for instance. This work has released powerful jolts of energy in the humanities, but many of these enterprises have also met their limits and revealed their own continuing assumption of a national or cultural home. The well-known discussion of the limited racial imagination in first-world feminism might serve as an instructive example here. Rather than obviating the search for postnational methods of study, theoretical approaches tend to revive the problem. "Theory" is one name for a methodological crisis in the humanities, not its resolution.

In this context, methods of analysis have continued to proliferate. Old historicists routinely sit across the conference table from new ones, while literary historians and "deconstructionists" argue over which "ism" should be added next to the hodge-podge list of "methods" studied in introductory courses. The grand promise of Theory as a meta-discourse that would unite and reposition the concerns of the humanistic disciplines has not utterly exhausted itself, but the wave of enthusiasm it inspired in the 1970s and 1980s does seem to many observers to have crested. We now find any number of so-called philosophical reactions—in the name of ethics, beauty, and so on—appealing to the logic of capitalist triumphalism and claiming to have won the day now that the period of struggle is over. Without some renewed commitment to identifying definite objects and methods of study, a drift into disorganized and unreflective pluralism can easily be imagined as the destiny of the humanities.

To this crisis, however, four solutions propose themselves. In the spirit of Samuel Huntington, for example, humanists might insist on preserving the categories of both "the human" and "the nation." Or, they might accept the political and philosophical critiques of the insufficiency of the category of "humanity" but retain, like Richard Rorty or Jürgen Habermas, some elements of the national tradition. Arguing for an essentially social democratic reform within the context of the nation, both Rorty and Habermas urge humanists toward finishing the project of modern nation-building in their academic forms. Alternately, we might remove "the nation" but retain a concept of "the human" as, arguably, Elaine Scarry has done in her well-known work on bodies in pain. Martha Nussbaum's neo-Aristotelian approach to emotions and human capabilities as universals might be understood in a similar vein. Finally, humanists might opt to revel in the uncertainty of a less charted alternative, operating with reference to neither the human nor the nation, inventing instead new provisional concepts from project to project, as need be. Each of these options has its benefits and promises to rebuild the humanities according to its own logic, but—faced with all of them—humanists still have the difficult task of sorting, ordering, and interpreting these options for our own enterprise.

It is for this vital task that the work of Fredric Jameson has been so immensely useful. Widely regarded as one of America's most important critics, and frequently described as America's most important Marxist thinker, Fredric Jameson has been at the forefront of the field of literary and cultural studies since the early 1970s. Author of such landmark texts as *The Political Unconscious: Narrative as a Socially Symbolic Act* and *Postmodernism, or, the Cultural Logic of Late Capitalism*, books that have literally transformed the critical landscape, Jameson is without doubt one of the leading humanistic intellectuals of our time. He is also one of the most eclectic—in the most positive sense of that term; he has written about philosophy, novelists from Proust to Stephen King, but also on drama, several different national cinemas, video art, easel painting, rock music, architecture and urban planning, as well as utopia and science fiction. In the process, Jameson's writing has produced an enormous map of cultural objects and theoretical schools, granting each some validity in its sector and coordinating each in relation to the others. Repeatedly throughout his career, Jameson has produced strong rewritings of major traditions with the explicitly pedagogical purpose of reinvigorating the humanistic or interpretive disciplines.

JAMESON'S CAREER

Perry Anderson explains what has made Jameson's scholarship so important and impossible to ignore during the late twentieth and early twenty-first centuries. Speaking of "Postmodernism, or, the Cultural Logic of Late Capitalism," the landmark 1984 *New Left Review* essay that would culminate in an award-winning book of the same title, Anderson wrote that it "redrew the whole map of the postmodern at one stroke—a prodigious inaugural gesture that has commanded the field ever since."[1] Here Anderson underlines the element most crucial to an understanding of both Jameson's career and the reception of his work: its essential boldness. In a similar vein, Colin McCabe also draws attention to Jameson's intellectual ambition; in the preface to *The Geo-political Aesthetic*, he remarks that "it can truly be said that nothing cultural is alien to him."[2] Indeed, any thorough review of Jameson's work cannot but marvel at its range. It uses materials in many languages, relies on familiarity with literally dozens of national histories, and exhibits knowledge of cultural texts that extends from urban planning and architecture through film and literature (in its many permutations) to contemporary video art. What distinguishes Jameson's work, then, is his ability to draw together this multiplicity of disparate strands, or straws in the wind as he put it, and reveal their integration. This totalizing impulse at once fascinates and infuriates his critics, but it is also what makes his writing so vital. By boldly and broadly synthesizing, Jameson has become one of those humanists who sets the agenda for critical discussion in our time.

For this reason, we can understand the history of Jameson's career as a sequence of Zeitgeist statements and the history of the reception of his work as a sequence of responses to those statements. To put it another way, the reception of Jameson's work can be divided between those who reset their compasses according to his successive mappings of the critical landscape and those who continue to use a preexisting map or propose their own. Critics in the first category do not necessarily accept Jameson's work uncritically; on the contrary, their work tends to be the most questioning. For instance, while in broad agreement with the general proposition that postmodernism is a left problem, Perry Anderson does not hesitate to offer his own criticism of its formulation. In the second category, we generally find critics who reject Jameson's totalizing view of history and (more important) historiography and therefore recoil from his paradigm shifting pronouncements. Critics of this orientation tend, for instance, to treat Jameson's work on postmodernism purely as style criticism and ignore its wider world-historical implications. What they ignore, in other words, is Jameson's central point: the idea that postmodernism is symptomatic of a deep historical undercurrent and therefore needs to be interrogated for what it can tell us about the new state of social and political organization. Instead, they approach it as an exposition on a certain moment in literary history and worry that Jameson has neglected particular exceptional texts.

This field-specific critical reception of Jameson's work on postmodernism is also instructive to consider because it reminds us of another crucial facet of his career—the fact that with each new book he speaks to a new audience and intervenes into a new field. This does not mean he ceases speaking to his current or past readers, only that he does not make a habit of preaching to the converted. In this sense, it could be said that with each new book Jameson builds an ever more complexly constituted audience. To summarize the nature of Jameson's relationship to his audience, we might turn to his remarks on Simmel in *The Cultural Turn*: "Simmel's subterranean influence on a variety of twentieth-century thought currents is incalculable, partly because he resisted coining his complex thinking into an identifiable system; meanwhile, the complicated articulations of what is essentially a non-Hegelian or decentred dialectic are often smothered by his heavy prose."[3] With the exception of the remark about Simmel being non-Hegelian, the main thrusts of this comment—the resistance to coining a brand-name system and the burying of ideas in heavy prose—clearly apply to Jameson himself, the former by his own admission and the latter by common consent. Perhaps most important, this quotation reminds us that Jameson's work, like Simmel's, has had an incalculable influence on a generation of scholars in a sometimes subterranean fashion.

In part this influence is due to Jameson's extraordinary work as a teacher of undergraduate and graduate students and his mentoring of junior scholars literally from all over the world. In interviews, Jameson has stated quite frankly that he understands the training of students as his essential task—that is, the task he can actually do, as opposed to those he might urge on others. What he invariably does as a pedagogue is give them the tools to carry out their own researches; thus, his students tend to work tangentially to his own oeuvre, though all the while retaining it as a touchstone. It would be an instructive, albeit difficult exercise to map the lines of flight Jameson's teaching has spawned, to see where his pedagogy has taken his students.[4] The essays brought together for this volume give a taste of that influence in just a few of the fields in which Jameson's work has been important.

Most consistently, Jameson's influence has been methodological. These methods of reading have been in evidence his first book, *Sartre: The Origins of a Style*. Although published at the height of the Cold War when a book on a Marxist was provocative in a way no longer properly recognizable to contemporary readers, the Sartre book has often been described by its critics as insufficiently political, or at least not *as* overtly political as its subject matter. And indeed it is true that Jameson does not dwell on the political content of Sartre's philosophy, but rather emphasizes the latter's style. This essential emphasis on the "unconscious" politics of style is developed further in his next book published a decade later, namely *Marxism and Form*. The second book is obviously political in both intent and content; it also changes the scale of the question of politics. While the first book concentrates on parts of the sentence, words, punctuation, and so forth, the next book tackles the sentence formation itself. In light of *Marxism and Form*, we can see that *Sartre* anticipates much of Jameson's later work in the way it analyzes style not as a problem of content, but rather as a problem of form.

This emphasis on form has been Jameson's principal means of politicizing the apparently non-political ever since. As he would put it in a later interview, "the form of the work of art—and I would include the form of the mass cultural product—is a place in which one can observe social conditioning and thus the social situation. And sometimes form is a place where one can observe that concrete social context more adequately than in the flow of daily events and immediate historical happenings."[5] In this sense, formal criticism provides the basis for his unique brand of dialectical criticism. In constructing this method, Jameson draws on a great many sources—Sartre, Adorno, Benjamin, and Lukács, to list only a few of the more notable—but none in so decisive a manner that we could resort to the shorthand of speaking in terms of direct influences. Jameson's work is no more Sartrean than it is Lukácsian, yet neither is it non-Sartrean or non-Lukácsian. Rather, in the best tradition of the dialectic, it is both at once, and of course it is also Adornian and non-Adornian, and so on. This is a long-winded way of saying that to simply describe it as Marxist-Hegelian lacks the subtlety, but more important the provocative ambivalence of Jameson's complex position. Caren Irr's essay in this volume addresses these questions further. And, as Roland Boer reminds us in his essay, Jameson coined the term "metacommentary" for a prize-winning MLA talk in 1971 to describe his method. Although in more recent years this term seems to have fallen into disuse, it has not ever been repudiated. The metacommentary's basic move is to conceive of the theory as a code, with its own rules of discursive production and its own logic of thematic closure. With the operating logic of the code in hand, Jameson then seeks to uncover the ideological pressures that are at work in this conception of text and textuality.

After *Marxism and Form*, *The Political Unconscious* was the next book to bring genuinely international attention to Jameson's work. *The Political Unconscious* was what contemporary publishers call a crossover book; it found readers on both sides of the Atlantic and in English Departments as well as Comparative Literature. The first of Jameson's published interviews were given in this period; likewise the first of many special issues of journals were dedicated to his work at this time. *The Political Unconscious* struck a chord in many quarters, as is obvious from its huge sales, but perhaps nowhere more so than in the then emergent field of cultural studies (in its Anglo-Australian permutation, rather than the American), which was establishing itself in the tradition of Raymond Williams, Richard Hoggart, and Stuart Hall. Cultural studies welcomed *The Political Unconscious*'s sophisticated method, which by synthesizing a number of concepts already familiar to the field, especially from the structuralist applications of Althusser and Lévi-Strauss, gave its early practitioners a means of exploring and articulating the ideological underpinnings of the popular and mass cultural texts they were engaging with.

Even as *The Political Unconscious* was being written, however, Jameson was already formulating his next major work. For many readers, this is the book that defines his work, although as Jameson himself has remarked it is rather peculiar to be associated with what one has criticized. This is of course the book on postmodernism, which began life as a lecture given at the Whitney Museum of Modern Art in New York in 1981.[6] The subsequent decade between the appearance of *The Political Unconscious* and its successor *Postmodernism, or, the Cultural Logic of Late Capitalism* was in many respects turbulent for Jameson: he moved from the French Department at Yale to the History of Consciousness program at U.C. Santa Cruz and from there to the Literature Program at Duke, with a short sojourn teaching in China as well. This restlessness was to a certain extent reflected in his work. His writing became more experimental in this period in that it branched into new areas and topics; in particular, he began to write more frequently and more directly on film. Until this point, he had only published two essays on film, one on *Zardoz* and the other on *Dog Day Afternoon*, but by the end of the decade he had two books on film.[7] He accepted a commission from Colin McCabe at the British Film Institute that resulted in a series of lectures given at the National Film Theatre in London in May 1990. This work was later published under the title *The Geopolitical Aesthetic*; in the same year, he also brought together a series of occasional essays on film and wrote a long piece on art deco to produce *Signatures of the Visible*. More interesting, though, and lending weight to the subterranean image previously given, he had at least four other substantial but ultimately unfinished projects ongoing throughout this period.

At the start of the decade, Jameson seems to have been preoccupied with completing or at least advancing a study of science fiction and utopias begun in a fairly ad hoc fashion in the previous decade. This preoccupation is visible in the conclusion to *The Political Unconscious*, but a short time after it seemed to stall, or else give way to newer or more urgent projects. At a conference held in Jameson's honor in 2003 it was announced that this project had at last reached the conclusion stage and that a book was imminent.[8] That more urgent project interrupting the science fiction and utopias book seems to have been a desire to write a kind of cultural history of the 1960s, which was begun but not completed—it did result, however, in three very important essays: "Periodizing the 1960s," "Wallace Stevens," and "Third-World Literature in the Era of Multinational Capitalism." The last of these three sparked a considerable furor, which Buchanan and Szeman examine in more detail in their contributions to this volume. Although Jameson himself designates "Periodizing the 1960s" and "Third-World Literature in the Era of Multinational Capitalism" as companion pieces to the program essay on postmodernism, that relationship has not yet been fully explored. By the same token, the Wallace Stevens essay has yet to be seen in its proper perspective as the first draft of an extended work on the birth and death of what Jameson calls "theoretical discourse." Not the least reason for this, of course, is that that extended work has not yet been published, although portions of it have been delivered under titles such as "What's Left of Theory?"

Other works in progress include one on Asian literature; in addition to the essay on third-world literature, which deals with Chinese and Indian writers as well as African writers, there are two other essays dealing with Asian authors.[9] Jameson also remains interested in rethinking modernist texts, particularly those with a postcolonial provenance or pertinence such as works by Joyce, Flaubert, and Rimbaud.[10] With regards to the latter, the 2002 publication of *A Singular Modernity* should not be seen as the conclusion to this project, but rather a late introduction that will perhaps hasten the project along.[11] Common to Jameson's most recent projects is the attempt to theorize a successor to modernism that is not yet properly a postmodernism; in this way they preface the postmodernism project in the typically Jamesonian manner of being "failures." What is curious about them is the fact that they followed the inaugural presentation of what Jameson himself describes as the program essay on postmodernism—it is almost as if having put forward that formulation, he had to then work around the edges of it, considering it from several different angles to see whether it really did hold up to scrutiny.

Since the mid-1990s, beginning with the last essays of *The Cultural Turn*, Jameson has begun to theorize the coming—some say achieved—transformation to the world-historical known as "globalization." In summary, Jameson's argument is that it may be useful to think of the concept of "globaliszation" as a "libidinalization of the market," by which he means that cultural production today increasingly aims to make the market itself desirable. There is, Jameson argues, no enclave left, aesthetic or otherwise, in which the commodity cannot reign supreme. Owing to the almost complete collapse of actually existing socialism and the generalized discrediting of Soviet communism that has followed, capitalism now imagines no actually existing alternatives. Indeed, Jameson fears that the very idea that there is or could be an alternative to capitalism has withered and died. As he puts it, today we find it easier to imagine the end of the world itself than an alternative to capitalism. Thus, more urgently than ever before, we are called on to uncover the inherent contradictions in the system and the ideological means by which they are papered over. In this respect, the Jamesonian project will always be, in the best sense of the word, an incomplete one.

CONCLUSION

It is to address the range, influence, and continuations of Jameson's work—especially the less widely considered work published since the celebrated *Postmodernism* book—that the essays collected here were assembled. These essays explore some of Jameson's central tenets, even as they reinterpret some of his legacy, turn some of his core concepts in other directions, and move out into worlds not necessarily encompassed by his own writings. These essays explore what his project can do and push the envelopes available in several of the humanistic fields influenced by Jameson's work—from Slavic studies, film criticism, literary history, to postcolonial studies and biblical criticism. These are also the essays of scholars who have come to Jameson's work because they are students of various corners of the Western Marxist tradition, and it might be best to describe this work as that of the "next generation" of the eclectic Western Marxist tradition. Centrally concerned with culture, politically disengaged from the Soviet experience, critically aware of the third worldist strains of the New Lefts of the 1960s, and deeply ambivalent about American claims to imperial authority, the contributors to this volume are, for the most part, members of a new generation of politically minded scholars of culture. This is a generation in the process of inventing its own predecessors and selecting its traditions from the arrays available in the so-called Supermarket of Theory. Having come intellectually of age at a time when poststructuralism was already a major institutional presence in the academy, this generation borrows and accepts some premises thereof, considering it as a fait accompli, a battle already fought and concluded, having left the usual detritus of battle strewn about. The essential act, then, for this intellectual generation is not the recovery of the materiality of the texts of culture or the affirmation of the so-called identities of the mid-twentieth century but rather the discovery, through the rich archives everywhere available, of the material operations of the present.

In short, the essays in *On Jameson* build on Jameson's central premises in hopes of addressing the contemporary crisis in the humanities with a reinvigorated version of critique: this Jamesonian critique is dialectical in character, rigorously conceptual and unafraid of polemic, materialist, and grounded (by various techniques) in the contradictory demands of particular discussions and national situations, while still reaching out toward global and fundamental questions. Together, these essays illustrate how and why politically conscious scholars think about global cultures today, how we teach, what objects we select, who we claim as methodological progenitors, and which future initiatives capture our imaginations.

With such big questions at issue, it should not be surprising that this collection ranges over Jameson's entire corpus and includes essays that consider everything from his early work on Sartre to his most recent on globalization, even though it focuses on the latter, newer material. This volume is especially concerned with reflecting on Jameson's most current work and demonstrating its potential to shape the emerging study of globalization. Furthermore, it treats Jameson's work as a complicated and interconnected whole. As the essays in this volume reveal in their aggregate, integrating these concerns is Jameson's emerging project of producing a critical theory of contemporary global cultures.

Following this introduction, the first set of essays is concerned with articulating four of Jameson's central concepts. Each essay in this section identifies the situation, tensions, and consequences of a core idea. Evan Watkins's essay situates Jameson's distinctive style of generalizing in relation to contemporary pragmatist assertions of the inconsequentiality of theory, arguing that Jameson's "generalization" operates as a distinctive form of historical abstraction. In her essay, Carolyn Lesjak contests a pro-praxis criticism of Jameson's work and underscores instead his distinctive form of socialist pedagogy. Roland Boer takes up the questions of interpretive method and outlines the derivation of Jamesonian exegesis, focusing on the crucial topic of "metacommentary." In his reconsideration of an argument made earlier in his monograph on Jameson, Sean Homer finds in *The Political Unconscious* in particular a concept of history and historicism especially suitable for the political situation of the new millennium.

The essays in the second part of this collection test particular Jamesonian concepts and hypotheses in readings of global cultures. Robert Seguin's essay considers a theory of cultural revolution latent within Jameson's work and outlines its consequences for an account of the work of intellectuals in the transition from an essentially feudal to a primarily industrial mode of production in the American South. Taking up the well-considered concept of cognitive mapping, Michael Rothberg reads a contemporary German documentary as a partial map of the transnational crisis of labor in newly integrated Europe. Taking the problem further east, Vitaly Chernetsky investigates the stalled encounter with Jameson's work and theories of postmodernism more generally in the post-Soviet sphere—especially Russia, the Ukraine, and the former Yugoslavia.

The third section turns most explicitly to the problems of globalization. It begins with a pair of essays reconsidering—from different directions and locations—Jameson's controversial discussion of third-world literature as national allegory. From Australia, Ian Buchanan situates these concepts in relation to the problem of the nation in contemporary theories of culture. From Canada, Imre Szeman traces the concept of national allegory through Jameson's work, arguing that both culture and "the nation" operate for Jameson as mediating categories; the nation in particular, Szeman argues, serves as an imagined alternative utopian space within globalization. Taking up the problem of utopianism, Caren Irr's essay reads Jameson's call for a return to Hegel not so much as a methodological regression but rather as a figure for his relationship to his American situation. These themes come together in Phil Wegner's synthesizing account of the twin drives of Jameson's work: historicization and totalization; Wegner aims to periodize Jameson's *oeuvre* to date and argue for the emergence of globalization as a new and central problem in his on-going meditation on the possibilities of the future.

Overall, it is the aim of this collection to consider Jameson's work, insofar as this is possible, in its own terms and with an eye to its pertinence for a problem likely to dominate the study of culture for some time to come: how to register simultaneously the commonalities and frictions that together have moved our present past a cultural condition we have sometimes called postmodernism and toward a political situation we are learning to describe as globalization.

NOTES

1. Anderson.

2. McCabe.

3. Fredric Jameson.

4. In a tantalizing couple of pages on the formation of the Marxist Literary Group, Sean Homer gives us the briefest of glimpses of what such a map might look like and in doing so demonstrates how useful a more comprehensive mapping would be. Sean Homer, *Frederic Jameson: Marxism, Hermeneutics, Postmodernism* (Cambridge: Polity, 1998), 27–31.

5. Jameson, "Marxism and the Historicity of Theory: An Interview with Fredric Jameson," *New Literary History* 29 (3) (1998): 360.

6. In private conversation, Jameson has suggested that, contrary to the public record, as set in place by Perry Anderson, the first airing of this piece actually took place in Germany. But this cannot be confirmed.

7. See McCabe, x.

8. See Jameson, "Nostalgia for the Present," *South Atlantic Quarterly* 88/2 (1929a): 517–537; "The Space of Science Fiction: Narrative in Van Vogt," *Polygraph* 2/3 (1989b): 52–65; "Science Fiction as a Spatial Genre: Generic Discontinuitues and the Problem of Figuraion in Vonda McIntyre's *The Exile Waiting*," *Science Fiction Studies* 14/1 (March 1987a): 44–59.; "Shifting Contexts of Science-Fiction Theory," *Science Fiction Studies* 14/2 (1987b): 241–47; "Science Fiction and the German Democratic Republic," *Science Fiction Studies* 11/2 (33) (1984b): 194–99; "Progress Versus Utopia; or, Can We Imagine the Future?," *Science Fiction Studies* 9/2 (27) (1982a): 147–58; "Towards a New Awareness of Genre," *Science Fiction Studies* 9/3 (28) (1982b): 322–24; "Futuristic Visions that Tell Us About Right Now," *In These Times* 6 (May 1982c): 17; "SF Novel/SF Film," *Science Fiction Studies* 713 (22) (1980): 319–22.

9. See Jameson, "Soseki and Western Modernization," *Boundary 2* 18 (3) (1991): 123–41; "Literary Innovation and Modes of Production: A Commentary," *Modern Chinese Literature* 1 (1) (1984): 67–77.

10. Jameson, "Modernization and Imperialism," *Nationalism, Colonialism and Literature (Field Day Pamphlet 14)*, Derry, 1988; "Flaubert's Libidinal Historicism: *Trois Contos*," *Flaubert and Postmodernism*, eds. N. Schor and H. Majewski (Lincoln and London: University of Nebraska Press, 1984a), 76–83; "Rimbaud and the Spatial Text," *Rewriting Literary History*, eds. T. Wong and M. A. Abbas (Hong Kong: Hong Kong University Press, 1984d), 126–41.

11. See Jameson, "Flaubert's Libidinal Historicism: *Trois Contos*," 76–83; "Wallace Stevens," *New Orleans Review* 11 (1) 1984c): 10–19; "Rimbaud and the Spatial Text," *Rewriting Literary History*, eds. T. Wong and M. A. Abbas (Hong Kong: Hong Kong University Press, 1984d), 66–93; "'Ulysses' in History," 126–41.

Part I

Central Concepts

1

Generally Historicizing

Evan Watkins

One of the many enduring legacies of New Criticism is the expectation that literary criticism as practiced in the university has "real world" consequences. It matters. Indeed, several decades of sustained critique of New Criticism has taken that expectation as a given, albeit different consequences than originary influences like Tate, Ransom, Blackmur, or Brooks might have imagined. Hence, whether critique took the form of identifying ideological congruities with Cold War politics or challenging the exclusionary closure of a high literary canon or the stratifying elitism of enforcing a higher literacy beyond the ordinary skills of everyday practices, the assumption remained that the parameters of New Criticism as normative critical practice in the university contributed mightily to the real world dominance of a reactionary politics. Correspondingly, if I can abbreviate rather melodramatically for effect, much of the excitement of a vast range of post-New Critical developments arose from a perceived potential to reorient critical practices toward a more radical politics or at least an alternative ensemble of counterhegemonic consequences.

Perhaps the most noticeable exception is Stanley Fish, who has balanced most of his late career on the premise that literary criticism as practiced in the university has almost no real world consequences beyond preserving the disciplinary coherence of a field of study to be inhabited by those who take great pleasure in the field of study. Not a popular position, needless to say, and I should make clear immediately that I have no intention in what follows of defending Fish's marvelously unreal severing of the real world from academic literary study. Nevertheless, keeping in mind Fish's often repeated injunction from *Professional Correctness* that interpreting the unique and inexhaustible specificity of literature supplies the necessary intellectual coherence of the field of study, it's worth remembering that a New Critical expectation of consequences was always a piggybacked dream in any case.

For the critical interface with the real world was made dependent on the immediate primacy value accorded to literature. Thus, as Edward Said has often remarked, the embedded chain would run its course from the value of the text to the value of what as critic. I can reveal about the value of the text to the assumption that the inexhaustibly specific value of the text could sustain inexhaustible consequences to whatever could be said about the text as criticism. Unlike Fish, however, whose logic requires him to jettison the last move of Said's ironic chain, a New Critical expectation of consequences bequeathed one of the more famous New Critical "ironies" for late followers like Murray Krieger to struggle over: on the one hand, literature had to be severed from its powers in the world or it couldn't legitimately be isolated as a special subject for critical expertise in the first place; but, on the other, if severed irrevocably, there'd be no ground or reason for critical expertise. Hence, Krieger's virulently proliferating imagery of "the text" as mirror turning into window turning into mirror that rivaled Tiffany at its most intricate.

Krieger aside, however, the forced dependence of an expectation of consequences on some version or another of inexhaustible specificity has long outlived New Criticism and helps account in part for what has become one of the more familiar narratives about post-New Critical "theory" reputations and influence. Taking Derrida as perhaps a key illustrative figure in this narrative, though arguably by now Foucault would serve almost as well, roughly the story goes like this. What had seemed to be Derrida's immense, pathbreaking intervention was nevertheless gradually assimilated into a routine of business as usual by a great many people in a great many academic departments around the country. As then fine-tuned to an always greater specificity indeed, subsequent Derridean-inspired work began to look like tap dancing in a smaller and smaller circle until finally the glare dissipated and we've been left with only an ultimately fruitless debate still surfacing here and there. Perhaps there was something inherent in his original efforts after all that predisposed the work toward a sadly routine assimilation, or, in the more sinister version, made it unfortunately susceptible to an ensemble of conservative interests eager to excise its more radical possibilities toward the end of preserving business as usual. Alternatively, there's the claim that what I've portrayed as a gradual assimilation was in fact a necessary task of extracting from all the excess and hyperbolic exaggeration a core of valuable insight that could be developed into the service of sound scholarship. Either way, for better or worse the thrill is gone and things have moved on. Whatever inexhaustible specificity available seems never to have been quite inexhaustible enough to sustain the initial momentum.

Although not very persuasive in such bald summary, as appropriately nuanced in detail, it's a narrative that has begun to appear almost a commonsense. By way of contrast, there's reason to recall that Jameson's career and reputation have followed a rather different itinerary. For while the arrival of *Marxism and Form*, *The Prison-House of Language*, and "Metacommentary" so close together seemed to make Jameson an instantly visible presence, even that initial impact registered differently. It was as if—inexplicably enough, given the dazzling range and the unfamiliarity at the time of much of his material in the United States—he was somehow already unfashionably belated, already a kind of immense and impressive monument at which subsequent generations of student tour groups would have to be detained at least briefly before they were encouraged to pass into the territories where the really new work was being done. I don't mean at all to downplay his influence on the work of others, myself included, and I certainly don't mean to ignore his own incomparable willingness over a long career to engage at length not only with every new arrival on the theoretical scene, but also with a multiplicity of material that might otherwise never have received much critical attention in the university at all. Nevertheless, I think his influence has been distanced rather than inaugural like that of Derrida or Foucault, or even those critics in the United States who positioned themselves directly in line with such figures. It was distanced in that he couldn't be ignored, especially given such an impressive range, but there were also always qualifiers that arrested the momentum of movement and direction almost before they were under way.

Consider, for example, the litany of nostalgias attributed over time to his arguments: nostalgia for "dialectic," for "Hegel," for "idealism," for "totalizing," for "master narratives," for "History" (in caps of course), for "modernism"—all have featured prominently as reason for arresting any momentum in the direction his arguments take. It seems almost perverse that someone who has so carefully forayed into so many new territories on so many occasions throughout such a long career should so continually be saddled with the label of *nostalgia*, of all things. But there it is, made all the worse perhaps by the fact that nostalgia has of course figured with greater and greater prominence in Jameson's own inquiries. It's tempting to remark that after all his characteristic morphing of disparate figures—as, for example, in the sequence from *The Political Unconscious* in which Althusser is folded backward piece by piece into a digitally remastered Lukács—positively invites a game of Name the Nostalgia behind the effort. There may indeed be a point to all this; I'm in no position to know exactly what Jameson is or isn't nostalgic about. But I want to argue first of all that the anomaly his career and reputation represent has to do more immediately with his refusing to assume, beyond the obligatory lip service required of all of us, the inexhaustible recesses of specificity. Or, to put it a little more bluntly, Jameson *generalizes*, inveterately and persistently. Second, I want to argue the political value of his peculiar way of generalizing, despite the trouble it causes.

Late in *Marxism and Form*, Jameson returns to a theme first stated in its preface: "The dominant ideology of the Western countries is clearly that Anglo-American empirical realism for which all dialectical thinking represents a threat, and whose mission is essentially to serve as a check on social consciousness. . . . The method of such thinking, in its various forms and guises, consists in separating reality into airtight compartments, carefully distinguishing the political from the economic, the legal from the political, the sociological from the historical, so that the full implications of any given problem can never come into view; and in limiting all statements to the discrete and immediately verifiable, in order to rule out any speculative and totalizing thought which might lead to a vision of social life as a whole."[1]

The language in this passage evokes a whole series of already long familiar conflicts between a British-dominated "analytic" philosophy and Continental philosophies, and behind that several centuries of contentious debates over empiricism and idealism. But of course the immediate reference—let alone the urgency of the message—isn't such philosophical oppositions at all. Rather, it involves what Jameson later in his career would identify as ideological "strategies of containment" whereby social conflicts could be "managed" by never being allowed full visibility within a network of "airtight compartments" that parceled out the limits of permissible inquiry. And, more directly, the passage points to the discipline-based academic structuring of U.S. universities such that economic issues, for example, could be treated as if they involved a separable economic "content" that required a special expertise to understand and that was unavailable as such even to those in flanking disciplines like political science, sociology, or psychology.

Yet, characteristically, Jameson doesn't choose to elaborate much of anything about the historical development of this academic structure, about its material conditions of existence within the complex ensemble of relations that both links and separates academic production of knowledge from other elements of the social formation, even about those "ideological" connections putatively embedded within the university through the culture at large. As I implied earlier, his language instead functions to reorient his readers' perceptions back onto the more or less familiar ground of philosophical debate, albeit now charged with a pointed political identification of the stakes as complicit with ideological practices. The effect can be deadening—well, so what, we've already been through all *that*—but perhaps more tellingly, given the urgency of the message, the passage can seem to foreclose precisely the kind of specific inquiry he would seem to be endorsing. That is, rather than turning with now "uncontained" eyes toward a thorough critical investigation that would make visible the complicated ideological complicities that have shaped the historical development of disciplinary structure in U.S. universities, we as readers are invited to revisit familiar debates with a heightened awareness of their political positioning. And in those circumstances it's perhaps little wonder that readers might well fasten on neither the argument nor the message, but instead begin to suspect behind the passage some deep-seated nostalgic investment in the *idea* of dialectic.

More immediately, however, the difficulty again is that Jameson generalizes. Rather than enabled by the Jameson passage to plunge directly into this rich potential for inquiry, as a reader one finds oneself instead pawing more and more frenetically at webbing after sticky webbing of ghostly philosophical debate thrown into the air by his language. Thus webbed and encumbered, it's hard to allow oneself the luxury even of daydreaming a drama of effects immediately at the payoff end. At the same time, however, without simply arresting the flow of the passage and ignoring the present urgency of his message entirely, it's never quite possible either to relax into a slow, sustained, sound scholarship revisiting the intricacies of those debates with a now slightly skewed fresh vision—and maybe as well getting the dates a little more accurate in the process. Denied both the inexhaustible specificity of potentially radical inquiry and the infinitely specific explorations of good scholarship, we're left instead to backpedal through wider and wider circles of generalization that seem to accumulate like a magnet glittering small particles of detail on every rhetorical turn.

I've picked my Jameson passage deliberately as dated and, while hardly an aside, perhaps nevertheless an acceptable kind of generalization about the implications of an argument whose primary substance lies elsewhere. Let me then turn to another passage in which the apparent generalizations at work seem far more integral to the initial unfolding of a long and complicated argument. I have in mind his notorious comparison of Van Gogh and Warhol that first paths readers into *Postmodernism, or, the Cultural Logic of Late Capitalism.* At this still very early moment in a long book, one finds the following: "But there are some other significant differences between the high-modernist and the postmodernist moment, between the shoes of Van Gogh and the shoes of Andy Warhol, on which we must now very briefly dwell. The first and most evident is the emergence of a new kind of flatness or depthlessness, a new kind of superficiality in the most literal sense, perhaps the supreme formal feature of all the postmodernisms which we will have occasion to return in a number of other contexts."[2]

This setup seems a rather simplistic compare-and-contrast between high modernism exemplified by Van Gogh's shoes and postmodernism exemplified by Warhol. That is, Jameson looks primed to begin a generalized account of typical postmodern characteristics by way of using Van Gogh and Warhol's images as conveniently shorthand examples. Nevertheless, the heightened rhetoric of comparison produces trouble almost immediately. From where exactly does "flatness or depthlessness" emerge? And what would be "the most literal sense" of superficiality? Why "*perhaps* the supreme formal feature," and who's ranking formal features—in contrast to content-features?—to begin with? How did "postmodernism*s*" suddenly acquire its "s?" And on and on. But of course none of this really matters, because before you know it with the casualness of "then," it appears "we must surely come to terms with the role of photography and the photographic negative in contemporary art of this kind; and it is this, indeed"—casual become causal—"which confers its deathly quality to the Warhol image, whose glaced X-ray elegance mortifies the reified eye of the viewer in a way that would seem to have nothing to do with death or the death obsession or the death anxiety on the level of content."

It's not entirely clear by any means, however, whether the referent for such a striking turn of phrase as "whose glaced X-ray elegance mortifies the reified eye of the viewer" is a newly glimpsed insight into the specificity of Warhol's image or of the photographic negative, where either might be pursued later in even more detail; or whether, instead, its peculiar turn offers a tentative limning of some much larger pattern, to be focused later, embracing both Warhol image and negative as the argument gradually widens its scope. In other words, what begins as a simple and rhetorically balanced compare-and-contrast seems rather quickly to have lost direction. Are we poised to go *into* the specificity of the Warhol image (or of the photographic negative) in all its distinctness from Van Gogh, or to spin *out* from both Warhol and negative toward a general pattern embracing a host of other examples as well, and that will gradually make conceptual sense of that distinctness? In any case, by the time one reaches the string of "or" phrases that follow immediately, the moment for decision seems to have slipped away.

Before pursuing this particular passage any further, however, I should say immediately that the prevailing response to the postmodern book would suggest that I'm already creating far more trouble than necessary. It has seemed clear enough that the ultimate direction of argument is toward the implacable generalization of the postmodern as now an historical dominant whose force field saturates the present such that no gesture can be even relatively immune. It may be true that this conclusion first makes an appearance under the sign of a rhetoric adopted from Raymond Williams parsing out residual, emergent, and dominant directions always coexisting in uneasy combination at any given temporal moment, with the outcome still up for grabs. But, by the end of the book, the circle seems snapped shut around the vast intricacies of postmodern presence evident everywhere, against which—as now great numbers of numbed themewriting students might attest—neither cognitive mapping, the reversal of ideology into utopia, nor the outside-in explosive force of the postmodern sublime seem to promise any particularly concrete effects at all, except maybe another theme/dissertation/book or two and some gleeful Fish-like "I told you so."

In other words, the response to *Postmodernism* has read Jameson's argument as conforming to the idea of generalization so easily targeted for critique by a pervasive assumption of inexhaustible specificity. For once that assumption is taken for granted, then it seems entirely obvious that generalization must involve a willed flight from the specific in all its historical embeddedness. One proceeds instead by a process of merely accumulating detail after disparate detail toward the goal of elaborating a pattern that can yield some larger conceptual intelligibility to the accumulated web of example. The proof of Jameson's complicity with generalization in this sense comes not only from the alacrity with which he leaves behind his own chosen textual examples like Warhol, but also in how he seems predisposed in any case toward reviving a value to the work of critics like Frye, for example, or those more openly taxonomic texts of a nascent structuralism, that in one way or another conform to such an itinerary of generalization. Like the predecessors he privileges, Jameson too seems driven by a desire to *over*generalize at the expense of ignoring the irreducible contingencies of specific texts and cultural moments.

Thus, not surprisingly, the book was greeted almost before publication with a proliferation of examples that "escape" Jameson's postmodern iron cage—as doubtless could be more clearly recognized had I had in this forum time to elaborate a reading of Crucial Text X a little further. Permission to generalize, that is, requires a casual dismissiveness like my own preceding sentences, hardly that characteristic Jameson unwillingness to leave anything behind as he wheels more and more widely from this year's sensation right on back through Sartre, Adorno, Lukács, even Frye and New Criticism. In marked contrast, several decades of theory work remind us over and over that if "history" can now mean anything at all, it must lie in the incomparably specific, from the "a" of difference to the microphysics of proliferating power and Deleuze's explosive singularity—not assuredly in receding waves of impedingly wider generalities. Like the passage I cited earlier from *Marxism and Form*, with the much larger scope of *Postmodernism* there is as well the all too familiar frustration of any expectation for immediate consequences. All this, and for what? Not a question, I would argue, ever posed in quite that way on first registering the initial impact of someone like Derrida or Foucault with any shock of understanding at all. For with the shock came something like the certainty of much further and still newer work that could be pursued with always greater specificity. And pursued it was, right into the sands of that familiar narrative of a triumphant Business as Usual/Sound Scholarship, depending on where you stand.

Stanley Fish's explanation for that pervasive narrative that I noted earlier of assimilation into business as usual is, as usual, elegantly simple. "Critics who begin with 'revolutionary' aspirations," he argues in *Professional Correctness*, "regularly lament the fact that their efforts have been appropriated—and, to add insult to injury, rewarded—by the very institution they sought to transcend."[3] The reason, again, is simple: "The face of the practice [of literary criticism] may continually change as new topics are drawn into its orbit, but, once in, anything 'new' is immediately rendered very familiar by the questions—with what does it cohere? of what is it a conversion? with what is it in tension?—the practice is obliged (by its own sense of itself) to ask."[4] Granting for the moment Fish's logic, arguably one immediate effect of Jameson's generalizing move is to forestall the temporal interval required by the narrative. That is, the long, slow decline from "revolutionary aspirations" to "very familiar" seems dramatically foreshortened as Jameson's ever-widening circles of generalization enact it at every rhetorical turn. Thus, perhaps what should strike readers most immediately about the "postmodern" conclusion is less the putatively implacable closure of a cultural dominant than the now immense and newly *familiar* web of cultural practices made visible in order to reach the conclusion.

For neither the visibility nor the familiarity depends on some reimportation of postmodernism back into the coordinates of the modern. Indeed, the much vexed question of whether typically postmodern characteristics might in fact have their origins much earlier seems barely to interest Jameson at all. What does interest him, I would argue, or maybe more exactly the rhetorical motivation of his generalizing turns, lies in the power of generalization to familiarize by lifting out and connecting the edges of otherwise embedded cultural forms and vectors of motion. Under the spell of that assumption of inexhaustible specificity, however, the "lifting out" can of course be isolated and denounced as the moment of fatal *abstraction*, forever marking the result as ahistorical, jerked free of history by the unseen force field of nostalgia for—whatever takes one on the occasion. But it's worth remembering that in Fish's logic at least, it's something very like that moment of abstraction that instead marks entry *into* the historical constitution of disciplinary practices.

Recall, again, the sequence of Fish's reasoning: "but, once in, anything 'new' is immediately rendered very familiar by the questions—with what does it cohere? of what is it a conversion? with what is it in tension?—the practice is obliged (by its own sense of itself) to ask." Those questions after all—"with what does it cohere? of what is it a conversion? with what is it in tension?"—function to lift out distinct sets of practices from their embedded temporal moment in the disciplinary field and into some arc of relation with the "anything 'new'" itself now rendered familiar by the emergent relation. Thus, by an extension of Fish's logic, the "shocking" conclusion to *Postmodernism, or, the Cultural Logic of Late Capitalism* isn't really the implacable dominance of the postmodern, but rather the implacable suturing of *postmodern study* into the disciplinary practice of literary criticism as that practice continually incorporates new topics and reorients itself accordingly.

Fish, however, is an epistemologically locked-in logician and not even a disciplinary historian, and with Jameson's argument available by way of contrast it's not particularly difficult to mark the magic moments that sustain Fish's unfolding argument—"but, once in," as if commas could do the work of history, and "obliged (by its own sense of itself) to ask," as if the ghost in the machine could spew its appropriate questions. For returning finally to that striking phrase I had isolated in the passage from very early in *Postmodernism*, I want now to suggest that it has to do with neither Warhol nor photographic negatives directly. Rather, it functions as a shorthand notation of effects that emerge into visibility as the passage lifts the edge of the Warhol image from the forced contact with Van Gogh toward connection with the photographic negative itself now similarly "abstracted" by edge. The passage moves on so rapidly because the rhetorical motivation, again, is neither "in" to Warhol or "out" to generalized pattern, but continually on around the suddenly released momentum of now visibly emergent effects. Little wonder that already by the end of the paragraph one finds oneself at "some more fundamental mutation" of both "the object world" and "the disposition of the subject," offered less as generalizations that might "explain" the impact of Warhol's image than as the functional means of registering generally the continual motion of things happening.

Because for Jameson the only specificity that really matters is an historical specificity of effects, and the effects that matter historically can never be determined by what's "in" anything—neither the inexhaustible text nor the disciplinary field. *There's no point* in testing Jameson's assertions by a reading of Van Gogh or Warhol or photographic negatives or any of the billion or so other texts that come swimming rapidly into view as the argument moves on. The question of whether "internal" textual evidence has been forced by Jameson's reading into conformity with his generalizing template of the postmodern is at best irrelevant and at worst an obstacle to recognizing where Jameson's rhetoric would lead us. Which is never "into" the text's irreducible specificity or "out of it" and toward some larger overarching pattern, but rather around the mazy web of effects made visible from the proliferation of contacts emerging at every turn of the argument.

Thus, what has already been left behind by Jameson in this after all still very early passage in a long book is not some now dated boundary line of "the literary," but rather the sustaining force of that inexhaustibility. That is, the lure of the inexhaustibly specific is always a trip in, to which Jameson opposes the powers of generalization as, precisely, the abstracting process of lifting out that can mark a limit to anything that emerges, however, only at the point of connection to something else. For the limit that becomes connection also marks the beginnings of effects that matter. Hence, if paradoxically, it is only through such a process of retrospective generalization that any ensemble of effects becomes conceptually visible as a specificity that matters as its limits, too, turn connection.

"Always historicize" comes at the expense of always having in view the limits of one's critical practices without ceasing for a moment to practice criticism of text after text. As retrospective generalization at its most politically urgent, the "postmodernism" of Jameson's argument is less an implacably overgeneralized description of an historical moment than an historicizing recognition of effectual tendencies. For effects as they register into the present are rarely over, nor would it be possible to mark such a moment with the means of retrospective generalization at hand. As the ending to the book should make clear, postmodernism in any case is far from over, even though it's impossible as yet to know where its effects will tend in the future. Against the grain of so much literary scholarship, Jameson's historicizing doesn't project description at all, any more than it works by example. Yet even though description and example remain the staples of the practice of criticism, it is as critic that Jameson directs us through the receding webs of passage from one text to another across the span of the argument.

For Fish it must be obvious that the practice of literary criticism is immediately and finally different from politics. "One might think," he argues in *Professional Correctness*, "that it would be possible to pay a double attention, at one moment doing full justice to the verbal intricacy of a poem and at the next inquiring into the agendas in whose service that intricacy has been put. But here one must recall the difficulty of serving two masters; each will be jealous of the other and demand fidelity to its imperatives."[5] In his "Afterthoughts" in *English as a Discipline*, responding to Fish, Paul Lauter remarks: "It is equally true that such a binary [between political work and the interpretation of meanings] obscures what we actually do both in figuring out what a poem 'means' and in carrying out political work."[6]

In refusing what he perceives as Fish's binary, Lauter would seem faithful to the imperative that governs that passage from *Marxism and Form* I quoted at the beginning of this essay. That is, when Fish seems intent on keeping literary criticism and politics in "airtight compartments," Lauter in contrast would insist on an inevitable intercontamination "so that the full implications of any given problem" *might* in fact begin "to come into view." Fish speaks as it were from a now rapidly disappearing disciplinary structure of distinctness; Lauter instead seems far more tuned to a set of circumstances where nearly every field from computational biology to TOESL training seems relentlessly determined to mobilize every conceivable energy of inter, trans, or adisciplinarity across boundary lines. Despite their obvious differences, however, there remains a sense in which the division of opinion between Fish and Lauter preserves a vision of the inexhaustibility of the literary, in much the same way that the putative interdisciplinarity of the contemporary university continues to feed on the structuring of the university into fields of expertise. For Lauter, the process of figuring out what a poem means inevitably intersects the political precisely because in all its specificity there are no ways to mark the limits of the literary text. If one goes far enough "in" with interpretation, and refuses the premature arrest imposed by Fish, political effects always happen.

In contrast, part of the great political value of Jameson's work is his refusal of this naturalized progression. Like Fish, he recognizes well enough that the further "in" to the literary text one proceeds by interpretation, the more locally literary, even disciplinary specific the whole process becomes. But while for Fish that forever excludes political practice as another and second "master," for Jameson literary texts can be the occasion for a critical politics. Texts *aren't* their effects; it's impossible to recognize the latter, no matter how well you've grasped textual meanings. By means of his historical generalizing, however,

Jameson can make available a visible means of recognition across the contact edges of his textual itineraries. The result is politics and it is literary criticism, without ever depending on the magical assumption that one just might turn into the other before your very eyes.

By implication, however, I've also suggested my reasons for positioning the anomaly of Jameson's career in the way I have at the beginning of this essay. Unlike Derrida or Foucault or other "masters" of theory, you can't follow this act. The historicizing of retrospective generalization doesn't open new territories in which to work, nor does it promise a still further specificity to engage. Likewise, rather than identifying an inevitable temporal arc of failure, "revolutionary aspirations" (to borrow Fish's phrase) and business as usual coincide almost from the beginning. The compensation, however, is that Jameson never becomes unavailable for use. Maybe you can't do this for yourself; it's not exactly clear what it might mean to "follow Jameson's direction." But it is always possible to learn from his work how to do what you do far better and in more historically responsible ways. Jameson generalizes. It's one of the only ways historical understanding has gotten "in" to the practice of criticism at all.

NOTES

1. Frederic Jameson, *Marxism and Form: Twentieth Century Dialectical Theories of Literature* (Princeton: Princeton University Press, 1971), 367–68.

2. Jameson, *Postmodernism, or, the Cultural Logic of Late Capitalism* (Durham, NC: Duke University Press, 1991), 9.

3. Stanley Fish, *Professional Correctness: Literary Studies and Political Change* (Oxford: Oxford University Press, 1995), 98.

4. Ibid., 99.

5. Ibid., 69.

6. Paul Lauter, "Afterthoughts," *English as a Discipline; or, Is There a Plot in this Play?*, ed. James C. Raymond (Tuscaloosa: University of Alabama Press, 1996), 184.

2

History, Narrative, and Realism

Jameson's Search for a Method

Carolyn Lesjak

We should always be bringing forth new things. Otherwise what are we
here for? What do we want descendants for? New things are to be found in
reality, we must grasp reality.

—Mao Zedong

In his essay on the politics of Fredric Jameson's style, Terry Eagleton identifies
the utopian dimension of Jameson's sentences as a "a shadowy presence coupled at every point to his analyses, a lateral gesture so all-pervasive that, like
utopia or desire itself, it refutes definitive figuration and echoes in the mind
simply as the rhetorical *verso* or buzz of inexhaustible implications of his grand
narrative themes."[1] After acknowledging the strength of this style, Eagleton
then goes on to address its more problematic aspects, suggesting that the
appropriative nature of Jameson's thought, its ability to voraciously absorb all
other critical perspectives like an "unrepentant bricoleur" finally weakens its
political import. As he concludes, "such appropriation too often leaves the
texts in question relatively untransformed, intact in their 'relative autonomy,'
so that the strenuously *mastering* Jameson appears too eirenic, easygoing and
all-encompassing for his own political good."[2] Indeed, in the final analysis,
Eagleton is concerned to show that Jameson isn't a very good (or at least not
the right kind of) Marxist, a claim for which he returns to Jameson's style
("The fact that he is in no sense a polemical or satirical writer—essential
modes, to my mind, for a political revolutionary—may be taken to confirm this
impression") and his reliance on the necessity of historicization.[3] With respect
to this latter point, historicization for Eagleton is in no way "a specifically
Marxist recommendation; and that even though Jameson would no doubt
gladly concede the point (since for him, as an Hegelian Marxist, 'Marx
includes Hegel'), such a concession merely blurs the specificity of Marxism

27

itself, which is not at all to 'historicize' . . . but in a word, to grasp history as structured material struggle."[4]

Although Eagleton's essay is dated in significant ways, published as it was in 1986 and hence a number of years before even Jameson's book-length study of postmodernism (1991), it sets out in ways that are still interesting—because still unresolved—a vocabulary with which to assess what would constitute a properly Marxist project. But, whereas Eagleton argues as if this project were almost self-evident, I want to suggest that it is anything but; and that, moreover, Jameson's work can best be considered as a timely search for an appropriate "method" of Marxist analysis adequate to the demands of postmodern culture and an increasingly globalized world system. Although other critics have highlighted many of the contours of Jameson's thought, I want in particular to focus on a term that remains submerged in Eagleton's essay (as well as others') and that offers, to my mind, a particularly rich reading of Jameson's import for contemporary Marxism: namely, the concept of realism.[5] By connecting Jameson's earlier work on realism to his later analysis of postmodernism and his study of Bertolt Brecht, I want to look at how "cognitive mapping" functions as Jameson's version of a new realism. Importantly, this realism is not "exactly mimetic in that older sense" but does retain what Jameson sees as the originality of the concept of realism: its "claim to cognitive as well as aesthetic status."[6] Unlike its nineteenth-century variants, this form of realism attempts finally to "produce the concept of something we cannot imagine."[7] As the indispensable third term of the triad forming my title, it embodies the most urgent of Jameson's pleas—the continuing *political* need for a revitalized "realist" aesthetics.

THE TERMS OF MARXISM, OR,
LEGITIMIZING A SOCIALIST DISCOURSE

To return first to Eagleton: if Jameson fails to promote the right kind of Marxism, this failing is not his alone, but rather that of Western Marxism in general, with its principal focus on commodification and philosophical concerns at the expense of political action.[8] As Eagleton argues, weighing the presence of Hegel, Lukács, and Adorno in Jameson's work against the absence of Lenin, Trotsky, and Gramsci, "too great an attention to 'commodification' links the economical to the experiential only at the cost of displacing the political; and in this sense it must be grasped as itself a political option, a partial displacement occasioned by the intractable problems of class struggle in the contemporary United States."[9] The effect of this "choice" is nothing less than the sapping of "vital, *political* energie*s*" and the reduction of Marxism to a form of academicism. In place of struggle, conflict, or opposition, he reads in Jameson's method an accommodation with a variety of theoretical discourses (he focuses primarily on structuralism and poststructuralism) that results, ultimately, in an ambiguous relationship between commentary and critique. In his ability to assimilate such divergent approaches, even when antithetical to Marxism, Jameson risks merely commenting on, rather than mounting, a clear critique of them. In short, what is missing or what gets lost in Jameson's magisterial style is the enemy and, with it, a determined political practice. Certainly, this must be the meaning of the triad Lenin, Trotsky, and Gramsci: while they represent theories of praxis, Jameson's threesome bespeaks an overemphasis on theory to the detriment of praxis.

These then, in essence, are the crucial coordinates of what for Eagleton would constitute a Marxist politics, ranging from what needs to happen at the level of the sentence to that of the superstructure: a certain polemical style adequate to the task of critique; a vision of political praxis not as an outcome of theorization but rather as its precondition;[10] a clear line of demarcation between bourgeois and Marxist theory; and a primary focus on class struggle as opposed to the twin processes of reification and commodification. Underlying these conditions, it seems to me, is a strong realist imperative: the desire for a kind of transparency between base and superstructure and for an older mass politics (and vanguard party)—with the implication that this is "real" politics. The basis for this distinction rests solidly on Eagleton's rejection of Hegelianism as the necessary framework for a contemporary politics. As he clarifies,

> For my part, it is not clear that there is anything inherent in late capitalism which spontaneously selects such philosophical issues as the relation between subject and object as the order of the day, as opposed, say, to questions of the character of the state and its repressive apparatuses, problems of proletarian organization and insurrection, or the role of the vanguard party.[12]

The opposition Eagleton posits clearly works to align the practical with the political and the real against the philosophical, the abstract, and the academic.

But, as I will argue, Jameson's evolving notion of a politically useful "realist" aesthetics, a term that gets refined and redefined as "cognitive mapping" and as a "geopolitical aesthetic," deals much more instructively with the deep problems afflicting a leftist politics, both in the United States and more widely; in other words, whereas Eagleton acknowledges the "intractable problems of class struggle" today, he seems unwilling to understand their intractability in terms of a radically altered social order in which an older form of politics— addressing "the character of the state and its repressive apparatuses" and so forth—is part of the problem rather than the solution. There is an irony in all this, too, I think, insofar as current debates among the left, especially with regard to various post-Marxisms, often label Jameson "old guard" in his insistence on the necessity of a concept of totality for a socialist politics. (This is where Jameson definitively parts company with poststructuralism and its critique of the colonizing, authoritarian character of any model of the totality.) In any case, Jameson's emphasis, as early as 1971, on the relation between subject and object, as well as "the relationship of part to whole, the opposition between concrete and abstract, the concept of totality, the dialectic of appearance and essence" would seem borne out by the shape of world politics since then.[12] With hindsight, it is hard to argue with a diagnosis of postindustrial or late capitalism that has as its centerpiece, as I want to suggest, the delegitimization of socialist discourse altogether, itself the product of a world more fully commodified than ever. After all, since the time of Eagleton's essay, we've witnessed, to name just a few events, the end of the Soviet state, the ascendancy of the intellectual Right, the declaration of the "death of Marxism," the destruction of the welfare state, the emergence of religious fundamentalism, and, most recently, its terrorist offshoots. Faced with what Jameson refers to, in the aftermath of September 11, as a "dialectics of disaster" (an idea to which I will return at the end of this essay), his notion of the need for a socialist pedagogy, which would attempt both to map the global structures determining our existence *experientially* (rather than abstractly) and to reinvest the social with a utopian desire all but nonexistent these days, seems, pace Eagleton, more than ever to be the order of the day. Responsive to globalization, and yet hardly utopian in assessing its current prospects, especially given the wholesale "genocide" of leftist movements by the United States worldwide, Jameson's emphasis on new forms of socialist pedagogy and the never-ending practice it implies (as we will see) appears to be the most realistic option we may have.[13] For, as Jameson earily reminds us, the other option of this dialectic between U.S. imperialism and anti-Western resistance is nothing short of our "common ruin."[14]

Realism as a Form of Cognitive Mapping

Jameson culls the key components for his theory of realism from the 1930s debates among Lukács, Brecht, Bloch, Adorno, and Benjamin over the controversy between realism and modernism. His interest in these debates, however, is hardly merely archival. In "Reflections on the Brecht-Lukács Debate" Jameson frames his comments on this classic series of exchanges by cautioning that there is no point in going back to these debates if we assume in advance who won (i.e., the modernists). Instead, he asks that we return to them with the view that the very terms of debate—and the political alliances attached to them in the initial exchange—may look radically different from our current vantage point. By refusing to prejudge either the damning denominations Lukács assigned to modernism or those Brecht equally vituperatively equated with Lukácsian realism, Jameson believes we can possibly learn something new not only about realism and modernism and their relationship to one another but about Marxist cultural criticism more generally. In keeping with Jameson's own method, "Reflections" can perhaps best be read as a series of interventions that take up the language of political critique in order to assess the strength of its various aspects, from the role of aesthetics in general to the more particular issues of "formalism," ideological analysis, and the relationship between form and content. My interest here lies both in the nature of these assessments as well as in the treatment of Brecht specifically. For it would seem with the publication of *Brecht and Method* (1998) that this essay must now take on new significance as an early (and singular) moment in which Jameson takes up, in writing, the question of Brechtian aesthetics. "Reflections on the Brecht-Lukács Debate" is thus worth returning to, as it were, not only because it is crucial in establishing the link between realism and "cognitive mapping" but because of what it says about Brecht—and how this relates to Jameson's later use of his aesthetic.

As with "the peculiar stamp of Jameson's contribution" to the postmodernism debate, to borrow Perry Anderson's phrase for his originality in linking postmodernism to late capitalism, Jamesons's reading of the Brecht-Lukács debate owes its élan to the radical difference he posits between the time of the debates in the 1930s and today.[15] While he will not yet have the language of "postmodernity," he nonetheless already fully has its concept, identifying this difference in the "emergence in full-blown and definitive form of that ultimate transformation of late monopoly capitalism variously known as the *société de consommation* or as postindustrial society."[16] It is not, however, the mere difference between these two moments that matters so much as the manner in which they alter the meaning of "realism" and "modernism" in terms of their respective political valences and "usefulness":[17] were we to simply rehearse the debate undialectically, we might easily claim Brecht as the winner, since surely Lukács's "reflection theory" of realism must appear far more inadequate—than Brecht's modernism—to the demands of representation in the wake of poststructuralism; but once we situate the controversy in the context of postindustrial society, it is not clear, according to Jameson, that it isn't Lukács with the "provisional last word for us today."[18] Or, as he captures the surprise in such a dialectical reversal, "there is some question whether the ultimate renewal of modernism, the final dialectical subversion of the now automatized conventions of an aesthetics of perpetual revolution, might not simply be . . . realism itself."[19]

The discussion of realism must begin, as Jameson suggests, with a recognition of its contradictions. An aesthetic unlike any other, realism makes dual claims to an aesthetic and a cognitive status:

A new value, contemporaneous with the secularization under capitalism, the ideal of realism presupposes a form of aesthetic experience that yet lays claim to a binding relationship to the real itself, that is to say, to those realms of knowledge and praxis that had traditionally been differentiated from the realm of the aesthetic, with its disinterested judgements and its constitution as sheer appearance.[20]

These two properties, nonetheless, exist in an uneasy coexistence, in which, in practice, one pole threatens to predominate, such that either the fictive nature of art (its aesthetic properties) or the "'reality' of realism" (its cognitive properties) is denied. Where the first imbalance leads to a naiveté about representation itself, and the ills of naturalism/social realism, the second tends toward seeing everything equally as representation and hence overwriting the referential nature of realism, as Roland Barthes, for instance, does when he turns realism into a "reality effect." In either case, the uniqueness of realism as an aesthetic-cognitive project is lost. In this light, Jameson commends Lukács's ability in his later work to "[walk] this particular tightrope, from which, even at his most ideological or 'formalistic,' he never quite falls."[21]

Yet, despite this, Jameson acknowledges that Brecht's positions within the debate over realism are, on the face of it, much more easily "transcoded" than Lukács's in our present context.[22] He locates two central issues in Brecht's charges against Lukács: his attack on "formalism"; and Lukács's use of his own method in the service of ideological denunciations. Both issues need to be considered as crucial to a Marxist aesthetics. First, in terms of "formalism," Brecht denounces Lukács for his seeming allegiance to form independent of content. Specifically, Lukács's championing of the novel—and Balzac more particularly—imbues its form with a (given) political content that would seem to undermine his recognition, more generally, of the necessarily mediated relationship between ideological structures and aesthetic phenomena. But, conversely, Brecht's claims, coming out of his work in the theater and directly opposed to the solitary process of novel reading, with its bourgeois public sphere, can equally look like a call for an unmediated aesthetic of performance. Rather than siding with one or the other, therefore, Jameson sees in this attack an important caveat about idealism in ideological analysis. As he weighs in,

It is probably best to take Brecht's attack on Lukács' formalism . . . as a therapeutic warning against the permanent temptation of idealism present in any ideological analysis as such, the professional proclivity of intellectuals for methods that need no external verification. There would then be *two* idealisms: one, the common-or-garden variety to be found in religion, metaphysics, and literalism; the other a repressed and unconscious danger of idealism within Marxism itself, inherent in the very ideal of science itself in a world so deeply marked by the division of mental and manual labor.[23]

This warning is important, first of all, for what it says about the notion of my titular "search for a method" and for Jameson's use of "method" in *Brecht and Method*. As this cautionary note implies, any claim to "method" in the abstract is always a self-founding move, bound to collapse into a kind of hermetic idealism—hence the necessity always for historicity, for without this touchstone of the practical, the concrete, or the material object-world, any "method" easily becomes nothing other than the production of its own premises. Thus, if we are to understand Jameson's own method, it must be in terms of an active search that, like Lukács at his best, attempts to "walk the tightrope" between the twin poles of realism, which is, in turn, a transcoding of method itself as a dialectical process that mediates between form and content, theory and practice.

Looking ahead, when Jameson turns his full attention to Brecht in the later book, he will tie his notion of a Brechtian "method" intimately to pedagogy and a particular form of "usefulness" (something to which I will return). For now, two examples will suffice. Crucial to Brecht's practice of the pedagogical, according to Jameson, is an awareness that all writing is subject to rewritings. As such, the pedagogical as method escapes the pitfalls of an empty formalism. Instead, this ceaseless "rewriting" is akin to Marx's description of the production of material life itself and the processes by which the base and superstructure mutually revolutionize each other as "concrete individuals . . . developing their material production and their material intercourse, alter, along with this their real existence, their thinking and the products of their thinking."[24] The material and the abstract are felt to be mutually productive of one another, made manifest through storytelling rather than production, or, in Jameson's terminology, "co-opted" for the narratological or a certain kind of "embodied storytelling" that will define Brecht's aesthetic practice. Another way of dramatizing this constantly revolutionizing process is through its obverse. Drawing on Brecht's *Me-ti, or the Book of Changes*, Jameson cites the following passage: "Master Hijeh [Hegel] thought that you can say such a sentence or a similarly constructed sentence for too long, that is that you can be correct at a given time and in a specific situation with such an enunciation, but after a while, and when the situation is altered, can then be wrong again."[25] The reversal of realism and modernism with which we began makes abundantly clear the value of this proverb.

Nevertheless, there is a crucial difference between "Reflections" and *Brecht and Method* regarding Jameson's assessment of Brecht's value for us today. In "Reflections," Jameson links Brecht's views on realism to a particular concept of science. Yet the kind of science Brecht envisions looks nothing like the science that threatens to collapse into idealism or formalism. Forestalling the dangers of abstraction, it embodies instead a notion more akin to popular mechanics and the kind of hands-on tinkering that entails. Like the vision of method, it "puts knowing the world back together with changing the world, and at the same time unites an ideal of praxis with a conception of production. The reunion of "science" and practical, change-oriented activity . . . thus transforms the process of "knowing" the world into a source of delight or pleasure in its own right."[26] Not only does this view of realism make the cognitive pleasurable—an idea that will be much more fully elaborated on in the book, especially with respect to Brecht's *Galileo*—but it tips the realist balance back toward the aesthetic in its emphasis on "play and genuine aesthetic gratification."[27] As a result, "the age-old dilemmas of a didactic theory of art (to teach *or* to please) are thereby also overcome, and in a world where science is experiment and play, where knowing and doing alike are forms of production, stimulating in their own right, a didactic art may now be imagined in which learning and pleasure are no longer separate from each other."[28]

This vision of a new kind of didacticism, which will form the center of the Brecht book, is striking in this earlier essay because of Jameson's final thoughts on its applicability. Asking whether this view of science is "still available to us as a figure today," Jameson, in essence, provisionally answers "no."[29] Seeing it as part of a much earlier moment of the second industrial revolution, he wonders whether it hasn't perhaps become outdated, much like "Lenin's definition of communism as 'the Soviets plus electrification,' or Diego Rivera's grandiose Rockefeller Center mural (repainted for Bellas Artes) in which, at the intersection of microcosm and macrocosm, the massive hands of Soviet New Man grasp and move the very levers of creation."[30]

What changes then between the time of this assessment in 1977 and *Brecht and Method* in 1998? While, of course, a certain amount of speculation is involved in such a question, a couple of developments would seem important to consider, one of them being the introduction of the notion of cognitive mapping itself, to which I will turn momentarily. But another development, perhaps less obviously related, involves Jameson's work on cinema in *Signatures of the Visible* (1990) and on Third-World cinema, more specifically, in *The Geopolitical Aesthetic* (1992).[31] What this latter work in particular suggests is that contemporary Third-World cinema is already reinventing a Brechtian aesthetics in its attempts to map First-World/Third-World relations. An example of cognitive mapping in action, these films project a renewed usefulness for Brecht's vision of science as popular mechanics, now in the changed world system of late twentieth-century global capitalism.

Exemplifying this shift is the Filipino filmmaker Kidlat Tahimik's *The Perfumed Nightmare*, in which a kind of Brechtian "science" reemerges, this time in the context of Tahimik's representational use of the jeepney—military jeeps left over from World War II that are refashioned into buses—and the form of transport it figures between village and metropolis. By virtue of its admixture of parts, the jeepney complicates the familiar binary relationship between First and Third World, as the third term of the dialectic, it moves the discussion of First-World/Third-world relations away from either a nostalgia for the traditional (and its premise of a pristine "other" uncorrupted by the First World) or a celebratory invocation of Western progress or technology. Instead, this third term "consists in the building, the unbuilding, the rebuilding, of the jeepneies—bricolage if there ever was, a scavenging for spare parts and home-made ad hoc solutions—the constant refunctioning (Brecht's *Umfunktionierung*) of the new into the old, and the old into the new."[32] Like the notion of science as popular mechanics, aesthetics and production are once more brought together, as an integral aspect of the jeepney is to be found in the remaking of "military machinery" into brightly painted objects that are, simultaneously, aesthetically pleasing and useful. They are after all the means by which Tahimik travels, in both a literal and a figurative sense: a new version of "a kind of Brechtian delight with the bad new things that anybody can hammer together for their pleasure and utility if they have a mind to," they are both the actual buses we see ("vehicles of war made into vehicles of life," as the film terms them) and Tahimik's film itself, "an omnibus and omnipurpose object that ferries its way back and forth between First and Third Worlds with dignified hilarity."[33]

Tahimik's film as jeepney: the significance of this claim lies in its envisioning of a "realist" aesthetic as a matter now of space rather than of time. Where classical nineteenth-century realism saw (imperialist) history as a developmental narrative unfolding in time and premised on a notion of historical continuity, this form of postmodern realism develops instead from a fully global history of uneven development and the "layerings of social time" produced by it.[34] Again, it is an admixture, this time of different social times, that is both represented in the film (part of its content) and constitutive of it (the nature of its form). The rough-and-ready look of the film—what Tahimik refers to as a "cups of gas" versus "full tank" approach to filmmaking—is integral, that is, to its content:[35] "Only a mode of representation which is not uncomfortable with clumsiness could accommodate such social developments. Kidlat's home-made movies handle them very well indeed, as a bonus or by-product allowing us to reflect on our own generic discomfort much as Brecht thought his audience should spend some time mulling over the meaning of the actions represented in the play."[36] Cinema and space are thus intimately linked; the unevenness of the processes of development, figured as a sedimentation of social times as well as generic conventions, writes itself into the form of Tahimik's film.

Significantly, a third dimension also arises from this "generic discomfort": the relationship between the writer/filmmaker and his or her materials. Indeed, realism here takes on a threefold nature, which, importantly, finds its theorization in "Reflections." Once again, too, it is Brecht who provides the grist for this analysis. As Jameson notes there, the "realistic" work of art is one in which "realistic" and experimental attitudes are tried out, not only between its characters and their fictive realities, but also between the audience and the work itself, and—not least significant—between the writer and his or her own materials and techniques. The threefold dimensions of such a practice of "realism" clearly explode the purely representational categories of the traditional mimetic work.[37]

At this point, it is hard not to see how the Brechtian aesthetic translates into what will become Jameson's notion of cognitive mapping. Once this third dimension is considered, the idea of realism is no longer simply mimetic in any traditional sense, but nonetheless retains its cognitive status in the experimentation with its characters, its audience, and its materials, each aspect of which, in different ways, entails experimenting with the work's relationship to reality. But, equally, late capitalism irrevocably complicates this relationship, as Jameson illustrates with respect to the project of modernism and its fate within consumer culture. Simply put, everything that was antibourgeois about modernism now characterizes commodity production itself. In this radically altered context, the concept of totality, by contrast, looks to be all the more revolutionary: "For when modernism and its accompanying techniques of 'estrangment' have become the dominant style whereby the consumer is reconciled with capitalism, the habit of fragmentation itself needs to be 'estranged' and corrected by a more totalizing way of viewing phenomena."[38] As Jameson's further articulations of cognitive mapping will show, the increasingly dire problem within this complex schema of a revitalized realism is thus one of cognition, of mapping human relations in a world made opaque by the mystifications of late capitalist society. In short, the reifying logic of capital impedes our ability to see contemporary capitalism as a total, now fully global system.

As this language of reification signals, it is in this respect that Lukács still has much to tell us. So, in an interesting dialectical twist, the Lukács we need is not that of the "realism debate" but of *History and Class Consciousness*. This Lukács allows for an analysis of the relationship of art and ideology equal to the task of capturing the complex mediations of class ideology in a way that his assignation of class ascription in the actual debate with Brecht could not. There, as Jameson underscores, "what is really wrong with Lukács's analyses is not too frequent and facile a reference to social class, but rather too incomplete and intermittent a sense of the relationship of class ideology."[39] The specific example he turns to is Lukács's condemnation of modernist works as "decadent," and his assessment of them, accordingly, as forms, essentially, of "false consciousness." In this equation, modernists like F. Scott Fitzgerald are therefore represented as devoid of all social and political content. In contrast, Lukács's analysis of reification opens up the possibility of unearthing this buried content—rather than declaring its nonexistence—in the midst of late capitalism's obfuscations precisely of these class relations.[40] Or, to relate back to our opening discussion of Eagleton's criticisms, for Jameson, via Lukács, class struggle can only be on the table once class relations are once again made visible and this can only happen by way of an analysis of the processes of reification obscuring those relations:

> Since the fundamental structure of the social "totality" is a set of class relationships—an antagonistic structure such that the various social classes define themselves in terms of that antagonism and by opposition with one another—reification necessarily obscures the class character of that structure, and is accompanied, not only by anomie, but also by that increasing confusion as to the nature and even the existence of social classes which can be abundantly observed in all the "advanced" capitalist countries today.[41]

The politics accompanying this transformed social situation will thus necessarily look different as well. As Jameson concludes,

> If the diagnosis is correct, the intensification of class consciousness will be less a matter of a populist or ouvrierist exaltation of a single class by itself, than of the forcible reopening of access to a sense of society as a totality, and of the reinvention of possibilities of cognition and perception that allow social phenomena once again to become transparent, as moments of the struggle *between* classes.[42]

To gain access to this "sense of society as a totality," new forms of narrative are required. And this necessity, too, of course relates directly to Lukács and his "[insistence] that problems in narrative are always related to limits in social experience."[43] In Jameson's own refunctioning of both Lukács and Brecht, "Reflections" ends fittingly with the adjuration to reinvent a conception of realism—and a warning that not doing so condemns us to repeating rather than moving beyond this debate.

The Brechtian recognition of the threefold nature of the practice of realism finds its full expression in the concept of cognitive mapping, which, in turn, combines and expands on the insights of Louis Althusser's model of ideology and Kevin Lynch's analysis of urban space. Since these aspects of Jameson's analysis have been treated widely, I am less concerned here with fully explicating them than I am with highlighting certain features that both draw on Jameson's injunction for a socialist pedagogy at the end of "Reflections" and extend it in important new ways. I am most interested finally in how the early essay, "Cognitive Mapping," positions aesthetics as central to the project of cognitive mapping.

The foundation for the crucial role aesthetics will play in Jameson's analysis lies in Althusser's definition of ideology as "the representation of the imaginary relationship of individuals to their real conditions of existence."[44] In this formulation, ideology mediates, in Lacanian terms, between the Imaginary and the Real. Yet once we recognize the Lacanian underpinnings of Althusser's definition, it becomes apparent that, like Brecht's method of realism, a third term must be added: the Lacanian Symbolic. Together, these three aspects of representation significantly complicate the notion of realism as simply mimetic insofar as the problematic nature of representation must now be part of any "realist" project. This then is the task that cognitive mapping has before it.

But Jameson's interest in Althusser also rests in transcoding his notion of ideology in spatial terms (and vice versa), with the help of Lynch's analysis of urban space. What Lynch adds to Jameson's theory is an emphasis on the inability of individuals within this dialectic to map their own position *as individual subjects* to the social structure as a whole. (While Lynch limits his discussion to the city, Jameson suggestively extends it to larger national and global spaces.)[45] The problem of reification, that is, takes on a decidedly spatial dimension within late capitalism. The project of cognitive mapping thus becomes as much about "placing" the individual subject within a fully global system as it is about simply describing that system. Indeed, existential as opposed to abstract knowledge becomes paramount, since this former way of knowing alone can connect individuals lived experience to the global structures determining that experience. When asked, therefore, why he doesn't focus, say, on a critical social science when defining the project of cognitive mapping, Jameson responds: "Now I think that you can teach people how this or that view of the world is to be thought or conceptualized, but the real problem is that it is increasingly hard for people to put that together with their own experience as individual psychological subjects, in daily life."[46] If, for Althusser, the distinction between science and ideology defines the difference between abstract knowledge and existential experience, then what Jameson claims, in effect, is that a "pedagogical political culture" must find a form for connecting these two kinds of knowledge. And this project, in Jameson's view is hardly "merely theoretical":

> they [difficulties in global mapping] have urgent practical political consequences, as is evident from the conventional feelings of First World subjects that existentially (or "empirically") they really do inhabit a "postindustrial society" from which traditional production has disappeared and in which social classes of the classical type no longer exist—a conviction that has immediate effects on political praxis.[47]

The social and the spatial thus figure one another, and signal an "experiential" impasse: the (First World) sensation that the world really is thoroughly reified—to the extent that production itself has disappeared.

Given this impasse, aesthetics, interestingly, begins to have a more central role. Certainly, narrative has always had primacy for Jameson; after all, as *The Political Unconscious* demonstrates, it is the means through which we apprehend history. But aesthetics in this context also registers something more specific: the need for new narratives or maps capable of locating the individual in the global, which Jameson equates with a "political form of postmodernism."[48] Indeed, this criteria distinguishes a socialist politics from other contemporary politics: "I am far from suggesting that no politics at all is possible in the new post-Marxian Nietzschean world of micropolitics—that is observably untrue. But I do want to argue that without a conception of the social totality (and the possibility for transforming a whole social system), no properly socialist politics is possible."[49] The definitive aspect of global cognitive mapping is thus a conception of the social totality, and, concomitantly, the ability, somehow, to represent the unrepresentable: the totality and its relation to lived experience.

Now, undoubtedly, this has been one of the most controversial of Jameson's claims. The invocation to totality at all counters prevailing poststructuralist wisdom regarding totalizing master narratives, dialectics, and the suppression of difference in the name of a progressive, teleological history. The most incisive criticism, surely, comes from Gayatri Spivak in *The Critique of Postcolonial Reason*, who sees in Jameson's focus on the cultural dominant in his analysis of postmodernism a "desire to keep heterogeneity at bay."[50] Reading Jameson's characterization of postmodern cultural production in terms of a "battle between marxism and deconstruction," she argues that any notion of an alterior cultural production, of the possibility of heterogeneous emergent or residual forms, is "forgotten" in the emphasis on the cultural dominant: "But if we only concentrate on the dominant, we forget that the difference between varieties of the emergent and residual *may* be the difference between radical and conservative resistance to the dominant, although this is by no means certain." In the context of the method of cognitive mapping specifically, this approach consigns all cultural production to a knowledge of this cultural dominant. In contrast, Spivak calls for a "transnational literacy" attentive to the heterogeneous.

If we return to Jameson's reading of *The Perfumed Nightmare*, it would seem, though, as if the practice of cognitive mapping belies Spivak's conclusions about its theoretical shortcomings.[51] There, as we recall, the jeepney/Tahimik's film figured as an alternative mode of travel between First and Third Worlds, "an omnibus and omnipurpose object" remaking the "new into the old, and the old into the new." Out of this process arose the possibility for a new relationship between aesthetics and production, one in which in the concept of use itself was radically refashioned. It is in this possibility, to my mind, that the expansiveness of cognitive mapping's potential is exhibited: once production and aesthetics are intimately linked, not only does use become something other than mere utility, but it also sheds its solely economic determination, incorporating numerous aspects of what would be considered extra-economic aspects of social life. In the film itself, this includes religion, ritual, politics, and power. All these areas, the film suggests, are equally open to being collectively remade and reused just like the jeepney.[52] And while this recycling of new and old certainly contains a knowledge of the cultural dominant, it would seem equally to be about what Spivak calls "varieties of the emergent and residual" and the kinds of resistance they might offer to the dominant. The invention of "new geotopical cartographies," in other words, doesn't have to preclude—at least in Tahimik's practice—the heterogeneous. If anything, it seems productive of it, both in its form and content.

The declaration that the fictional Tahimik issues when he resigns as president of the Werner Von Braun fan club attests to this heterogeneity in its assertion of independence: "I declare myself independent from those who would build bridges to the stars . . . I am Kidlat Tahimik. I choose my vehicle. I choose my bridge." This independence is hardly reducible to a knowledge of the dominant. Indeed, the choosing of vehicle and bridge alter the possibilities of how "travel" between First and Third Worlds can be imagined and the means by which such traveling can take place. The potential difference this implies is perhaps best marked in the enigmatic saying Tahimik repeats at the end of the film, as he literally blows the last scene into chaos with his breath and declares, "When the typhoon blows off its cocoon, the butterfly embraces the sun." Our inability to fully grasp what this means or to know exactly what to do with it surely lies in part with the "strangeness" of its language and imagery as a "politics." In its very inscrutability it would thus seem consonant with Spivak's invocation regarding a transnational literacy: "We must learn to learn."[53]

But the task of pedagogy, as Jameson reminds us, is at once more necessary and more difficult in the current political climate. It finally involves nothing less than legitimizing socialist discourse at a moment when it has lost all currency:

> while people know that a socialist discourse exists, it is not a legitimate discourse in this society. Thus no one takes seriously the idea that socialism, and the social reorganization it proposes, is the answer to our problems. . . . Our task . . . has to do with the legitimation of the discourses of socialism in such a way that they do become realistic and serious alternatives for people.[54]

Within this larger context, the aesthetic of cognitive mapping finds its place. Its timeliness as a reinvented realism that is also a pedagogy thus rests on its being both descriptive and utopian, an aesthetic that is simultaneously about the possibility of such an aesthetic. As Jameson concludes in "Cognitive Mapping," "even if we cannot imagine the production of such an aesthetic, there may, nonetheless, as with the very idea of Utopia itself, be something positive in the attempt to keep alive the possibility of imagining such a thing."[55] At the same time, it suggests that part of our learning to learn will necessarily entail a fuller theorization of pedagogy. In this light, Jameson's book on Brecht, to which I will now turn, seems, despite being published to coincide with Brecht's centenary, more than occasional in its timing.

PEDAGOGY AS METHOD

If, as we saw earlier, Brechtian aesthetics helped to define for Jameson the multiple levels or coordinates of "cognitive mapping" (by way of the Brecht-Lukács debate), it should perhaps come as no surprise that Jameson "returns" (if there can be a return to something that has never been left) to a full-length study of Brecht in *Brecht and Method*. While in his earlier discussion Jameson emphasizes Brecht's refiguring of realism as "experimental and subversive" rather than "passive and cognitive" (as it can look in Lukács's version), in this newer work, these notions are expanded to encompass a theory and practice of didactic art itself. From the outset, the question posed both to the Brechtian aesthetic and, in turn, to our reading of Brecht in the 1990s, is "Is it 'useful' and, if so, how?"

A dynamic combination of the "didactic," a "sly method," and an immanent form of activity ("activity becomes worth doing in its own right"), the concept of "usefulness" links the aesthetic and the political in its concern with *praxis*.[56] At first sight, this claim might seem odd, given the overwhelming forces allied against the possibilities of *praxis* at all today—Jameson's prognosis of postmodern society attests to the lack even of any desire for change, let alone any program for it—but, as he cautions,

> it is important to remember that the Brechtian doctrine of activity— if it was once energizing because activity and praxis were very precisely on the agenda—is now urgent and topical precisely because they are not, and because so many people seem immobilized in the institutions and the professionalization which seem to admit of no revolutionary change, not even of the evolutionary or reform-oriented kind. Stasis today, all over the world—in the twin condition of market and globalization, commodification and financial speculation—does not even take on a baleful religious sense of an implacable Nature; but it certainly seems to have outstripped any place for human agency, and to have rendered the latter obsolete.

So, on the one hand, restoring to the aesthetic a concept of "usefulness" will be about putting activity and agency back "on the agenda," but in a radically altered form, given the particular idiosyncracies of Brechtian activity. Less a programmatic doctrine or a politics of the "party," activity designates instead a nonreified relationship to the object world, in which "immanence and transcendence become indistinguishable (or their opposition transcended, if you prefer); or, in other words, in such a way that 'the thing itself' appears." Indeed, as Jameson underscores, "the thing itself" [die Sache selbst] is precisely what we've forgotten, the "enfeebled memory, the word-on-the-tip-of-the-tongue, that Brecht reminds us about, and offers to help us reconstruct, if not re-create." Thus, where "cognitive mapping" serves as a code word for "class consciousness," the Brechtian conception of activity embodies, in one name for its utopian calling, the "construction of socialism."

On the other hand, and again because of the "helpless period like our own, where destiny seems once again disconnected from history," the "usefulness" of Brechtian activity will also entail the revival of what Jameson calls "the older precapitalist sense of time itself, of the change or flowing of all things: for it is the movement of this great river of time or the Tao that will slowly carry us downstream again to the moment of praxis."[57] The conception of time as perpetual change upsets the means by which capitalism convinces us of its ubiquity, thereby making the eternal ephemeral and the natural historical.[58] But perhaps most important, it involves a kind of change that will inevitably include our own passing, without which new possibilities, or, better yet, the New itself, is irredeemably foreclosed. It thus incorporates, simultaneously, the pain of Becoming and its pleasures—a form of dialectical overcoming in which activity/agency enacts its own passing through its reemergence as a subject of history (a process akin to Brecht's recommendation "to tell the story of individual experience like the history in the history books").[59] The joining of concrete "objectness" with its continual, dialectical overcoming thus constitutes a Brechtian vision of change that is always about the new and, with it, the "ever-so-desirable property of wanting to learn, of eagerness for the doctrine," which is, as we saw earlier, "simply the method itself."[60]

The autoreferential nature of method necessitates a pedagogy equally about form and content, or, rather, one in which the two have become inseparable, since its goal must be nothing short of teaching the New, which is finally less about any sort of specific content than it is about learning how to learn—and the eagerness of wanting to learn. Brecht's theater, according to Jameson, offers a most productive site for such learning precisely because it functions as "the 'experimental' attempt to ward off reification": "The well-made production is one from which the traces of its rehearsals have been removed (just as from the successfully reified commodity the traces of production itself have been made to disappear): Brecht opens up this surface, and allows us to see back down into the alternative gestures and postures of the actors trying out their roles."[61] Many of the various techniques of Brecht's theater support this attempt, from the notion of *Gestus* (which organizes the middle section of the book) and the *Lehrstücke* (learning plays) to the more familiar *Verfremdungseffekt*. What these techniques share is a de-reifying function, the ability to peel away second nature by opening it up to scrutiny and revealing it as historical. In Brecht, this extends to such things as emotions themselves: "The emotions always have a quite definite class basis; the form they take at any time is historical, restricted and limited in specific ways. The emotions are in no sense universally human and timeless."[62] But, crucially as well, the work of Brecht's theater is collaborative and as such a "collective experiment" that, for Jameson, still has much to teach us, not least in its figuring of a "collective *praxis*": "the promise and example of a utopian cooperation, down to the very details of those literary sentences which our tradition has attempted to reserve as the last refuges of true creation and the individual genius. It is a lesson whose Brechtian pleasures will surely return in future generations, however unfashionable it may feel to contemporaries in the current age of the market."[63]

Teaching, as this passage makes clear, is never far from pleasure; in fact, pedagogy is all about pleasure. Yet, it is not pleasure for its own sake exactly that is emphasized, but rather the way in which pleasure is used or to what ends: "not, pleasure, but its function, is the issue in thinking historically about aesthetics and culture."[64] In *Mahagonny*, for instance, pleasure, like Brecht's method, is both in the content and the form of the play. As Brecht himself describes it: "As for the content of this opera, *its content is pleasure*. Fun, in other words, not only as form but as subject-matter. At least, enjoyment was meant to be the object of the enquiry even if the inquiry was intended to be an object of enjoyment. Enjoyment here appears in its current historical role: as merchandise."[65] The content of this particular fun—pleasure as merchandise—is all important, marking, as it does, a "gap" between the form of pleasure—its inquiry—and its reduced content. This gap enables activity at the same time that it inspires it. Counterposed to the marketing of pleasure are other Brechtian pleasures, such as those of Galileo in *Life of Galileo*, which enact the pleasures of learning and its gustatory affiliations. (In the play, the Pope says about Galileo, "He enjoys himself in more ways than any man I have ever met. His thinking springs from sensuality. Give him an old wine or a new idea, and he cannot say no.")[66] Within this context, Galileo's discoveries, as Jameson stresses, are as social as they are scientific; moving between these registers, what is displayed, in effect, is "the breaking in of the *Novum* upon the self: a dawning both of a new world and of new human relations."[67]

The discovery of these pleasures is inseparable from the process of de-reification, which, in turn, involves the pleasure or "slyness" of turning things inside out. And, as we've seen, that process is at once about the "autonomiza-tion" or breaking down of everything from individual gestures to the separate moments that constitute an action or event and their rebuilding. An autoref-erential lesson, it

> underscores the need, in change, for pedagogy as such, projecting the latter outward on an immense social scale, and thereby anticipating the fundamental discovery of cultural revolution—the conviction that objective transformations are never secure until they are accompanied by a whole collective reeducation, which develops new habits and practices, and constructs a new consciousness capable of matching the revolutionary situation.[68]

Like Brecht's theater, "collective reeducation" in this sense is hardly the teach-ing of any specific doctrine, such as Stalinism or Maoism; instead, it is a col-lective form of learning to learn anew, which will involve, as we recall, our own passing. Unlike the specter of the gulag or reeducation camps, however, this passing will come by way of the experimental tinkering associated with Brechtian "science," and, as such, hold out the possibility of a radical new Becoming.

In all this, Brecht's "slyness"—and by extension, Jameson's—gains its import. Early in the book, Jameson admits that

> it is tempting to suggest that it is precisely Brecht's well-known sly-ness that is his method, and even his dialectic: the inversion of the hierarchies of a problem, major premiss passing to minor, absolute to relative, form to content, and vice versa—these are all operations whereby the dilemma in question is turned inside out, and an unex-pected unforeseeable line of attack opens up that leads neither into the dead end of the unresolvable nor into the banality of stereotypi-cal doxa on logical non-contradiction."[69]

At this point, it is equally tempting to see in this slyness Jameson's method and dialectic as well. Just as with this series of inversions, Jameson's realism, rein-vented once again through Brecht, "turns inside out" the very Lukácsian prob-lem it was marshaled to combat: reification. Envisioned now as a kind of Brechtian "autonomization," Jameson's realism dialectically refashions mod-ernism itself. Modernist fragmentation, and its collusion with the market, becomes a precondition for an "unexpected unforeseeable line of attack": the Brechtian project of reassembly. Reification is "refunctioned" as a condition of possibility for the "autonomization" of the social order (and the aesthetic as well) so that it, too, can be reassembled much like Galy Gay is broken down and rebuilt in various guises in Brecht's *Mann ist Mann*. This rebuilding is, of course, part and parcel of a socialist pedagogy.

With this "line of attack's" emphasis on "usefulness" and the pleasures attendant on use, it is also tempting to see in *Brecht and Method* a relaxation of what Steven Helmling, in his recent study, characterizes as Jameson's "success/failure dynamic" regarding critique in general and Marxist critique in particular (and exemplified by the question of "how a 'revolutionary' critique [can] be said to succeed in a period when revolution itself is failing").[70] "Inevitable failure," he notes, "here sounds less inevitable than before."[71] But reading *Brecht and Method* in light of recent events, it's hard not to read that "failure" in the broader context of the "dialectics of disaster" and its movement, potentially, toward our "common ruin." Like the lesson of Mother Courage, the failure here involves a "negative learning process," whose direness consists in a "failure to learn": "in Brecht what is fatal is always the failure to learn: as witness the alleged tragedy of Mother Courage, for Brecht a fundamental illustration of the deadliness of the idea you can't give up (the little nest egg, the capital of the wagon that cannot be lost, hanging on to your investment no matter what happens)."[72] Although the utopian might seem to carry the day in Jameson's reading of Brecht, this larger failure looms over Jameson's analysis. But the coexistence of change and doom also has a long history, and one that may offer the only opening we now have for a late-capitalist Brechtian "slyness," or turning of the system inside out. "Reading an underlying Maoism into what is standardly termed Brecht's 'Stalinism,'" this dialectic

> folds back into the sheerest celebration of change, change as always revolutionary, as the very inner truth of revolution itself. This is what the dialecticians have always understood and clasped to their hearts. . . . History puts its worst foot forward, Henri Lefebvre taught us; it proceeds by catastrophe rather than by triumph. So the true dialectician—of whom Brecht, and behind him the tutelary scroll of the ancient Chinese sage, is emblematic here—will always wish patiently to wait for the stirrings of historical evolution even within defeat.[73]

These "stirrings," to which Jameson's own search for a method attest, will entail a new kind of didacticism—the "teaching" of "a particular mental *Haltung*" (stance)—and new forms of pleasure.[75] For as Me-ti in *The Book of Changes* makes clear in his preference for "rogue's tales," "When you have a country in which strength and cunning can only be exercised in trickery and knavishness, then naturally enough I must indulge my pleasure in strength and cunning in their application to such things."[75] In our roguish present, Jameson's "realism" is finally, like Brecht's method, the holding open of the possibility, dim as it may seem, of alternative histories.

Notes

1. Terry Eagleton, *Against the Grain* (London: Verso, 1986), 66.

2. Ibid.

3. Ibid., 71. It seems important to note that Jameson does not, however, eschew the polemical, but rather sees it as a crucial tactic of a Marxist criticism. As he clarifies in the introduction to *The Political Unconscious*, "the unavoidably Hegelian tone of the retrospective framework of *The Political Unconscious* should not be taken to imply that such polemic interventions are not of the highest priority for Marxist cultural criticism. On the contrary, the latter must necessarily also be what Althusser has demanded of the practice of Marxist philosophy proper, namely 'class struggle within theory.'" See Fredric Jameson, *The Political Unconscious: Narrative as a Socially Symbolic Act* (Ithaca: Cornell University Press, 1981), 12.

4. Eagleton, 72–73.

5. A selection of books on Jameson include Sean Homer, *Fredric Jameson: Marxism, Hermeneutics, Postmodernism* (New York: Routledge, 1998); Perry Anderson, *The Origins of Postmodernity* (London: Verso, 1998), Clint Burnham, *The Jamesonian Unconscious: The Aesthetics of Marxist Theory* (Durham: Duke University Press, 1995); Douglas Kellner, ed., *Postmodernism/Jameson/Critique* (Washington, D.C.: Maisonneuve Press, 1989); and William C. Dowling, *Jameson, Althusser, Marx: An Introduction to the Political Unconscious* (Ithaca: Cornell University Press, 1984).

6. Jameson, *Postmodernism, or, the Cultural Logic of Late Capitalism* (Durham: Duke University Press, 1991), 51; "Reflections on the Brecht-Lukács Debate" (1977), *The Ideologies of Theory*, Vol. 2 (Minneapolis: University of Minnesota Press, 1988), 135.

7. Jameson, "Cognitive Mapping," *Marxism and the Interpretation of Culture*, ed. Cary Nelson and Lawrence Grossberg (Urbana: University of Illinois Press, 1988), 347.

8. Perry Anderson makes a similar claim about Western Marxism in *Considerations on Western Marxism*. In his later assessment of Jameson, however, he sees in his integration of the cultural and the economic (captured in Jameson's notion of the cultural logic of late capitalism) the "most complete consummation" of Western Marxism. Central to this broadening of Western Marxism's approach to culture was Jameson's use of Ernest Mandel's Late Capitalism. See Perry Anderson, *Considerations on Western Marxism* (London: Verso, 1979); and *Origins*, 72.

9. Eagleton, 75.

10. Eagleton differentiates Jameson from Lukács even in this respect: "The distance from History and Class Consciousness is notable indeed: the dispelling of reification which for that work was an indispensable concomitant and effect of class struggle has become, in Jameson, its theoretical prolegomenon." Ibid., 75.

11. Ibid., 75.

12. Jameson, *Marxism and Form: Twentieth-Century Dialectical Theories of Literature* (Princeton: Princeton University Press, 1971), xix.

13. Jameson, "The Dialectics of Disaster," *The South Atlantic Quarterly* 101 (2) (Spring 2002): 301. The list of places in which the United States participated in

destroying communist parties includes, as Jameson notes, not only the better known repressions in Latin America but also those in Africa and Asia, only more recently being brought to light. As he goes on to state, the "physical extermination of the Iraqi and Indonesian communist parties, although now virtually forgotten, were crimes as abominable as any contemporary genocide."

14. Jameson, "Dialectics of Disaster," 304.

15. Anderson, Origins, vii.

16. Jameson, "Reflections," 143. This statement also echoes the opening of *Marxism and Form* in which Jameson elucidates more fully the nature of the 1930s, asserting that

> The reality with which the Marxist criticism of the 1930's had to deal was that of a simpler Europe and America, which no longer exist. Such a world had more in common with the life-forms of earlier centuries than it does with our own. To say that it was simpler is by no means to claim that it was easier as well: on the contrary! It was a world in which social conflict was sharpened and more clearly visible, a world which projected a tangible model of the antagonism of the various classes toward each other, both within the individual nation-states and on the international scene as well—a model as stark as the Popular Front or the Spanish Civil War, where people were called on to take sides and to die, which are, after all, always the most difficult things.

See Jameson, *Marxism and Form*, xvii.

17. As I will discuss, the issue of "usefulness" surfaces centrally in *Brecht and Method*—but the emphasis here in the earlier essay is mine rather than Jameson's.

18. Jameson, "Reflections," 146.

19. Ibid., 146.

20. Ibid., 135.

21. Ibid., 135.

22. At the beginning of this volume of *The Ideologies of Theory*, Jameson explains that all the essays in some way deal with a changed intellectual space occasioned by poststructuralism and the proliferation of various theoretical codes. As he describes the process of transcoding, it is a necessary result of the shift from ontology or metaphysics to theory:

> It will . . . today be less a question of finding a single system of truth to convert to, than it will of speaking the various theoretical codes experimentally, with a kind of Whorf-Sapir view toward determining what can and what cannot be said in each of those theoretical "private languages." What is blurred, left out, what does not compute or is "inexpressible," in this or that theoretical language may then be a more damaging indictment of the "theory" in question than traditional ontological or metaphysical critiques. (ix)

Moreover, Marxism must "measure its range" by means of this transcoding. Indeed, transcoding is the name Jameson gives to what, as we saw earlier, Eagleton criticizes as a form of intellectual "bricolage." See Jameson, *The Ideologies*, viii–ix.

23. Jameson, "Reflections," 137.

24. Jameson, *Brecht and Method*, 27.

25. Ibid., 116.

26. Jameson, "Reflections," 140.

27. Ibid., 140.

28. Ibid., 140–41.

29. Ibid., 141.

30. Ibid., 141.

31. In an interview with Eva Corredor about Lukács's place "after communism," Jameson directly addresses his return to realism (and modernism) in this book in the context of considering whether we can still use the word "realism" or "whether the word is not too strongly identified either with Dickens and Balzac or with Lukács himself, either one now being thought of as old-fashioned and taking us back to a period that is over and done with." As he concludes here, "on the other hand, I continue to think that the problem raised by this realist discussion remains a very interesting one, and it would be a pity to lose that, to lose the problem, which is a rich one and turns on cognitive mapping, whereas we might very well wish to lose all the solutions that were proposed in that particular period. I think it is worth pursuing the debate in this sense, even if one has to mark this word and ask oneself questions about it." See Eva L. Corredor, *Lukács After Communism: Interviews with Contemporary Intellectuals* (Durham: Duke University Press, 1997), 82.

32. Jameson, *The Geopolitical Aesthetic: Cinema and Space in the World System* (Indiana: Indiana University Press, 1992), 209.

33. *The Perfumed Nightmare*, prod. and dir. Kidlat Tahimik, 90 min., 1978, videocassette; Jameson, *Geopolitical Aesthetic*, 211.

34. With regard to nineteenth-century realism, Franco Moretti, for instance, characterizes the bildungsroman as a form that "held fast to the notion that the biography of a young individual was the most meaningful point for the understanding and the evaluation of history." See Franco Moretti, *The Way of the World* (London: Verso, 1987), 227.

35. Kidlat Tahimik, interview by Loris Mirella, *Polygraph* I (Fall 1987): 61. As Tahimik phrases this difference, "I'm really talking about making films with all the money there, which is the 'full tank' approach; whereas when I make it, I get a cup of gasoline, put it in my car, drive as far as I can get. When it conks out I wait—beg, steal or borrow the next cup of gasoline."

36. Jameson, *Geopolitical Aesthetic*, 195.

37. Jameson, "Reflections," 141.

38. Ibid., 146.

39. Ibid., 137.

40. Lukács states the issue thus: "Reification requires that a society should learn to satisfy all its needs in terms of commodity exchange. The separation of the producer

from his means of production, the dissolution and destruction of all 'natural' production units, etc., and all the social and economic conditions necessary for the emergence of modern capitalism tend to replace 'natural' relations which exhibit human relations more plainly by rationally reified relations." See Georg Lukács, *History and Class Consciousness*, trans. Rodney Livingstone (Cambridge: MIT Press, 1971), 91.

41. Jameson, "Reflections," 146.

42. Ibid., 146.

43. Corredor, 86. This understanding of narrative, in fact, defines Lukács's "greatness" for Jameson.

44. Louis Althusser, *Lenin and Philosophy and Other Essays*, trans. Ben Brewster (New York: Monthly Review Press, 1971), 162.

45. Jameson also complicates Lynch's discussion in *The Image of the City* by developing it in relation to the history of cartography. As he suggests, Lynch deals primarily with itineraries, whereas the narrative of mapmaking incorporates more fully the threefold nature of realism. Tracing the development of cartography, Jameson adds to the itinerary (existential data) the invention of the compass (the ability to map the totality) and the globe (the complexities of representation). See Jameson, *Postmodernism, or, the Cultural Logic of Late Capitalism* (Durham: Duke University Press, 1991), 51–52.

46. Jameson, "Cognitive Mapping," *Marxism and the Interpretation of Culture*, ed. Cary Nelson and Lawrence Grossberg (Urbana: University of Illinois Press, 1988), 358.

47. Jameson, *Postmodernism*, 53.

48. Ibid., 54.

49. Jameson, "Cognitive Mapping," 355.

50. Gayatri Chakravorty Spivak, *A Critique of Postcolonial Reason: Towards a History of the Vanishing Present* (Cambridge: Harvard University Press, 1999), 314. The next quoted passage follows shortly after this one, also on p. 314.

51. Interestingly, in *The Critique of Postcolonial Reason*, Spivak does not ever directly address any of Jameson's essays about Third-World cultural production, but limits her discussion to his analysis in *Postmodernism, or, the Cultural Logic of Late Capitalism*.

52. This idea comes in part from an unpublished manuscript by Christopher Pavsek on "Memories of Overdevelopment: The Films of Kidlat Tahimik."

53. Spivak, 391.

54. Jameson, "Cognitive Mapping," 358–59.

55. Ibid., 356.

56. Jameson, *Brecht and Method*, 4. The following three quotes also come from p. 4.

57. Ibid., 6; and 4.

58. In a different context, Jameson points, in his analysis of Friedrich Schiller and Herbert Marcuse, to the value of hermeneutics in performing a similar kind of defamiliarizing of the present: "For hermeneutics . . . is also a political discipline, and provides the means for maintaining contact with the very sources of revolutionary activity during a stagnant time, of preserving the concept of freedom itself, underground, during geological ages of repression." See Jameson, *Marxism and Form*, 84.

59. Jameson, *Brecht and Method*, 44.

60. Ibid., 99.

61. Ibid., 11–12.

62. *Brecht on Theater: The Development of an Aesthetic*, ed. and trans. John Willett (New York: Hill and Wang, 1964), 145. Brecht also goes through a series of examples of the A-effect (Alienation-effect) from being asked whether you've looked carefully at your watch ("I realize I have given up seeing the watch itself with an astonished eye") to expecting one thing and getting something else, to driving an old car after a modern one. This latter example is worth quoting as exemplary of how both objects, the old and the new, are made strange: "Suddenly we hear explosions once more; the motor works on the principle of explosion. We start feeling amazed that such a vehicle, indeed any vehicle not drawn by animal-power, can move; in short, we understand cars, by looking at them as something strange, new, as a triumph of engineering and to that extent something unnatural. Nature, which certainly embraces the motor-car, is suddenly imbued with an element of unnaturalness, and from now on this is an indelible part of the concept of nature," ibid., 144–45.

63. Jameson, *Brecht and Method*, 10.

64. Ibid., 38.

65. Ibid., 96.

66. Bertolt Brecht, *Life of Galileo*, trans. John Willett (New York: Arcade Publishing, 1994), 93.

67. Jameson, *Brecht and Method*, 92.

68. Ibid., 92–3.

69. Ibid., 25.

70. Steven Helmling, *The Success and Failure of Fredric Jameson: Writing, the Sublime, and the Dialectic of Critique* (Albany: SUNY Press, 2001), 2.

71. Helmling, 157.

72. Jameson, *Brecht and Method*, 91.

73. Ibid., 16; and 17.

74. Ibid., 24.

75. Quoted in Jameson, *Brecht and Method*, 116.

3

A Level Playing Field?

Metacommentary and Marxism

Roland Boer

Jameson's work embodies a tension at the heart of contemporary literary criticism and theory—namely, between what has been called the ban on master narratives and the continued existence of those narratives as such. What we find, on the one hand, are the suspicions of poststructuralists and postcolonial critics against any totalizing theory and, on the other, the construction of ever more totalizing theories in the work of writers such as Slavoj Žižek, Michael Hardt, and Antonio Negri. Politically and economically, the tension takes the form of a rampant globalization over a host of regionalisms and cultural specificities. That globalization may be the oft-derided and yet feared global dominance of the United States, or the acephalous "empire" of Negri' and Hardt's argument, whereas a scale of regionalisms, from Quebec and Scotland to the Asian region, seems both to oppose such globalization and yet feed off it. In other words, apart from an interest that we might have in the particular content of Jameson's writing and the positions he espouses, his work also has a bearing on these tensions or contradictions in literary and cultural criticism, politics, and economics.

And what we find is that Jameson weaves a fine line between an open-ended mode of interpretation and espousal of an overarching Marxist method. On the first count, Jameson's approach may be regarded as an ad hoc venture, always constructing his method at the moment of critical evaluation, taking the key terms of Marxism as problems rather than fixed categories that must be applied. Marxism, then, becomes a political and theoretical program that is always on the move, multifarious and restless. Jameson attempts to deal with the increasing pluralism of methods and theories by advocating an approach that compares the various available methods for their strengths and weaknesses. Another way of casting such an openness is in terms of what he calls at various times metacommentary or transcoding: the ability to move from one critical method or code to another, learning the language anew each time in order to assess the coherence of the method in question, but never assuming an overarching or superior method. It is a little like floating shares on the stock market or sending one's team out onto a "level playing field." In this case, however, we are talking about methods of criticism, whose fortunes wax and wane like shares or a team, largely beyond one's own control.

But then we can flip the coin and find another story, one in which Marxism is, as he famously puts it, the "untranscendable horizon"[1] of all interpretation. Once we begin to read in this way, no matter how many methods one might encounter, testing their strengths and weaknesses against each other, Marxism will turn out to be the superior method, able to absorb the insights of other approaches at a more comprehensive level of interpretation. More specifically, it is a dialectical Marxism, one that traces its heritage back through Hegel, that is the final horizon of interpretation.

I argue that the openness of Jameson's approach stands in a crucial, if fascinating, tension with the political necessity of taking Marxism as superior to other forms of criticism, politics, and socioeconomic practice. The tension comes ins sharpest in his effort to retool Marxism so that it loses its hoary and dogmatic form to become a thoroughly postmodern and less determinate strategy of interpretation and cultural politics. In following through my argument, I will be using on Jameson's work a crucial practice of his own: the identification of a contradiction, a tension that becomes constitutive of the whole. That contradiction is a key feature of dialectical criticism, particularly of the dialectical Marxism that Jameson takes up from Adorno, Lukács, and Sartre, means that my own analysis becomes a form of immanent criticism, an entry into the fabric of the thought and argument itself in order to use precisely that thought to interpret itself. It is a more rigorous approach than the easy path of applying external categories of criticism from the first moment, although it is impossible in the end to seal off any system of thought, let alone one as encyclopedic as that of Jameson.

As far as the structure of my discussion is concerned, I have divided it into three parts. The first part outlines the function of what Jameson variously calls metacommentary or transcoding. Subsequently, I develop a genealogy for his explicitly Marxist method of interpretation. Both sections seek to show how these two related strategies in Jameson's critical labor are nevertheless distinct. In the third section, I consider more closely the tension between metacommentary and Marxism, which forms the crucial nexus of his work, being both a source of some problems and its powerful promise.

Metacommentary and Transcoding

Jameson's own suggestion[2] is to distinguish between two terms—"metacommentary" and "transcoding"—that roughly follow the lines of literary and cultural criticism, being distinguished more by the objects of analysis—texts and critical theories, respectively—than by the process itself. Metacommentary is "a reflexive operation proposed for staging the struggle within an individual literary and cultural text of various interpretations that are themselves so many 'methods' or philosophies or ideological worldviews."[3] Transcoding, on the other hand, breaches the barricades of literary texts and moves out into the relations between theories or "codes" in the wider cultural sphere, although specific cultural products appear reasonably often in transcoding analyses: "When the polemic leaves the ground of an individual text . . . it seems to me increasingly desirable to stage such conflicts in terms of a rather different framework, which I will call *transcoding*."[4] Despite the differences between them, metacommentary and transcoding constitute variations on the same basic approach: for this reason, I will consider them together, even more so since transcoding brings into greater relief some basic criticisms of Jameson.

Metacommentary itself evokes the distinction made by the Alexandrian librarians between the volumes of physics and those of—for want of a better term—metaphysics: metacommentary, as it were, describes those items that are located "next to" the volumes of commentary and interpretation. Meta-commentary widens its perspective, steps back from, abstracts itself from the commentary process and comments on the commentaries and interpretations. It is interested in how various interpretations are set up and organized and where their conditions of possibility might be located. The term is also the title of an article that received the prestigious William Riley Parker Prize from the Modern Language Association.[5] This article formed the basis of the much longer theoretical section at the end of *Marxism and Form*,[6] which in turn was elaborated on for the first chapter of *The Political Unconscious*. The "Metacom-mentary" article therefore lies at the beginning of this published process of theoretical development and, thus, contains many themes and ideas that would later be developed as well as distinguished more sharply: metacommentary itself, combined with the use of a Freudian depth model (the repressed and its symptom) and a debt to formalism.

As previously noted, metacommentary becomes transcoding when analy-sis leaves the specific boundaries of the text and moves out into the vast field of contemporary theory and culture. The term "transcoding" describes the process of leaping from one method or mode of analysis to another; it is the activity of "measuring what is sayable and 'thinkable' in each of these codes or ideolects" in order to "compare that to the conceptual possibilities of its com-petitors."[7] With the increasing rate of change in interpretive fashion (charac-teristic of late capitalism), as well as the multiplicity of methods such change generates, the ability to transcode becomes a necessity for the critic. Transcod-ing is in this light the postmodern (in Jameson's terms) variant on metacom-mentary; the concern of both, however, remains that of the pluralism of methods and interpretations.

Apart from a suggestive connection with organ transplanting and architecture,[8] transcoding bears many resemblances, and is indeed explicitly likened, to the activity of translation. Jameson's linguistic skills—he comes from languages first and has been variously professor of French and Romance languages—are significant for the whole strategy of transcoding and of its base, allegory. Indeed, many of the texts he deals with and some of the texts he has written are outside the English language, whether of first world Europe or of third world regions.

Transcoding assumes the existence of various methods or ideological codes, and it requires the ability to speak those various codes, a skill comparable to speaking and translating a foreign language:

> (I have to learn to speak it, for example; I can say some things more strongly in one foreign language than in another, and vice versa; there is no Ur- or ideal language of which the imperfect earthly ones, in their multiplicity, are so many refractions; syntax is more important than vocabulary, but most people think it is the other way round; my awareness of linguistic dynamics is the result of a new global system or a certain demographic "pluralism").[9]

Transcoding, however, brings me to the verge of the tension I am exploring in Jameson's work. Thus far, I have been interested in the genesis and workings of metacommentary/transcoding. Yet the other major dimension of his work is an elaborate method: this is not to say that metacommentary is not a method in itself, or that there aren't some interesting connections between metacommentary and the Marxist method, but what interests me are the tensions between the two. Before I can do that, let me trace the development of the explicit Marxist method.

Genealogy of a Marxist Method

Jameson's clearest statement of a detailed Marxist method comes in the third and final section of the long, and justly famous, first chapter of *The Political Unconscious*. Alongside the general preparation for the Marxist method with its well-known political, social, and historical levels, there is a more specific preparatory thread running through the first two of the three sections of this chapter: medieval allegory and its reinterpretation by Northrop Frye. To this preparatory pair, I will add a few other developments that serve to explain the genealogy of Jameson's method: a study by Jameson of Walter Benjamin and the traditional Marxist approach to interpretation.

There are, however, some other contributions to the three levels to which Jameson occasionally alludes or that have some deeper structural association.

To begin with, the idea of an interpretive schema operating according to levels has some roots in Jameson's work on Sartre, particularly the latter's undeveloped suggestions of a "hierarchy of heterogeneous significations,"[10] echoed by Jameson's "hierarchy of motivations, in which the various elements of the work are ordered at various levels from the surface . . . so that in the long run everything in the work exists in order to bring to expression the deepest level of the work which is the concrete itself."[11] Two specifically threefold schemas—apart from the classic formulation of Hegel's dialectic— on which Jameson has written are Lacan's imaginary, symbolic, and real[12] and Althusser's mechanical, expressive, and structural causality. It is particularly the Althusserian reflections that are of interest, coming as they do in the great juxtaposition of Althusser and Lukács. Yet the final influence of Althusser is oblique, since Jameson's method claims to be a development of the last or structural mode of causality into which the others (mechanical and expressive) are subsumed.

With these sorts of precursors, the proper logical beginning of Jameson's theory of literary criticism is medieval biblical allegory. The section on medieval allegory in *The Political Unconscious*[13] comes in the context of the discussion of Althusser's proposals on causality; more specifically, it is part of a recuperation of expressive causality (the idea that an object may express the inner truth of a larger whole, such as a period of time) against Althusser's strictures. Briefly stated, the four levels of medieval exegesis were first the *literal* level, which in principle remains the base from which the other levels move. This first level was generally understood to be the Hebrew Bible or Old Testament. The second level—normally designated the *allegorical*—works through the New Testament, especially the life of Christ in light of which the New Testament writers themselves often rewrote Old Testament sections. We might take as an example the invasion of the promised land, after the Exodus from Egypt, in the books of Joshua and Judges, or the analogous return from the Babylonian exile in 537 BCE, both of which become in the New Testament the resurrection of Christ. The third level is the *moral*, which focuses on the life of the individual believer: thus, the promised land and the return from exile become the conversion and salvation of the sinner, as St. Paul on the road to Damascus in the Acts of the Apostles, or the final destination of the believer in heaven. The fourth is the *anagogic*, which jumps to the sweep of history, specifically that of the church, moving from creation to the end of history. At this level, what was previously the arrival in the promised or return from Egypt, the resurrection of Christ and the salvation of the individual believer, shuffles its meaning to refer to the eschaton, the culmination of the trials of the church in the return of Christ, the end of history, and the realization of the kingdom of God.

A number of significant points emerge from this schema. First, the insistence on recovering and maintaining the literal (first) level constitutes the innovation of the medieval allegorists over the Hellenistic procedures that readily left the uncomfortable literal text behind in the search for more acceptable allegorical meanings (Homer and the gods are the usual examples). While exponents may have been tempted to dump the literal in practice, as the medieval precursor Origen was prone to do, it remained an essential anchor if the allegorical scheme was to function properly. Indeed, the development of the four levels based on the literal level seems to have been an effort by interpreters in the early church to contain—by means of both retaining the literal and providing for all interpretive possibilities with a comprehensive program (all other suggested levels being variations on these four)—the wilder flights of interpretive practice.

Second, Jameson asserts the importance of the second or allegorical level of interpretation, an importance that is due to its role in cracking open the literal level to other stages of interpretation, namely, the moral (third) and anagogical (fourth) levels. As I will argue later, this allegorical key looms large in Jameson's appropriation of the medieval schema.

Third, Jameson's attraction to the medieval procedure lies in its ability to totalize, to incorporate the individual dimension within the concrete totality of history, to reconnect the public and the private, the sociological and the psychological. This schema is able to relate the individual and the collective through the inverted, or chiastic, symmetry between the first and second levels (collective history of Israel and the individual life of Christ) and the third and fourth (the individual believer's life and the collective history of salvation) that not only relates the believer to the religious collective of the past (Israel) and the major Christian salvation event (Christ), but also inserts the individual believer within the span—from creation to the end of history—of the history of salvation. In this way, the medieval schema performs a similar function to the definition of ideology that Jameson borrows from Althusser: the representation of the subject's imaginary relationship to her or his real social and historical conditions of existence. Another dimension of totalization lies in the challenge to, on the one hand, a liberal pluralism that appears to allow equal validity to any interpretation and method but in fact works to block the moves that would connect interpretations to their political, social, and historical place, and, on the other hand, a ban on master narratives that attempts to allow marginalized voices to speak, yet is so often unable to do so. For Jameson, a Marxist method inspired by medieval allegory would make the connections between interpretation, politics, and history, and provide space for marginalized voices.

My suggestion is that the four levels of medieval allegory are transformed into the three levels of Jameson's own approach. Part of this transformation is enacted in the encounter with Northrop Frye's recasting of the fourfold medieval interpretive scheme.[14] Frye represents for Jameson the positive dimensions of modern—over against medieval—religious interpretation, specifically due to his emphasis on the collective and social implications of religion and its interpretive strategies. This collective emphasis operates in two ways: first, the terms and debates of religion refer in a symbolic manner to the various questions concerning the nature of community; second, if literature is understood as a paler and later version of myth and ritual, then literature also must ultimately be understood as a "symbolic meditation on the destiny of community."[15]

To my mind, Jameson's appropriation of Frye operates at a number of its own levels, not all of which are articulated by Jameson. The appropriation is, as expected, a dialectical affair with critique and praise mixing it up together. Jameson is taken by a number of points in Frye's approach: the flexibility with which Frye reinterprets the older scheme; the existence of an allegorical key that generates the other levels of interpretation; and the notion that the various levels are in fact "phases." In comparison to medieval allegory, Frye feels that "[i]t is better to think . . . not simply of a sequence of meanings, but of a sequence of contexts or relationships in which the whole work of literary art can be placed. . . . I call these contexts or relationships 'phases.'"[16] Jameson describes the levels of his own approach as phases in this sense.

However, the major issue for Jameson is the relation in Frye's work between individual and collective elements, an issue that comes to the fore in the third (mythical) and fourth (anagogic) phases of Frye's scheme. Jameson's explicit argument is that Frye removes with one hand what he provides with the other, namely, an emphasis on the collective: in comparison with the medieval scheme, Frye inverts the last two levels, making the third a collective level and the fourth an individual one. Skipping past Frye's first (literal and descriptive) and second (formal) phases, Jameson presents Frye's third or mythical phase as the locus of the various collective and social concerns that are the strength of Frye's reinterpretation. Due to its displacement, the value of this third phase of Frye's scheme is equivalent to that of the final level of medieval allegory (termed by the medieval exegetes the "anagogic"). It is Frye's own final or (misnamed) anagogic phase—equivalent for Jameson to the third or moral level of the medieval scheme—that causes all the disappointment.

Frye is, however, undertaking a more comprehensive task, in which he wishes, in characteristic symmetrical fashion, to relate the four allegorical phases (or the "theory of symbols") with the five modes of fiction discussed in his first essay on the "theory of modes":[17] myth, romance, high mimetic, low mimetic, and ironic, which correspond to phases in Western literature as much as to types or modes of literature. To make five fit into four, Frye has smuggled a second phase into the arena of the first. A table expresses it best:[18]

Fictional modes (1st essay):	Allegorical phases (2nd essay)	Medieval levels
Ironic	1. Literal and descriptive	–
Low mimetic		Literal
High mimetic	2. Formal	Allegorical
Romance	3. Mythical	Moral
Myth	4. Anagogic	Anagogic

Jameson seizes on the terminological uncertainty. The attempt to fit five fictional modes into four allegorical phases (second column) creates some instability: five phases are grouped under four headings. Jameson's argument is that Frye has inverted the medieval moral and anagogic phases while introducing terminological confusion as well (Frye's "anagogic" does not have the same content as the medieval "anagogic"). Further evidence for Jameson's argument is in the shift of myth from the final fictional mode (first column) to the penultimate allegorical phase (second column): a more rigorous scheme would have located the mythical as the final allegorical phase and then renamed the anagogic, which would now be in the penultimate position.

Despite the ambiguities of this final level—combining a universal apocalyptic perspective with that of the individual body and providing a useful interplay between the social and libidinal bodies—Jameson finds that the individual ultimately dominates: "The essentially historical interpretive system of the church fathers has here been recontained, and its political elements turned back into the merest figures for the Utopian realities of the individual subject."[19]

Alongside this explicit argument are two dimensions of Jameson's discussion of Frye that are not articulated. First, although he criticizes the perceived inversion of the medieval system, Jameson also unconsciously draws out some important features for his own system. In the latter, the crucial middle phase, as we will see, is the social: here, Jameson would seem to be following Frye in locating the social in the middle phases rather than at either end of the process as in the medieval system. Further, Frye's final or anagogic level moves beyond society to consider issues of universal significance. While Jameson is unhappy with the dominance of the individual body at this level, his own system moves from the social to the universal (minus the libidinal body) in its final phase. The essential factor in this implicit appropriation of Frye is the distinction between the social and the universal, a distinction that operates in Frye's scheme and in the later elaboration of Jameson's, but is absent from Jameson's assessment of Frye, in which everything is lumped under the "collective" label. Thus, at a less conscious level, Jameson is indebted to the order of Frye's phases as they exist. In fact, he is able to achieve, or rather slip in, such an appropriation while the reader's attention is focused on the critique leveled at Frye.

Second, the tension between the criticism and the positive use of Frye's ordering of allegorical levels indicates another debate operating behind Jameson's arguments. On the surface, Jameson asserts the medieval order over against Frye, thereby making the cluster of questions associated with the individual a figure of, or an element on the way to, the greater domain of the social. I would suggest that this is a coded way of asserting the priority of Marxism over the temptations of a Freudian analysis; in other words, Freudian insights will ultimately be understood in the Marxist context and not vice versa. That Freud is a partner in this discussion is indicated by the treatment of Freud that immediately precedes that of Frye.

In light of Jameson's complex appropriation of Frye, what then happens to the relationship between individual and collective in Jameson's own hermeneutic scheme? Contrary to the expectations that follow the critique of Frye, Jameson does not develop a level or phase in which the individual person or body is the major concern. There is no Freudian level preceding the Marxist one. Rather than returning to the medieval order in which the individual—both Christ and the believer—received their own space, Jameson lops off, as it were, the final stage of Frye's allegorical scheme, or at least the parts concerned with the individual. Those concerns are then redirected to the two other phases of Jameson's three-phase approach, but in each case the individual is situated within a wider collective. Thus, in the first phase we find an important place given to the individual text in the context of specific historical developments. The all-important struggle between the individual person and society is contained within Jameson's second, or social, level. He has been able to achieve such containment in part because of Frye's own foregrounding of the individual-social interplays in his own system. Jameson signals his appreciation of Frye's treatment in this respect, digging into the Marxist tradition to locate the importance of both individual or libidinal liberation and social revolution, and this appreciation has spilled over into the construction of Jameson's allegorical system.

I have argued for two stages thus far—medieval allegory and Frye's reinterpretation—in the genealogy of Jameson's method. The third logical—as opposed to temporal—stage comes from a study on Walter Benjamin[20] in which Jameson interprets Benjamin by means of the fourfold mode of medieval exegesis. However, there is a crucial slippage in this study: whereas the four medieval levels were the literal, allegorical, moral, and anagogical, in the Benjamin article Jameson cites them as the literal, moral, allegorical, and anagogical. The levels are reinterpreted as follows: the literal becomes the psychological; the moral remains as such; the allegorical becomes the aesthetic or the religion of art; and the anagogic is transformed into the level of history or politics. The middle two levels have been interchanged, swapping the moral and the allegorical. The net effect is to fuse these two middle phases, leaving us with the literal, allegorical/moral, and anagogical.

The importance of this switch and fusion for the development of Jameson's Marxist allegorical method lies in two related areas: the reduction from four levels to three, and the role of the key allegorical level. Regarding the former, the medieval system had two levels that dealt with the individual, namely, the allegorical (Christ) and the moral (individual believer). In light of the Benjamin study, the distinction has effectively been collapsed and the new middle phase will be invested with all the concerns of the collective inherited from Frye's own reinterpretation. As far as the important allegorical level is concerned, I noted earlier that it was this level in the medieval approach that opened up the text for the other interpretive levels. The interchange in the Benjamin article between the second and the third levels serves to share the allegorical key between them, and with the folding of these two levels into one another, the second or middle phase of a three-level system becomes the new allegorical code breaker.

In this genealogy, there remains one final stage, in which a more traditional Marxist hermeneutic makes its contribution. Thus far, some of the elements in Jameson's own three-phase approach have slipped into place: from medieval allegory has come the emphasis on the literal at the first phase and the concern with the whole of history in the final level; from Northrop Frye also comes the importance of the literal at the first level as well as the individual-collective relationship; in the Benjamin study, the threefold system becomes clearer with the middle phase taking on the nature of an allegorical key. The remaining question is the nature of that second or middle phase: traditional Marxist hermeneutics supplies Jameson's option for the social as the allegorical key of his interpretive schema. For, in that tradition, the social, or "relations of production," functions as the prime mediation between the superstructure and the other dimensions of the base. In other words, as the following diagram illustrates, elements from culture, ideology, or politics relate to the economic by means of the social, whose major concern is class conflict.[21]

	Superstructure	Culture Ideology Legal system Political structures and the state
Mode of production		
	Infrastructure (economic)	Mediation: relations of production (social class) Forces of production (technology, ecology, and population)

Jameson's second level is also the social, and its prime interest is also the dynamic of class conflict. It is both allegorical key and mode of mediation between the levels.

Without going into the details of the base-superstructure relationship, or Jameson's favored situation-response model for the relation between the two, or even the reconstitution of the various levels as semiautonomous zones, my genealogy of Jameson's Marxist method—moving through medieval allegory, Northrop Frye, the Benjamin study, and the mediatory role of the social—has made its point. I leave Jameson's summary of the method itself as its best brief statement, for I want to pick up the tensions between metacommentary and Marxism in the final part of this essay. In specifying the argument that Marxist critical insights expand the understanding of texts by providing their ultimate semantic preconditions, Jameson argues that

> such semantic enrichment and enlargement of the inert givens and materials of a particular text must take place within three concentric frameworks, which mark a widening out of the sense of the social ground of a text through the notions, first, of political history, in the narrow sense of punctual event and a chroniclelike sequence of happenings in time; then of society, in the now already less diachronic and time-bound sense of a constitutive tension and struggle between social classes; and, ultimately, of history now conceived in its vastest sense of the sequence of modes of production and the succession and destiny of the various human social formations, from prehistoric life to whatever far future history has in store for us.

> These distinct semantic horizons are, to be sure, also distinct moments of the process of interpretation, and may in that sense be understood as dialectical equivalents of what Frye has called the successive "phases" in our reinterpretation—our rereading and rewriting—of the literary text. What we must also note, however, is that each phase or horizon governs a distinct reconstruction of its object, and construes the very structure of what can now only in a general sense be called "the text" in a different way.

> Thus, within the narrower limits of our first, narrowly political or historical, horizon, the "text," the object of study, is still more or less construed as coinciding with the individual or literary work or utterance. The difference between the perspective enforced and enabled by this horizon, however, and that of ordinary *explication de texte*, or individual exegesis, is that here the individual work is grasped essentially as a *symbolic act*.

> When we pass into the second phase, and find that the semantic horizon within which we grasp a cultural object has widened to

include the social order, we will find that the very object of our analysis has itself been thereby dialectically transformed, and that it is no longer construed as an individual "text" or work in the narrow sense, but has been reconstituted in the form of the great collective and class discourses of which a text is little more than an individual *parole* or utterance. Within this new horizon, then, our object of study will prove to be the *ideologeme*, that is, the smallest intelligible unit of the essentially antagonistic collective discourses of social classes.

When finally, even the passions and values of a particular social formation find themselves placed in a new and seemingly relativized perspective by the ultimate horizon of human history as a whole, and by their respective positions in the whole complex sequence of the modes of production, both the individual text and its ideologemes know a final transformation, and must be read in terms of what I will call the *ideology of form*, that is, the symbolic messages transmitted to us by the coexistence of various sign systems which are themselves traces or anticipations of modes of production.[22]

Marxism and Metacommentary

There are, then, two great lines in Jameson's method with a whole series of overlaps. (For instance, the Marxist method performs a "metacommentary" for other Marxist methods, and the perpetual shifting of metacommentary/ transcoding is comparable to the levels of Jameson's literary method.) But, as I have been arguing, there is also a significant tension between the two. Let me begin from the side of transcoding/metacommentary, for here lies a dilemma that Jameson has not been able to resolve. The advantages of the approach are considerable: the shift from one interpretive method or theory to another serves to demystify each of those methods by comparisons that show up the weak spots and the optionality of each of the methods through which one passes. The disadvantage, at least for a Marxist, such as Jameson, is the rapid enlistment of metacommentary and transcoding as advocates for a liberal tolerance of all viewpoints. In this liberal climate, an impossible situation develops: any maneuvers toward dominance and authority (as is attempted by Jameson by means of Marxism) are ruled illegitimate and totalitarian. But with self-criticism and admissions of relativity "the media excitement falls away, everyone loses interest, and the code in question, tail between its legs, can shortly be observed making for the exit from the public sphere or stage of that particular moment of History or discursive struggle."[23]

The problem here lies in Jameson's explicit advocacy of Marxism as the way to control and order the pluralism of methods and interpretations on which metacommentary, and transcoding rely. Looking at the problem from the side of metacommentary we can see that its basic assumption is to recognize the limited validity of a range of textual interpretations without granting any interpretation an exclusive claim to truth. The clash is quite clear, as also with transcoding, which deals with contemporary theory in a similar fashion. If a Marxist approach is included in the array of methods available for metacommentary or transcoding, then that approach must take its chances among the crowd of other options and approaches.[24] However—and here the difficulties begin—if Marxism were genuinely to be floated among the rising and falling success of other codes or methods, then it must be open to the risk of failure in comparison to other methods. The problem is that this never takes place: for Jameson, Marxism is not just another theory for open exchange on the methodological market. A number of grounds are presented for the argument that Marxism is more than a theory, the main one being its ability to provide a total picture within which other methods and interpretations may find their place; that is, a Marxist method does not displace other theories but subsumes them within its own program. The ability to do so relies in part on showing—by means of comparison with the Marxist method—how the appearance of complete readings by other methods is pretense and illusion. The basic problem may now be restated: if one method is assumed to be superior, then it is difficult for metacommentary to continue its path of comparing methods and interpretations.

I will restate the dilemma yet again, but this time in terms of the criticisms others have directed at Jameson. The dialectical activities of metacommentary and transcoding are other ways of describing a perpetually moving target—Jameson's interpretive strategy—that resists being pinned down in any one place. For some critics, this is a strength and a weakness: the ability of self-transformation or transcoding is useful and necessary to evade arrest, but it makes identification by comrades extraordinarily difficult.[25] The problem is that Marxism must take its polemical chances along with all the other codes, a situation that leaves open the possibility of being outmaneuvered and outplayed, and of having nothing that distinguishes it from, or makes it superior to, any other code or method.[26] Thus, with no means of transforming the other methods into more useful tools, they remain as they are.[27]

If this is a genuine suggestion—that is, that Marxism will not necessarily triumph at the close of play—then the suspicion is, given the contrast between the strong assertions of the priority of Marxism in *The Political Unconscious* and the more tempered comments in *Postmodernism*, along with his continued interest in reactionary figures such as Wyndham Lewis[28] and especially Heidegger,[29] that Jameson may be inadvertently selling out to liberalism or he may be covering a nocturnal border crossing into post-Marxism. This suspicion most often translates into concerns from critics of the Left over Jameson's political quietism and absence of a working-class base, which is reflected in his method and style.[30] For others, he is too Hegelian and thus idealist,[31] or simply too established and mainstream.[32] Those less sympathetic to Marxism feel that, in more recent work, his Marxism has been subsumed by postmodernism.[33] Jameson is caught: if he allows that Marxism must jostle for position in the theoretical marketplace, then he has de facto accepted liberal pluralism; if he asserts the superiority of Marxism, then there is less room to be open to the possibilities of other methods. Jameson's initial response has been a variation on the insistence of the privileged place of Marxism in interpretation. In its weaker form, this insistence becomes an inescapable yet unthinkable conviction, however momentarily held, that the method in use is privileged to some extent.[34] In a stronger sense, Jameson advocates, like Lukács before him,[35] the acceptance of a number of central problems of Marxism before an interpretation may be said to be Marxist:

> the nature, dynamics, and polarizing logic of social class; the labor theory of value; the commodity form and the four types of exchange value; alienation and commodity reification; the hidden logic of historical dynamics, most specifically in relationship to social evolution, but also in more static situations of domination or hegemony, national and international; a commitment to the problem of ideology (but not necessarily to any particular model of it), as well as to the problem of superstructures, in short, to the whole problem of the "determination of consciousness by social being"; finally, a sense of the great overall organizing concept of Marxism which is the notion of the mode of production, a concept which ought to end by raising the most urgent issues of the difference between capitalism and precapitalist societies, of the originality or not of present-day consumer or late monopoly capitalism as against the classical kind, and of course, last but most important, the possible nature of socialism or communism as a social formation.[36]

This first response, in either its weaker or stronger forms, may satisfy some of the questions, but it does not solve the problem I identified in the preceding paragraph. The more involved response might run as follows. The objection itself—that the Marxist membership card is difficult to decipher—is a modernist one, since it assumes enclaves, retreats, and pockets of resistance that have withstood the eradication campaigns or have been inadvertently bypassed by capitalism. The notion of resistance and of belonging to a resistance group generally works in such a modernist context, but it does not work in the present reality of postmodernism in which such pockets and corners have been finally eliminated. A new approach is required, and some of its features are those of Jameson's approach, namely, familiarity with contemporary theories and strategies and the taking on, even if temporarily, of their form and function. It might in fact be argued that transcoding constitutes the postmodern replacement of the older "critical distance." But this is no longer possible due to the invasion of the last enclaves by capital, Nature and the psyche, or, as Jameson puts it, the collapse of culture into society.[37] To make this whole argument more difficult to counter, it also might be argued that Marxism is a product of and response to capitalism: without capitalism, Marxism would not be identifiable in its present form. Thus, the third and thus far purest stage of capitalism—termed, following Mandel, "late capitalism" with the associated cultural dominant of postmodernism—might also be the time for the purest and strongest form of Marxist analysis itself.

However, lest metacommentary be viewed as a gentle comparative exercise, undertaken in comfort under a pluralist umbrella, more liberal than Marxist, Jameson's depiction of the violence of each interpretive act and of the conflictual nature of metacommentary comes as a timely warning. Thus, "all 'interpretation' in the narrower sense demands the forcible or imperceptible transformation of a given text into an allegory of its particular master code."[38] As far as metacommentary is concerned,

> Interpretation is not an isolated act, but takes place within a Homeric battlefield, on which a host of interpretive options are either openly or implicitly in conflict. . . . As the Chinese proverb has it, you use one ax handle to hew another: in our context, only another, stronger interpretation can overthrow and practically refute an interpretation already in place.[39]

Even in this quotation, the tension in Jameson's approach—between a desire to be open to a pluralism of methods and the "desire called Marx"—rises once again to the surface, for the "stronger interpretation" will in the final analysis be the Marxist one. In contrast to the depictions of Marxism as just one more method struggling for its place among a host of others,[40] Jameson suggests that Marxism is superior because it is more than just another method: it is "neither a contemporary *theory*, in the historically specific sense of this word, nor a contemporary *philosophy* (but rather, like Freud, that particular thing sometimes called a unity-of-theory-and-practice)."[41] Even more strongly, Marxist interpretation is superior due to its "semantic richness"; it provides the "necessary preconditions for adequate literary comprehension," indeed an "ultimate semantic precondition for the intelligibility of literary and cultural texts."[42]

Yet, as I have pointed out, Jameson does not wish to abandon a commitment to pluralism, so he distinguishes between what might be termed a "lazy" pluralism—each method assumes that it will be left alone in its own corner to pursue its own agenda without any interference from other methods or social and historical questions—and a conflictual pluralism of the battlefield and marketplace. Such a distinction indicates the difficulties under which he is working, not the least of which are those of his own situation.

I would suggest that the tension between pluralism and Marxism is in part due to Jameson's position in North America and the academy. There are three elements to this: his work responds, first, to the needs of the New rather than Old Left;[43] it is also a vigorous program to deal with and make Marxism relevant to the proliferation of theories and methods that began in the 1950s and 1960s (mostly in France, with an appropriate translational time lag into the 1980s and 1990s) and has since become known as "theory." Finally, it constitutes a response to and a massive effort to overcome the marginalization of Marxism in the United States and in the university, with the extent of that response functioning as a dialectical register of Marxism's exclusion from public and academic life. So, Jameson must hold onto a form of pluralism in order to remain within the bounds of critical and theoretical discussions that systematically exclude Marxism, while at the same time push his own significant critical skills to their limit in claiming for Marxism an overarching and central role over and within those discussions.

Marxism, it seems, staggers out of the conflict for the most part intact and ready to assume a new mantle, for this argument is an alternative way of stating Jameson's own solution: the very existence of transcoding and the optionality of the codes means that no code or ideology any longer braces our social system. In other words, neither a unifying ideology of society nor a collection of authoritative texts (the canon) remains to bolster this system. Jameson locates the major reason for this ideological and canonical collapse in the process of reification: as interpretations and methods become more obviously commodified, they become exchangeable with one another (hence metacommentary and transcoding). This means that no one interpretation, ideological construct, or canon is able to dominate the field; instead, all that is left is the celebratory and pleasurable act of consuming other interpretations or methods. That is, the commodity form—in its own right the reification of social relations—has been reified. Transcoding and metacommentary therefore become the methodological and textual projections, respectively, of the activity of commodity consumption. All of this suggests that the possibility of transcoding and metacommentary indicates a more fundamental unity of the historical situation of the various codes and methods—namely, late capitalism and its cultural dominant, postmodernism. With renewed vigor Marxism returns to map this postmodern situation, for it always was more of a union of theory and practice rather than a mere code or theory; or, to use Jameson's words, "when Marxism is dialectical enough it is superior."[44]

NOTES

1. Fredric Jameson, *The Political Unconscious: Narrative as a Socially Symbolic Act* (Ithaca: Cornell University Press, 1981), 10.

2. Jameson, *The Ideologies of Theory, Essays 1971–1986*. Volume 2: *Syntax of History*. *Theory and History of Literature* 49 (Minneapolis: University of Minnesota Press, 1988), iii–ix.

3. Ibid., viii.

4. Ibid.

5. Jameson, "Metacommentary," *PMLA* 86/1 (Jan 1971): 9–18. Reprinted in *The Ideologies of Theory, Essays 1971–1986*. Volume 1: *Situations of Theory*. *Theory and History of Literature* 48. Foreword by Neil Larsen (Minneapolis: University of Minnesota Press, 1988), 3–16.

6. Jameson, *Marxism and Form: Twentieth-Century Dialectical Theories of Literature* (Princeton: Princeton University Press, 1971), 306–416.

7. Jameson, *Postmodernism, or, the Cultural Logic of Late Capitalism. Post-Contemporary Interventions* (Durham: Duke University Press, 1991), especially 391–99.

8. Jameson, *The Seeds of Time* (New York: Columbia University Press, 1994), 137–38.

9. Jameson, *Postmodernism*, 394.

10. Jean-Paul Sartre, *Critique de la Raison Dialectique* (Précédé de Question de Méthode) Vol. 1: *Théorie des Ensembles Pratiques* (Paris: Librairie Gallimard, 1960), 92–93, trans. and Intro. Hazel E. Barnes (New York: Vintage Books (Random House), 1963), 146.

11. Jameson, *Marxism and Form*, 409.

12. Jameson, *Ideologies of Theory* I, 75–115. See also Michael Clark, "Imagining the Real: Jameson's Use of Lacan," *New Orleans Review* 11/1 (Spring 1984): 67–72.

13. Jameson, *Political Unconscious*, 23–50.

14. Ibid., 69–74.

15. Ibid., 70.

16. Northropp Frye, *Anatomy of Criticism* (Princeton: Princeton University Press, 1957), 73.

17. Ibid., 33–67.

18. Based on ibid., 115–16.

19. Jameson, *Political Unconscious*, 74.

20. Jameson, *Marxism and Form*, 60–83.

21. Jameson, *Political Unconscious*, 32.

22. Ibid., 75–76. See the restatement in *The Geopolitical Aesthetic: Cinema and Space in the World System* (Bloomington and Indianapolis, and London: Indiana University Press and British Film Institute, 1992), 212.

23. Jameson, *Postmodernism*, 397.

24. See *Ideologies of Theory* II, ix; as also with Jameson's proposal for postmodernism in "Afterword—Marxism and Postmodernism," in *Postmodernism/Jameson/Critique*, ed. Douglas Kellner (Washington: Maisonneuve, 1989), 383–84.

25. See James H. Kavanagh, "The Jameson Effect," *New Orleans Review* 11/1 (Spring 1984): 20–28; Neil Larsen, "Metadorno," (Review of *Late Marxism*) *Postmodern Culture* 2/2 (Jan 1992). Retrieval: Larsen.192 at http://jefferson.village.virginia.edu /pmc/contents.all.html; Jim Merod, *The Political Responsibility of the Critic* (Ithaca and London: Cornell University Press, 1987), 145.

26. See J. Fisher Solomon, *Discourse and Reference in the Nuclear Age* (Norman: University of Oklahoma Press, 1988), 252–59.

27. See Terry Eagleton, "Fredric Jameson: The Politics of Style," *Diacritics* 12/3 (Fall 1982): 17–18.

28. See Denis Donoghue, Review Fables of Aggression. *New York Review of Books* 29/7 (29 Apr 1982): 28–30.

29. Jameson, "Marx's Purloined Letter." *New Left Review* 209 (Jan/Feb 1995): 75–109.

30. Jonathan Arac, *Critical Genealogies: Historical Situations for Postmodern Literary Studies* (New York: Columbia University Press, 1987), 305–307; Eagleton, 14–22; Philip Goldstein, *The Politics of Literary Theory: An Introduction to Marxist Criticism* (Tallahassee: Florida State University Press, 1990), 154; Dan Latimer, "Jameson and Post-Modernism," *New Left Review* 148 (1984): 117; Victor Li, "Naming the System: Fredric Jameson's 'Postmodernism,'" *Ariel: A Review of International English Literature* 22/4 (Oct 1991): 137; Edward Said, "Opponents, Audiences, Constituencies, and Community," *Critical Inquiry* 9/1 (Sep 1982): 13–14; Susan Wells, *The Dialectics of Representation* (Baltimore: Johns Hopkins University Press, 1985), 16; Cornell West, "Fredric Jameson's Marxist Hermeneutics." *Boundary* 2 11 (1982): 177–200. See, in response, Jameson's comments on "single-shot, single-function" views of political action: "Interview: Fredric Jameson," by Leonard Green, Jonathan Culler, and Richard Klein. *Diacritics* 12/3 (Fall 1982): 75; Jameson, *Postmodernism*, 264.

31. Chimnoy Banerjee, "Review of Marxism and Form," *West Coast Review* 7/3 (Jan 1973): 63; Hentzi, "Faces of Totality," 61; Jay Murphy, "'The Wrong State of Things': Adorno's Marxism for the '90s," *Afterimage* 18 (May 1991): 12–13.

32. Dan Latimer. "Jameson and Postmodernism," 116–27; Curtis White, "Jameson out of Touch?," *American Book Review* 14 (Dec-Jan 1993): 21, 30.

33. Geoffrey Galt Harpham, "Postmodernism's Discontents," *Times Literary Supplement* June 28 (1991): 7–8; Mark Krupnick, "Review of Postmodernism," *Journal of Religion* 72 (1992): 636–37.

34. Jameson, "Demystifying Literary History," *New Literary History* 5/3 (Spring 1974): 611–12; *Ideologies of Theory* II, 148–49.

35. Georg Lukács, *History and Class Consciousness: Studies in Marxist Dialectics*, trans. Rodney Livingstone (Cambridge: MIT, 1971), 1–26.

36. Jameson, "Marxism and Teaching," *New Political Science* 2–3 (Fall–Winter 1979): 31.

37. Jameson, "Rimbaud and the Spatial Text," *Rewriting Literary History*, ed. Tak-wai Wong and M. A. Abbas (Hong Kong: Hong Kong University Press, 1984), 93; "Andrea Ward Speaks with: Fredric Jameson," *Impulse* 13/4 (Winter 1987): 8.

38. Jameson, *Political Unconscious*, 58.

39. Ibid., 13.

40. Ibid., 10, 31.

41. Jameson, *Ideologies of Theory* II, ix.

42. Jameson, *Political Unconscious*, 75.

43. Personal communication, November 1994.

44. Personal communication, November 1994.

4

Narratives of History, Narratives of Time

Sean Homer

> The historical materialist understands that the abstract mode in which
> cultural history presents its material is an illusion, established by false
> consciousness. He approaches this abstraction with reserve.
>
> —Walter Benjamin

In my study of Fredric Jameson, I advanced a series of criticisms of Jameson's conception of history, as formulated in *The Political Unconscious*.[1] First, I argued that Jameson enacts a spurious conflation of the Althusserian conception of history as an absent cause with the Lacanian notion of the Real. Drawing on the work of certain post-Marxist theorists, I contended that such a conflation was untenable and undercuts the view of history presented in *The Political Unconscious*. Second, I took issue with the assertion of history as a singular great narrative to wrest the realm of freedom from the realm of necessity or, to put it another way, as the narrative of class struggle. Deploying Hayden White's notion of emplotment[2] and recent work from postcolonial studies, I insisted that history was not a singular narrative as such but a multiplicity of potential narratives depending on how one emplots or narrativizes the given historical material. Finally, I insisted that if we take Althusser's critique of historicism seriously, and in particular his conception of differential temporalities, this would again undermine the singularity of history and posit a multiplicity of histories. Today, I would want to approach these criticisms, as Walter Benjamin puts it, with more reserve. There are primarily two reasons for this: the first is theoretical and the second political.

The initial impulse behind my critique was to advance an open, pluralist view of Marxism sensitive to a politics of difference and otherness. Indeed, I still do but I am no longer convinced of the validity and political implications of some of the arguments I used against Jameson, or that his own position is not more open and sensitive to the pulse of history than these critiques. At the time I was influenced by the project for radical democracy advanced by Laclau and Mouffe, whereas today that "radical" agenda has foreclosed on the possibility of universal social transformation and unashamedly returned, at best, to the traditions of European liberalism and, at worst, to the legacy of fascists.[3] What now constitutes a dialogue on the post-Marxist left, as witnessed in the recent exchange between Judith Butler, Ernesto Laclau, and Slavoj Žižek, is a rather arcane debate around Kantian formalism that stubbornly eschews discussion of the economic.[4] While all three theorists agree on the need to move beyond the particularity of specific identities in order to reconstitute a collective subject of historical change, for both Butler and Laclau this must take place within the constraints of the present horizon, yet only Žižek (rather naively from Laclau's point of view) insists on the need to demand the impossible and challenge the parameters of the horizon itself.[5] Within a globalized economy today the primary political objective must be to think the fundamental contradiction as the precondition upon which identity politics can arise, that is, class conflict. "With the rise of the anti-globalization movement," writes Žižek, "the era of the multitude of particular struggles that one should strive to link in a 'chain of equivalence' is over. This struggle (the only serious opposition movement today)—whatever one's critical apprehensions towards it—is clearly focused on capitalism as a global system."[6] It was in part, therefore, through a more sustained engagement with the work of Žižek that I began to rethink my criticisms of Jameson, but also from the persistence of history itself.

History, Jameson observed, tends not to forget us, however much we might want to ignore it; and today, history has returned with a vengeance few could have thought possible just a few short years ago. The final decade of the twentieth century—from the collapse of the Soviet Union in 1989, through the first Gulf War, the "humanitarian" intervention in Somalia, the carnage of Chechnya and the Balkans to September 11 and the obscene sight of the only remaining superpower on earth bombing, what was left of one of the poorest countries on earth back into the middle ages to the naked and cynical hypocrisy of the second Gulf War—has unequivocally forced history in that old-fashioned, modernist sense back onto the agenda. That is, history not as a set of competing narratives or genres but a single catastrophe piling wreckage upon wreckage.[7] It seems to me today politically more astute and ethical to contest the notion that history is simply competing constructions and narratives and, loosely paraphrasing Hardt and Negri, to cling to the primacy of the concept of historical truth as a necessary and powerful form of resistance.[8] It is now the Right who want to rewrite their atrocities as humanitarian narratives, "just wars," or a spurious defense against terror and to which the Left must oppose the reality of the event itself. As NATO and its allies seek to extend their war on the weak and impoverished around the globe,[9] a growing anticapitalist movement—apparently impervious to the sophistication of the postmodern world we live in—insistently links global exploitation, environmental degradation, and military expansionism to the economic imperative of capital. Postmodern history as a collection of "more or less plausible fictions"[10] looks pretty thin today and as Hayden White, the original influence behind much contemporary historiography, has observed, Marxism has emerged from this period of political and economic turmoil not discredited but as really the only explanatory framework that can adequately account for the global transformations of our age.[11] I want to reconsider, therefore, the three interrelated issues of history, narrative representation, and time and suggest that Jameson is much closer to the "truth" of history than the arguments I advanced. Let me briefly recapitulate Jameson's position in *The Political Unconscious* and my arguments before undertaking that self-critique.

MARXISM AS AN ABSOLUTE HISTORICISM

In *The Political Unconscious*, Jameson argued that Marxism alone can reveal to us the essential mystery of the past because only Marxism can restore, in the present, the real sense of urgency of past historical events as a single great collective narrative. Marxism is not an historicism but an absolute historicism, the untranscendable horizon of all interpretation and understanding. In an extraordinary display of dialectical thought, Jameson formulated a conception of *structural historicism* that incorporated Althusserian Marxism and Lacanian psychoanalysis (among a number of other contemporary theoretical discourses) within an overarching Hegelian philosophy of history. This was a theoretical gesture that many of Jameson's more postmodern and postcolonial critics saw as evidence of Marxism's oppressively totalizing logic and will to power.[12] What was seen as particularly scandalous in Jameson's text within a British context was the attempt to reconcile the antithetical traditions of Althusserian and Hegelian Marxism, especially since it was Althusser himself who, more than any other figure within Western Marxism, had discredited the Hegelian Marxist conception of history.[13] In *Reading Capital*, Althusser had argued that there were two fundamental errors of the Hegelian philosophy of history. First, it posited a *homogenous continuity of time* and, second, it fell prey to *contemporaneity*. In brief, Hegel saw history as essentially Spirit's biography and just as in the philosophy of mind consciousness dialectically transcends itself to achieve ever greater levels of awareness and reflexivity, history can be seen to proceed through a series of stages, each period succeeding the next as one dialectical totality after another. According to Althusser, Hegel's notion of totality was *expressive* in the sense that "all the elements of the whole always co-exist in one and the same time, one and the same present, and are therefore contemporaneous with one another in one and the same present."[14] History is thus reduced to a temporal continuity in which "events" take place in a succession of continuous presents or, as Jameson would characterize it, history is just one damned thing after another. Against this view of history as the unilinear evolution of a fixed sequence of periods, Althusser opposed the new "scientific" concepts of complex contradiction, overdetermination, structural causality, and *Darstellung* (presentation). *Darstellung* designates the mode of *presence* of the structure in its *effects*, and therefore designates structural causality as such. History, in other words, is an "absent cause," something that we know, not as the thing-in-itself, but through its effects. We cannot have empirical knowledge of history, only as a concept, and must therefore maintain at all times the distinction between the object of knowledge (the concept of history) and the real object (the empirical events of history).

Jameson conceded that on its own terms the Althusserian critique was quite unanswerable, but then suggested that this was to miss the point: Althusser's critique is not an attack on historicism as such. What is really at issue here is a dual problem around the nature of periodization and the representation of history—that is, the way in which the concept of an historical period presents everything as a seamless web of phenomena, each of which, in its own way, "expresses" some unified inner truth, and correspondingly, the way we are presented with a representation of history as merely the succession of such periods, stages, or moments. For Jameson, the second problem represents the prior one, for the reason "that individual period formulations always secretly imply or project narratives or 'stories'—narrative representations—of the historical sequence in which such individual periods take their place and from which they derive their significance."[15] What Althusser was attacking under the rubric of expressive causality, and historicism generally, suggests Jameson, is in fact allegorical interpretations that seek to rewrite given sequences or periods in terms of a hidden master-narrative. If we understand allegory, however, not as the reduction of the heterogeneity of historical sequences to a predetermined narrative but as an opening up of multiple horizons, then the concept of an historical narrative can be rehabilitated. Indeed, Jameson proposes that his conception of the political unconscious can resolve this dilemma of accommodating the Althusserian critique within a teleological, or more accurately *narrative*, vision of history if we acknowledge that:

> interpretation in terms of expressive causality or of allegorical master narratives remains a constant temptation, because such master narratives have inscribed themselves in the texts as well as in thinking about them; such allegorical narrative signifieds are a persistent dimension of literary and cultural texts precisely because they reflect a fundamental dimension of our collective thinking and our collective fantasies about history and reality.[16]

Our role as critics is not to abolish these faint murmurings of history and reality from texts but to retain them and open ourselves up once more to the reception of history through cultural texts. As Benjamin writes, our task as historical materialists is to "conceive of historical understanding as an after-life of that which is understood, whose pulse can still be felt in the present."[17] It is this sense of the living presence of history that, for Benjamin at least, distinguishes historical materialism from the purely contemplative approach of historicism. I will return to this issue later. According to Jameson, we can reformulate Althusser's conception of history, taking account of both his critique of expressive causality and interpretation generally while at the same time retaining a place for these operations, if we acknowledge that "history is *not* a text, not a narrative, master or otherwise, but that, as an absent cause, it is inaccessible to us except in textual form, and that our approach to it and to the Real *itself* necessarily passes through its prior textualization, its narrativization in the political unconscious."[18] As with the Althusserian conception of structure, history is not immediately present, not graspable in itself, but something we know through its effects or textualizations. Let me now turn to my three critiques of Jameson.

HISTORY AS REAL

As is evident from the previous quotation, there is an equivalence posited in Jameson's text between history as an absent cause and the real in Lacan. Throughout *The Political Unconscious*, this equivalence remains implicit, taking the form of an analogy between Jameson's own dialectically expanding horizons of interpretation, the text, the social and history, and Lacan's three orders: the imaginary, the symbolic, and the real, but the implications of this analogy are never fully elucidated. Primarily, Jameson utilizes Lacanian categories to ground cultural texts in history and retain access to history without recourse to either naive realism or vulgar materialism. The structural analogy between the text and history and the symbolic and the real is further supported through the function of contradiction and desire within each theorist's system. The presence of history within a given text manifests itself as a particular form of contradiction; history is that which resists desire. In short, contradiction serves "as the measure of the effect of History on its 'narrativization' and functions in much the same way as that of desire for Lacan, that is, as an 'anchoring point' that orients the symbolic toward the real."[19] For Jameson, the Lacanian real is simply history itself, albeit for psychoanalysis this will mean the history of the subject and for Marxism the history of class struggle.[20]

Jameson was by no means the first critic to attempt a rapprochement between structural Marxism and Lacanian psychoanalysis. The move was instigated by Althusser himself in his important 1964 essay "Freud and Lacan" as well as his influential reformulation of ideology as a system of representation and subjectification,[21] and it is through this problematic of ideology and the subject that Jameson himself came to incorporate Lacanian ideas within his text. The critique of Althusser's use of Lacan is now well established and I do not want to rehearse it again here.[22] From a post-Marxist perspective, the gulf separating Althusser from Lacan was seen to be completely unbridgeable, and certainly Althusser's conception of the ideological subject was emphatically not the Lacanian subject of the unconscious.[23] However, the gulf separating the Marxian problematic of historical agency and social production on the one hand and Lacanian psychoanalysis on the other has now, at least in part, been bridged through the work of Slavoj Žižek, who has, more than any other contemporary theorist, reorientated our understanding of Lacan around the concept of the real. As Žižek has increasingly come to distance himself from his former post-Marxist affiliations, the real has come to operate in his work as history in the Jamesonian sense. In *The Sublime Object of Ideology*, Žižek explicitly aligned the real with Laclau and Mouffe's conception of *antagonism*:

> the precise definition of the real object: a cause which in itself does not exist—which is present only in a series of effects, but always in a distorted, displaced way. If the Real is the impossible, it is precisely this impossibility which is to be grasped through its effects. Laclau and Mouffe were the first to develop this logic of the Real in its relevance for the social-ideological field in their concept of *antagonism*: antagonism is precisely such an impossible kernel, a certain limit which is in itself nothing; it is only to be constructed retroactively, from a series of its effects, as the traumatic point which escapes them; it prevents a closure of the social field.[24]

For Laclau and Mouffe, antagonism was to be clearly delineated from any Marxian conception of dialectical or determinate contradiction in the sense that Jameson would use it.[25] A couple of years later, Žižek identifies the real, with an Althusserian conception of history as an absent cause:

> The symbolic order is "barred," the signifying chain is inherently inconsistent, "non-all," structured around a hole. This inherent non-symbolizable reef maintains the gap between the Symbolic and the Real—that is, it prevents the Symbolic from "falling into" the Real— and, again, what is ultimately at stake in this decentrement of the Real with regard to the symbolic is the Cause: the Real is the absent Cause of the Symbolic.[26]

More recently, the real has come to be associated with the underlying logic of global capital itself. For instance, reflecting on recent ecological crises in the introduction to *The Ticklish Subject*, Žižek remarks that "this catastrophe thus gives body to the Real of our time: the thrust of Capital which ruthlessly disregards and destroys particular life-worlds, threatening the very survival of humanity."[27] Elsewhere, the real is associated directly with the Marxian conception of class struggle as the ultimate limit of history. Class struggle is real in the sense that it is unsymbolizable (one Lacanian definition of the real); there is no neutral position from which one can stand outside of class struggle and thus symbolize it. The real, writes Žižek, is the nonhistorical kernel of a historical situation: "The Lacanian Real is not some eternal essence, but strictly an historical Real. Not a Real that is simply opposed to quick historical changes, but the Real that generates historical changes while at the same time being reproduced by these changes."[28]

I have argued elsewhere that Žižek's deployment of the real raises certain difficulties in terms of articulating a Marxian political strategy, that is, a strategy of solidarity in which different groups in struggle come to recognize their common interest in opposing capital.[29] What *is* clear, however, is that the real for Žižek is precisely Jameson's understanding of history as radically unsymbolizable and at the same time constantly threatening to erupt in our symbolic universe as the violence of class conflict and social struggle. The real as that which is beyond the symbolic and radically unsymbolizable is the nondiscursive kernel of history that forestalls a purely narrative or constructivist view of history. If this is the case, though, in what sense can history be said to be a narrative.

HISTORY AS NARRATIVE

Jameson emphasizes that history is fundamentally nonnarrative and nonrepresentable, history is not a text but remains inaccessible except through its prior (re)textualizations. This raises a number of questions and specifically, "if history is accessible only through discursive or epistemological categories, is there not a real sense in which it therefore has only a discursive existence?"[30] Jameson, rightly I think, is at pains to avoid such a conclusion as this would lead down the poststructuralist path of textuality, discursive determinism and postmodern relativism. One does not have to argue the reality of history, he writes, "necessity, like Dr. Johnson's stone, does that for us."[31] History, for Jameson, is the experience of necessity, it is not a narrative in the sense that it represents the content of a story but rather the form through which we experience necessity, the formal effects of an absent, nonrepresentational, cause. History as a properly narrative political unconscious paradoxically needs no justification:

Conceived in this sense, History is what hurts, it is what refuses desire and sets inexorable limits to individual as well as collective praxis, which its "ruses" turn into grisly and ironic reversals of their overt intention. But this History can be apprehended only through its effects, and never directly as some reified force. This is indeed the ultimate sense in which History as ground and untranscendable horizon needs no particular theoretical justification: we may be sure that its alienating necessities will not forget us, however much we might prefer to ignore them.[32]

History is not so much a process we can know, but a structural limit on consciousness and agency, a limit we constantly come up against whether or not we intend it. The danger here, however, is that it risks precipitating the theory of history back into real history, or the conflation of the object of Knowledge with the real object. To put it another way, the reduction of the theory or science of history to history itself continually runs the risk of "collapsing into empiricism."[33] In an attempt to avoid this slide into empiricism, I turned to contemporary theories of "emplotment."

We do not need to completely abandon the concept of history as narrative, I argued, but we must distinguish between the essentially narrative characteristic of history and the assertion that history is itself a narrative. Narrative's particular value, as Paul Ricoeur has shown, lies in its "intelligibility," in its ability to organize the bewildering mass of historical data into a form that is readily understandable. Indeed, if history were to shed its narrative links, it would cease to be historical. There is an irreducible gap introduced with the advent of the narrative between itself and lived experience, between living and recounting, a gap—however small it may be—is opened up. "Life is lived, history is recounted."[34] While both human experience and narrative share a temporal quality, temporality does not constitute a narrative and neither, as I will argue, does it constitute history. In other words, our experience of life does not necessarily have the form of narrative, except and insofar as we give it that form through processes of selection and organisation, or the various ways in which that lived experience is emploted. The notion of emplotment is politically very appealing, it raises the possibility that we can overturn our received representations of history, which, to quote Benjamin again, is always the history of the victors, and attempt to brush against the grain of history. In other words, we can begin to retrieve and recount those very histories of the oppressed, the colonized, racial and sexual minorities who have been marginalized by traditional historical accounts. The notion also foregrounds the inherently ideological component of history, that narrative form is not neutral or scientifically objective but rests on certain ideological presuppositions. As historians and critics, we not only select and organize the discrete events and actions we are choosing to recount, but we also make certain narrative decisions on where a particular historical account commences and ends, or what we select to include and exclude from that account. These narrative decisions will confer a sense of coherence and completion on a given historical sequence and, above all, construct the "meaning" of history.

These debates, which were initially fought out between Marxism and postmodernism in the 1980s, have found greater political resonance today in the expanding field of Holocaust studies.[35] In the early 1960s, Adorno observed that there could be no poetry after Auschwiz and that the Holocaust marked the limit of representation; the suffering of the Holocaust is at once on a scale that cannot be represented but at the same time it must be, and this is the paradox of the Holocaust as an historical event.[36] In the 1980s, the postmodernists took up this debate, but not the dialectic that grounded it in history itself. Lyotard suggested that the Holocaust marks the ultimate limit of our discursive horizon, the point at which rational discourse comes to a stop. Moreover, if we enter into discursive struggle with the Holocaust revisionists, then we have already lost the argument, we have conceded the ground to the revisionists because the Holocaust, as an event, cannot be accounted for within the limits of rational discourse and inquiry.[37] In other words, Lyotard prioritized one side of Adorno's paradox, its unrepresentability, at the expense of the other, that is, the absolute need for serious artists to try and represent the Holocaust truthfully. Stephen Greenblatt has succinctly and, to my mind, successfully countered Lyotard's argument that Holocaust revisionism is essentially an epistemological problem; for Greenblatt it is rather an "attempt to wish away evidence that is both substantial and verifiable." I will come back to this later.[38] A few years ago, the theoretical issues raised by Holocaust Studies reached the front pages of the British press when in 2000 the revisionist historian David Irving sued Deborah Lipstadt for slandering his reputation as a legitimate historian. In *Denying the Holocaust: The Growing Assault on Truth and Memory*,[39] Lipstadt had accused Irving of being a Holocaust denier and misrepresenting historical truth; what is interesting about the trial and the debate that surrounded it was not so much what was said but precisely that *no* debate actually took place. Lipstadt would not enter into a discussion with Irving, she would not be interviewed in the press or on television, and she would not allow Irving, who conducted his own case, to cross-examine her in court. Her reasoning was strangely reminiscent of Lyotard's argument for not entering into discussion with revisionists in that Holocaust denial is beyond reasonable and rational argument. I say strangely because in *Denying the Holocaust*, Lipstadt identifies the skepticism of Lyotard and postmodern historiography in general with not Holocaust revisionism as such, but contributing to the intellectual climate in which it can flourish. Unlike Lyotard, however, this is not because the Holocaust marks the end of discursive possibility, but because the empirical evidence for the event is so overwhelming that no reasonable or objective person can deny the facts. To deny the Holocaust is not a more or less plausible narrative position to be discursively negotiated, but an overtly ideological and anti-Semitic stance. While I am politically more sympathetic to Lipstadt than to Lyotard in this instance, I find the idea of not engaging with racists and anti-Semites precisely because they are racists and anti-Semites problematic, as this potentially cedes the ground to the revisionists from which their ideas can proliferate. From a Jamesonian perspective, we are still left with the problem that the Holocaust is not a narrative and remains fundamentally unrepresentable, but at the same time we only have access to it through narrative representation. Hayden White has tried to formulate a compromise position between the theory of historical tropes or emplotment and asserting the reality of the Holocaust as an historical event. I want to follow White's argument as it highlights the difficulties encountered with a purely discursive approach to history.

According to White, there is an inevitable and "inexpugnable" relativity to historical representation because historical accounts, like factual statements, remain linguistic entities and of the order of discourse. "The relativity of representation," writes White, "is a function of the language used to describe and thereby constitute past events as possible objects of explanation and understanding."[40] Unless we adopt a naively realist position and see historical accounts as literally the representation of real events, then we are not in a position to criticize that representation on the grounds of its "true" or "false" presentation of facts. This is where the Holocaust poses certain problems, for if we are to take White at his word, then we cannot refute the recent trend of revisionist historiography that has sought to rewrite or even deny the events of the Holocaust through an appeal to the reality of the events themselves (i.e., Lyotard's position). White, understandably, does not want to accept such a politically ambiguous position. If there are indeed competing narratives of history, he argues, these are essentially competing "modes of emplotment," but to avoid absolute relativism he qualifies this assertion with an acknowledgment that there are limits imposed on particular modes of emplotment by given historical events. The specific genre one chooses, for example, whether tragedy, comedy, farce, and so on, will also determine the events to be included and the sequence in which they will be recounted. Thus, it is inconceivable that the Holocaust can be emploted as a comedy or a romance and, if it was, we can legitimately argue that this is a falsification of events. Although, clearly Mel Brooks's 1968 film *The Producers* or Roberto Benigni's *Life Is Beautiful* (1997) make this argument difficult to maintain. White suggests, however, that to adopt this approach is really to miss the point about the Holocaust. Debates over the possibility or impossibility of its representation are not in fact over the reality or otherwise of specific historical events but rather over the kinds of language we use to represent these events. In short, we are overly preoccupied with a mode of historical representation indebted to notions of verisimilitude and literary realism for what is an essentially modernist event. "It is not that history is no longer represented realistically," he argues, "but rather that our conceptions of both reality and history have changed."[41] In a formulation reminiscent of Jameson's conception of the logic of content, White insists that older forms of "realistic" representation are simply inadequate to articulate an experience that was unique to our century and that new, more modernist, modes of historical representation will be required to fully express or present this experience.

White's argument is persuasive but does not appear to resolve the issue so much as displace it. He once more brackets the question of historical reference and shifts the debate to the order of discourse and competing modes of representation. In a response to White, Perry Anderson has insisted that there are both extrinsic and intrinsic limits to emplotment set by the historical evidence itself.[42] Narrative strategies are only credible if they operate within certain exterior limits and subject to the control and rules of historical evidence. Intrinsically, narrative strategies are subject to the dual restraint of, on the one hand, and as White acknowledged, specific kinds of evidence ruling out certain forms of emplotment, and, on the other, the relative weakness of generic forms to determine the selection of evidence. For example, Lipstadt did not refuse to debate with Irving simply because she did not like the narrative he presented but because he failed to abide by the extrinsic constraints, the weight of historical evidence, that render his narrative meaningful as historical discourse and he refused to acknowledge the intrinsic constraints of historiography around the selection, interpretation, presentation, and validation of evidence. We may not therefore be able to constitute our historical narratives quite as we choose because of constraints on the potential forms of narrativization. This is not to deny what White calls the "inexpungable relativity in historical representation," but it is to suggest that it is more historically constrained and limited than he may be prepared to accept. We can agree, I think, that historiography involves processes of interpretation, narrativization, and construction without having to accept that it is reducible to these processes; historical facts are not given, but neither are they the starting point for historical inquiry—they are its outcome.[43] Whether we deem those "facts" to be true or false depends not on the structure of discourse but on the nature of the world to which they apply.[44] In short, we can accept White's "inexpugnable" relativism of historical discourse without relativizing history itself or committing what Roy Bhasker calls the epistemological fallacy.[45] Theories of emplotment tend to elide the separation of the real and the symbolic. In other words, the real, or history, is simply folded back into the representation of history. Whereas I had sought to forestall the slide into empiricism, I only succeeded in severing any genuine link between history and the text, reducing history to a text in precisely the manner Jameson was seeking to avoid. What has been lost in this maneuver is that creative tension that Jameson defines as contradiction and Lacan desire, and it is within that irreducible gap between the real and the symbolic, or, text and history, that we as subjects and social agents find a space to act and intervene in events. What I want to suggest is that if we accept the notion of history as real, we can avoid this theoretically and politically debilitating collapse and avoid identifying history with its representation.

LACAN AGAINST THE HISTORICISTS

Jameson has always maintained that Marxism is not a theory of history or a historicism, as it does not relativize the past in terms of the present but rather sees history as the fundamental and intractable limit of the social. This critique of historicism, I would now argue, is fully consistent with a Lacanian conception of the real and would forestall the more constructivist elements of postmodern historiography. In *Read My Desire*, Joan Copjec defines historicism as "the reduction of society to its indwelling network of relations of power and knowledge" without any reference to a principle or a subject that "transcends" that regime of power and knowledge.[46] Her critique is explicitly aimed at Foucault, but can be extended to contemporary historicism in general. The dilemma facing historicism is that the past as such is irretrievable and therefore must be "constructed." In the attempt to avoid a teleological representation of history, historicism tends to foreground the radical *discontinuity* of history, conceptualizing history, not in the Hegelian/Lukácsian sense of a "progressive longitudinal totality" but rather as a series of displacements, ruptures, and breaks. As Copjec points out, the abandonment of historical continuity immediately falls prey to contemporaneity:

> Its stolid denial of any 'transcendence', of any notion that there is a beyond *internal* to historical reality, or that there is something that will forever remain inarticulable in any historical text, is what leads new historicism to isolate each historical moment from the one preceding and following it, and to reduce it to its contemporaneity with itself—that is, to an account of what is conceivable at any particular moment, to what it was possible to think at a certain time.[47]

Historicism is condemned to what Copjec calls "presentism" precisely because it fails to countenance a "beyond" to historical reality (in Lacanian terms, the symbolic), a moment that forever remains inarticulable or, to put it another way, something that escapes our representations of history. What psychoanalysis teaches us through notions of unconscious desire and fantasy is how such a coincidence between subject and object, between the representation and the real, can never fully succeed. The representation can never be fully self-identical to what it represents; there will always be something that escapes it, an excess, a leftover. It is this excess or leftover that Žižek defines as the "non-historical kernel of history," or the real. The attempt to comprehend history on its own terms will be perpetually stalled as "the circuit of self-recognition or coincidence with itself which would enable such comprehension is deflected by an investment that cannot be recuperated for self-knowledge."[48] Historicity, argues Copjec, is grounded in this constitutive gap between history and its own self-recognition; the error of historicism is to mistake the representation for the thing itself or, to put it another way, to confuse the social reality of the symbolic with the radical historicity and alterity of the real.[49]

From the Lacanian/Žižekian perspective I am developing here, the political imperative is not to attempt to restore those moments of historical amnesia to give a fuller, truer, account of history—an impossible endeavor and fundamental misrecognition of the nature of the problem itself—but rather to recognize the constitutive nature of that failure. Briefly and rather schematically, teleological accounts of history rest on the presupposition of an objective historical process, independent of human consciousness, the necessary laws of which can be discerned through their repetition. Žižek argues that historical necessity is not the repetition of independent objective laws but instead a process of misrecognition. In other words, it is not the objective laws of history that are repeating themselves but rather an initial failed encounter with the real. Symbolic repetition is the repetition of a contingent traumatic and *unsymbolizable* encounter with the real that is only retrospectively, through its repetition, posited as the cause of historical process.

> The crucial point here is the changed symbolic status of an event: when it erupts for the first time it is experienced as a contingent trauma, as an intrusion of a certain non-symbolized Real; only through repetition is this event recognized in its symbolic necessity— it finds its place in the symbolic network; it is realized in the symbolic order.[50]

Necessity is not on the side of history as such, the contingent trauma of an unsymbolizable encounter, but on the side of the symbolic where "these past failed [events] which 'will have been' only through their repetitions, at which point they become retroactively what they already were."[51] The notion of historical necessity therefore does not work proleptically but rather analeptically. Historical necessity cannot tell us how things may be in the future, how the inevitable laws of history may unfold to reveal to us the future that always remains open, but only how things have been and *how they could have been no other way*. It is certainly true to say that historicity in this sense is a construction, it is something that is retrospectively posited and continually reappraised, but what is constitutive of historicity is not symbolic repetition as such but that initial failed encounter "experienced as a contingent trauma, as an intrusion of a certain non-symbolized Real." It is this sense of the real that divides historical materialism from historicism:

> We have a certain tension between historicity and the non-historical,
> where, to avoid any misunderstandings (and this I think is the ulti-
> mate of the historical dialectic), it is not simply that everything is his-
> torical (this is false historicism), it is that each historical epoch—we
> must historicize eternity itself, if I can put it that way, in the sense
> that we still have to retain the opposition between eternity and his-
> toricity—that each historical epoch produces or posits its own eternal
> presupposition. Within each epoch, you have a certain antagonism, a
> certain dramatic point around which this epoch turns. But it is not
> eternal, it is just constructed as eternal.[52]

For Žižek, that presupposition that defines our epoch today is class struggle,
not in the sense of a nonhistorical essence but as the "nonfoundational" foundation of all other struggles, that which defines and sustains the field of all
other struggles today. Moreover, there is only one figure in the whole history
of Marxism who has recognized "this non-historical 'ex-timate' kernel of history" and that is Walter Benjamin, a figure who uniquely conceived of "history
as a text, a series of events which 'will have been'—their meaning, their historical dimension, is decided afterwards, through their inscription in the symbolic network."[53] I would want to add to this, however, that Benjamin does not
see the past as simply a text but as a unique "living" experience; in "Theses
XVI" he writes, "Historicism gives the 'eternal' image of the past; historical
materialism supplies a unique experience with the past."[54] It is this sense of
urgency of the past in the present that marks out for Benjamin the historical
materialist from the historicist and it is this sense of urgency that is recognized
by Jameson today. History, from a Lacanian perspective, is not reducible to the
symbolic, to social reality, but is that which exceeds the symbolic. History is
the leftover, the hard impenetrable kernel resisting symbolization, but at the
same time only knowable through its effects on the symbolic. History is not
images of so-called smart bombs destroying mosques in Iraq, or lines of deso-
late figures crossing snow-covered mountains in the Balkans. It is not the
images of post-apocalyptic ruins of Chechnia or Afghanistan but the trace that
remains sedimented within those ruins, as we see in Iraq today, the excess and
violence that are unrepresentable and unassimilable that constantly threaten to
erupt and blast us out of the postmodern complacency of our contemporary
discursive regime.

TIME AND HISTORY

Let me now conclude with my final criticism of Jameson's structural historicism. Althusser, as I said earlier, rejected the Hegelian conception of a *continuous and homogenous time*, insisting that as it posited an immediate and

continuous present it could not be regarded as the *time of history*. In contrast to the contemporaneity of the Hegelian philosophy of history, Althusser posited a *differential* conception of historical time. That is, if we consider the social whole as a structural totality in the Althusserian sense, then we can posit for each of its various levels (economic, political, judicial, etc.) a specific temporality particular to that level. Althusser writes:

> it is no longer possible to think the process of the development of the different "levels" of the whole *in the same historical time*. Each of these different "levels" does not have the same type of historical existence. On the contrary, we have to assign to each level a *peculiar time*, relatively autonomous and hence relatively independent, even in its dependence, of the "times" of the other levels.[55]

In this sense, we can speak of the time and history of philosophy, for example, or the time and history of aesthetics, each specific level has its own particular temporality and its own history. Thus, for Althusser we must not only conclude that there are differential temporalities, but also that there are different *histories* corresponding to the different levels of the social totality. Following the logic of Althusser's arguments, I suggested that this rules out any conception of history as a singular unending narrative as formulated by Jameson. Again, though, I am no longer entirely convinced that a differential conception of temporality and the historicity of specific levels of the social totality automatically rules out a conception of the singularity of history itself.

There are two principal grounds for this. First, my criticism rests on an unfounded conflation of temporality and history. Second, my arguments fail to acknowledge the different levels of analysis and abstraction that both Althusser and Jameson are working with. Let me consider the question of temporality first. As Peter Osborne has pointed out, there are three broad conceptions of time and they are not all historical.[56] These three conceptions Osborne identifies as the objective or cosmological perspective, that is, the relationship of time to nature; the subjective phenomenological perspective, which is primarily concerned with lived experience and individual time-consciousness; finally, what he designates as the intersubjective or social perspective, and it is this third category that is associated with a historical multiplicity of forms of time-consciousness that together make up the time of history or "historical time." In other words, not all time is historical, neither objective nor subjective phenomenological time are historical in the sense that we understand historical time as a relationship to the past as well as nature. Furthermore, historical time is associated with a multiplicity of temporalities and in fact encompasses two quite different kinds of historical temporality: "There are the multiple temporalities associated with the historical and geographical diversity of social practices, and there is the single overarching temporality—

the time of History with a capital H—through which these multiple temporalities are unified, they are unified, into a single complex system."[59] According to Osborne, it is unavoidable that some form of totalization of social times
into history, in its emphatic sense, takes place.

In other words, it is not inconsistent to posit a differential notion of temporality, or what Osborne calls alternative temporalizations of history, with an
insistence on history as a collective singular. We are simply referring to different levels of experience and abstraction here. Indeed, what I had overlooked in
my original reading of Althusser's conception of differential time was that his
insistence on the *relative autonomy* of specific temporalities and histories does
not completely sunder their relations from each other. Relative autonomy does
not imply that these histories are totally independent of each other or the
whole itself but rather "their relative autonomy and independence—is based
on a certain type of articulation in the whole, and therefore on a certain type
of dependence with respect to the whole."[58] There is, in short, a level at which
the multiplicity of temporalities and histories are unified and articulated as a
whole. As Etienne Balibar puts it, "in the history of different social formations
there is a multiplicity of 'times,' each contemporary with one another, some of
which present themselves as a continuous progression, whereas others effect a
'short circuit' between the most ancient and the most recent. This 'overdetermination' . . . is the very form assumed by the *singularity* of history."[59] It is this
level of abstraction, not as something we can immediately experience, or know
as a thing-in-itself, but as a contradictory and overdetermined space that
encompasses both identity and difference, singularity and multiplicity, that
Jameson designates History with a capital H.

THE RETURN OF THE REPRESSED

On October 2, 2003, the Iraq Survey Group (ISG) presented its eagerly
awaited report to the U.S. Congress about weapons of mass destruction in
Iraq. This report would retrospectively provide George W. Bush's "smoking
gun" and justification for the massive bombing of Iraq in the second Gulf War.
What was striking about the report, however, was that they found no "shining
weapons." Indeed, the report claimed that Saddam Hussein's chemical
weapons program had been disbanded long before the war, that there has been
no attempt to resume his nuclear weapons program after the first Gulf War,
that there was no evidence to confirm that Iraqi military units were prepared
to use biological weapons, that Iraq had no long-range weapons, or that Iraq
had any stocks of banned weapons at all. None of this would come as any surprise to the antiwar movement that had been arguing just this case for the previous year, and one might have expected the Bush and Blair administrations to

be a little embarrassed, to say the least. Far from it. Jack Straw, the British foreign secretary, claimed that the report offered "incontrovertible evidence" that the Iraqi regime was in breach of UN resolutions, Tony Blair insisted that had the UN seen this report before the war, it would have supported the invasion, and the U.S. State Department claimed that a ten-year-old vial of Botulinum B found in a scientist's refrigerator constituted a weapon of mass destruction. What is striking about this barefaced rewriting of history is the degree of discrepancy between the representation and the represented. Despite attempts by the United States and the United Kingdom to retrospectively justify their imperialistic aggression and present the new Iraq as peaceful, democratic, and law abiding, or at least better than it was under Ba'ath regime, the determinate contradiction between history and text is too great. The discursive narrativization of the second Gulf War is presently collapsing under the weight of its own contradictions and the insistence of history itself. Both the Bush and Blair administrations are struggling to represent the war as a success while the body count mounts and the chaos spreads. The real of this event cannot be *sutured* and stitched neatly back into symbolic network and it is this radical antagonism for Žižek and contradiction for Jameson that finally appears to be bringing the U.S. and British administrations to account for their actions. Bush and Blair cannot emplot this event in any way they choose because the real of the event is still disrupting and restructuring the symbolic framework through which we understand it. The value of Jameson's notion of the political unconscious was to hold open that gap between history and text, to refuse to collapse history back into discourse or narrative, and to insist on the determinate contradiction between the two. History, as that ultimate horizon of understanding, may be forever out of reach and unknowable as a thing-in-itself, but at the same time it stands in judgment of our discrete narrative constructions. And as Jameson and Žižek persist in reminding us, it is only against this horizon, the universalization of capital, that these discrete narratives of history make sense. More important, though, the lesson we should take from Jameson and Žižek today is that for the historical materialist, the purpose is not just to understand the logic of capital, but to intransigently oppose it at every opportunity and challenge the very limits of that horizon.

NOTES

1. Sean Homer, *Fredric Jameson: Marxism, Hermeneutics, Postmodernism* (Cambridge: Polity Press, 1998).

2. Hayden White, *Metahistory: The Historical Imagination in Nineteenth Century Europe* (Baltimore: John Hopkins University Press, 1973).

3. See Chantal Mouffe, *The Return of the Political* (London: Verso, 1993) and the edited volume *The Challenge of Carl Schmitt* (London: Verso, 1999).

4. Judith Butler et al., *Contingency, Hegemony, Universality: Contemporary Dialogues on the Left* (London: Verso, 2000).

5. Butler et al., *Contingency, Hegemony, Universality*, 205.

6. Slavoj Žižek, "'What Some Would Call . . .': A Response to Yannis Stavrakakis," in *Umbr(a)* 1 (2003): 131–35. For a succinct overview of the current state of debate on the economic, military, ideological, and political aspects of globalization see Michael Mann, "Globalization and September 11," *New Left Review* 12 (November/December, 2001): 51–72 and for Jameson's analysis see "Notes on Globalization as a philosophical Issue," *The Cultures of Globalization*, ed. Fredric Jameson and Masao Miyoshi (Durham: Duke University Press, 1998) and "Globalization and Strategy," *New Left Review*, 4 (July/August, 2000): 49–68.

7. Walter Benjamin, "These on The Philosophy of History," *Illuminations* (London: Fontana, 1992).

8. Michael Hardt and Antonio Negri, *Empire* (Cambridge: Harvard University Press, 2000), 156.

9. Ellen Meiksins Wood, "Infinite War," *Historical Materialism* 10 (1) (2002): 7–27.

10. Christopher Norris, "Postmodernizing History: Right-Wing Revisionism and the Uses of Theory," *Southern Review* 21 (2), (1988): 123–40.

11. White, "Hayden White Talks Trash: An Interview by Frederick Aldama," *Bad Subjects*, 55 (May, 2001) <http://eserver.org/bs/55/white.html>.

12.1See Linda Hutcheon, *The Politics of Postmodernism* (London: Routledge. 1989), especially chapter 3.

13. See Robert Young, *White Mythologies: Writing History and the West* (London: Routledge, 1990).

14. Louis Althusser and Etienne Balibar, *Reading Capital*, trans. Ben Brewster (London: Verso, 1970), 94.

15. Fredric Jameson, *The Political Unconscious: Narrative as a Socially Symbolic Act* (London: Methuen, 1981), 28.

16. Jameson, *The Political Unconscious*, 34.

17. Benjamin, "Eduard Fuchs, Collector and Historian," 252.

18. Jameson, *The Political Unconscious*, 35.

19. Michael Clark, "Imagining the Real: Jameson's use of Lacan," *New Orleans Review* 11 (1) (1984): 68.

20. Jameson, "Imaginary and Symbolic in Lacan: Marxism, Psychoanalytic Criticism and the Problem of the Subject," *Literature and Psychoanalysis, The Question of Reading: Otherwise*, ed. Shoshana Felman (Baltimore: John Hopkins University Press, 1982), 387.

21. See Althusser, "Freud and Lacan" and "Ideology and Ideological State Apparatus (Notes towards an Investigation)," *Essays on Ideology* (London: Verso, 1984).

22. See, for example, Paul Hirst, "Althusser and the Theory of Ideology," *Economy and Society* 5 (4) (1976); Slavoj Žižek, *The Sublime Object of Ideology* (London: Verso, 1989) and Michele Barrett, "Althusser's Marx, Althusser's Lacan," *The Althusserian Legacy*, ed. E. Ann Kaplan and Michael Sprinker (London: Verso, 1993). A slightly longer version of this paper can be found in Michele Barrett, *The Politics of Truth: From Marx to Foucault* (Cambridge: Polity Press, 1991).

23. Barrett, "Althusser's Marx, Althusser's Lacan."

24. Žižek, *The Sublime Object of Ideology*, 163–4.

25. See Ernesto Laclau and Chantel Mouffe, *Hegemony & Socialist Strategy: Towards a Democratic Politics* (London: Verso, 1985) and Ernesto Laclau "New Reflections on the Revolution of Our Time," *New Reflections on the Revolution of Our Time* (London: Verso, 1990).

26. Žižek, *The Metastases of Enjoyment: Six Essays on Women and Causality* (London: Verso, 1994), 30.

27. Žižek, *The Ticklish Subject: The Absent Center of Political Ontology* (London: Verso, 1999), 4.

28. Žižek, "Interview," *Historical Materialism* 7 (2000): 194.

29. Homer, "It's the Political Economy, Stupid! On Žižek's Marxism," *Radical Philosophy* 108 (2001): 7–16. See also in this respect Alex Callinicos, "Review of Žižek, The Ticklish Subject," and Butler, et al., "Contingency, Hegemony, Universality," *Historical Materialism* 8, (2001): 373–403.

30. John Frow, *Marxism and Literary History* (Oxford: Basil Blackwell, 1986), 39.

31. Jameson, *The Political Unconscious*, 82.

32. Ibid., 102.

33. Michael Sprinker, *Imaginary Relations: Aesthetics and Ideology in the Theory of Historical Materialism* (London: Verso, 1987), 159.

34. Paul Ricoeur, "On Interpretation" *Philosophy in France Today*, ed. Alan Montefiore (Cambridge: Cambridge University Press,1983), 179.

35. See Hutcheon, *The Politics of Postmodernism* and Ellen Meiksins Wood and John Bellamy Foster, *In Defense of History: Marxism and the Postmodern Agenda* (New York: Monthly Review Press, 1997) for a summary of the debates between Marxism and postmodernism on history. Dominick La Capra, "Representing the Holocaust: Reflections on the Historians' Debate" *Probing the Limits of Representation: Nazism and the "Final Solution,"* ed. Saul Friedlander (Cambridge: Harvard University Press, 1992) provides a useful overview of the early debates in Holocaust Studies. For an interesting analysis of Holocaust representation that uses Jameson's ideas see Michael Rothberg, *Traumatic Realism: The Demands of Holocaust Representation* (Minneapolis: University of Minnesota Press, 2000).

36. Theodor Adorno, "Commitment," *Aesthetics and Politics*, ed. Ernst Bloch (London: Verso, 1977), 188.

37. Jean-François Lyotard, *The Differend: Phrases in Dispute* (Manchester: Manchester University Press,1988), 57.

38. Stephen Greenblatt, "Towards a Poetics of Culture," *The New Historicism*, ed. H. A. Veeser (London: Routledge, 1989). See also Alex Callinicos, *Theories and Narratives: Reflections on the Philosophy of History* (Cambridge: Polity Press, 1995), chap. 2.

39. Deborah Lipstadt, *Denying the Holocaust: The Growing Assault on Truth and Memory* (Harmondsworth: Penguin, 1994).

40. Hayden White, "Historical Emplotment and the Problem of Truth," *Probing the Limits of Representation: Nazism and the "Final Solution,"* ed. Saul Friedlander (Cambridge: Harvard University Press, 1992), 37.

41. White, "Historical Emplotment and the Problem of Truth," 52.

42. Perry Anderson, "On Emplotment: Two Kinds of Ruin," *Probing the Limits of Representation: Nazism and the "Final Solution,"* ed. Saul Friedlander (Cambridge: Harvard University Press, 1992).

43. Callinicos, *Theories and Narratives: Reflections on the Philosophy of History*, chap. 2.

44. For a defense of historical reference and the distinction between historical and fictional discourse see J. Fisher Solomon, *Discourse and Reference in the Nuclear Age* (Norman: University of Oklahoma Press, 1988) and Gregory Currie, *The Nature of Fiction* (Cambridge: Cambridge University Press, Currie 1990).

45. Roy Bhasker, *Reclaiming Reality: A Critical Introduction to Contemporary Philosophy* (London: Verso, 1989).

46. Joan Copjec, *Read My Desire: Lacan Against the Historicists* (Cambridge: MIT Press, 1994), 6–7.

47. Copjec, "Introduction" to *Supposing the Subject*, ed. Joan Copjec (London: Verso, 1994), viii–ix.

48. Copjec, "Introduction," ix.

49. For a Foucauldian response to Žižek's deployment of the real, see Butler, "Arguing with the Real" in *Bodies that Matter: On the Discursive Limits of Sex* (London: Routledge 1993). See also Žižek, *The Ticklish Subject*, chap. 5, and Butler et al., *Contingency, Hegemony, Universality*.

50. Žižek, *The Sublime Object of Ideology*, 61.

51. Ibid., 141.

52. Žižek, "Interview," 193.

53. Žižek, *The Sublime Object of Ideology*, 136.

54. Benjamin, "These on The Philosophy of History," 254.

55. Althusser and Balibar, *Reading Capital*, 99.

56. See Peter Osborne, "The Politics of Time," *Radical Philosophy*, 68 (1994): 3–9 and also *The Politics of Time* (London: Verso, 1995).

57. Osborne, "The Politics of Time," 6.

58. Althusser and Balibar, *Reading Capital*, 100.

59. Etienne Balibar, *The Philosophy of Marx* (London: Verso, 1995), 108.

Part II

Reactions and Readings
around the World

5

Cultural Revolution, the Discourse of Intellectuals, and Other Folk Tales

Robert Seguin

"We are unknown to ourselves, we knowers, we ourselves, to ourselves, and there is a good reason for this. We have never looked for ourselves."[1] So Nietzsche begins his brilliant polemic *On the Genealogy of Morality*, a text insistently addressed to the "knowers" of the world, the philosophers, psychologists, and anyone else engaged in the propagation of those "ascetic" systems of value (whether bourgeois or socialist, Christian or agnostic) that Nietzsche sees at the root of the decay of the contemporary West. In short, it is the domain of intellectuals that Nietzsche wishes to examine, in particular the very substance and structure of intellectual discourse. He will do this in part by telling the tale of what he notoriously calls the "slave revolt in morality," that is, the overturning by Christianity's "ascetic priests" of the aristocratic ideals of strength and heroic action and their replacement by the weak and sickly plebeian thematics of sin, conscience, and pity. In effect, an entire transvaluation of cultural norms takes place in Nietzsche's philosophical just-so story, a kind of reeducation program that reshapes the very "ethical substance" (*Sittlichkeit*) of the lifeworld. Here, then, in one of the inaugural moments of the modern discourse of the intellectual, Nietzsche fashions in jagged outline the contours of the problematic of what a rival tradition will call cultural revolution.

That rival tradition is of course Marxism, and indeed, the term itself occupies a central if perhaps uncertain place in Fredric Jameson's work. The phrase possesses two distinct but related senses in his work, the first of which frames the matter in essentially hermeneutic terms. In his 1979 essay "Marxism and Historicism," he attempts to retrieve the notion from the then-recent Chinese experience and apply it to the problem of the articulation of differing modes of production with one another. What he wishes to gather under one conceptual rubric are thus the enormous and varied efforts required to remold and retrain whole populations for life under novel and unfolding social and economic circumstances. The traditional examples he adduces include Bachofen on the transition from matriarchy to patriarchy (a neolithic cultural revolution)

and Weber on the Protestant ethic (an element of bourgeois cultural revolution). "Let me add in passing," he continues, "that this new unifying category
of historical study seems to me the only one in terms of which the so-called
human sciences can be reorganized in a properly materialistic way."[2] At once
offhand and sweeping, Jameson proposes here nothing less than a new paradigm for humanistic study. He expands on this theme in a few important pages
in *The Political Unconscious*, where he specifies more clearly the lineaments of
the concept. It is not strictly a matter of transitions between modes of production, which might be the immediate implication; rather, he insists that distinct modes and their associated cultural forms always coexist in a complex and
contradictory layering, and that cultural revolution represents an always ongoing process among dominant, emergent, and residual forms. The task of cultural hermeneutics, then, will be to decode texts in terms of these competing
sign systems—the ultimate representational dynamics Jameson calls the ideology of form.

The second sense of cultural revolution in Jameson's work revisits the
aforementioned problem of cultural reeducation and emphasizes more social
questions. Here, the central text is that widely denounced, if I think poorly
understood, essay, "Third-World Literature in the Era of Multinational Capitalism." If we are to grasp the meaning of the interventions of Third-World
artists and intellectuals, Jameson argues, we are going to have to grasp the precise situations these interventions address, situations all marked in one form or
another by the problem of what Gramsci called subalternity, the habits of subservience and obedience that have been instilled over many decades in
exploited and colonized peoples. "Subalternity is not in that sense a psychological matter, although it governs psychologies," he notes, and hence it cannot
adequately be dealt with through either private therapy or objective changes in
the socioeconomic context alone: "This is a more dramatic form of that old
mystery, the unity of theory and practice."[3] What is foregrounded here is the
active praxis of intellectuals in situation, as they strive to cognitively and allegorically map peculiar national conditions where fresh imaginations of possible futures are sorely needed, all the while that the distorted realities of the past
exercise their baleful hold. In terms of cultural analysis, this sense of cultural
revolution would seem to resonate less with the abstractions of the ideology of
form than with the second interpretive level Jameson proposes in *The Political
Unconscious*, that having to do with the narrative translations of social class: in
this context, what we track are the complex movements and machinations of
social groups as they maneuver across shifting and uncertain terrain.

Such, in any case, is the direction I wish to move in these pages. I want to
explore the possibility of generalizing from Jameson's remarks on Third-World
writers toward a more encompassing sense of the "writer as intellectual," and
in so doing flesh out his notion of cultural revolution: despite Jameson's evident ambitions for the concept, one nonetheless has the sense that his varied

remarks on it do not quite add up to a full-dress theory. The long reading of Conrad in *The Political Unconscious* does, I suppose, model for us the *bon usage* of the concept, with its demonstration of the revelation of history in the Conradian narrative machinery. Still, there remains, I think, a tension between the admittedly retrospective framework of Jameson's text and a category whose most immediate inspiration, in China, so vividly dramatizes the problems of the "actual"—of praxis, invention, and the construction of the new. I want to come at this through a consideration of some American writers, a national focus that offers some advantages in this context. Lacking both an aristocratic ideological rationale for artistic production and any sense of necessity or vocation for the modes of bourgeois realism, writers in the United States faced early on the dynamics of professionalization and marketplace rationalization, leading to a precocious articulation of "alienated" aestheticist ideologies (think of Poe's influence on Baudelaire, for instance). Moreover, the political currents we today refer to as the new social movements (the struggle for racial and sexual equality, among other) have had a long and vibrant tradition in the United States, and have in crucial ways subtended and intersected with intellectual and writerly situations across the decades. Finally, the insistent doctrines of democratic possibility and Emersonian self-reliance—such foundations of American public ideology—have worked to sharpen the U.S. writer's sense of the essential mystery of political sovereignty as such, and intimate that subalternity is not merely a matter for the so-called undeveloped areas of the world. In such a context, writers such as Mark Twain and Zora Neale Hurston (whom we will examine later), despite their great differences, are equally attuned in to the multilayered problematic of what Jameson calls cultural revolution.

On the Genealogy of Morality, meanwhile, suggests itself as a potential pathway into the more general theoretical parameters of this problem, not only because of its fortuitous coupling of the intellectual with cultural revolution, but also because of its essentially narrative frame, the way it peoples its philosophical discourse with lusty noblemen, cringing peasants, and conniving priests. This cast of characters is drawn from a distinct topography of social class and hierarchy, in keeping with the long-evident reality of the intellectual's role in the elaboration and maintenance of social structure. Indeed, a prominent strand of the literature on intellectuals has pondered the extent to which intellectuals form a coherent social grouping, and whether such a group can ever manifest the characteristics and functions of a class as such. Drawing on the experience and situation of the Soviet Bloc countries, for instance, Konrad and Szelenyi argued that the structural locations made available to knowledge workers by a labyrinthine state bureaucracy effectively constituted them as a new social class. At about the same time, sociologist Alvin Gouldner reached a similar conclusion about a putatively postindustrial North America, where a now knowledge-based economy would bestow new social power on intellectuals (the "symbolic analysts" in Robert Reich's later, well-known formulation).[4] I tend to remain skeptical of such analyses, not only because of their limited national frameworks, but because their restriction to empirical sociology overlooks the more figural and allegorical dimensions of the problem of intellectuality, precisely the realm to which Nietzsche's hothouse polemical tale gives us some access.

Nietzsche's text appeared in 1887, only a decade before the advent of the Dreyfus Affair in France, the event that ushered into the public sphere the intellectuals in their modern guise, the intellectuals so-called, who, for better or for worse, are typically the referent of the discourse of intellectuals. We will thus faithfully reproduce here the split between those Gramsci described as intellectual functionaries—lawyers, scientists, and technocrats of all sorts who staff both the public and private knowledge apparatuses of bourgeois society—and those who, through an historically variable combination of self-nomination, felicitous conditions of employment, and active interpellation by the organs of the public sphere, come to occupy a space of critical distance on contemporary society and politics and who work to ally themselves with various sectors of the disenfranchised. The long-standing conceptual tension between these two descriptions and accounts of intellectuals, one inclusive and one exclusive, is, as John Guillory notes, more than just a methodological matter: "[T]he discrepancy between inclusive and exclusive definitions of intellectuals in Gramsci's account, or in theories of the Professional-Managerial Class, describes a social reality—the occlusion of intellectual functionaries by the discourse of 'intellectuals'—and is therefore not a mere defect in theory."[5] The relation of Nietzsche's "ascetic priests" to the intelligentsia of the Dreyfus Affair might on the face of it seem uncertain at best, however the insistent rhetoric of plebeianization and proletarianization in *On the Genealogy of Morality* suggests the kinship, and hence behind the religious functionary must surely be ranged the intellectuals of the burgeoning working-class movement of the later nineteenth century, avatars of a socialism Nietzsche loathed fully as much as he did Christianity.

Emile Zola, the most noteworthy of the intellectual figures who defended Dreyfus, stands as something of a symptomatic figure in our present context. I have in mind Lukács's juxtaposition of Zola's naturalist aesthetic with what he takes as the more successful realisms of Balzac and Tolstoy. While the latter display true narration, and hence map the social totality in all its complexity, Zola's much more detailed and exhaustive practice ends up as mere description, forever at a fatal distance from the social world it seeks to capture. But this is not a matter of talent, but rather of historical situation, and what effectively intercedes between Zola's sentences and concrete social life is something like theory as such—that is, Zola possesses an elaborate "scientific" doctrine of novelistic art that he follows closely, whereas Balzac and Tolstoy elaborate their work in a manner unburdened or at least ungoverned by whatever ideas about the writer's craft that they undoubtedly have. Zola's writerly predicament thus oddly echoes his emergence as the emblematic modern intellectual, in that both facets of his situation have their root in the central political dynamics of capitalist modernity. Previous social systems and modes of production developed "naturally," without an articulated self-conception (feudal barons would not have thought of themselves as engaged in "fashioning and extending the feudal mode of production"), and hence we might say that in premodern times all thought and action, however far-flung, was essentially local. Capitalism, as Marx stressed in any number of ways, represents an historic break, not only in its dynamic of expansion and universalization, but also in its bringing to consciousness of itself precisely as a system, one that must seek to suppress or subsume competing ones. Indeed, the historical continuum is henceforth fractured conceptually into a range of alternative modes of production, including communism, perhaps the most drastic alternative of the lot.

There is thus something quite unprecedented in the idea of actually trying to replace one mode of production with another. But having the idea engenders thoughts on how to realize it, and hence the dialectic of theory and practice is bequeathed to the modern discourse of intellectuals as one of its constitutive elements. Marx, in his moments of high political passion, liked to imagine the advent of new social forms as a kind of organic unfolding, as in his famous remarks on the Paris Communards: "They have no ideals to realize, but to set free the elements of the new society with which old collapsing bourgeois society itself is pregnant." Rousing rhetoric, to be sure, and while Marx's sense of capitalism's unwitting laying of the groundwork for socialism remains important, the stubborn fact remains that intellectuals, at least, will *always* have ideals to realize. Indeed, Marx suggested—and cautioned—as much in the third of the Thesis on Feuerbach (a text that is itself very much directed, of course, at the philosophers and "knowers" of the world): "The materialist doctrine that men are products of circumstances and upbringing, and that, therefore, changed men are products of other circumstances and changed upbringing, forgets that it is men who change circumstances, and that it is essential to educate the educator himself. Hence, this doctrine necessarily arrives at dividing society into two parts, one of which is superior to society."[6] The materialism Marx criticizes here might just as easily be called the inherent idealism of the discourse of intellectuals, one that has the noteworthy operational effect of dualizing and polarizing the social field—not, however, in the Marxian class sense but with, I think, affinities to the latter that require investigation. The epithet "superior," meanwhile, while true enough in one sense, remains only half the story, as we will see.

A certain energy of bifurcation is also visible in Nietzsche's story of the birth of morality. To recall the basic plot: Nietzsche famously renders the ethical binary, good versus evil, into a projection of a more basic sociopolitical distinction, that between the high-born or noble and the low-born or base (or slavish). The revolution he describes entails a transvaluation or inversion in the essential meaning of this binary. In earlier noble society, the social distinction resulted in the binary good versus bad, which, according to Nietzsche's speculative ethnography, possessed no ethical content as such: it simply assigned positive or negative value to the two social realms (the high, of course, is valued). The slave revolt in morals happens when the lower orders seize on this binary and transform it into a matter of ethics. One notices here the effort Nietzsche puts into fashioning the original aristocratic "good" as the only active term of the binary, as the sole locus of concrete meaning. "Bad" is in effect a remainder term, an empty and uninteresting afterthought derived negatively from "good." With the term good, Nietzsche wishes to hold together in synthesis things that the conditions of modernity threaten to break apart, a wish that can be glimpsed in remarks like the following:

> And just as the common people separates lightning from its flash and takes the latter to be a *deed*, something performed by a subject, which is called lightning, popular morality separates strength from the manifestations of strength, as though there were an indifferent substratum behind the strong person which had the *freedom* to manifest strength or not. But there is no such substratum; there is no "being" behind the deed, its effect and what becomes of it; "the doer" is invented as an afterthought,—the doing is everything.[7]

Recent poststructuralist thought has fastened onto this passage as a principal exhibit in its critique of the subject, which is all well and good, but tends to overlook the precise contours of Nietzsche's tale. He is trying to imagine desire, thought, and action as essentially *immanent* to one another, forming an indivisible continuum that structures the very ground of his "premodern" lifeworld, and whose enabling condition is the coherence of aristocratic class position and consciousness. There is no *individual* subject because the agency in question is the manifestation of a form of collective social being. The decay or devolution of this plane of immanence into a social field riven by the machinations of intellectuals and the masses they control figurally marks in Nietzsche the emergence of both class struggle in its modern form and the conundrum of theory and practice that will henceforth shadow the very question of historical agency in all its guises.[8]

Yet the deepest expression of these semantic and conceptual trends lies not so much with the dramatis personae of the text but rather with the abiding paradox that emerges from it: how is it that the "weak" of the world, with their "slave morality," manage to undermine the noble incarnation of action and strength in the first place? The weak have, it seems, displayed a measure of strength, without thereby becoming strong in any fashion that Nietzsche will countenance. Or, as Geoffrey Harpham phrases the question in his suggestive analysis of the text, "Why do the weak triumph? What is strength if it does not prevail?"[9] While Nietzsche does speak of the preternatural cunning with which ressentiment imbues the ascetic priests, this hardly seems sufficient to explain the remarkable reversal of fortune that is narrated. Strength and weakness eventually begin to shade willy-nilly into one another, and Harpham concludes that Nietzsche's text provides no real answers to these questions. What Harpham discerns to be at work is, rather, a kind of textual self-immolation even more resolute and implacable than anything in Derrida or de Man.

The aporia might be productively dislodged, however, if, rather than take the terms strength and weakness as names for reified substances or properties, we instead read them as terms for *something else*, as words that are grappling with what is essentially a generic problem—the genre of intellectual discourse as such. The problematics of "strength in weakness" are thus less conceptual confusions than markers of discursive form, one whose roots lie in the social positioning of intellectuals: the priests and the slaves over whom they hold sway figure the paradox because the priests are structurally weak—they need masses of one sort or another to carry out what for Nietzsche are their sickly and ressentiment-ridden designs. But the discourse thereby generated encodes a dimension of *superiority* as well, as Marx's comments above on Feuerbach indicated, and which in Nietzsche is embodied in the ascetic ideals that the priests and philosophers self-regardingly invoke to elevate their moral status above all others. This peculiar tension would emerge later, in Sartre's still resonant theory of the intellectual as an objective traitor (on which Jameson has commented in several places), as someone caught ineluctably between antagonistic social spheres. As products of the bourgeois educational system (and very likely middle class themselves), intellectuals are forever outside of those subaltern groups that they would wish to represent, concretely learning middle-class habits of mind and manner of which they may not even be aware. Their efforts of political advocacy and ideological critique, however, condemn the intellectuals in the eyes of that class that materially supports them. The intellectuals occupy a certain social space in a society in which intellectual functions (to invoke Gramsci again) are—despite the hype about new armies of Reichian "symbolic analysts"—doled out quite sparingly indeed, awaiting the day when such functions might be more generally disseminated throughout the social body (and no doubt qualitatively transformed in the process).

Beyond the dynamics of genre, which we will explore more fully, I want to open a brief parenthesis and suggest an allegorical dimension to the matter of strength in weakness, whereby the political unconscious of the *Genealogy* forges further striking connections. I have in mind Giovanni Arrighi's work on what he calls the American "systemic cycle of accumulation," which provides us with another means of returning the fundamental conceptual incoherence of Nietzsche's text back to its concrete material ground. Arrighi revisits Marx's conception of capital's structuring of the labor process and its concomitant impact on the shape of the proletarian movement articulating a seeming contradiction in Marx's thinking on these matters. On the one hand, Marx contends that capital will render the daily life of the proletariat ever more precarious, with increasing immiseration and insecurity—a scenario of mounting powerlessness. On the other hand, Marx observes that the advance of modern industry will socialize production ever more thoroughly, bringing workers together in common situations and making clear their mutual interests and interdependence. Given this basis for stable working-class institutions, this scenario envisions the growing social strength of the proletariat. The former depiction thus imagines the working class as more fractious, but less able to coordinate its political ambitions while the latter sees it as more organized, but less inclined to challenge the system overall. This seeming split, in Arrighi's view, is the unacknowledged heart of the many contentious and sometimes crippling debates in the socialist tradition over reformism versus revolution, as if the working class composed two entirely separate and incompatible modes of being. The contradiction becomes less severe, however, when one takes into account that the two descriptions—one corresponding to the active army of labor (the side of strength), the other to the reserve army—embrace the identical populations: "For in Marx's view the Active and the Reserve Armies consisted of the same human material which was assumed to circulate more or less continuously from one to the other. The same individuals would be part of the Active Army today and of the Reserve Army tomorrow, depending on the continuous ups and downs of enterprises, lines and locales of production."[10] Hence, Marx envisioned a certain determinate interplay of "strength and weakness" as a ground for the development of political consciousness. The problem historically has been that, with the development of imperialism, the mass immiseration of workers was increasingly a feature of life in the periphery, while labor in the core countries tended to enjoy greater social power—over time, two contrasting populations did indeed come into existence. As imperialism gives way to globalization, however, Arrighi suggests that matters are gradually returning to something closer to Marx's original conception, with labor on the periphery gaining (albeit with painful slowness) greater institutional leverage, while mass deprivation begins to loom larger in the core countries. The key point, finally, for our purposes is that Nietzsche's text, in the course of elaborating a paradox around cultural change and the place of social and intellectual agency, unwittingly thinks a problem whose "solution" lies in the field of materialist discourse and the theory of class.

We are now perhaps in a position to specify more concretely the loose connections between intellectuals and class that have hitherto been noted fitfully. Indeed, I am tempted to put this in a strong form and posit that, within the Marxian lexicon, the notions of class in general (and proletariat in particular) and intellectual are effectively symbolic cognates. Both notions are deeply structured by the logic and figurality of strength in weakness, in several ways. If there has been much discussion about how intellectuals might constitute a class, the very same might be observed of the working class. Indeed, as several observers have noted, there is, strictly speaking, only one class in Marx's *Capital*, namely, the bourgeoisie; the proletariat is posited as both inside and outside of capital, as part of the machinery of value extraction and as a point of negation (the famous "gravediggers"), and thus lacks a stable representational determination.[11] Both notions also crucially encode within themselves a certain protocol of abolition: the point of classes is to get rid of them, just as we must also make good on Gramsci's great claim that everyone is an intellectual (and thus in Utopia there will be no separate group of them). Finally, their structural parallelism is rooted in their function as general names for agency, as terms that point to the very social actors charged with following that path of eradication that they conceptually encode. Much like Marx's early notion of "communism" as the name for the movement to abolish the present state of things, "class" and "intellectual" enjoin a thinking of process that targets the reification secreted by the concepts themselves (those ossified social entities of classes and intellectuals). Hence, the *figural* charge of the terms must also be taken account of: aside from their analytic role, both concepts, through their imbrication with agency, and whatever the historical shortcomings and failures of the actual entities they designate, stand as figures for the *construction* of universality as such (as distinct from any achieved universality). To those who would identify the institutional situatedness and specificity of the intellectual as mitigation against such wild-eyed talk, I would invoke Žižek's insistence that it is only through the specific role, the specific political demand, the specific site, that the universal achieves any measure of substance and articulation: universality never manifests itself universally, but, paradoxically, through local contingencies.[12] In any event, the parallels outlined here seem to me to explain the persistent and, I believe, mistaken temptation to see intellectuals as a class unto themselves, the confusion arising, again, not from the social behavior or functioning of the groups but rather from their conceptual and metaphorical congruity.

It is via the vexed and much maligned dimension of the universal that we are at length returned to where we began, the question of cultural revolution.[13] For this phrase, too, names a universalizing project, the heady and seemingly impossible one of a universal *culture* (a culture that would surely have to strive to make a place for those hybridities and heterogeneities that are today routinely cited against the notion of the universal as such). Such a *project* (to invoke the Sartrean term), while it has premodern, mostly religious, antecedents, becomes under capitalism linked to a necessary economic mode of realization (modernization and consumerism would be two bourgeois forms), with socialism claiming the—imaginary yet genuine—right to the "true" universal. "You are nothing, therefore you can be everything," exclaimed Marx about the working class, in one of his more dramatic articulations of the figure of strength in weakness. "The ascetic priest is the incarnate wish for being otherwise, being elsewhere,"[14] Nietzsche asserts in a striking passage that, while in a different key, chimes richly with Marx's words. In both, power emanates through the drive of negation, and a constitutive dimension or horizon of futurity opens out before us. What would it mean to imagine a concrete, putatively realizable future radically different from one's present? What does such fantasizing suggest about the shape of desire itself? What matters of responsibility come into play in relation to present action and behavior? Such are a few of the questions engendered by the effort to take poetry from the future, and by the intrusion of the *concept* between the current state of affairs and the desired future. *On the Genealogy of Morality* draws these questions within the bounds of its signifying field, in typically oblique or even occulted fashion, through the whole discussion of the function of "bad conscience." "To breed an animal *which is able to make promises*—is that not the paradoxical task which nature has set herself with regard to humankind?"[15] asks Nietzsche. A being, then, in contrast to the realm of aristocratic caprice and present-oriented immanence, whose actions are now tied to a future dispensation, who promises to see to it that a certain future action takes place, "someone who is answerable for his own future."[16] This "breeding," then, represents more work for the knowers, a mighty "shaping of a population"[17] is signified by this particular cultural revolution. His tale then takes a remarkable turn into antiquity, where the origins of guilt and conscience are discovered to lie *in the exchange relationship itself*—a relationship whose universalization under capitalism has made the notions of production and cultural revolution thinkable in the first place.

But it is finally the figural and generic elements of all this in which I am most interested, in the precise senses of these terms. When Foucault dismisses the "faded" notion of the left intellectual as an "individual figure of a universality whose obscure, collective form is embodied in the proletariat," he means something like a literal embodiment or incarnation.[18] But the effect is discursive: when the intellectual turns to linguistic production, something of his or her social and conceptual space manifests itself in language and narrative, in the forms of utterances and story units. So I do not wish to produce another map of the "class situation of intellectuals," or to pull out magic formulae of the sort scornfully derided by Gayatri Spivak: "As we used to hear from the knee-jerk Marxists: theory and practice are united in the concept."[19] Rather, what I would like to extract from these reflections, for the more humble purposes of literary analysis, is something like the generic or folk form of the discourse of intellectuals, on the model of Vladimir Propp's formalist analysis of Russian folk tales. In Propp's basic scheme, what he regards as the fundamental pattern of folk storytelling, the Hero initially starts off weak, beset by a lack that can variously encompass strength, courage, desire, or the will. Before he can successfully engage either the Villain or the series of arduous tasks that will confront him (mutually exclusive options, in Propp's view) and gain his Reward, help, in the form of spells, potions, or powders, must be bestowed on him by the crucial figure of the Donor. In Jameson's early appraisal of Propp, he notes that the Donor is the most compelling narrative operator, the one who furnishes much of the "storyness" to the tale in the form of change and eventhood.[20] Given the emergence of the folktale from the immemorial reaches of peasant existence, it is perhaps naturally tempting to see in the Donor a figure of alienated subaltern political consciousness. Hence, we can imagine the Donor as a repository for various magical and religious impulses, powers that can defeat the Villain (frequently a figure for the aristocracy) or overcome the grim pressure of material scarcity represented by the Hero's labors. But the Donor is really the peasantry itself, projecting the strength of the multitude into the fantasy sphere of storytelling, into a narrative category that is not that of the Hero itself—the reified figure of strength and victory— but that of a catalyst, one that can emerge into the light and then retreat into shadow, who confers power but does not act on it. In thus cleaving more to process and event, and in keeping open the promise of erasure (for in Utopia, the subaltern classes will not stand triumphant but will have disappeared), the Donor reveals its cognate Other as the notion of revolution as such, as attested to by all the slave and peasant rebellions that have left their scattered traces on the paths of history. Zora Neale Hurston (who had a dual career as novelist and anthropologist) echoes this line of thought when she asserts that the characters of folklore are "wish fulfillment projections," and that the tales are the production of weak people "to compensate for their weakness."[21]

So, we have elements of weakness in/and strength here, too—a narrative kernel evident in discourses of the subaltern and the intellectual alike. The difference is that the solution to the conundrum for the peasants and proletarians is themselves, as it were, whereas for the intellectual, it is exactly these same social groups and precisely *not* themselves—though, as we will see, signals here are frequently crossed. What precipitates from this impasse is what we might characterize as a drive for completion in the discourse of intellectuals, a discourse constitutively marked by a variously absent/present "other" that would somehow complete and transcend them as a formation. But this is something that can take many forms, and that becomes especially susceptible to allegorical investment when it is enacted within literary discourse. What I want to explore now are the ways that such generic dynamics offer fresh perspectives on social form and class process in literature. As I noted earlier, the authors I have in mind are American, products of a society that is in many respects both the "purest" modern class society and the one wherein the imagination and the expression of class have been most thoroughly occluded and diverted.

Twain and Hurston, the writers I will (all too briefly) examine, both undoubtedly conform, through social location and specific position-taking alike, to the more exclusive sense of the political intellectual invoked earlier.

Indeed, criticism of their work has not been unaware of the salience of this point, but it has tended, as so often happens, to circumscribe the matter within the frame of the individual subject, such that we might isolate and parse the set of social and political opinions they held and then "apply" them to their work. Let us see, rather, where the preceding reflections might take us. Mark Twain's *A Connecticut Yankee in King Arthur's Court* (appearing in 1889, only two years after the *Genealogy*) might seem at first almost too perfect for our purposes, since it is nothing less than an extended satiric disquisition on the riddles of revolutionary social renewal. The hero, Hank Morgan, wakes after a blow to the head to discover himself transported to Arthurian England (though there is nothing consistent in Twain's portrayal, which is a mishmash of historical elements from a number of centuries). Unlike the scenario of *Star Trek*, with its (suspiciously flexible) Prime Directive designed to prevent interference with technologically less-advanced societies, Morgan quickly realizes that his nineteenth-century knowledge and outlook place him in a vastly superior position with respect to the denizens of Camelot. He contrives to have himself installed as the king's lieutenant (refusing, in good democratic fashion, any sort of royal title and opting simply for Boss instead), with the aim of making society over in his American image. While Twain's purpose is clearly more directed at revealing the limitations and prejudices of U.S. society than it is at poking fun at the Arthurians, the satiric registers are frequently uncertain, something amplified by the first-person narration. Hank Morgan is both a proud proponent of the ideals of the eighteenth-century revolutions (as was in large measure Twain himself) and a ruthlessly practical and incipiently violent foreman of a firearms factory, the bourgeois modernizer par excellence. So while he charts a clear course for disaster, Twain nonetheless gives to Morgan a number of pointed and sympathetic ruminations.

What appalls Morgan most about the medieval kingdom is the poisonous effect that the absolute and unbreachable power of the church and nobility has on the common people. Deferential and dependant in all matters, the habits of subalternity run deep in the populace indeed. Hank's early efforts to instill the desire for freedom among the commoners are fruitless, and he seethes openly at the perverse consequences of the feudal class structure (that all around defer to the Boss as much as to any king is of course an irony quite lost on him). Watching a group of peasants toil "gratis" for the bishop, he reflects on the glorious advances wrought by the French Revolution:

> Why, it was like reading about France and the French, before the ever-memorable and blessed Revolution, which swept a thousand years of such villainy away in one swift tidal wave of blood—one: a settlement of that hoary debt in the proportion of half a drop of blood for each hogshead of it that had been pressed by slow tortures out of that people in the weary stretch of ten centuries of wrong and shame

and misery the like of which was not to be mated but in hell. There were two "Reigns of Terror," if we would but remember it and consider it; the one wrought murder in hot passion, the other in heartless cold blood; the one lasted mere months, the other had lasted a thousand years; the one inflicted death upon ten thousand persons, the other upon a hundred millions; but our shudders are all for the "horrors" of the minor Terror, the momentary Terror, so to speak; whereas, what is the horror of swift death by the ax, compared with lifelong death from hunger, cold, insult, cruelty, and heartbreak?[22]

This passage strikes sparks even today, in this age of the *Livre noir du communisme* and the insistent ideological effort to discredit the very idea of revolution as inherently murderous and terroristic. Even after the historical advent of philosophies of nonviolent resistance (which might enjoin us to seek alternatives to the "terror" here lauded), such a forthright defense of revolutionary violence remains bracing. Still, in Morgan's "accounting ledger" grasp of the matter some of the pragmatism that Twain mocks comes through.

Hank realizes, however, that things are very far from the volatile political dynamics of late eighteenth-century France. While he might wish to force the issue more quickly, he understands that a certain level of social development must first be attained:

And now here I was, in a country where a right to say how the country should be governed was restricted to six persons in each thousand of its population. . . . It seemed to me that what the nine hundred and ninety-four dupes needed was a new deal. The thing that would have best suited the circus side of my nature would have been to resign the Boss-ship and get up an insurrection and turn it into a revolution; but I knew that the Jack Cade or the Wat Tyler who tries such a thing without first educating his materials up to revolution grade is almost absolutely certain to get left.[23]

Here, in the interstices of this passage, in this most unlikely of places, precipitate all the old questions about voluntarism versus determinism, about the role of the vanguard party, and, crucially, about the functions of pedagogy, all framed by the enduring mystery of the sources of political consciousness. Not unlike dialectical writing, where, as Jameson memorably puts it, before you can say one thing you first have to say everything, the paradox here circles around the phrase "revolution grade," as if, before you can stage a revolution, you first need a revolution. But such moments are probably best grasped as the aporias of the discourse of the intellectual as such, as it seeks affiliation with the idea of revolution and with the social substance that would be its avenue of enactment. Morgan's task here is of course doubly difficult, since he must initially inculcate a sense of injustice among the commoners before the institutions of feudalism can properly be dealt with.

The catastrophe that finally ensues finds its truth in a similar aporetical register. Hank's long-term solution to the abhorrent situation is education and modernization. He erects a "man factory" where selected commoners are taught basic literacy and technology skills, introduces the trappings of advertising to teach the virtues of cleanliness ("Use Peterson's Prophylactic Toothbrush"), and establishes media networks like newspapers and telegraphy. Things proceed apace, and Morgan's confidence grows until at length he believes he "could easily have the active part of the population of that day ready and eager for an event which should be the first of its kind in the history of the world—a rounded and complete governmental revolution without bloodshed."[24] The reigning powers, however, have other ideas, and the church eventually issues an interdict declaring the Boss and his works blasphemous and heretical. Morgan's carefully trained minions, save for a few, desert him and close ranks with their feudal masters. It is a minor object lesson in the Althusserian "permanence of ideology" and a remarkable foretaste of the still-vexing actions of the European working classes a quarter century after the appearance of the novel: well drilled in the internationalism of a social democratic movement they strongly supported, they instead fell in with the bellicose jingoism of their national governments when hostilities were declared in August 1914. A similar fate awaits the legions of Camelot as well, since Morgan and his band, despite their paltry numbers, retain an enormous technological advantage. Unleashing gatling guns, high explosives, and electrified fences, many thousands are slaughtered. The bloodshed shatters Hank Morgan's dream, and he subsequently falls prey to madness.

This bleak conclusion has been almost universally ascribed to Twain's own personal cynicism and misanthropy (qualities often opportunistically adopted by legions of bourgeois critics, who are only too happy to endorse Twain's putative revelation of the fundamental and indelible corruption of humanity). However, it would be more productive to frame the matter once again in generic terms, as an inherent crisis point of intellectual discourse. The claims and efforts of pedagogy and Gramscian moral and intellectual leadership here develop increasing internal tensions, like a reactor slowly going critical, until an eruption of (not exactly cathartic, in this case) violence ensues. The principal fault line seems to run through the metaphor of automata: Hank consistently characterizes the medieval Britons as machines, as manipulable drones awaiting fresh programming. Indeed, he posits human as pure tabula rasa: "Training—training is everything; training is all there is to a person. We speak of nature; it is folly; there is no such thing as nature. . . . We have no thoughts of our own, no opinions of our own; they are transmitted to us, trained into us."[25] These sentiments issue in more of the intellectualist folk form, which implicitly arrogates to itself the donor function and busily secretes images of subaltern passivity and, as a paradoxical but in reality empty mirror image, recalcitrance. In this sense the discourse of the intellectual remains a greater vehicle for purely individual libidinal investment than does its more anonymous folk counterpart. Hence, it cannot register the dynamics of collective fantasy that subtend group existence, what Žižek would call the stubborn kernels of enjoyment that groups abide by and that frequently look irrational and atavistic to the outside gaze. The nexus of enjoyment in intellectual discourse, one very much given to narrative elaboration, would I think be political fantasy as such, something most often taking the form of inventing new—and often minimally distinguishable—political programs and "visions" (like inventing new diets, as Virilio once acidly put it). In any event, the events in *Connecticut Yankee* themselves move finally toward our central conundrum of weakness and strength, for when Hank unleashes the force of modern armaments, he brings the dualism to an unstable head: like Samson destroying the temple, he wields a godlike power utterly incapable of furthering his designs. The narrative oscillation of pedagogy and violence is undergirded by the structural aporia of strength in weakness, in the sense that the sought-after allegorical completion of intellectual discourse provided by the figure of the masses is undermined by a representational structure that inexorably posits the masses as dolts incapable of carrying the charge of revolution.

Another instance of the fraught narrative dynamics of pedagogy and revolutionary desire—one elaborated, however, within a significantly different context—occurs in Hurston's *Moses, Man of the Mountain* (1939). The shift to an African American figure at once introduces a host of new questions to confront, not least of which is the relation of the black writer and intellectual to a culture and collectivity that is much more than purely theoretical. Hurston struggled her whole career in positioning herself within the almost gravitational force field of this community, sometimes ecstatically acceding to its power, at others fitfully distancing herself. Indeed, the two impulses circle each other and intertwine throughout much of her work, though this has sometimes been obscured by the discourse of canonization that has engaged her writing over the last two decades. This understandably celebratory critical effort, led principally by Henry Louis Gates, Jr., has rightfully restored Hurston to curricula and scholarly analysis, though it has done so at the cost of ignoring much of her work and fetishizing instead a single text, her 1937 novel *Their Eyes Were Watching God*. While some place is occasionally made for her folk tale collection *Mules and Men* and some of her short stories, critics nonetheless frequently dismiss her other novels and texts as the products of illness, bad judgment, or a somewhat craven attempt to garner a wider (and whiter) readership. But, as with most writers, the tensions and contradictions in Hurston are the more compelling objects of interpretation, and it is only by widening the critical frame that we can begin to reflect on some of these.

Like *Connecticut Yankee, Moses, Man of the Mountain* is a work of mytho-
logical history, a retelling of Moses leading the Israelites out of slavery in
Egypt and (almost) into the promised land. The theme was a common one in
African American storytelling, with its obvious redemptive implications, but
Hurston is here more interested in the problems of political and intellectual
leadership in its charismatic mode than in fashioning a triumphal tale of salvation. Indeed, a case could be made for all her novels—save, partially if crucially, for *Their Eyes*—as explorations of this thematic, one likely afforded by
what she characterized as her own displacement from inside to outside, from
the all-black Eatonville of her childhood, with its singular (if incomplete)
insulation from the white gaze and racial geometry, to her engagement with
Boasian anthropology and its self-conscious embrace of intellectual distance
and the outsider principle: "It was only when I was off in college, away from
my native surroundings, that I could see myself like somebody else and stand
off and look at my garment. Then I had to have the spy-glass of Anthropology to look through at that."[26] What she sees through that spyglass is a group
that only ambiguously includes herself, namely the *folk*, a much discussed and
almost talismanic term in the analysis of African American culture. The folk
are rural agricultural workers, arising directly from the institutions and situations of slavery, in (often silent) contradistinction to later urban factory workers. Their musical and storytelling traditions, which form such a vital
component of Hurston's work, are frequently taken to be the wellspring of
whatever is most valuable and unique in black culture. Yet a troubling uncertainty attends their status as links to a "premodern" world in the context of an
increasingly urbanized and industrialized society: what might they represent
for a now postmodern polity, and how are they and their achievements to be
valued? How is the modern *intellectual* to relate to them? All the problems of
subalternity that Jameson invoked, and that Twain wrestled with, return here
once again.

Here indeed is the rub for Hurston, since she works in complicated ways
both to link herself to the folk and distinguish herself from them. Her situation was by no means unique: the writers and intellectuals of the Harlem
Renaissance, in the wake of the Great Migration from rural South to urban
North that began in the later years of the nineteenth century, faced what might
be called a general crisis of organicity that called forth complex new strategies
of discursive representation and social positioning. But Hurston has been
identified with the folk more insistently than any other writer of this era, partly
as a result of her own efforts and partly, as Hazel Carby has argued, from the
academic discourse of the 1980s and 1990s, which tended to fetishize supposed rural authenticity as a kind of imaginary bulwark against the disastrous
condition of contemporary urban African American life.[27] Walter Benn
Michaels, meanwhile, has with typical extravagance a functional equivalence
between Hurston and (the seemingly very different) Langston Hughes in

terms of their solution to what Michaels himself describes as "the intellectual's relation to the masses." He argues that the two rearticulate Gramsci's notion of the organic intellectual, with its orientation around a shared class experience and project, in relation to a purely racial bond instead: the bourgeois or petit-bourgeois intellectual effectively mimics, through the use of vernacular dialect and narrative materials, the presumed racial authenticity of the working-class folk and thereby cements his or her organic link to them.[28] While Hurston's own ambivalence about the folk unsettles this argument (as does her continuing attention to class categories), Michaels is surely right to insist that such a problematic lies at the heart of Hurston's work.

What we find, then, when we begin to take a broader view of Hurston's overall output, is a much more vexed relation to those folk she is usually thought to champion. No doubt Hurston cherishes the immemorial subaltern wisdom reflected in the oral tales she recounts, with its clear-eyed sense of life's vicissitudes and wisecracking disrespect for discourses of authority. Such attitudes, however, cause much trouble for Hurston's charismatic leaders, such as John Pearson (from *Jonah's Gourd Vine*, a character modeled on her father) and Moses, ambitious men who seek to lead the masses into a more "advanced state." Here the other dimension of Hurston's relation to the folk makes itself felt, a relation indeed marked by the characteristic dilemmas of the intellectual's relation to the masses. The other shoe that drops in Hurston's portrait of the folk involves their recalcitrant refusal to embrace the ways of modernity, their suspicion of new economic and technological programs being in some ways a figure for their inability to "rule themselves," that is, to seize responsibility for their own destinies. In other words, the very conditions of oppression that have inculcated a dynamic oral culture have bred an equally strong condition of stasis in the folk, marked by a lack of social ambition and an acceptance, albeit grumbling, of white tutelage. Moses, John Pearson, and Jim Meserve (from *Seraph on the Suwanee*) confront such resistance with both sympathy and exasperation, knocking their sconces repeatedly against what comes to seem the very deadweight of history.

In *Moses, Man of the Mountain*, these issues reach a kind of crisis point. The Lord charges Moses with a very clear task: lead the people—who, in their vernacular speech are indistinguishable from the porch sitters of *Their Eyes* —out of bondage and mold them into a new nation. With varieties of nationalism flourishing across both the world and the political spectrum during the 1930s (including the centrality of the so-called national question to black political thinking), the word *nation* in the novel assumes intensely contemporary overtones. The very sense of nationhood insisted on by Hurston's Moses—a bounded territory, housing a racially mixed and even polyglot population, administered by a settled written law—underplays the ethnoreligious dimensions of nationhood and emphasizes instead the strains of a progressive American modernity.[29] Another fascinating index of this is

Hurston's characterization of Moses's god-given powers: the discourse of conjuring from Afro-American folklore she deploys here, with its mixture of sorcery together with feats of prestidigitation and sleight of hand, introduces an uncertainty with respect to Moses's exploits—is he a conduit of divine will or just a talented practitioner of an essentially secular magic? This sceptical potentiality emerges full-blown in the very people Moses would lead, who are depicted as a most thickheaded and resentful lot, whiny and conniving, quick to change allegiances and become nostalgic for life under Pharaoh after a day's hungry marching through the desert. In effect, the substance of Hebrew cultural life remains slavery, even though its formal shackles have been cast off: the successful founding of the nation will thus also entail a cultural revolution that would dissolve the craven habits of subalternity to which the people cling. Moses attempts to discipline his reluctant charges and keep them with the program with displays of powers and occasional expulsions; however, things reach a head after Moses descends the mountain with the golden tablets. Finding "his" people lost in idolatry, Moses, the modernizer, adopts the same course as Stalin when faced with the fractious Kulaks: extermination, the liquidation of all those who resist the new dispensation.[30] It is a terrible moment, as the very folk who had been such a vital presence in *Their Eyes* are grimly but, in Moses's and I think the text's view, justly puts to the sword.

To suggest a Stalinist moment in a writer who consistently disparaged the communist movement is only to observe the global force field of the 1930s in which her narrative practice is enmeshed and its power to employ an ancient tale to vehiculate new social content. The impasse reached here, so reminiscent of the end of *Connecticut Yankee*, resides in the problematic of charismatic authority Hurston interrogates and its inability to imagine a cultural transformation of the masses that is undertaken in any fashion by the masses themselves. It is this very conceptual and political dilemma—what I've referred to as cultural revolution—that I believe informs the most vital layers of Hurston's general narrative mode. While a Hurston imagined under the sign of modernization (both bourgeois and Soviet-style), with its valorization of economic development and individual autonomy, might seem unfamiliar, the ideological investments here are very real; the contradictions they entail with her acknowledged investments in folk collectivity signal the emergence of a genuine *problematic* in her work, a properly modernist narrative machine that "maps" the dynamics of cultural revolution in all their complex manifestations.

The full description and analysis of such a problematic, however, lie beyond the scope of the present essay.[31] What I wish to do in conclusion is merely suggest some of the directions in which these exploratory reflections might be developed. The problem of the "writer as intellectual," in terms both of his or her social position as such, as well as the dynamics of narrative apparatuses and character fields, unfolds potentially in several ways. I think, for example, of the "intellectual workers"—the doctors, lawyers, scientists, and sundry bookworms—who densely populate American realism, who have typically been read as mimetic indices of the burgeoning professionalization of bourgeois life, but who might be more fruitfully grasped as markers that map the contours of the new problem of theory and practice, of knowledge and historical agency. Such dynamics are likely only exacerbated under modernism, and offer new ways of framing an American modernism hitherto resistant to clear conceptualization. Cultural revolution in this context would mean, not so much a hermeneutic of the trace of older social forms as proposed by Jameson, but rather something closer to an active imagination of the possibilities and restrictions of historical form and agency in the present, as if the spectrum of modes of production and the particular narrative machinery become enmeshed and begin generating figures and allegories of social change and political horizons. But much of this remains coded: the previous examples suffer from a certain obviousness, and the challenge would be to detect, for example, more stealthy figurations of strength and weakness or intellectual machination. Above all, establishing the linkage of all this to the frequently repressed class texture of the social and of literary form would be the ultimate desideratum of such investigations.

NOTES

1. Friedrich Nietzsche, *On the Genealogy of Morality*, trans. Carol Diethe (Cambridge: Cambridge University Press, 1994), 3.

2. Fredric Jameson, "Marxism and Historicism," *The Ideologies of Theory*, vol. 2, *Syntax of History* (Minneapolis: University of Minnesota Press, 1988), 174.

3. Jameson, "Third-World Literature in the Era of Multinational Capitalism," *Social Text* 15 (Fall 1986): 76.

4. See Georg Konrad and Szelenyi, *Intellectuals on the Road to Class Power* (New York: Harcourt Brace Jovanovich, 1979); Alvin Gouldner, *The Future of Intellectuals and the Rise of the New Class* (New York: Seabury, 1979). It is interesting to note that the fate of "new class" theories—promulgated initially from a Left-wing perspective—has been one of expropriation and rearticulation by the Right. Irving Kristol and the culture warriors following in his wake routinely rely on a "theory" of liberal academics and media moguls as constituting a new class that governs cultural discourse in the United States. One notices here the evaporation of any economic underpinnings and the reduction of the original sociological research to a purely cultural ideology.

5. John Guillory, "Literary Critics as Intellectuals," in *Rethinking Class*, eds. Dimock and Gilmore (New York: Columbia University Press, 1994), 107–49. I draw on Guillory's superb account at several points in my essay. See also the wide-ranging discussion in John Frow, *Cultural Studies and Cultural Value* (Oxford: Oxford University Press, 1995).

6. Karl Marx, "Theses on Feuerbach," *The Marx-Engels Reader*, 2nd ed., ed. Robert Tucker (New York: Norton, 1978), 144.

7. Nietzsche, 28.

8. As Stanley Aronowitz remarks, "however important their work is for various state institutions prior to the contemporary epoch, intellectuals begin to occupy a unique political position when the question of the 'masses' enters political discourse," *The Politics of Identity: Class, Culture, and Social Movements* (New York: Routledge, 1992), 132.

9. Geoffrey Galt Harpham, The Ascetic Imperative in Culture and Criticism (Chicago: University of Chicago Press, 1987), 209. Analogies might be drawn here with Gianni Vattimo's pensiero debole and Bruno Latour's notion of the "politics of explanation" who seeks in his work on the sociology of science: "Our quandary is similar to that of a non-violent pacifist who still wishes to be 'stronger' than a violent militarist. We are looking for weaker, rather than stronger, explanations, but we still would like these weak accounts to defeat the strong ones." Bruno Latour, "The Politics of Explanation: An Alternative," *Knowledge and Reflexivity*, ed. Steve Woolgar (London: Sage, 1988), 155–76.

10. Giovanni Arrighi, "Marxist Century, American Century," *After The Fall: The Failure of Communism and the Future of Socialism*, ed. Robin Blackburn (London: Verso, 1991), 126–65. Arrighi has more recently placed this discussion within a wider context of global capitalist history in *The Long Twentieth Century* (London: Verso, 1994).

11. See especially Etienne Balibar's discussion in his essay "In Search of the Proletariat," *Masses, Classes, and Ideas* (New York: Routledge, 1994), 125–50.

12. See Slavoj Žižek, *The Ticklish Subject: The Absent Centre of Political Ontology* (London: Verso, 2000), esp. 221–28.

13. For recent reconsiderations of the question of the universal, see Balibar, *Masses, Classes, Ideas*, 177–226, as well as his essay "Ambiguous Universality," *Differences* 7:1 (1995): 48–74; Alain Badiou, *Ethics*, trans. Peter Hallward (London: Verso, 2001).

14. Nietzsche, 93.

15. Ibid., 38.

16. Ibid., 39.

17. Ibid., 62.

18. Michel Foucault, 'Truth and Power," *Power/Knowledge*, ed. Colin Gordon (New York: Pantheon, 1980), 126.

19. Gayatri Spivak, "From Haverstock Hill Flat to U. S. Classroom, What's Left of Theory?" *What's Left of Theory? New Work on the Politics of Literary Theory*, ed. Judith Butler et al. (New York: Routledge, 2000), 1–39.

20. Jameson, *The Prison-House of Language* (Princeton: Princeton University Press, 1971), 64–69.

21. Zora Neale Hurston, *Go Gator and Muddy the Water: Writings by Zora Neale Hurston from the Federal Writers' Project*, ed. Pamela Bordelon (New York: Norton, 1999), 78.

22. Mark Twain, *A Connecticut Yankee in King Arthur's Court* (New York: Signet, 1963), 83.

23. Ibid., 85.

24. Ibid., 285.

25. Ibid., 114.

26. Hurston, *Mules and Men* (New York: Harper Perennial, 1990), 1.

27. Hazel Carby, "The Politics of Fiction, Anthropology, and the Folk: Zora Neale Hurston," *New Essays on Their Eyes Were Watching God*, ed. Michael Awkward (Cambridge: Cambridge University Press, 1990), 71–94.

28. Walter Benn Michaels, *Our America: Nativism, Modernism, and Pluralism* (Durham: Duke University Press, 1995), 93.

29. Indeed, it is tempting to see Hurston's work as a precise expression of what Jameson, in his essay on Third-World literature, calls national allegory.

30. Hurston, *Moses, Man of the Mountain* (Urbana: University of Illinois Press, 1984), 292–94.

31. I attempt this larger argument in "Cosmic Upset: Cultural Revolution and the Contradictions of Zora Neale Hurston," forthcoming.

6

Construction Work

Theory, Migration, and Labor in an Age of Globalization

Michael Rothberg

It would be interesting . . . to write a general history of the modes of production from the standpoint of the workers' desire for mobility (from the country to the city, from the city to the metropolis, from one state to another, from one continent to another) rather than running through that development simply from the standpoint of capital's regulation of the technological conditions of labor. This history would substantially reconfigure the Marxian conception of the stages of the organization of labor.
—Michael Hardt and Antonio Negri, *Empire*

The village must teach us to make the globe a world.
–Gayatri Spivak, *Critique of Postcolonial Reason*

In the following, I read Fredric Jameson's theory of cognitive mapping through the lens of Lourdes Picareta and Jacinto Godinho's 1996 documentary film *lohn–macht–angst: Arbeiter auf der globalen Baustelle* ["wages–power–fear" or "wages–produce–fear: Workers on the Global Construction Site"] in order to consider the complex status of migrant labor in the new Europe and in the new global economy.[1] *Lohn–macht–angst*—which documents the lives of construction workers and their families in Germany, Portugal, and Guinea-Bissau—suggests insights into the inextricability of economic processes, political analysis, collective praxis, and representation, insights that correspond to Jameson's call for a project of "cognitive mapping." Although the concept of cognitive mapping was originally developed in the context of urban studies and redeployed in Jameson's work on postmodernism, it has become even more obviously relevant during the last decade of globalization. In its linking of politics, pedagogy, and aesthetics, cognitive mapping stands as one of the most significant of Jameson's theoretical interventions, one in which he weaves together the most important strands of his thinking. A reading of Picareta and

Godinho's film can contribute to Jameson's project of mapping contemporary capitalism, a project still in need of exemplary aesthetic texts that would both clarify the historicity of our situation and contribute to the development of a corresponding theoretical discourse.

Like the Jamesonian theory of cognitive mapping, *lohn–macht–angst* produces paradoxical effects. On the one hand, both Jameson's theory and the critical aesthetic practice of the film confront us with the harsh realities of the times in which we live, times defined by the seemingly uncontested power of capital and the dramatic impoverishment of the vast majorities of the world's population. Such representations and theories can easily lead to despair about possibilities for substantive change. On the other hand, both Jameson and *lohn–macht–angst* provide means through which the times can be grasped as historically contingent—that is, as potentially open to resistance and reconstruction through individual and collective agency. In bringing together Jamesonian theory with Picareta and Godinho's film, we approach several significant questions signaled by my epigraphs: What would it mean "to write a general history of the modes of production from the standpoint of the workers' desire for mobility" (Hardt and Negri)? How might the adoption of such a standpoint transform Marxist theory from within? Can this theoretical reformulation help us "to make the globe a world" (Spivak)? To address such questions, I begin by providing a genealogy of Jameson's theory of cognitive mapping and then place that theory in dialogue with Gayatri Spivak's notion of transnational literacy. In the following sections, I turn to a close reading of Picareta and Godinho's film in order to illustrate and test the efficacy of Jamesonian theory within the evolving conditions of global economic production.

Although he has co-edited an important collection, *The Cultures of Globalization*, and written a series of relevant essays, Jameson may seem not to have made the kind of definitive intervention into the question of globalization that he did in 1984 with the publication of his essay "Postmodernism, or, The Cultural Logic of Late Capitalism." And yet Jameson's writings on postmodernism, cognitive mapping, and what he later termed "the geopolitical aesthetic," with their emphasis on the spatial relations of culture and economics, anticipate much important work that has been done on the phenomena of global culture and transnational capitalism and remain surprisingly timely twenty years after their composition. Here I want to focus in particular on how the concept of cognitive mapping might assist in the critical interrogation of globalization. Jameson first publicly used the concept at the 1983 Illinois conference that led to the important volume *Marxism and the Interpretation of Culture* (1988). By the time of that publication, the concept had appeared at the conclusion of the postmodernism essay; a few years later, the "Cognitive Mapping" essay itself would be folded into the conclusion of the 1991 postmodernism book.[2]

Jameson describes cognitive mapping as an aesthetic function that owes debts both to Althusser and the urbanist Kevin Lynch. Lynch's notion of cognitive mapping is meant to describe how city-dwellers are able to move through alienating urban spaces of daunting complexity that exceed experiential capabilities. For Lynch (in Jameson's characterization), "disalienated" movement through urban space "involves the practical reconquest of a sense of place and the construction or reconstruction of an articulated ensemble which can be retained in memory and which the individual subject can map and remap." In formulating his own version of cognitive mapping, Jameson moves several steps beyond this project. First, he remarks on the suggestiveness of Lynch's model for spaces beyond the urban, which can never be experienced directly, such as the national and global realms. Second, he articulates Lynch's notion of cognitive mapping with an Althusserian account of ideology; this allows Jameson to connect the mapping function to the crucial Marxist theme of the social totality. Like the map, ideology—understood by Jameson in a "positive," knowledge-producing sense—"enable[s] a situational representation on the part of the individual subject to that vaster and properly unrepresentable totality which is the ensemble of society's structures as a whole."[3] As the telos of a particular political and pedagogic aesthetic practice, the cognitive map would mediate between what is knowable (through "scientific knowledge" of the system) and what is unrepresentable and thus inaccessible to the "existential experience" of the subject. The space between knowledge and experience is designated by Jameson as "a gap, a rift."[4]

While cognitive mapping thus appears as the response to an a priori crisis in representation (linked to the "eternal" necessity of ideology in the Althusserian problematic), Jameson also adds a crucial historical dimension to the question of the mapping function that is somewhat in tension with the antihistoricist Althusserian framework. A pressing need for cognitive mapping arises, he argues, with the restructuring of capitalism in its second, monopoly or imperialist stage. In its "classical or market" phase, capitalism generated a grid-like space of "geometrical and Cartesian homogeneity." This space of industrial "Taylorization" corresponds, according to Jameson, to the decoding, demystifying representational schemes of realism, but does not (at least in this account) raise particular problems of representation. It is with the outward expansion of capital during the epoch of colonialism that the representation of capital's space becomes problematic because of the "growing contradiction between lived experience and structure."[5] This contradiction corresponds to new problems of perception and conceptualization that the project of cognitive mapping is meant to address. In the wake of colonial expansion,

the phenomenological experience of the individual subject . . . becomes limited to a tiny corner of the social world, a fixed-camera view of a certain section of London or the countryside or whatever.

But the truth of that experience no longer coincides with the place in which it takes place. The truth of that limited daily experience of London lies, rather, in India or Jamaica or Hong Kong; it is bound up with the whole colonial system of the British Empire that determines the very quality of the individual's subjective life. Yet those structural coordinates are no longer accessible to immediate lived experience and are often not even conceptualizable for most people.[6]

In its strong drive to coordinate diverse social and geographical realms, this passage provides one of the key moments out of which we might formulate Jameson's contribution to the analysis of globalization, but it also illustrates some of the possible limits to that contribution (to which I will return). As can be imagined given the terms of this argument, the difficulties of representation that emerge in the age of empire are only redoubled in the neocolonial third stage of late capitalism, "a moment in which not merely the older city but even the nation-state itself has ceased to play a central functional and formal role in a process that has in a new quantum leap of capital prodigiously expanded beyond them, leaving them behind as ruined and archaic remains of earlier stages in the development of this mode of production."[7] I will leave aside for the moment the question of the roles of the city and the nation within multi-national capitalism—a question by no means resolved among observers of the global economy.

Most valuable in this theory of cognitive mapping from my perspective here is the recognition that the gap between knowledge and experience can only be bridged through coordinating practices of representation that are necessarily contingent and imperfect. The contingent bridging of the gap is simultaneously the place of politics and the place of aesthetics (concisely brought together in the concept of the "pedagogical political culture" that defines cognitive mapping.[8] While the theory thus locates politics and aesthetics in the same space, it also guards against their facile equation or, at least, their reduction to a single model of form or practice. Whatever one thinks of the claims to totalize knowledge on one side of the gap, the cognitive map itself—the bridge, the aesthetico-political practice—is ultimately closer to the situational "experience" on the other side, because its construction cannot be fully grounded in certainty and stability. Jameson's dual framework, which address at once synchronic/universal and diachronic/contingent problems of representation, seeks to coordinate structural analysis of the economy with the singularity of aesthetic and political performativity.[9]

And yet, while Jameson's conceptualization of cognitive mapping suggests the need for a differential politics attuned simultaneously to different levels of the social, his language sometimes betrays him and puts forward a more unitary vision not commensurate with his perception of the necessary "gap" between knowledge and experience. Jameson's proposal for cognitive mapping has come under scrutiny in Gayatri Spivak's *Critique of Postcolonial Reason* for two related problems.[10] In the project of cognitive mapping, Spivak first identifies a particular, class-specific Western male subject.[11] If Spivak's complaint sounds like a familiar brand of "theoretical correctness," she also locates a significant ambiguity in Jameson's formulations. The slippage between the universal necessity—and ultimate failure—of the bridging of knowledge and experience and its location in a particular subject position becomes clear in the previous passage in which Jameson charts the historical emergence of the gap. The "phenomenological experience of the individual subject," he writes, "becomes limited to a tiny corner of the social world, a fixed-camera view of a certain section of London or the countryside or whatever." History, in this passage, seems to reside only on the side of the metropolitan subject, who is "fixed" in "a certain section of London or the countryside or whatever." Is the "whatever" meant to gesture at a subject differently situated with respect to the imperial project? It seems unlikely that that is what is intended here, but perhaps the more crucial question would be, does it matter politically, aesthetically, or experientially—once contingency is inscribed into the mapping project—where the subject is situated in relationship to the social totality? Now, it is clear that in his work as a whole, Jameson has shown significant interest in exploring those subject positions that here fall into the "whatever" position—I'm thinking, for instance, of the controversial essay on "Third World literature" or the more global scope of *The Geopolitical Aesthetic*.[12] But do those investigations change the fundamental problematic of cognitive mapping? Should they?

Spivak argues that they should change the terms of the argument, but that they ultimately do not (although she herself does not consider Jameson's other, more globally inflected works). She links the problem of subject position to a second issue of relevance here—the historical narrative in which it is embedded—and focuses in particular on the question of the "dominant" that grounds Jameson's analysis. As is well known, the project for cognitive mapping is articulated within the larger theorization of postmodernism as the cultural logic of the third stage of capitalism (even if, as we have seen, its necessity is already inscribed in an earlier moment). This theory relies in turn on a narrative of capitalism's fundamental stages (already alluded to) and on Raymond Williams's nuanced account of residual, dominant, and emergent forces that coexist and interact within any allegedly synchronic structure. In contrast to the cognitive mapping of the culturally dominant postmodernism proposed by Jameson, Spivak argues that we "cannot afford to ignore the irreducible heterogeneity of the cultural in the name of the 'cultural dominant' simply because it is dominant."[13] Her reasoning is political and pragmatic as well as theoretical: "a power-analysis of cultural dominants is bound to make visible the repression of emergent heterogeneity: unless careful, the analysis can itself collaborate in that repression by refusing it access to the status of the idiom of cultural description. . . . [I]f we only concentrate on the dominant, we forget that the difference between varieties of the emergent and residual *may* be the difference between radical and conservative resistance to the dominant, although this is by no means certain."[14] Spivak's multiply hesitating language stands in contrast to Jameson's complex, but more straightforwardly indicative mode. Not just a matter of style, the different means of expression correspond to what I would read as different theories of politics—Jameson's grounded in a dialectical, but ultimately progressive vision of historical change; Spivak's in the uncertainties and hesitations that emerge at once from her deconstructive commitments and her attempt to think the exclusion of subalternity (the definitively non-dominant) through a "productive acknowledgment of complicity."[15]

To be sure, Jameson's commitment to the cognitive mapping and critique of the dominant does not in any way exclude engagement with marginal positions. Indeed, the initial example of cognitive mapping involved Marvin Sukin and Dan Georgakis's account of the League of Black Revolutionary Workers, *Detroit: I Do Mind Dying*, as just such a representational problematic.[16] Rather than excluding marginal positions, cognitive mapping's insistence on the epistemological salience of subject position sometimes leads to a version of the standpoint epistemology that has often proven productive in feminist and minority studies. As Jameson observes in the course of his fine analysis of Kidlat Tahimik's film *Perfumed Nightmare*, "[w]hat the First World thinks and dreams about the Third can have nothing whatsoever in common, formally or epistemologically, with what the Third World has to know every day about the First. Subalternity carries the possibility of knowledge with it, domination that of forgetfulness and repression—but knowledge is not just the opposite of forgetfulness, nor is domination the opposite of oppression."[17] While the invocation of the subaltern seems to reference Spivak's famous essay "Can the Subaltern Speak?"—given at the same conference during which Jameson presented "Cognitive Mapping"—what differentiates Jameson from Spivak in their approaches to subalternity also becomes clear here.[18] For Jameson, subaltern knowledge is always knowledge of the dominant, while for Spivak, subaltern knowledge is precisely and structurally heterogeneous to the dominant framework. Hence, for instance, what Tahimik's film "knows," according to Jameson, is that under conditions of late capitalism "the economic dimension has come to take precedence over a political one which is not left out or repressed, certainly, but which . . . is for the moment assigned a subordinate position and role."[19] Whether or not this is a convincing reading of *Perfumed Nightmare*—and in the occasion I find that it is—what is characteristic here is the move of subordinating questions of the political and of power to the critique of capitalism (a move that is explicit throughout Jameson's writings of the last decades). Knowledge of the overwhelming determination of the economic is by no means foreign to Spivak's work, and yet, as the famously enigmatic conclusion to "Can the Subaltern Speak?" illustrates, subaltern knowledge and knowledge of the subaltern undermine the certainty evinced by Jameson's reading that first-world subjects can so easily know what it is that the subaltern knows.

In place of cognitive mapping, Spivak proposes "transnational literacy," which "keeps the abstract as such, the economic, visible under erasure." Characteristically, Spivak does not provide a simple definition of transnational literacy; rather, readers are left to induce its contours by tracking its effects through her reading practice. For my purposes here, I want to suggest that the concept of transnational literacy supplements (in the everyday as well as Derridian senses) Jameson's project of cognitive mapping by translating the responsibility of the first world critic beyond engagement with the already unrepresentable dominant into the differently inaccessible realms of the exploited, the suppressed, and even the subaltern. The need for literacy, in other words, is not located in the possibly illiterate subaltern, but in the educated first world reader: at the very moment Spivak seeks to instruct "dominant" readers in the pitfalls of turning subalternity into exploitable resources for "information retrieval," she also suggests the necessity for those same readers to develop ethical reading practices or "literacy" with which to reapproach the spaces of subalternity. These heterogeneous realms are not "pure" sites of "resistance" because they are in no way separate from the dominant—hence, the importance of keeping the economic "visible under erasure." And yet, they are not only structurally necessary to the dominant—the concept of which could only be misapprehended without them, as Jameson certainly recognizes. They are also potential (but by no means certain) sites of rearticulation and agency, and they are windows into alternative narrative frames, into what Arjun Appadurai calls the "imagined worlds" of the subordinated.[20] Turning to Picareta and Godinho's film will provide an opportunity to test this proposed concatenation of cognitive mapping and transnational literacy with reference to a work that allows neither a romanticization of resistance and subalternity nor a forgetting of the overarching power of the global dominant.

On June 16, 1995, thousands of Germans marched through the streets of Berlin to protest the hiring of foreign workers. This was not a demonstration organized by neo-Nazis; nor did it lead to the kind of racist violence that has riddled post-unification Germany. Rather, the demonstration was organized by the construction workers' union IG-Bau-Steine-Erden and was a response to some of the social and economic contradictions attendant on the increased integration of the European Union (EU). At stake was not primarily race, as we are used to thinking about it in relation to xenophobic violence in the new Europe, but especially issues of class and the nation-state in an era of increasingly transnational social relations. The union was protesting the practice of so-called wage dumping in which subcontracted workers from other EU countries are "posted" to Germany. Because they are technically employed in another EU state, posted workers could at that time be paid the lower wages of their homeland—in this case, primarily Britain, Ireland, and Portugal—while competing with the relatively high-waged German workers. Furthermore, such posted workers were not entitled to any of the social benefits of the German state, and thus were an even greater bargain for the construction industry than the comparison of wages suggests. The possibility of wage dumping arises from a 1993 EU provision for "freedom of services" among corporations based anywhere in Europe. Given these conditions, in the mid-1990s, there were approximately 200,000 construction jobs in Germany filled with workers from other EU countries and a similar number of unemployed German construction workers.[21]

One year after the German construction workers' protests in Berlin, the EU issued a directive "to guarantee contract workers migrating between member states nationally prevailing wages and social rights." This decision, according to two commentators, Jytte Klausen and Louise Tilly, "signals the need of the still-important nation-state—acting as a member of a union of states—to protect national actors and prevent national standards from eroding."[22] The stakes of this 1996 directive are high, since construction work is no minor industry in Europe: in 1988, "7 percent of all persons employed in the EU were active in construction,"[23] and the post-unification boom in Germany (and in Berlin in particular) brought the figure to more than 8 percent in the mid-1990s.[24] Nevertheless, a year after this significant directive, high unemployment in Germany led the leftist opposition of that time to press for a further crackdown on foreign workers.[25] Indeed, the minimum wage agreed on in 1996, against the protests of labor-source countries, such as the united Kingdom and Portugal, remains well below the wage negotiated earlier by German unions. Despite the evolution of supranational institutions and policies, the governing of capital and labor in post-Cold War, post-unification Europe continues (and no doubt will continue) to involve crises of the sort at issue in the construction workers' protests.

Taking the conflict over the wages of construction workers in Berlin as its point of departure, Lourdes Picareta and Jacinto Godinho's *lohn–macht–angst: Arbeiter auf der globale Baustelle* moves between countries and continents in order to provide a cognitive mapping of the unequal impact of contemporary economic and political realities on differently situated individual and collective subjects. An analysis of this documentary, made for the German television series "Blickpunkt Europa" [Focus Europe], helps render visible the relationship between work, race, space, gender, and the nation-state in an age of globalization. Although the construction industry does not ordinarily come to mind as one of the representative sites of the "new" economy, considering the fate of construction workers in Europe can lead to a more "concrete" understanding of social relations under globalization.

While *lohn–macht–angst* is by no means a formally experimental work, focusing on the film's aesthetic strategies, as well as the material realities it documents, will also allow consideration of the relationship between representation and the workings of transnational capitalism. Such a consideration is in order, for as the account of Jameson's approach to cognitive mapping should have made clear, even when the dynamics of regional and global economic relations can be understood and described, efforts to resist the imposition of such relations must soon confront problems of representation. Jameson's oeuvre as a whole—and especially his writings on postmodernism—put forward a strong case that questions of representation are not supplementary to considerations of globalization, but are rather intrinsic to them. As a primary instance of this argument, consider how the new technologies of communication that undergird global economic processes render certain social relations hypervisible while leaving others in the shadows. The case of migrant workers illustrates both sides of this ambivalent relationship between representation and globalization: on the one hand, migrant workers are consistently made visible through processes of ethnicization and racialization, yet, on the other hand, the trajectories of migrant workers' lives are erased from collective representations and thus isolated from potential solidarity with other workers.[26]

Before looking in more details at the film, let me clarify the particular context in which I will consider Picareta and Godinho's work. While paying attention to the local histories depicted in the documentary, my focus will not primarily be on the German context of its production and reception. If we were to foreground that context, we might note that, although depicting global processes, *lohn–macht–angst* is enabled by a specifically national organization of television production, and intervenes first at both regional and national levels. The film was made for German television by Südwestfunk Baden-Baden, a regional television station in the southwest, and broadcasted on some channels of the third program, a series of public stations dedicated to regional German productions. The film had, in other words, a regional provenance, but an interregional circulation. Taking advantage of the German public sphere's relatively greater openness to critical perspectives on social issues (in relation, at least, to the contemporary United States), the film intervenes in ongoing tensions with respect to the status of "foreigners" in Germany and the integration of the country's eastern and western halves.[27] It produces an enlightening regional, even subnational, "take" on global processes that unsettles local (as well as international) presuppositions about post-unification Germany. For instance, when asked how unemployment has changed his life, Karl-Heinz, the white German worker featured in the film, remarks that he has become quite "aggressive, although I don't want to be," and his wife adds that now "he hates foreigners and East Germans." The unexpected conjunction of "foreigners and East Germans" demystifies and recontextualizes the racialization of various groups of diverse origin in Germany by referring racist discourse to an economic substructure too often overlooked in liberal antiracism.[28] As important as such insights are, my essay moves beyond the local German context to situate the film within larger debates about globalization. When we view the film from the broader, not specifically German perspective of its commentary on transnationalism, as it also deserves to be considered, the mix of political and economic factors becomes more complex than the example of Karl-Heinz suggests. It is precisely in sorting out the various levels of *lohn–macht–angst*'s approach to globalization that the theoretical work of Jameson is both indispensable and, at certain moments, limited.

Lohn–macht–angst opens with an image of sparks flying on a construction site in Portugal. A voice-over narrative immediately introduces the three representative figures and the framework of displacement that run throughout the film: "The African in Lisbon. The Portuguese in Berlin. The German without work." This opening setup simultaneously establishes symmetry and asymmetry in its depiction of Francisco, José, and Karl-Heinz, the three workers alluded to, and in the political and economic networks that connect them. While all suffer displacements, that of the German is already marked as different in nature from those of the workers from Guinea-Bissau and Portugal. Central to the film is this articulation of coexisting proximity and distance—both between locations in what the film's subtitle calls "the global construction site" and between the workers who toil or, like Karl-Heinz, desire to toil in those sites. The global construction site is another name for the "new geography of power" identified by Saskia Sassen and characterized by new relationships of sovereignty and territory that necessitate a remapping of social, political, and economic spaces.[29] The film's opening sequence establishes the two key axes of this remapping that will be relevant here: on the one hand, the explicit opposition between mobility and stasis, and, on the other, the implicit importance of gender, marked here by a foregrounding of the particularly masculine-coded industry that is the film's subject. The remainder of the film constitutes a reflection on the interwoven status of these two axes of movement and gender.

How does the film's representation of these two axes of the global construction site correspond to Jameson's sketch of a political pedagogy? We have seen how his call for cognitive mapping emerges out of the historical context of classical imperialism and then receives heightened impetus from the transnational reach of contemporary capitalism. While Jameson deliberately orients his narrative from above—it is "capital itself," and not "the Hegelian Absolute Spirit, nor the party, nor Stalin," writes Jameson ironically, that guides his materialist analysis[30]—Picareta and Godinho follow capital's underside, the movement of workers, without in any way discounting how economic power shapes the narratives of those lives. The film's focus is not only on the imprint left by the systemic on the situational, but also on the particular resources brought to bear in local contexts.

While the three workers share a trade, just as they share anxieties about their lives and labors, the film demonstrates how separate and disparate are the lifeworlds they inhabit. It takes a staged dialogue between José and Karl-Heinz at a food stand in Berlin to bring them into the same frame; but, although the workers frequently express similar analyzes, fears, desires, and prejudices, it is not clear that communication has taken place between them, despite the filmmaker's audible translation between German and Portuguese. If, to the moderately xenophobic Karl-Heinz, the meeting in Berlin between a Portuguese and a German worker seems unlikely or worse, it also serves as a microcosm of the film's strategies of representation. In a compact forty-five minutes, *lohn–macht–angst* stages an encounter between the center, periphery, and semiperiphery of the global economy.[31] The filmmakers travel between nations and continents, and conduct interviews in at least five languages, in order to demonstrate that Karl-Heinz is only removed by three degrees of separation from villagers in Guinea-Bissau, the West African nation and former Portuguese colony that is one of the world's poorest places.[32]

All the workers depicted in the film are caught in one of the central paradoxes of global social relations, as articulated by Sassen: "Economic globalization denationalizes national economies; in contrast, immigration is renationalizing politics."[33] Or, as sociologist Douglas Massey puts it, "in essence, today's global economy is characterized by the deregulation and internationalization of all markets save one," the labor market.[34] Picareta and Godinho's film depicts the contradictions that riddle such a paradoxical situation. After the title sequence, the film performs a partial cartography of the world system. It first depicts the African Francisco working in Lisbon and then shifts to Berlin, where José and Karl-Heinz confront each other in the tense economic climate of mid-1990s Germany. In Berlin, the film documents celebrations of the reconstruction of the new capital—backed by a gospel choir singing "Oh Happy Day!"—as unemployed workers look on bitterly. If Karl-Heinz's potential job has gone to the posted Portuguese worker José, who can be hired at about half the price of the unionized German worker, the conditions of José's potential job in Portugal have been eroded by the exploitation of African workers like Francisco, who labors illegally and without protection in Lisbon for half the wages José is making in Berlin.[35] Just as José sends money back home to his family in Portugal, with the intention of building his own house, Francisco sends money to his family in Africa. Yet here again asymmetry enters the picture.

While both the Portuguese and German workers express desires to remain at home—and blame the presence of foreigners on their inability to do so happily—Francisco's money is intended to help his nephew and ultimately his immediate family come to Europe. Those who desire mobility, however, are the least likely to achieve it. A cousin of Francisco interviewed in Guinea-Bissau, the only member of his family to have completed his education, has already tried and failed to travel to France; his entire family saved for years to facilitate that attempt and he doesn't believe he'll ever have another opportunity. Meanwhile, his degree in agriculture has prepared him for a career he cannot afford to begin, so instead he drives a bus, his daily rounds through the city an ironic echo of his frustrated desire for upward mobility and a self-reflexive instance in a film whose own production relies precisely on the mobility denied some of its subjects. The contrast that the film's montage evokes between Karl-Heinz, Francisco, José, and Francisco's cousin demonstrates that, in conditions of globalization, neither movement nor stasis is inherently privileged.[36] Rather, for the vast majorities of the world's workers, the very terms movement/stasis have themselves been rendered unstable in a more fundamental expropriation by the global system.

The film's montage creates a fictive (though by no means fictional) connectedness between workers otherwise isolated from each other by a combination of historical contingency and corporate manipulation. Yet the film's fiction of connectedness turns out to mirror—not so much mimetically as allegorically—its object. Despite all of the unevenness in access to mobility or stasis depicted by the film, both Francisco, from Guinea-Bissau, and many of the Portuguese workers in Berlin turn out to be working for the same subcontractor, a Portuguese multinational called Engil with business on three continents. While making a point of the ease with which Engil moves across borders and takes on and drops workers according to the needs of its bottom line, the film does not attempt to represent the corporation as such.[37] The nondescript corporate headquarters are shown briefly from the outside at one point, but no representative of high level management appears in the film; the only nonlaborers involved in the construction industry who speak are a German foreman and a site manager. In choosing not to attempt to represent corporate power directly, while everywhere evoking its effects, *lohn—macht—angst* works at the problem of representation for which Jameson introduces cognitive mapping as the potential solution.

In Jameson's account, we recall, it is important to distinguish between the ability to understand the global system and to represent it. While the world system is, for Jameson, knowable, it remains unrepresentable; thus, there is "a gap, a rift, between existential experience and scientific knowledge." Cognitive mapping has "the function of somehow inventing a way of articulating those two distinct dimensions with each other."[38] Does the film reproduce the gap between experience and knowledge or does it constitute an attempt to find a new mode of representation adequate to the conditions of globalization? I think it does both. That is, it represents the social relations of late capitalism as precisely the gap between the transnational experience of workers and the invisible but determining power of the multinational corporation. The film thus demonstrates the necessity of moving cognitive mapping beyond its crucial concern with the dominant—the map produced here takes shape precisely in the space between systemic coherence and subjective contingencies.

The cognitive map constructed by *lohn–macht–angst* is more than a tracing of the circuits of transnational migrations of capital and labor, however. Two other dimensions need to be taken into account in our reading of the film: the coexistence of different historical temporalities and the coexistence of a parallel, but discontinuous narrative track. The contemporary movements of capital are, first of all, depicted against a backdrop of complex, longer-term histories of colonialism, slavery, and genocide. These histories emerge through the strategic choices made in the production of the film about which locations to investigate and which circuits to follow. Crucial to the film's significance is not only who is at work on the global construction site, but also the relationship between the history of each particular site and what is being constructed there now.

In Portugal, the film documents the construction of the grounds of Lisbon's 1998 World Expo. As Francisco discusses his fragile working conditions there, Picareta places him in front of a monument celebrating Portugal's role in 500 years of exploration and, we might add, conquest. Indeed, Francisco's very presence at this site is a result of just this history. A former subject of Portugal's erstwhile colonies in Africa, Francisco now helps construct a vision of globalization that is at once nostalgic and oriented toward a particular future. When the Expo leaves, it will also have left in place a luxury living quarter with a massive shopping mall, as well as entertainment and transportation centers. Like other workers throughout the world, Francisco helps construct a site of prosperity from which he will be systematically excluded. But in a particular irony, the site of the World Expo he produces will also reproduce the distorted image of the national and transnational conditions and histories that have formed him and under which he labors. The racist comment of another of Picareta's interviewees, a Portuguese builder working in Lisbon, about his time in Germany reminds us that the memory of slavery is also conjoined with the Portuguese celebration of its past: "The Germans should get Negroes from Tanzania or central Africa if they need slaves." Moving imaginatively between Germany and Africa, this vision provides a distorted map of Portugal's semiperipheral position and its status as a former colonial power and as a current exporter *and* importer of labor.

The situation in Berlin is equally ironic. There, an even more transnational work force is involved in what was at the time the largest construction site in Europe—the one surrounding the former Potsdamer Platz. Taking place on the grounds of the former no-man's land constituted by the Berlin Wall and the border between East and West Germany, this construction process literally and allegorically manages the crisis of the post–Cold War world.[39] Before the Nazi period, during the Weimar Republic and earlier, the cafés, traffic, and commerce of Potsdamer Platz had come "to symbolize above all the bustle, speed, and motion of the modern metropolis."[40] While during those years Potsdamer Platz had a significant claim to be *the* site of modernity and modernism, it now might be seen as one of the emblematic sites of post-modernity and late capitalism. But if Potsdamer Platz did once seem to represent the modern tout court, it can no longer be understood as representative in that fashion. The center-periphery disjunction alluded to by Jameson in his discussion of monopoly capital still permitted the metropole to see modernity reflected in its own urban image. However, under the contemporary conditions of transnational capital represented in the film—including large-scale labor migration and the global circulation of cultures—the periphery has become more visible in the center, just as elements of the center have been partially deterritorialized and relocated outside of Europe and North America (none of which implies a lessening of hierarchy or exploitation—to the contrary). Today's global cities are not singular, but part of an inseparable constellation of sites, as Sassen has argued.[41]

Both the urbanity of the modern metropolis and the East/West ideological rift marked by the Wall that used to cut through the square have been replaced by a new conglomerate of corporate and state spaces constructed on a North/South axis (again, both literally and, given the presence of workers like José, allegorically). Interestingly, the North/South axis of construction, of which Potsdamer Platz forms the southern zone, was once "the site of Hitler's Reichkanzlei [Chancellery] and the space to be occupied by [Nazi architect Albert] Speer's megalomaniac north-south axis from the Great Hall in the north to Hitler's triumphal arch in the south . . . the power center of the empire of a thousand years."[42] Stretching from the Brandenburg Gate and the Reichstag, once again the home of the German Parliament, through Leipziger Platz and Potsdamer Platz, the site in which José and his international array of coworkers labor is part of a reconstruction of Berlin that has since made it both the new capital of a unified German state in a rapidly unifying Europe and the center of an entertainment/shopping/business complex owned primarily by Sony and Daimler-Chrysler (still Daimler-Benz at the time of the film). At the time of writing, many of the buildings in this area have been completed, but much construction remains. Already, however, the conglomeration of governmental, business, and tourist functions in this area of the city weaves politics, economics, and culture into a dense web that is simultaneously national and defined by regional (European) and global flows. While some of these construction projects cannily integrate past and present—for example, the new Reichstag with its glass dome meant to suggest the transparency of democracy over against the abuses of the recent past—the overall effect, especially in Potsdamer Platz, is of a "branded," mall-like space that seeks to erase the history upon which it is built. Nevertheless, the construction of these national and transnational spaces is inseparable from the history that led to the gash in the city's fabric now being mended, including especially the Cold War and the National Socialist war of annihilation [*Vernichtungskrieg*] that, after irreparable murder and destruction, boomeranged on Germany itself.

Taken together, the sites of global construction in *lohn–macht–angst* are also sites that index the multiple constructions of global history over the past half-millennium. These are sites that beg for cognitive mapping, but of a sort that must be able to wrestle with traumatic historical losses that complicate the meaning of contemporary capitalist restructuring. Because the subjects that labor and consume in them are the products of overlapping long-term histories, the maps that chart the Lisbon Expo and Potsdamer Platz must aspire to multidimensionality; they must be able to move into the depths of time as well as across the surface of economic flows. Furthermore, the layering of histories in the film's locations—and the particular nature of the histories of slavery, genocide, and colonialism to which they allude—suggests that problems of knowledge as well as representation are at stake. The certainty with which Jameson poses "scientific knowledge" against the unrepresentable may prove an impediment to cognitive mapping if it is not recognized that no singular scientific knowledge will be able fill in the voids to which those places of construction give form. As in Daniel Liebeskind's Berlin Jewish Museum (another recently completed and controversial architectural project), empty places will remain in the memory and unconscious as well as the geography of cities, such as Berlin and Lisbon. In fact, the very rush to reconstruct urban space in the post-Cold War era—as documented by *lohn–macht–angst*—puts into play a complex combination of memory and forgetting that may, among other things, serve as a fetishistic denial of the disruptions of genocide and colonialism.[43] Cognitive mapping provides an impetus to begin to chart such disruptions, but without the risk of entering into the heterogeneous excavations necessitated by transnational literacy, it also threatens to reduplicate capitalism's fetishization of the present.

While those multiple urban histories become part of the film's materials because they constitute the "setting" for its site of enunciation, they coexist with another narrative strand that also demands that we complicate the map of global capital. At its exact midpoint, the film shifts dramatically, although this can only be understood retrospectively. While the first half of *lohn–macht–angst* moves back and forth between work sites in Portugal and Germany, using the links between these spaces as an occasion to track the logic of capital in its globalized form, the rest of the film, starting with a scene in the Berlin hostel where the foreign workers live, turns toward more "domestic" spaces. The effect of this turn is not, however, a simple immersion in a private sphere separates from the world of work. Rather, this shift constitutes an opening up of another loop in the film's mapping project, one that demonstrates that the space of globalization is even more complex than the transnational relations of production at first suggest. Indeed, the hostel or *Heim* where the workers in Germany spend their scant off-work time might serve as the first figure of a situation in which work space and home space are no longer separable, which is not to say that they are identical. Can these nonseparable, non-isomorphic spaces be written into the same seamless narrative?

At one point in the depiction of the Portuguese workers' *Heim* in Berlin, the camera dwells momentarily on a pair of boots sitting on the floor next to a radiator on which men's underwear is drying. The iconography of the boots recalls Van Gogh's well-known painting of the peasant shoes, which, through Heidegger's discussion in "The Origin of the Work of Art" and Jameson's writings on postmodernism, has played a large role in discussions of the periodization of cultural production. Jameson famously reads "A Pair of Boots" in tandem with Andy Warhol's "Diamond Dust Shoes" in order to distinguish, somewhat didactically, between modernism and postmodernism. Jameson reads the Van Gogh painting twice, seeing it first as a "Utopian gesture" that enacts a "willed and violent transformation of a drab peasant object world into the most glorious materialization of pure color in oil paint,"[44] and then, paraphrasing Heidegger, as the calling forth of an organically rooted peasantry and "the whole missing object world which was once [its] lived context."[45] Compared to these respectively utopian and nostalgic readings, Jameson reads Warhol's shoes as "shorn of their earlier life world" and argues that the depthlessness and affectlessness of the commodified images of Warhol's work correspond to the cultural logic of late capitalism.[46]

Where does the image of the shoes in a Berlin migrant workers' hostel fit into this scenario? In their worn appearance and close connection to the presence of actual workers, the shoes approximate the modernist vision of Van Gogh, or perhaps the work of Walker Evans, in a photograph alluded to by Jameson as a realist alternative version. Yet their "situation" is certainly closer to the eviscerated late capitalist "life world" that Jameson decodes in the Warhol than to that of Van Gogh's farmer or even Evans's worker. Nevertheless, the construction worker's shoes belong to a very different sector of that late capitalist world, one in which material production still very much takes place despite the omnipresence of the society of the spectacle dramatized by "Diamond Dust Shoes." The worker's boots, and the adjacent undergarments registered by the camera, call for an understanding of how contemporary capitalist relations penetrate well beyond the "global construction site" alluded to in the film's subtitle. Or rather, the global reach of construction does not refer only to the international division of labor and the transnational flow of capital. Rather, today's construction site is global also in that it has come to encompass life itself. "Life itself" is neither the "life world" of the peasant depicted by Van Gogh nor the domestic sphere of bourgeois society, but rather what is left when the public/private distinction inherent to an earlier era is eroded by transformations in the means and relations of production. The shoes are there, along with the underwear, to allude to the intimacy and embeddedness of capitalist relations, to their ability to remake life itself, especially for those migrant workers for whom the concept of "home" has become separated from any fixed domicile.

At this point, montage becomes a significant, if still understated, formal feature of the film and questions of gender come to figure centrally. Sitting with his fellow workers in the *Heim*, José articulates the elements of the dream of upward mobility that has brought him to Berlin: to live in his own house with his wife and children "like a normal person," never to have to emigrate again.[47] Following this statement, the film jumps to Portugal, where José's wife Maria is interviewed as she knits sweaters that she sells for a small profit. Although the film focuses on a particularly masculine-gendered industry, it also portrays women as workers in various scenarios involving homework, seasonal labor, subsistence farming, and unpaid affective and domestic labor. As Spivak points out, the reemergence today of homework in particular, depicted here in the figure of Maria, simultaneously complicates the temporality of capitalism and grounds globalization:

> This type of woman's labor dates from before capitalism and thus is prior in a linear trajectory. It is the exacerbation, in globality, of a residual phenomenon already accompanying industrial capitalism. Under international subcontracting and now post-Fordist capitalism, it extends from Aran Islands sweaters to high-tech computer terminal work at home. . . . We must therefore learn not to treat homeworking as a peripheral phenomenon, as if it is no more than a continuation of unpaid service in the home. We must keep trying to deconstruct the breach between home and work in the ideology of our global struggles to reach this female grounding . . . layer that holds up contemporary global capital.[48]

To be sure, given the heterogeneous forms women's work takes in the contemporary world (and has taken in the past), there is something troubling about the way that *lohn–macht–angst* persistently locates women in the home. The film might nevertheless be a text through which we can deconstruct the breach between home and work insofar as it situates women at once inside and outside the transnational flows represented, and associates the violation of domesticity both with "male" and "female" spaces. Despite being staged in primarily gender-segregated spaces, the film allows no one-to-one coding of the binaries it mobilizes: male/female, work space/domestic space, movement/stasis, first world/third world. Instead, we can find in the film an image parallel to the scene in the hostel that permits an evocation of the ambivalent positioning of women's (and men's) work in globalization and the havoc the latter wreaks with traditional notions of public/private spaces: a final shot of José's family, filmed at dusk, depicts their house as warmly lit from within, yet with window and doors open to the penetration of the outsider's gaze. Whether at home or in a hostel, the film seems to suggest, workers live in an exposed, naked space.

But the film does not stop there; it adds several more links to the discontinuous chain of domestic spaces that it maps. The openness of the Portuguese house is immediately contrasted to the cramped interior of the unemployed German worker's apartment in Berlin, where Karl-Heinz and his wife live with their cats and tacky figurines. Oddly, this German woman is the only unnamed figure among the film's principal interviewees. She is also the only one whose work status is never discussed. From this depiction of northern domestic space, threatened, nonetheless, by a precarious economic situation, the film returns to Portugal, but this time to the shantytown where Francisco and his brother, along with other migrant African workers, have constructed shacks out of wood and metal with their own hands. Like the Berlin hostel, this is again a male space, populated by groups of workers, many undocumented and without any kind of social safety net. Finally, the film moves to Francisco's hometown of Cachungo in Guinea-Bissau, close to the Senegalese border. In Guinea-Bissau, where the monthly salary of workers is equivalent to one or two hours of wages for the construction workers in Portugal, we meet Francisco's wife and the other thirty people who barely subsist from contributions sent home by Francisco and his brother. Here, in a much more desperate form than in Portugal, work—performed overwhelmingly by women—is geared toward basic survival, physical well-being, and the elimination of hunger and disease.

It is difficult to describe the shock of recognition that takes place when the film moves to Africa in its final seven minutes. Although the film has spent a great deal of time documenting the lives of African workers in Europe, it has, until these final minutes, only shuttled back and forth between Portugal and Germany. That particular intra-European, transnational movement from center to semiperiphery has seemed logical, given the film's focus on issues apparently particular to the European Union (of the sort that I summarized earlier). However, in moving to Guinea-Bissau, the film simultaneously exposes and breaks through the Eurocentric frame that has thus far determined its representational space. This move reveals the very notion of European union as fictional at its core: it is premised on a process of simultaneous selective inclusion and exclusion of the labor of Africans and other allegedly non-European peoples. In a film concerned so obviously with labor migration, this final move—coupled with the image of Maria's homeworking—warns us against fetishizing the movement of people in our attempts to map globalization.[49] Indeed, the film does suggest the entry into a new phase of labor migration—that of the posted worker whose much more temporary, "flexible," and isolated status should be distinguished from the more familiar guest worker of the 1960s and 1970s. However, such a new mode of migration is revealed as made possible by the grounding and grounded labor of reproduction—often, although not always, performed by women in the villages and peripheries of the world system. While reproduction obviously had to take place under previous regimes of production and migration, it now also enters into a new mode under the altered conditions of production depicted in *lohn–macht–angst*.

In its second half of the film, we can reconstruct the presence of a series of women that parallels the series of male workers presented in the first establishing shots of the title sequence. The two series, however, are of a different order. While I have already pointed to the discontinuities and asymmetries that divide Francisco, José, and Karl-Heinz, the film seems to imply a greater isolation, premised on radically shrunken possibilities for movement, in the sphere of women. While the workers really do compete, however unequally, on the same stratified terrain of the labor market, their wives occupy radically heterogeneous spaces even as they perform related acts of production and reproduction. They are in no sense outside of global capitalism, yet they occupy their marginal position within it differently.[50] The film's bracing portrait of the reconfiguration of domesticity does not suggest a privileged location of resistance or authenticity. Rather, the blurring of the domestic/work divide suggests the need for a theory of history that could account for women's integrated, but nonsynchronous relationship to capitalist accumulation; homework of the sort portrayed here both precedes capitalist modernity and appears as the effect of its most contemporary modulations. A cognitive map of such a situation must be able to account for the presence of such ironic returns and discontinuities— elements that exceed Jameson's narrative of the stages of capitalism even as they take on definition precisely in relation to it.

By reconstructing the film's discontinuous shadow narrative of women's work, we can draw attention to what Michael Hardt and Antonio Negri define as affective, immaterial labor as well as to the regime of power that Hardt and Negri identify as characteristic of late, globalized capitalism: biopower. Following Foucault's formulation in *The History of Sexuality* and other late works, Hardt and Negri identify biopower as "a form of power that regulates social life from its interior, following it, interpreting it, absorbing it, and rearticulating it. . . . The highest function of this power is to invest life itself through and through, and its primary task is to administer life. Biopower thus refers to a situation in which what is directly at stake in power is the production and reproduction of life itself."[51] In what ways is the production and reproduction of life itself susceptible to cognitive mapping? What forms of transnational literacy does it demand?

Lohn–macht–angst provokes these questions and in doing so helps to shift our thinking about the local and translocal dynamics of globalization. The film does not simply portray globalization from the perspective of capital, as Jameson tends to, or from the perspective of "the workers' desire for mobility," as

Hardt and Negri would have it. It does both of these things to a certain extent, but it also does more: it reveals contemporary history as cross-cut by multiple desires and framed by the determinations of layered histories. The narrative of the reproduction of life in the second half of the film does not simply "reproduce" the narrative of production in the first. They are coextensive, but not continuous. The women featured in the second half of the film do not link up in the same logic of substitution and displacement that the men do. Their stasis is essential to the movements mapped and performed by the film, but it cannot be fully subsumed or rendered intelligible by the film or the logic of globalization—it is of a partially different order.

Tracking the shadow narratives of gender and domesticity, as well as the layered histories of the construction sites themselves, does not lead immediately to insights about resistance to the forces of globalization. But the inclusion of these heterogeneous elements does offer another form of resistance: it resists the narrative and analytic frameworks that portray globalization as a singular process, whether these frameworks derive from globalization's celebrants or critics. These marginal elements suggest that there are also other stories to tell, stories that will certainly include the subsumption of new areas of social life and indeed of life itself into capitalism but that will also have to grasp the multiple political and cultural dynamics that constitute the terrain of human history. The film does provide a partial cognitive map of global capitalism, yet it also teaches us that the globe is not an enclosed representational space but rather a world with multiple entries and exits, a world that demands heterogeneous forms of knowledge, representation, and literacy.[52]

In conclusion, it is worth pausing for a moment to consider what *lohn–macht–angst* does not depict. One way in which the film's cognitive map remains partial concerns its silence about the question of Americanization and U.S. hegemony, a question that plays a large role in Jameson's approach to postmodernism and globalization, as well it must. This silence, which should by no means be understood as a refusal of the issue, can be a salutary one for U.S.-based critics to reflect on. Indeed it teaches us that, even if there is a large degree of overlap between the forces of Americanization and the forces of globalization, there are also regional process that proceed in semiautonomy from the one world superpower. The European-African axis explored by the film can usefully decenter the subject positions of North American Anglophone critics. The film reveals daily lives and struggles that, while surely not free from American hegemony or without analogy to the American context, nevertheless take place within historical conditions and political and economic structures that retain their specificity.

Concatenating the Jamesonian theory of cognitive mapping with a notion of transnational literacy allows us to track the dominant and to factor in various differently situated minority and subaltern positions (not to mention other dominant positions, in this case European ones). For those of us based in the

United States, the workers depicted by Picareta and Godinho are a reminder that the development of new theoretical models as well as new forms of international solidarity will have to take account of histories and experiences of transnational migration and political organization that are not immediately available to us. Even, and perhaps especially, in a moment of ascendant and aggressive U.S. neo-imperialism it is important that critical thinking does not reproduce American hegemony on the level of theory. Jameson's writings—on postmodernism, globalization, and the geopolitical aesthetic—constitute a call for just such a critical internationalism and provide the tools to continue the difficult construction work that it entails.

NOTES

I am grateful to Caren Irr and Ian Buchanan for their comments on earlier versions of this essay, and to Lourdes Picareta for generously making her film available to me. Thanks also to Beth Drenning and Yasemin Yildiz for discussions of the film and the essay. Kristin Schoenfelder deserves special thanks for helping to secure materials and for her report from Lisbon.

1. Lourdes Picareta and Jacinto Godinho, *lohn–macht–angst: Arbeiter auf der globalen Baustelle* (Südwestfunk Baden-Baden, 1996).

2. Fredric Jameson, *Postmodernism, or, the Cultural Logic of Late Capitalism* (Durham: Duke University Press, 1991); "Cognitive Mapping," *Marxism and the Interpretation of Culture*, ed. Lawrence Grossberg and Cary Nelson (Urbana: University of Illinois Press, 1988). The title essay on postmodernism was originally published in 1984 in *New Left Review*. On globalization, see Fredric Jameson and Masao Miyoshi, ed., *The Cultures of Globalization* (Durham: Duke University Press, 1998), especially the preface and essay by Jameson. See also Jameson, "Globalization and Political Strategy," *New Left Review* 4 (July-August 2000): 49–68.

3. Jameson, *Postmodernism*, 51.

4. Ibid., 53.

5. Jameson, "Cognitive Mapping," 349.

6. Ibid., 349.

7. Ibid., 350.

8. Jameson, *Postmodernism*, 54.

9. The issues of contingency, structure, and universality as they relate to political practice are usefully debated in the collective volume by Judith Butler et al., *Contingency, Hegemony, Universality* (New York: Verso, 2000).

10. Gayatri Chakravorty Spivak, *Critique of Postcolonial Reason* (Cambridge: Harvard University Press, 1999).

11. Jameson, "Cognitive Mapping," 411.

12. See Jameson, "Third World Literature in the Era of Multinational Capitalism," *Social Text* 15 (Fall 1986): 65–88; and *The Geopolitical Aesthetic: Cinema and Space in the World System* (Bloomington and London: Indiana University Press and BFI, 1992).

13. Jameson, "Cognitive Mapping," 315.

14. Ibid., 314.

15. Ibid., Ibid., xii.

16. See Jamseon, "Cognitive Mapping"; *Postmodernism*, 413–15.

17. Jameson, *Geopolitical Aesthetic*, 199.

18. Spivak, "Can the Subaltern Speak?," *Marxism and the Interpretation of Culture*, ed. Lawrence Grossberg and Cary Nelson (Urbana: University of Illinois Press, 1988), 271–313.

19. Jameson, *Geopolitical Aesthetic*, 212.

20. For Appadurai's argument about the existence of imagined worlds among the diasporic groups of contemporary globalization, see Appardurai, *Modernity at Large: Cultural Dimensions of Globalization* (Minneapolis: University of Minnesota Press, 1996), esp. chaps. 1 and 2.

21. For an account of labor migration in contemporary Europe that pays particular attention to the situation of construction work in Germany, see Thomas Faist, "Migration in Contemporary Europe: European Integration, Economic Liberalization, and Protection," *European Integration in Social and Historical Perspective: 1850 to the Present*, ed. Jytte Klausen and Louise Tilly (Lanham: Rowman and Littlefield, 1997), 223–48. For a longer historical perspective on migrant labor in Europe, see, in the same volume, Leslie Page Moch, "Foreign Workers in Western Europe: The 'Cheaper Hands' in Historical Perspective," Klausen and Tilly, 103–16. For a brief account of the 1995 protest, see "Berlin construction workers stage demo," *Deutsche Presse-Agentur*, June 16, 1995, (February 9, 2004). <http://web.lexis-nexis.com/universe>. For an account of wage dumping and posted workers, see Wolfgang Munschau, "Wage dumping irks German jobless: Immigrant construction workers are 'posted' from one EU country to another," *Financial Times* (March 30, 1996): 2.

22. Klausen and Tilly, "European Integration in a Social and Historical Perspective," *Euopean Integration in a Social and Historical Perspective*, ed. Klausen and Tilly, 3–21; quotation p. 20. See also, Munschau, "Wage dumping."

23. Faist, 231.

24. The 1990s statistics come from the website of the Statistisches Bundesamt Deutschland, (December 3, 2002), <http://www.destatis.de> the official bureau of statistics in Germany. Since the mid-1990s, the construction industry has been hit hard by falling rates of employment; as of late 2002, the percentage of construction workers had fallen to 6.3 percent. While the number of workers in construction has been falling more sharply than in other sectors of the economy, the only sector that has registered any gains at all in the past few years is the service sector. During that period, unemployment has climbed to 4 million.

25. See "Tough line on foreign construction workers needed, says opposition," *Deutsche Presse-Agentur*, September 25, 1997, (February 9, 2004). <http://web.lexis-nexis.com/universe>.

26. For a provocative argument about the links between labor and ethnicization, see Rey Chow, *The Protestant Ethnic and the Spirit of Capitalism* (New York: Columbia University Press, 2002), esp. 33–38.

27. For some helpful general remarks by Jameson on differences between the American culture industries and those of national (European) traditions, see his "Notes on Globalization as a Philosophical Issue," *The Cultures of Globalization*, ed. F. Jameson and Masao Miyoshi (Durham: Duke University Press, 1998), esp. 60–63.

28. I am grateful to Yasemin Yildiz for helping me to unpack the film's resonance in a German context.

29. Saskia Sassen, *Losing Control? Sovereignty in an Age of Globalization* (New York: Columbia University Press, 1996).

30. Jameson, "Cognitive Mapping," 348.

31. The vocabulary of "center, periphery, and semiperiphery" should not be understood as indicating a return to teleological models of development. To the contrary, the film demonstrates that those locations are not translatable into a progressive narrative of development, but rather exist simultaneously and in a relationship of mutual determination.

32. Guinea-Bissau achieved independence from Portugal after an extended armed struggle led by nationalist hero Amilcar Cabral and his movement for the liberation of Guinea-Bissau and Cape Verde. According to the CIA's *World Factbook 2000*, Guinea-Bissau is one of the twenty poorest countries in the world, with a per capita GDP of $900 for its population of 1,285,000. The nation's economy is based on farming and fishing (it is one of the world's largest cashew producers), but has been further eroded by a civil war that took place in the late 1990s.

33. Sassen, 59.

34. Douglas S. Massey, "To Study Migration Today, Look to a Parallel Era," *The Chronicle of Higher Education* (August 18, 2000): B4-5; quotation B5.

35. This is a complex and difficult point, both economically and politically. It is easy in this context to see how racist rhetoric evolves around the loss of jobs to immigrants, since it is clear that in both Germany and Portugal, the conditions of labor for local workers are undermined by the transnational labor migrations. This is a double bind in which workers are set against each other in a system that works through legal and extralegal channels to maximize profits. Picareta and Godinho's choice of these particular transnational links in order to explore the problem is quite apt since Portugal is involved both in the exporting and importing of labor. In fact, according to Thomas Faist, "Intra-European migratory movement, such as that to Germany from Portugal pursuant to the freedom to provide services, is only a small fraction of the immigration to Portugal herself from third countries; indeed, Portugal has become one of the magnets for immigration from North Africa" (236).

36. The often true, but ultimately simplistic notion that movement is a prerogative of privilege is a common one even though it is belied by the vast numbers of refugees, asylum seekers, and migrant workers who can be found throughout the world. See, for example, Zygmunt Bauman, *Globalization* (New York: Columbia University Press, 2000).

37. If the film does not attempt to represent the corporation, it might be said to enact the corporation's practices through its own cross-border movements; that is, the film producers enjoy an ease and voluntarism of movement denied to their worker-subjects, but characteristic of the forces behind the workers' situation. By self-reflexively foregrounding their distance from the experience of the workers, the film producers evoke the "gap" between knowledge and experience which the project of cognitive mapping seeks contingently to bridge.

38. Jameson, *Postmodernism*, 53.

39. For two fine accounts at different moments of the reconstruction of Potsdamer Platz in the context of the larger transformation of the urban fabric of Berlin, see Andreas Huyssen, "The Voids of Berlin," *Critical Inquiry* 24 (Autumn 1997): 57–81; and "After the War: Berlin as Palimpsest," *Harvard Design Magazine* (Winter/Spring 2000): 72–77. These essays have now been collected in Huyssen, *Present Pasts: Urban Palimpsests and the Politics of Memory* (Stanford: Stanford University Press, 2003).

40. Brian Ladd, *The Ghosts of Berlin: Confronting German History in the Urban Landscape* (Chicago: University of Chicago Press, 1997), 116.

41. See Saskia Sassen, *The Global City: New York, London, Tokyo* (Princeton: Princeton University Press, 1991).

42. Huyssen, "The Voids of berlin," 65.

43. Drawing on Freud, Eric Santner has produced the concept of narrative fetishism: "the construction and deployment of a narrative consciously or unconsciously designed to expunge the traces of the trauma or loss that called that narrative into being in the first place." The construction projects depicted in *lohn–macht–angst* might be seen as, among other things, related versions of a spatial or urban fetishism. See Eric Santner, "History beyond the Pleasure Principle: Some Thoughts on the Representation of Trauma," *Probing the Limits of Representation: Nazism and the "Final Solution,"* ed. Saul Friedlander (Cambridge: Harvard University Press, 1992), 143–54; here, 144.

On the play of memory and forgetting in the reconstruction of Berlin, see the two essays by Huyssen cited earlier. Huyssen also usefully links larger questions of urban reconstruction to the design of Liebeskind's musuem; see "Voids" 73–81.

It is also interesting to remark in this context that the word "fetish" arose out of the Portuguese contact with West African traders in the sixteenth century. See Ioan Davies, "Negotiating African Culture: Toward a Decolonization of the Fetish," *Cultures of Globalization*, ed. Jameson and Miyoshi, 137. Davies also notes that both Jameson and David Harvey have employed the concept of the fetish in their discussions of the depthlessness of postmodern architecture.

44. Jameson, *Postmodernism*, 7.

45. Ibid., 8.

46. Ibid., 8–9.

47. For a helpful discussion and contextualization of the situation of Portuguese migrants in Germany, see Andrea Klimt, "European Spaces: Portuguese Migrants' Notions of Home and Belonging," *Diaspora* 9.2 (2000): 259–85. Klimt, however, does not discuss the experience of posted workers like José.

48. Spivak, *Critique of Postcolonial Reason*, 390–91.

49. See Spivak, *Critique of Postcolonial Reason*: "Increasingly and metaleptically, transnationality, a new buzzword for cultural studies, is becoming a synonym for the movement of people. To recode a change in the determination of capital as a cultural change is a scary symptom of cultural studies" (412); "transnationality [does] not primarily mean people moving from place to place, although labor export [is] certainly an important object of investigation. . . . There can be labor migrancy associated with transnationalization, but in fact it is not necessary—with postfordism and export processing zones. The demographic determining factors for labor migration lie elsewhere" (414).

50. It is, of course, important to remember that the forms of women's work depicted in the film are quite limited and by no means exhaustive. Considering labor performed by women in other contexts—such as in the maquilladoras of the U.S.–Mexican border region—would have led to a very different kind of film. *Lohn–macht–angst* does not seek to provide an all-encompassing representation of globalization; instead it maps a particular region and set of connections within the context of global flows.

51. M. Handt and A. Negri, *Empire* (Cambridge: Harvard University Press, 2000), 23–24.

52. Here I am thinking of Deleuze and Guattari's concepts of the map as an "experiment in contact with the real" and of the rhizome as constituted by multiple entries and exits. See Gilles Deleuze and Félix Guattari, *A Thousand Plateaus* (Minneapolis: University of Minnesota Press, 1987).

7

Postmodernism, or the Cultural Logic of Postcommunism?

The Cultures of the Former Soviet Bloc Encounter Jameson

Vitaly Chernetsky

The story of the encounter between the Western academic Left and the intellectuals from the ex-USSR and its former East European satellites has been complex and at times traumatic for all the parties involved. Initial enthusiasm about a possibility of dialogue across the weakening Iron Curtain for many soon gave way to bitter comments about frustrated attempts at communication. Surely the two sides shared a familiarity with at least some aspects of the Marxist intellectual tradition; why this was not a sufficient common ground for developing a fruitful dialogue? For looking in retrospect at such attempts, now that more than a dozen years separate us from the initial attempts at contact with possible collaboration in mind, we are forced to acknowledge that, for the most, these attempts, save for a few isolated exceptions, have failed. Was this failure unavoidable? And most important, is there still a common ground and a possibility for a resumption of such dialogue? While not claiming to provide exhaustive answers to these questions,[1] the present essay attempts bringing us closer to being able to tackle them, by tracing the engagement with the work of Fredric Jameson in several Slavic postcommunist countries, Russia in particular.

An exploration of this topic is fraught with many difficulties, largely because to tell the story of such engagement is to tell one of a failure to engage (especially in the case of Russia). This would seem particularly unusual since Jameson, in addition to being widely recognized as the leading American Marxist intellectual, is viewed by many, to quote the cover of Perry Anderson's *The Origins of Postmodernity*, as "theorist supreme of postmodernism"—and both postmodernism and Western theoretical thought have garnered a considerable amount of attention in the Second World in general and in Russia in particular. Indeed, the word "postmodernism" for a good part of the 1990s was ubiquitous in the Russian mass media, and translation of many theorists, particularly Barthes, Baudrillard, and Foucault, but also Derrida, Deleuze, and Lyotard, has been a veritable cottage industry. And the translation activities have not been limited to French-language texts: the Russians recently discovered, among others, Stephen Greenblatt and Harold Bloom. Why is it then that the only published Russian translation of Jameson's writing until very recently was a four-page occasional piece entitled "Theory in a New Situation," part of a Soviet-American roundtable on the role of theory in literary scholarship published in 1990 in the leading Soviet journal of literary criticism, *Voprosy literatury* [Questions of Literature], a piece, moreover, that is a response to a similarly short "provocation" essay by J. Hillis Miller, "The Triumph of Theory and the Production of Meanings"?[2]

This bizarre Russian avoidance of Jameson stands in stark contrast to the cases of two other communist-ruled states, Yugoslavia in the 1970s and 1980s, and mainland China in the 1980s and 1990s, where Jameson's writing attracted significant attention and was copiously translated and much discussed. But the cases of both "exceptions," Yugoslavia and the PRC, are easily explained: both, at the time of their engagement with Jameson's thought, were outside Soviet-style dogmatic, "orthodox" interpretation of Marx. In Yugoslavia, neither Soviet-style "dialectical materialism" nor Soviet-style "socialist realism" ever became the officially prescribed norm—a consequence of Tito's break with Stalin in 1948;[3] in China these two underwent significant modification (which famously resulted in the falling out between the USSR and the PRC in the 1960s and copious ideological diatribes directed against each other; in the Soviet case, "Chinese revisionists" were portrayed in the official media as scarcely less menacing than "American imperialists"). In both countries, as a result, non-Soviet Marxisms attracted considerable attention. The case of China is outside the scope of this essay, for linguistic and other reasons, but I will dwell briefly on the example of Yugoslavia, which is truly impressive: *Marxism and Form* was translated into Serbo-Croatian in 1974, *The Prison-House of Language* in 1978, *The Political Unconscious* in 1984; additionally, several essays by and interviews with Jameson appeared there as well. A large international symposium on postmodernism, with Jameson's participation, took place in Zagreb in March 1986.[4] Finally, it was in Dubrovnik, then still part of Yugoslavia, in October 1990, that the much commented on and very traumatic (mis)communication between Soviet and American intellectuals (Jameson among them) took place.[5]

After the disintegration of Yugoslavia, however, the stream of translations of Jameson into Serbo-Croatian (in either Serbian, Croatian, or Bosnian standard) dries up for almost a decade—I have not been able to trace any publications of such material between 1992 and 1999; only very recently does Jameson's name reappear, this time in the discussion of globalization.[6] Else-

where in the newly postcommunist Eastern Europe, though, like in the former
Soviet Union, the discourse on postmodernism undergoes a boom, spilling
over even into the tabloid mass media. Thus, several of Jameson's essays, in
particular his early and extremely influential formulations of his theory of
postmodernism, the 1983 "Postmodernism and Consumer Society" and the
1984 "Postmodernism, or, the Cultural Logic of Late Capitalism," are widely
translated—for instance, in Slovenia (the most "Western" of ex-Yugoslav
nations), where a small volume of Jameson in translation, entitled simply *Postmodernizem* [Postmodernism], came out in 1992, and was reissued in an
expanded version in 2001, or in Poland, where both essays were translated, in
1996 and 1988, respectively.[7] Why not in Russia?

Thinking about this frustrated communication, both Jameson and
Susan Buck-Morss acknowledged that this was in part a product of the radically different versions of the impact of the upheavals of the 1960s in the
First and the Second World: if in the West, they pushed many intellectuals
toward Marxism, in the Soviet bloc (in the USSR, Czechoslovakia, and
Poland in particular) it by and large signaled the *end* of attempts at creative
engagement with and development of Marx's ideas.[8] Only the dogmatic official version of Marxism-Leninism, or the branches of inquiry that were as
far removed from considerations of ideological or class issues as possible, in
particular the driest possible form of structuralist/semiotic scholarship, continued to flourish. There was one important exception to this rule: small
groups of researchers within various Academy of Sciences research institutes
were supposed to follow Western intellectual developments and produce
judgmental expert discourse about them, usually published in collections of
essays under the titles like *Criticism of the Western Bourgeois Perversions of*
[your branch of scholarship here]. Naturally, not all of these experts wrote
their denunciations wholeheartedly—in fact, many of them were sympathetic to the ideas they found in these foreign texts to which they had privileged access. Several tried and true strategies did exist for conveying some
of this "forbidden fruit" to a broader domestic audience. Publications of full
translations of actual Western texts were out of the question—but one could
"smuggle" in a large amount of quotes if the censors were not in a particularly draconian mood. Alternatively, a critique could be dressed in a vocabulary so dry and dense that a censor would find it forbidding and let it
through simply out of belief that the writing was too esoteric and would not
achieve wide resonance—or sometimes the censor would be careless enough
to allow a text as long as the requisite quotes from the "classics of Marxism-
Leninism" and present party leaders appeared in their obligatory places in
the opening and closing sections of the text. Still, if some of French poststructuralism or of the Frankfurt school made it into Russia in such a mediated way, the Anglo-American Marxist scholarship seemed to have had the
gates firmly shut in front of it.

Yet, when the Iron Curtain became more porous in the second half of the 1980s, it was the Marxist-oriented scholars from the West who were among the first who hoped to discover and establish ties with the representatives of what was considered cutting-edge thought in the Second World; this brought both Jameson and Buck-Morss to Moscow in 1988, for example. The intellectuals they encountered were primarily philosophers, not literary scholars or, say, sociologists; naturally, these were not the knee-jerk "denunciators of perversions," but instead, those who found it fascinating to engage with Western scholarship, and—being part of elite institutions based in the imperial capital—had relatively free access to the latter. At the initial stage of mutual curiosity, the dialogue seemed promising; however, problems soon became almost insurmountable. By 1991, Jameson's impressions of the situation were grim:

> Unfortunately Cold War anticommunism has lavishly supplied all possible and imaginable stereotypes . . . so that even experiential truth from the East now looks indistinguishable, not merely from media commonplaces and simulacra but from its most ancient Cold War forms. . . . The more their truths are couched in Orwellian language, the more tedious they become for us; the more our truths demand expression in even the weakest forms of Marxist language—that of simple social democracy say, or even the welfare state or social justice, or equality—the more immediately do the Eastern hearing aids get switched off. . . . To put it briefly, the East wishes to talk in terms of power and oppression; the West in terms of culture and commodification. There are really no common denominators in this initial struggle for discursive rules, and what we end up with is the inevitable comedy of each side muttering irrelevant replies in its own favorite language.[9]

The East in question, though, was listening—and learning. The Russian participants of the Dubrovnik 1990 conference that prompted these remarks soon launched a publishing house named Ad Marginem; for several years, the name of Jameson, along with those of Susan Buck-Morss and Annette Michelson, appeared on the list of its advisory board. There was talk about producing a volume of Russian translations of Jameson's selected writings. To a large extent, however, this was an attempt to curry favor from what the Russian side perceived as the Western intellectual establishment. The presence of the names of Jameson and others appeared to be purely decorative; to my knowledge, none of the publishing house's projects were an actual product of his "advice." Indeed, the publishing house from the outset behaved in an unabashedly capitalist fashion, trying to strike gold through controversy: its first two books were a collection of essays entitled *The Marquis de Sade, Sadism, and the Twen-*

tieth Century and a translation of Sacher-Masoch's *Venus in Furs*, accompanied by Deleuze's study of this text, *Coldness and Cruelty*. By the second half of the 1990s, my attempts to talk to representatives of Ad Marginem about reviving the idea of a volume of Jameson in Russian elicited no enthusiasm: there would be no market for such a book, I was told, and it would be impossible to support a publication of an American Marxist with a grant from any Western foundation active in Russia—or indeed from any other source.

I was surprised by such skepticism on behalf of the publishers, since by then the discourse on postmodernism in Russia was slowly maturing from mass-media exchanges to scholarly monographs on the topic. And in these publications, mentions of Jameson's name were indeed recurrent. But this was not the case for Ad Marginem despite the fact that in 1990, it was excited about postmodernism as a concept and its applicability to the Second World, in the face of the initial reluctance of Western scholars, Jameson among them, to extend the applicability of the term outside the West (Jameson's studies of magic realism in Second and Third World film, which, he believed at the time, was "to be grasped as a possible alternative to the narrative logic of contemporary postmodernism,"[10] testify to this).

Indeed, the only discussion of Jameson I was able to trace in the publications of Ad Marginem was of an anecdotal nature, in an essay by Mikhail Ryklin that offers a reading of the Dubrovnik conference markedly different from those by either Jameson or Buck-Morss.[11] The Dubrovnik of 1990, a resort town turned into "a press for squeezing out foreign currency," is seen by Ryklin as an epitome of postmodernist simulacric transparency, of commodity culture reigning supreme (while, for Buck-Morss, Dubrovnik's "pleasures of sensory immediacy" were only a contrasting background against which to consider the conference's problems). "I could not rid myself from the feeling," writes Ryklin,

> that I was put inside a tourist "view" or a postcard. . . . Everyone inhabiting this tourist landscape could be proud of breathing through his—and his only—skin, but he had no means to differentiate himself from the other: everything was the same and synthetically-edible. You consumed the world that in turn was consuming you. . . . Thus our seminar on postmodernism took place in an ideally postmodern space.

The key sign of postmodernness of this space, for Ryklin, was that "Fred Jameson, one of the fathers of American postmodernism, a Marxist and a fighter against colonialism" was, he says, the only conference participant housed in Dubrovnik's luxurious Hotel Imperial.[12]

It was this postmodern space, in Ryklin's opinion, that encouraged one to think "postmodern thoughts," and, in turn, provoked knee-jerk responses and conflicts. This, for him, was "the Dubrovnik effect," a réssentiment of the Soviet bloc participants, as it were, against immersion into a refined version of consumer society (apparently quite pleasurable for the Western participants, and probably for a good many of the Soviet bloc ones as well), desperate attempts at resisting the encroaching simulacrum—a simulacrum that proved so fragile when two years later the city was bombed by the Yugoslav navy.[13] Paradoxically, in Ryklin's text, Jameson's name, pace his scholarly contributions, becomes a signifier for an intellectual form of American imperialism and is basically dismissed in a sarcastic one-liner.

What is peculiar about this reaction is that postmodernism (more specifically, "Philosophical Problems of Postmodern Discourse") was the title for the Dubrovnik conference proposed by the Soviet bloc participants.[14] Indeed, the rather active embrace of the term and the extension of its use to the Second World context generated surprise and a degree of resistance from the Western participants in this dialogue. If postmodernism is indeed a phenomenon pertaining *only* to late capitalist societies, then attempts to use the term in discussions of Third World and especially Soviet bloc cultures are patently absurd. In the early 1990s, Susan Buck-Morss considered this coupling an "apparent anomaly"; Marjorie Perloff called it "an oxymoron"; and Katerina Clark, while agreeing that "gestures in that direction [i.e., towards the 'postmodernizing' of Soviet literary sensibility] have been made," insisted that those who were making those gestures were by no means near to arriving at their destination.[15] However, these warnings were voiced in the face of a fait accompli: over the course of just a couple of years, the term "postmodernism," if not the phenomenon itself, was actively embraced by a large numbers of Second World intellectuals. Perhaps not coincidentally, this embrace coincided with the disintegration of the Soviet bloc: by early 1992, the term was all over the pages of the now ex-Soviet cultural media, and used overwhelmingly for a discussion not of foreign but of local (Russian, Ukrainian, and so forth) cultural phenomena.

Jameson himself at the time expressed a very cautious sympathy with this use. Indeed, the two big projects that resulted from his interest in Soviet culture in those years, the chapters "On Soviet Magic Realism" in *The Geopolitical Aesthetic* and "Utopia, Modernism, and Death" in *The Seeds of Time*, testify to his complicated stance on the issue. The bulk of the first of the two is devoted to a reading of the 1988 film *Days of Eclipse* by the Russian director Aleksandr Sokurov, loosely based on a science fiction novel by the Strugatsky brothers, *A Billion Years to the End of the World*. From the outset, Jameson stresses the "instructive difference" of both Soviet science fiction and Soviet "new wave cinema" from their Western counterparts, something that he sees in danger of disappearing with "the new Western-style commercialization heralded by *perestroika* films and the influence of the market." He goes on to assert that "Modernist traditions . . . are still very much alive in the Soviet

Union today";[16] however, he stops short of identifying the film as either modernist or postmodernist. Still, the aims of Jameson's interpretation of the film are clear. In both the novel and the film, characters who are on the verge of breakthroughs in knowledge find that an unexplainable external force is trying to thwart their efforts; the main characters receive mysterious packages and telegrams of unknown provenance, meet strange, surreal characters, and so forth; at least one of them kills himself. What is narrativized here, believes Jameson, are external attempts to block and thwart "the construction of socialism itself, a society in control of its own destiny, that sets its own, human agenda for itself." Yet as the Soviet Union disintegrates, the forces that can be tied to this blockage can no longer be allegorically interpreted as Stalinism or the Party as a totalitarian institution—"it is the capitalist world system into which the Soviet Union has decided to integrate itself." Thus, it appears that within the context of this reading, if one may talk about the Second World entering postmodernity, it is only as a consequence of the collapse of communist rule and its entry into the situation in which "late capitalism weighs on the world like a doom" and "the Soviets are in danger of becoming neocolonial subjects."[17]

The logical accent in Jameson's engagement with Soviet culture shifts in *The Seeds of Time*. Each of the three large chapters of this book, he asserts, "attempts a diagnosis of the cultural present with a view toward opening a perspective onto the future," a project much needed in the context where "any attempt to say what postmodernism is can scarcely be separated from the even more problematic attempt to say where it is going."[18] It comes as a bit of a shock then that while the first and the last chapters of the book indeed concern themselves with very contemporary—and Western—phenomena, the middle one devoted to Second World culture focuses on the 1920s modernist fiction of Andrei Platonov, a fascinating writer to be sure, but hailing from a very different time period. Jameson's logic in including a reading of Platonov is that it allows a glimpse into an alternative form of modernity that was represented by Second World culture, and that this latter is indeed a distinct phenomenon, "an emergent socialist culture whose development, in its Eastern or Slavic form, has been cut short." It is important for Jameson to assert that there is indeed such a thing as a distinct Second World culture, since such possibility "has been ignored, if not passionately repudiated" in most attempts at presenting global cultural models. This is a culture that is fast disappearing, "now that socialist institutions and property systems . . . have everywhere in the Soviet east been rolled back." Still, in his view, "in the former Soviet Union (although not necessarily in the former Soviet east as a whole), modernism is still alive and continues to coexist with forms of postmodernism as fresh and sassy as anything current in the West"; moreover, the inhabitants of the ex-USSR are for him "the last surviving modernists in world culture, over whose shoulders we postmoderns are still in a position to peer."[19] This enigmatic statement, however, is left unsubstantiated: no examples of such "enduring modernism" in post-Soviet spaces are adduced.

What seems foreign to Jameson's vision of postmodernism is what by now has become the doxa in the discourse on Second World postmodernist culture, namely, that the first signs of the break between modernism and postmodernism arose in the USSR more or less simultaneously with the West: the fiction of Abram Tertz (Andrei Sinyavsky) and Venedikt Erofeyev serving as important harbingers in the late 1950s–1960s, and a major development in both visual and verbal arts occurring in the 1970s, all of them the consequence of the waning of the utopian impulse.[20] When Jameson's writings about postmodernism have been used to construct models of postmodernist culture, frequently they were made to support discussions of local, national models, as in Russia in particular, the discourse about postmodernism overwhelmingly has been the discourse about Russian culture as a postmodernist phenomenon. As I have noted earlier, however, references to Jameson are sprinkled very lightly on the pages of such publications, and in the face of an absence of Russian translations of Jameson, they often take rather peculiar forms. I would like to share with you the results of my attempts to trace such references.

The first relatively substantial introduction of the Russian-language readership to Jameson occurred in 1990 on the pages of the first—and only—Russian-language edition of the magazine *Flash Art*. The issue contained an essay by John Rajchman, "Postmodernism in a Nominalist System of Coordinates," accompanied by the photos of the "culprits," Jameson among them. The overall tone of the piece is of mild sarcasm; Jameson is described as "a literature professor who does Marxist social theory and writes about art shown in New York"; his "search for new critical work to embody his historical hopes," according to Rajchman, "was at odds with the meaning the term postmodern had meanwhile acquired in actual artistic practice: that of a style with an ideology."[21] This piece, however, remained the only published Russian-language text to date in which the figure of Jameson is at the center of the discussion of postmodernism; indeed, in later studies, it is sometimes quoted uncritically as a source for introducing Jameson's ideas, as, for example, in Irina Skoropanova's *Russkaia postmodernistskaia literatura: Uchebnoe posobie* [Russian postmodernist literature: a textbook].[22]

The parameters of the Russian discourse on postmodernism were to a large extent set with the January 1991 publication of an essay by Mikhail Epstein, "Posle budushchego: O novom soznanii v literature" [After the future: on a new consciousness in literature], a work that combines elements of a manifesto and an analytical article.[23] A literary critic by training, Epstein developed his scholarly persona in the liminal space between the officially sanctioned and the dissident/underground realm of intellectual activity. Throughout the 1980s, he wrote prolifically about contemporary experimental Russian writing (especially, but not only, poetry) and its philosophical underpinnings, producing texts intended both for immediate publication and underground circulation (eventually published in the 1990s). By the end of the 1980s, he was widely considered a leading interpreter of this new "alternative" writing for a wider reading public.

In the essay in question, Epstein attempts to diagnose some key features in current Russian writing and goes on to compare it with "Western post-modernism." The common features, he asserts, are abundant, from the over-all feeling that one inhabited a "posthistory" and the spatial axis supplanted the temporal one in its importance, to the propensity for simulacra-making and abundant quoting of clichés and styles of previous eras. If anything, Russia is even more postmodern than the West. "Is it not the case that 'sim-ulacra'—that is, maximally lifelike likenesses that have no original—began to be created by our culture much earlier and in greater quantities than in the West?" asks Epstein rhetorically. Without naming names, he expresses his strong disagreement with theorists who see postmodernism as an exclusively Western phenomenon:

> The features of Western postmodernism are fully confirmed by the experience of our literature. This is why it is impossible to concur with those scholars (Soviet as well as foreign) who limit postmod-ernism only to the field of activity of "late capitalism," "multinational monopolies," "computer civilization," or "the schizophrenia of postin-dustrial society." Postmodernism is a phenomenon of a much broader scale, which has emerged on the basis of both total technologies and total ideologies. The triumph of self-valorizing ideas, which both imitate and abolish reality, has been no less conducive to the post-modern way of thinking that the predominance of video communi-cations, which also create a world of arrested time, rolled up in itself.[24]

It is obvious that Jameson is one of the main addressees of this passage (par-ticularly since Epstein had an opportunity to meet and argue with him at the March 1990 conference at Duke).

Epstein continued publishing prolifically on the topic of Russian post-modernism in the 1990s.[25] His later work has displayed some influences of the writing of the Russian émigré philosopher and art critic Boris Groys, most importantly of the book *The Total Art of Stalinism* and the essay "A Style and a Half: Socialist Realism between Modernism and Postmodernism."[26] For Groys, the strategies of socialist realism display a use of proto-postmodernist means ("cannibalizing" appropriation) for the modernist ends ("historical exclusiveness, internal purity, and autonomy from everything external"); hence its hybrid position as "a style and a half."[27] Epstein pushes Groys's thesis even further, substituting communism for socialist realism in this argument. In an

essay suggestively titled "The Origins and Meaning of Russian Postmodernism," alluding to Nikolai Berdyaev's classic study *The Origins and Meaning
of Russian Communism* (which argues that the indigenous religious underpinnings determined the Russian interpretation of the idea of communism and its
local adaptation from the Western model), Epstein asserts that what has come
to be known as the distinguishing features of postmodernism—a propensity for
simulacra-making (as in the famous "Potemkin villages"), a view of the sign as
radically autonomous, a fondness for pastiche, and so forth—constitute the
general characteristic of Russian culture, at least beginning with Peter the
Great's attempts to Westernize the country in the late seventeenth–early eigh-
teenth centuries. After the interruption of the early twentieth-century avant-
garde, these features are reasserted in the Stalin era, and the Soviet project of
building communism is for him is an "explicitly heroic" form of Soviet postmodernism that anticipates the later, "implicitly ironic" one. Thus, he concludes, "postmodernism may be seen as a cultural orientation that has developed
differently in the West and the Soviet Union. The Western version came later
chronologically, but was more self-aware from a theoretical standpoint."[28]

A cogent critique of this theory can be found in Mikhail Berg's recent
volume *Literaturokratiia: Problema prisvoeniia i pereraspredeleniia vlasti v literature* [Literaturocracy: the problem of appropriation and redistribution of
power in literature]. Berg sees Epstein's approach as an implicit discreditation
of both postmodernism (of which the Soviet communist project is "an unripe
barbaric variant, as it were an 'Oriental' version") and Russian culture (which,
like the communist project, is judged to be "consciously secondary"):

> Like every paradoxical comparison, the comparison of postmod-
> ernism to communism (and, in essence to the entire post-Petrine
> period of Russian culture) turns out to be correct in its details but
> contradictory in its entirety. Naturally one can find in Russian culture
> traces of borrowings and imitation, but this does not mean that it has
> been a culture of *self-conscious* secondariness and pastiche-making.
> Roughly speaking, the difference here is between a copy and a simu-
> lacrum, even if one agrees with the reductionist assertion that Russ-
> ian culture [attempted to] copy that of the West.[29]

Berg here seizes on what I believe to be an overarching problem of Epstein's
theoretical project: extremely perceptive in his detailed observations, he is
often strikingly off mark in his generalizations. For Epstein continuously tries
to advocate a rigid systemic view of global culture, a latter-day incarnation of
Goethe's *Weltliteratur*. He tries to distill some sort of Platonic essence of this
global culture, an essence that has to be ideology-free in his belief (silently
alluding back to Matthew Arnold's "the best that has been known and

thought"). He terms this essence "transculture" and advocates a search for this latter as a more productive approach than the Western pursuit of multiculturalism.[30] Finally, he comes up with a bizarre "periodic table of Russian literature" in which postmodernism turns out to be merely the last phase of one cycle among many, itself to be invariably supplanted by a return to a new cycle that will return to a condition akin to an expression of modernist energies[31]—hence his sympathy to Lyotard's somewhat cryptic assertion that postmodernism can be viewed as something that is "proto-modern," an expression of a nascent form of modernism.

This view of Lyotard's Epstein contrasts with that of Jameson—his only open engagement with Jameson's writing. Epstein notes Jameson's critical comment on this statement by Lyotard in his preface to the English translation of *The Postmodern Condition*, which suggests that Lyotard's "very commitment to the experimental and the new ... determine an aesthetic that is far more closely related to the traditional ideologies of high modernism than to current postmodernisms."[32] He goes on to quote a truncated sentence from the cultural logic essay, which for him summarizes Jameson's conception of postmodernism: "with the collapse of the high-modernist ideology of style ... the producers of culture have nowhere to turn but to the past: the imitation of dead styles, speech though all the masks and voices stored up in an imaginary museum of a now global culture."[33] While Epstein concedes that "the postmodernism known to us is closer to Jameson's characterization ... the subsequent evolution of postmodernism," in his opinion, "approaches the boundary of 'what will have been done' described by Lyotard."[34]

Although one can sympathize with Epstein's utopian vision of contemporary Russian culture as "the protostage of some as yet unknown cultural formation,"[35] his particular vision of that culture, namely, as some wizened and refined phenomenon that is "beyond ideology," strikes one as a reductive—and reactionary—phenomenon, a consequence of his desire to squeeze a multicultural world into his rigid "transcultural" system. No wonder he reduces Jameson's vision of postmodernism basically to the notion of pastiche and completely ignores—as inexplicably have all the Russian critics quoting Jameson—the notion of an aesthetic of cognitive mapping as a positive postmodernist project. For it is envisioned as a pedagogical political culture, and the fact that *any* culture does indeed have a political dimension is not something that attracts Epstein's attention (that Russian culture has served as a tool of imperialist oppression, for example, does not figure in his model in any way).

While Epstein was extremely influential in the Russian discourse on postmodernism in the early 1990s, by the middle of the decade, the spotlight shifted to other figures. In particular, with the publication of his two books, *Poststrukturalizm, dekonstruktivizm, postmodernizm* [Poststructuralism, deconstructivism, postmodernism, 1996] and *Postmodernizm ot istokov do kontsa stoletiia* [Postmodernism from its origins to the end of the century, 1998], Ilya Ilyin has emerged as one of the experts on this topic. One of the main reasons behind Ilyin's rise was that his books were indeed couched in a form of authoritative expert discourse familiar to Soviet-schooled readers; indeed, they constituted extended surveys of Western literary and cultural theory of the recent decades (the 1970s and 1980s). Ilyin's books seem to be designed with intent to overwhelm an unprepared Russian reader, make him or her awestruck at the sheer number of names of Western scholars that appear on their pages. Yet therein also lies the main problem with his works: they are, by and large, a collection of snippets and brief paraphrases made to fit a relatively strict taxonomy. Ilyin generously bestows labels like "American neomarxist leftist deconstructionist" on various Western scholars (this particular label is given to Jameson, Frank Lentricchia, and Michael Ryan[36]); his intention is to produce a kind of navigational manual for the sea of contemporary theory, yet, the judgmental position "above the fray" that he assumes in these books seriously undermines his effort. For instance, the second volume, the one supposedly dedicated to postmodernism, is subtitled "an evolution of a scholarly myth" (*evoliutsiia nauchnogo mifa*), and from the outset postmodernism is referred to as a "chimera" (*khimera*). As a consequence of such decisions, his books focus entirely on the critical discourse itself, as postmodernism for him is only "a peculiar philosophy of cultural consciousness." "The contradictory nature of contemporary life is such," believes Ilyin, "that it cannot be fit into any limits comprehensible to the human mind, and willy-nilly generates, in the attempts at theoretical interpretation, explanatory approaches no less phantasmagoric than itself," with postmodernism serving as the prime example.[37]

Ilyin appears to have been trained in the Soviet-style judgmental expert discourse I mentioned earlier, and while the need to assume the position of a Soviet-style "Marxist" is now gone, residues of that approach are strongly manifest in his books, particularly when he touches upon Western Marxist scholarship (in other words, the anathema of "revisionism"). In the case of Jameson, it appears that the only work of his that Ilyin consulted extensively was *The Political Unconscious*. It is mentioned in Ilyin's first book in the list of texts influenced by Deleuzian "schizoanalysis," and is considered next to Lyotard's *The Postmodern Condition*, as a text that has established the view that history is only available to us in the form of a narrative. By affirming narrative as an epistemological category, Jameson, according to Ilyin, "further develops Lyotard's idea."[38] While it is laudable that Ilyin brings this seminal study to the attention of the Russian public, I find it altogether surprising that, in his two books supposedly primarily concerned with the discourse on postmodernism, the only work by Jameson that is given extensive consideration is the one that *predates* his formulation of a theory of postmodernism (not to mention the bizarre assertion that *The Political Unconscious* is a book that develops the ideas first formulated by Lyotard in *The Postmodern Condition*). From the later work, the only thing Ilyin finds worth quoting is the definition of pastiche (footnoted to the 1983 "Postmodernism and Consumer Society" essay).[39]

In Ilyin's second book, Jameson first makes a brief appearance within a long chapter on Lacan (on the occasion of Jameson's assertion in his essay "Imaginary and Symbolic in Lacan" that the Lacanian Real can be analogized to History itself).[40] Jameson is now labeled as a "postmodernist" (along with Lyotard and the generic "feminists") as distinct from the "poststructuralists" (Derrida, Foucault, Deleuze, and Guattari).[41] Later, however, Jameson is accorded more extensive treatment within a critique of Western Marxism; here, once again, the main spotlight shines on *The Political Unconscious*.

Ilyin begins with an extensive discussion of a book by Christopher Butler, *Interpretation, Deconstruction, and Ideology*. He notes that Butler tries to avoid "holistic systems of convictions" and that he criticizes Jameson's position in *The Political Unconscious* as "unacceptably holistic." This discussion serves as a prelude to the following statement:

> Of course, Jameson himself is not at all such a consistent Marxist or even materialist as he seems to Butler, who accuses him of attempts to endow Marxism with the features of "an integral explanatory methodology"; *as is demonstrated by analysis*, Jameson's own statement that "Marxism subsumes other interpretive modes or systems" remains on the level of a declaration rather than a concrete research methodology.[42]

The reader would be hard pressed to detect any such "demonstrative analysis" in the vicinity of this passage in Ilyin's book. Throughout, he engages instead in sweeping judgmental statements like:

> In the USA one can name a wide range of scholars of the leftist, or rather, "pseudo-leftist" [*levatskii*—an adjective with distinctly pejorative connotations in Russian] persuasion, who have undertaken attempts to combine various neomarxist concepts with poststructuralism, creating, depending on their own views, either sociologized or openly extremist sociological versions of the latter. The most popular among them are Fredric Jameson, Frank Lentricchia, Gayatri Spivak, John Brenkman and Michael Ryan. . . . Naturally there are all the necessary reasons to doubt the extent to which such Marxism can be called authentic.[43]

Such sweeping denigration in passing is actually not the main drive of this section of Ilyin's book. This passage is followed by an extensive quote from Derrida's 1980 interview in which he expresses sympathy to Marxism, which allows Ilyin to make the point that surprising as it may sound to the Russian audience, the leading Western intellectuals have actually been taking Marxism (as they understood it) seriously, that "in the 1980s, Marxism was an inalienable part of Western consciousness." Still, he emphasizes,

> only very conditionally one may speak of a presence of a certain element of Marxism in the views of the sociologically-oriented American critics that belong to the circle of poststructuralist-deconstructivist views. . . . Thus, irrespective of the fact whether this or that critic is called a Marxist, or even if he tends to define himself as such, only concrete analysis of his philosophical and political views can provide an answer to the question *who he really is*.[44]

Note the menacing distinctly Stalinist overtones of "revealing the enemies of the people that masquerade as Marxists" in this last passage. And the "concrete analysis," once again, is merely invoked, not practiced. A few pages later, the reader does find a relatively lengthy paraphrase of the first and third chapters of *The Political Unconscious* (the theoretical introduction and the discussion of Balzac).[45] Yet some of the accents Ilyin places in his paraphrase may surprise those familiar with Jameson's work. He begins by noting "the essential influence of Paul Ricoeur's book *De l'interpetation* [translated into English as *Freud and Philosophy*—VC]" as a defining feature of both *Marxism and Form* and *The Political Unconscious*, in its serving as a source for the distinction between the negative and positive hermeneutic. He goes on to register, and rightly so, the importance for Jameson of Bloch's "principle of hope." However, the judgmental is not far behind. Ilyin seizes on the following sentence in the final pages of *The Political Unconscious*:

> When properly used, the concept of the "text" does not, as in garden-variety semiotic practice today, "reduce" these realities to small and manageable written documents of one kind or another, but rather liberates us from the empirical object—whether institution, event, or individual work—by displacing our attention to its *constitution* as an object and its *relationship* to the other objects thus constituted.[46]

Here is Ilyin's rendition of it:

> Working in the tradition of the so-called "cultural criticism," Jameson tried to create his own variant of poststructuralism, where hermeneutics's and deconstructivism's methodology of analysis would play an important part. In particular, the latter [deconstructivism], despite its obvious ahistoricity, in the critic's opinion "liberates us from the empirical object—an institution, event or an individual work of art—by attracting our attention to the process of its constitution as an object and its relationship to other objects similarly constituted."

The unwarranted substitution of a crudely understood "deconstructivism" for Jameson's careful introduction of the notion of the "text" allows Ilyin to declare that this passage "immediately removes from the agenda the question of any belonging of the American critic to Marxism, except maybe on the declarative level." He then generously allows Jameson to be considered a good, productive poststructuralist who was able to "integrate in his work into a coherent whole the ideas of Derrida, Frye, Greimas, Lacan, Ricoeur, Althusser, Macherey, Lévi-Strauss and Bakhtin," and "attempted to soften the textualist approach to history and reality."[47] Only after this judgmental/taxonomical prelude does Ilyin go on to talk about the appropriation of Althusser in the first chapter of *The Political Unconscious* and of the Greimasian semiotic square in the third.

I am not sure what prompted Ilyin to engage in this practice of distortion in his book—it is entirely possible that he sympathized with a number of aspects of Jameson's argument in *The Political Unconscious* but, as an ex-Soviet intellectual, found the presence of Marxism, and especially the effort to revitalize the latter, too hard to stomach. Still, one remains puzzled as to why in a volume supposedly devoted to the account of the history of the discourse on postmodernism he ignores all of Jameson's contributions to it from 1983 onward—for after the lengthy discussion of *The Political Unconscious* Jameson is cursorily mentioned only once more (on page 186), again in connection with this same work. One may conclude that the titles of Ilyin's books are deceptive; it would have been more appropriate to call them "an attempt of a critical overview of some debates in the Western literary and cultural theory in the 1970s—early 1980s." Postmodernism, even if evaluated negatively, enjoys only a very marginal presence on their pages.

An attempt to engage thoroughly with the Western discourse on postmodernism and postmodernity and to develop an original take on them that would also account for the Russian cultural practices did come soon, though, with the publication in 2000 of Nadezhda Man'kovskaya's *Estetika postmodernizma* [The aesthetics of postmodernism]. This volume, a product of a trend in post-Soviet Russian intellectual life to "re-embrace" the ties to Western cultural and intellectual riches, traces the development of some "key words" in this discourse, such as "irony," "deconstruction," "simulacrum," "desire," "schizoanalysis," Kristevan "polylogue," and "virtual reality," as well as such phenomena as "the diffusion of high and mass culture" and "the aesthetization of science and of the environment." Man'kovskaya's vision of postmodernism is overwhelmingly positive, as something that interrogates the cultural Canon and various *idées reçues*; underlying postmodernism, she sees "a drive to humanize art" and the "increase in subjectiveness, humanism and self-criticism in scholarly endeavors."[48] Perhaps, as a logical consequence of such approach, in difference from Ilyin's lumping Jameson together with Lyotard and a host of other "postmodernists," Man'kovskaya singles Jameson out as one of the "opponents of postmodernism," the only exhibit of such attitude in her book besides Habermas.

In her presentation of Jameson's views, Man'kovskaya refers to the 1988 version of the "Postmodernism and Consumer Society" essay. She asserts that in it "the American neomarxist aesthetician F. Jameson criticizes postmodernism as an aesthetic of the consumer society that exists in an 'eternal present'; an aesthetic that has substituted for the sense of history an illusory pseudohistoricism, mimicry, pastiche, blind irony, which leads to the atrophy of the innovative potential of art, the deindividualization of creativity and a schizophrenization of culture." She goes on to say that Jameson "sees the philosophical fiasco of postmodernism" in its "ignoring of the human being with its feelings, emotions, worries, pathologies," providing instead the absence of feeling that finds its most concrete manifestation in pornography. According to Man'kovskaya, "Jameson sees the cultural-aesthetic deficiency of postmodernism in its expansive treatment of culture and art that strips them of their relative autonomy," as a result of which "culture dissolves in politics, ideology, economy . . . losing the critical distance towards social reality and hence the ability to impact the latter. The aesthetic consciousness of the artist and his audience is now dominated by the sense of being lost, by a loss of identity, a submersion into a real/irreal world which can be symbolized by the commercial channels of American television." The list of "postmodernist evils" also includes "the robotization of creativity, purely quantitative false pluralism, asociality, freedom from responsibility, an orientation toward commercial success."[49] While in this paraphrase, one may recognize some traces of Jameson's text, the accusatory tone is entirely Man'kovskaya's introduction, as is a certain "darkening of the shades," so to speak. This constructed "image of the enemy" allows her to proclaim that, although "not only the polemical jibes but also some theoretical remarks by the opponents of postmodernism are based on reality," this still does not allow postmodernism to be considered a "cancer of contemporary culture" or "an artistic dead end." Man'kovskaya concludes by asserting that

> the objective analysis of this aesthetic phenomenon in its original, and not caricatured, form allows to judge both the shortcomings of the transitional stage in culture's development that are mostly connected with eclecticism and secondariness of artistic devices and principles, and also the pertinent return into aesthetics and art of the language of aesthetic feeling, of beauty as reality, of the context of global culture and of the daily life.[50]

Once again, Man'kovskaya's ends may be laudable, but the misrepresentation of Jameson's position used for rhetorical purposes in her argument is unwarranted. I do not recall Jameson ever proclaiming postmodernism a "cancer" or a "dead end"; he does not deny originality to postmodern art (I refer the reader, for example, to his discussion of experimental video), nor does he declare himself to be "an opponent of postmodernism." Indeed, he has emphatically responded to the accusations of being "a vulgar Marxist hatchet man" by emphasizing the need to distinguish between the dimensions of taste, analysis, and evaluation in approaching culture: "as far as taste is concerned," he insists, "culturally I write as a relatively enthusiastic consumer of postmodernism." Jameson is far more cautious and "passionately ambivalent" (as he himself described Foucault) in the dimension of analysis, famously proposing that the political edge of postmodernist culture for him lies in the development of "an aesthetic of cognitive mapping—a pedagogical, political culture that seeks to endow the individual subject with some new heightened sense of its place in the global system."[51]

Another, rather curious Russian book that appeared in 2000 and invoked Jameson in its discussion is the earlier mentioned *Literaturokratiia* by Mikhail Berg. This volume is not centrally focused on the notion of postmodernism; it only serves as one of the illustrations of the author's thesis, namely, that literature as an institution constitutes a battlefield between authors vying to accumulate symbolic capital and assume a position of power. Power is seen here in a somewhat Foucauldian sense as a force-field or a network that pervades the entire society, and institutionalization is regarded as a key element in its redistribution. One is struck, however, by the relentlessly grim tone of Berg's study. The notions of pleasures of the text seem radically alien to him; his truly seems to be a loveless book, driven by a vision of power that slips from the Foucauldian to the Machiavellian.

In contrast to Man'kovskaya, Berg offers a generally negative assessment of postmodernism, in particular as it has played out in Russian literature. He sees postmodernism as a manifestation of its crisis and as something that is now undergoing a crisis of its own (there is a certain irony in this, in combination with the grim tone, given that author over the course of the last two decades produced several overtly postmodernist novels that, however, failed to put him into the front ranks of contemporary Russian literature). Still, for Berg, "that which is called postmodernism constitutes a radical form of work with the boundary, with discourses of power, the power zones of the social space that is characteristic of any relevant form of activity in the era of Modernity, no matter the name it is given." The crisis of Russian postmodernism, for Berg, is

> the consequence of the interrupted (or incomplete) processes of transformation of the society, which failed to generate either a value-based artistic market or the necessary social conditions for the legitimation of intellectual and artistic activity that generates innovational impulses in culture. The reason [for this] is the state's dominant position in the field of power, pushing other players, the society first of all, to the side, away from the struggle for the redistribution and

appropriation of power discourses—and the value of any, including literary, practice lies in the amount of power that this practice can redistribute and appropriate.[52]

In the course of his analysis, Berg invokes Jameson's name several times, but while such recourse, as I have noted earlier, is productive in his critique of Epstein's theoretical model (his contrasting of Jameson and Lyotard), when he does it to advance his own argument, we once again encounter a strange distortion. In his study, he intends to demonstrate that

> the more or less universal features of a successful authorial strategy are: 1) the overcoming and verification of culturally relevant boundaries; 2) the search for and determination of the mechanisms for appropriation of various forms of capital—cultural, social, symbolic, which in the course of an exchange for an investment of reader's attention may assist in the increase of the latter's social status and the level of the latter's psychological stability.

This assertion is supported with a reference to Jameson's "complaint that today 'one cannot take the cultural act outside the massive Being of capital, to a point from which capital could be attacked.'"[53] Remarkably, once again we are faced with a distortion, not only of Jameson's text (which reads: "No theory of cultural politics current on the Left today has been able to do without one notion or another of a certain minimal aesthetic distance, for the possibility of the positioning of the cultural act outside the massive Being of capital, from which to assault this last. What the burden of our preceding demonstration suggests, however, is that distance in general [including 'critical distance' in particular] has very precisely been abolished in the new space of postmodernism."[54]), but also of its message, through introducing the gesture of complaint and, most important, by substituting for a Marxian understanding of capital (as something to be critiqued or "assaulted"), a "de-fanged" metaphorical notion of symbolic and/or cultural capital that may only be accumulated or expended. Indeed, the extent to which Berg avoids any possibility of a Marxian formulation while widely employing both economic and sociological metaphors in his study is truly remarkable.

Although I object to Berg's use of Jameson's work in his text and cannot accept his book's grim tone (understandable as it may be in the context of Putin's Russia), as I noted earlier, Berg makes a number of valid points in his critique of some Russian theorists of postmodernism. Still, his vision of culture as determined by a restricted economy of scarcity is not, in my opinion, an adequate approach to the discussion of postmodernism. Nor does he take into account the unprecedented possibility of speaking out that postmodernism in Russia provided for the previously marginalized groups, such as women, sexual and ethnic minorities.[55] As a counterpoint to Berg's vision, I would like to offer another example of what may be considered an instance of a Russian response to Jameson, taken from the work of Arkady Plotnitsky, an American theorist of Russian émigré background.

In his *Reconfigurations: Critical Theory and General Economy*, Plotnitsky sketches out a model of theoretical practice (including theories of the postmodern) based on Georges Bataille's theory of general economy. "General economy," writes Bataille, "makes apparent that excesses of energy are produced, which by definition cannot be utilized. The excessive energy can only be lost without the slightest aim, consequently without any meaning."[56] Plotnitsky juxtaposes the general economy as a theoretical practice

> to classical theoretical systems or *restricted economies*, such as Hegel's philosophy or Marx's political economy. Such classical theories configure their objects and the relationships between those objects as *always meaningful* and claim that the systems they present avoid the unproductive expenditure of energy, containing within their bounds multiplicity and indeterminacy. The general economy exposes all such claims as finally untenable; it demands—and enacts—a different form of theoretical practice.

Plotnitsky ties in the notion of general economy with Niels Bohr's principle of complementarity, generalized beyond quantum mechanics into "a mode of theorizing."[57] Working in this framework, he mounts a critique of the theoretical underpinnings of Jameson's model of postmodernism as restrictive and overdetermined, and argues that

> the understanding of the political and cultural landscape of postmodernism demands a general economy. Postmodernism may indeed demand it as "the cultural logic of late capitalism" . . . or late socialism, or indeed late communism, postcommunism even—postcapitalism, postsocialism and postcommunism. Against Jameson's logic, however, all these appear to coexist, or rather, in the mode of a general economy, are all simultaneously at play, the play that can never be quite simultaneous, although not without simultaneities, either. Obviously, such terms, and specifically "late capitalism," have complex relations to the cultural logic of the modern, or the postmodern, or any period.[58]

Although I do not share the somewhat combative intentions of Plotnitsky's argument, it does seem to me that an understanding of postmodernism within the terms of general economy could be extremely productive, since it accounts for the excess of signification and the overflowing of images of both Soviet and

Western kind, the general "explosion of culture," as well as the multiplication of alternate realities of cyberpunk. It also may help sketch out an approach to postmodernism that does not limit the latter within late capitalist societies, that is, the First World. Sadly, though, Plotnitsky's work is yet to be read in his country of birth.

While these examples of Russian responses to Jameson's work may certainly put one into a bad mood, they do not exhaust the post-Soviet approaches to Jameson—although many, in Russia and sometimes even beyond its borders, persist in the prejudicial colonialist belief that it is the only post-Soviet state with an intellectual discourse of note. Such prejudices highlight the persistence of imperialist attitudes in Russia that survived remarkably well over the course of Soviet rule, and explain why Russian intellectuals remain by and large deaf not only to Western Marxism but also to another critical discourse—that on postcolonialism. It was nowhere to be found on the pages of Russian scholarly publications until the early 2000s, and among the scholars whose work I have discussed in this essay, Ilyin is the only one to mention Edward Said and Gayatri Spivak, only to quickly label the latter a "socially *éngagée* feminist deconstructionist" and the former "a well-known literary scholar of a leftist-anarchist orientation" and quickly move on. [59]

Perhaps, one of the greatest ironies of post-Soviet culture is that it was Belarus—a country notorious for its dictatorial rule, restrictions on press freedoms, the most entrenched endurance of residues of Soviet ideology and the weakness of resistant discourses—that attempted to present the most comprehensive engagement with both the discourse on postmodernism and that on postcolonialism. Its capital, Minsk, hosted the first major intellectual gathering devoted to postcolonial theory anywhere in the former Soviet Union (a summer school, in 2001), and it also produced a mammoth encyclopedia of postmodernism (also published in 2001), which features lengthy articles on Jameson and, separately, on his 1991 *Postmodernism* volume.[60] But just as the "postcolonial" summer school evidenced numerous instances of "cognitive dissonance,"[61] the encyclopedia presentation combined breathless de-individualized "Sovietese" scholarly prose style with lengthy unmarked quotations from the original, a sui generis abridged "ventriloquization" of Jameson. The judgmental inserts are rare, but telling, as in the assertion that Jameson "first calls to social action aimed at changing the situation, then advanced a less practical idea of a cultural cartography of the world of late capital."[62] Thus, one of the crucial constituent parts of Jameson's theoretical vision—namely, the project of cognitive mapping—receives, in a typical fashion, a one-line dismissal.

In marked contrast to the curious but telling case of Belarus, another post-Soviet nation proved very receptive both to the discourse on postmodernism and the discourse on postcolonialism, and provided a home for some rather constructive engagement with the two: Ukraine. In the case of postcolonialism, we can even speak of an initial excessively euphoric appropriation that resulted in an uncritical use of the term that even spilled into the mass media, similarly to the fate of the term "postmodernism" in Russia at the same time. Yet when the time came for a calmer scholarly consideration of these discourses, Ukraine provided what can be seen as a model approach. Rather than engage in judgmental expert discourse adorned with twisted snippets of quotations, a large team of scholars, led by the literary theorist Mariya Zubryts'ka, prepared a comprehensive critical anthology of contemporary theoretical thought, *Slovo, znak, dyskurs* [Word, sign, discourse]. In it, for instance, we find a representative section on postcolonial criticism and theory, containing selections from the work of Spivak, Said, Homi Bhabha, Simon During, and several other scholars, accompanied by an informative introductory essay and extensive commentary.[63] This section is followed by another one, specially devoted to "postmodernism as interpreted by F. Jameson," which likewise includes a contextualizing two-page introduction (by Zubryts'ka) and a translation, by Mykhailo Stasiv, of the essay "The Politics of Theory: Ideological Positions in the Postmodernism Debate."[64] The choice of this essay alone is a welcome difference from the Russian approach, as it precludes the facile labeling of the theorist as an "advocate" or "opponent" of postmodernism, and, together with the calm, measured introduction and informative commentary, fosters the practice of cognitive mapping as envisioned by the author.

Another welcome instance of maturing of the Ukrainian discourse on postmodernism is provided in a 1999 essay by Yuri Andrukhovych, one of the nation's leading contemporary writers. This text, entitled "Chas i mistse, abo moia ostannia terytoriia" ("Time and Place, or My Last Territory"), opens with a condensed and "carnivalized" presentation of stereotypical views on postmodernism (as "irresponsible," "parasitical," "death of literature," "rejection [through pervasive irony] of each and every ethical system," "dumb, mechanical experimentation," "vulgar tastelessness," etc.). Andrukhovych supplies a parodic list of negative epithets that have been attributed to postmodernism beginning with each and every letter of the Cyrillic alphabet, as well as considers the views that postmodernism is merely a manifestation of literary narcissism that has existed throughout history and thus nowhere in particular. This flood of stereotypes, in Andrukhovych's opinion, can be dealt with only through personal, subjective features and signifiers, through asking the question "Where am I?"[65] In other words, he arrives at the paradigm of cognitive mapping.

In Andrukhovych's case, this leads to a reflection on the cultural composition of his native region, Halychyna (or Galicia), a region paradoxically located in the center of Europe geographically and at its margins culturally. Halychyna, for him, is characterized by a certain superficiality of cultural patterns in the context that is "ironic and immoral"; it is, he says, an instance of "plagiarism, all the more pitiful since the plagiarist has chosen the deadest of all possible objects," "classic" European culture. However, realization of being placed as a subject into this "suspicious and despised world" leaves one no choice but to attempt to put together, to recombine the fragments that constitute this place as a cultural phenomenon. Central Europe in general, he asserts, is nearly a figment of the imagination, it "almost doesn't exist," just as Halychyna "almost doesn't exist" within Central Europe.

This particular territory, he asserts, allows one to approach postmodernity as the "great promising void" following the crumbling or active destruction of various modernities and modernisms. It can also be described, he believes, as the "not fully formed, but already sensed posttotatilarianness," combined with "a continuing neototalitarian threat" that still can, "amoeba-like," "fill with itself anyone in this space and all of this space in its entirety."[66]

On yet another level, this is also the manifestation of a tradition of multiculturalism (Halychyna historically has been one of the most ethnically, religiously, and culturally heterogeneous regions of Europe), which, however, itself has been nearly obliterated. In other words, one now faces a "post-multiculturalism" manifested through ruins ("of castles, holy places, factories, bridges, observatories, and especially of cemeteries"), a palimpsest of cultures and "anticultures," and likewise, through fragments, "of lost languages, writing systems, dialects, burnt manuscripts." It is a "province at the center, for the center is everywhere and nowhere," a representation of the "chaotic nature of being." The task of a postmodernist practitioner of culture, asserts Andrukhovych, is to address the particular location where one finds oneself today. This may be a "dangerous territory," yet one has no choice but to address it.[67]

The imperative articulated in Andrukhovych's essay provides one of the clearest articulations of what I believe to be the most productive—and the most badly needed—postmodernist project in the context of the Second World within the shifting global political, social, and cultural contexts. One hopes that such examples will indeed be more numerous in other Second World spaces, for, perhaps, one day it will enable a wide community of readers there to discover an affinity to a prescient feature of Jameson's writing—what Perry Anderson has named its ability "to conjure what might be thought impossible—a lucid enchantment of the world."[68] And just perhaps such turnaround may in turn encourage Fredric Jameson himself to consider engaging again with Second World culture.[69] But for now, I believe the history of this "almost but not quite" encounter suggests several possible conclusions.

The one that I believe bears emphasizing would be that while often failing in attempts at engaging directly with Western intellectual discourses, Russia and Eastern Europe often generated cultural artifacts, and demonstrated sociocultural processes, that reflect and respond to these Western intellectual impulses in an intricate, rich, and often unpredictable fashion. These "indigenizations" of globally dominant cultural and intellectual trends call us to rethink our conceptualization of the cultural aspects of globalization, our readings of strategic employments of the paradigm of national allegory, as well as numerous other constituent parts of contemporary thought associated with Fredric Jameson's intellectual project—and thereby to resist a temptation to reproduce and reify the strangely persistent oxymoronic binary between the First and the Third World. A key task for cultural criticism in this dramatic time remains to be attuned to the dynamics of Second World's evolvement and to go on with a project of cognitive mapping of this development. Without it, any attempt at constructing a global cultural model is bound to remain fatally flawed.

NOTES

A note on the transliteration from the Cyrillic: in the main body of the text, personal names are spelled in the way that makes it easiest for the English speakers to pronounce them correctly, while in the footnotes the Library of Congress transliteration is followed, to enable the readers to consult the sources with the help of bibliographic databases. Hence, for example, "Ilya Ilyin" in the main body of the text and "Il'ia Il'in" in the notes.

1. The most thorough and compelling attempt at approaching these questions to date is Susan Buck-Morss's *Dreamworld and Catastrophe: The Passing of Mass Utopia in East and West* (Cambridge: MIT P, 2000).

2. See F.R. Dzheimson, "Teoriia v novoi situatsii," *Voprosy literatury* 6 (June 1990): 86–89, and Dzh. Khillis Miller, "Triumf teorii i proizvodstvo znachenii," *Voprosy literatury* 5 (May 1990): 83–87, both translated by O. Soloukhina. Russian transliterations of the names of Western critics deserve a separate saga. In the case of Jameson, they have produced (in reverse Library of Congress transliteration) Fredrik and Frederik, Dzheimison, Dzheimeson, and Dzheimson. Only in late 2000 was an anonymous translation of the 1983 version of "Postmodernism and Consumer Society" published in the journal *Logos* (Fredrik Dzheimison, "Postmodernizm i obshchestvo potrebleniia," *Logos* 4 [2000], <http://www.ruthenia.ru/logos/number/2000_4/10.htm>), and no new translations have appeared since then.

3. Another consequence of 1948 was the wide availability of American mass culture, in particular Hollywood films, in post–World War II Yugoslavia (part of the Marshall Plan). In combination with the country's intellectual climate, it makes the emergence of a thinker like Slavoj Žižek quite logical and not at all unexpected.

4. Fredric Jameson, *Marksizam i forma*, trans. Dušan Puhalo (Beograd: Nolit, 1974); *U tamnici jezika*, trans. Milivoj Solar and Antun Šoljan (Zagreb: Stvarnost, 1978); *Političko nesvesno*, trans. Dušan Puhalo (Beograd: Rad, 1984). The materials of the Zagreb symposium were published as Ivan Kuvaćió and Gvozden Flego, eds., *Postmoderna: Nova epoha ili zabluda* [Postmodernity: a new era or a mirage?] (Zagreb: Naprijed, 1988). The most substantial interview is "Postmoderni prostor" [Postmodern space], by Mladen Kozul and Ivailo Dichev, *Quorum* 7 (1) (1991): 3–18.

5. For the most informative accounts of the Dubrovnik conference, see Buck-Morss, *Dreamworld and Catastrophe*, 230–43, and Mikhail Ryklin, *Iskusstvo kak prepiatstvie* [Art as an Obstacle] (Moscow: Ad Marginem, 1997), 49–52.

6. Jameson, "Globalizacija i politička strategija," trans. Dag Strpi?, *Politička Misao: Croatian Political Science Review* 37 (4) (2000): 89–104.

7. Jameson, *Postmodernizem*, trans. Lenca Bogović et al. (Ljubljana: LDS, 1992); 2nd ed., corrected and expanded (Ljubljana: Društvo za teoretsko psihanalizo, 2001); "Postmodernizm albo kulturowa logika póznego kapitalizmu," trans. K. Malita, Pismo Literacko-Artystyczne 4 (1988); "Postmodernizm i spoleczenstwo konsumpcyjne," trans. Przemyslaw Czapliński, in Ryszard Nycz, ed., *Postmodernizm: Antologia przekladów,* [Postmodernism: an anthology of translations] (Kraków: Baran i Suszczynski, 1996), 190–213.

8. "In the Soviet Union . . . we are given to understand that the Khrushchev generation was the last to believe in the possibility of a renewal of Marxism, let alone socialism; or rather, the other way around, that it was their failure which now determines the utter indifference to Marxism and socialism of several generations of younger intellectuals," Jameson, *Postmodernism, or, the Cultural Logic of Late Capitalism* (Durham: Duke University Press, 1991), 274; a similar observation can be found in Buck-Morss, *Dreamworld and Catastrophe,* 220.

9. Jameson, "Conversations on the New World Order," *After the Fall: The Failure of Communism and the Future of Socialism,* ed. Robin Blackburn (New York: Verso, 1991), 260, 265.

10. Jameson, *Signatures of the Visible* (New York: Routledge, 1990), 129.

11. Buck-Morss's fascinating and informative account of the conference is a retrospective attempt to "work through" its traumas and to see the miscommunication not as a manifestation of differences, but as a symptom of the breakdown of the Cold War era's version of the East–West antinomy.

12. Ryklin, 50–51 (all translations are mine unless otherwise indicated—VC).

13. Ibid., 51–52.

14. See Buck-Morss, *Dreamworld and Catastrophe,* 231–32.

15. Buck-Morss, "Is There a Common Post-Modernism Culture?" presented at the conference Soviet Culture Today: Restructuring the Past or Inventing the Future?, Duke University, March 1990; Perloff, "Russian Postmodernism: An Oxymoron?" *Postmodern Culture* 3 (2) (January 1993), <http://muse.jhu.edu/journals/postmodern_culture/v003/3.2perloff.html>; Clark, "Changing Historical Paradigms in Soviet Culture," *Late Soviet Culture: From Perestroika to Novostroika,* ed. Thomas Lahusen and Gene Kuperman (Durham: Duke University Press, 1993), 304.

16. Jameson, *The Geopolitical Aesthetic* (Bloomington: Indiana University Press, 1992), 87, 90.

17. Ibid., 109, 111.

18. Jameson, *The Seeds of Time* (New York: Columbia University Press, 1994), xii–xiii.

19. Ibid., xvi, 73–74, 79–80. Without succumbing to the temptation to dwell at length on the strategies of inclusion and exclusion at work in this "we," I would like to note here that it does not seem feasible to pinpoint a "pure" postmodernist culture

without modernist residual elements anywhere in the world. That modernist energies are still at work within postmodernity can be demonstrated even on the basis of the fact that a coherent understanding and "solidification" of the concepts of modernism and modernity has become ultimately possible only in the postmodern era: see, for example, Astradur Eysteinsson, *The Concept of Modernism* (Ithaca: Cornell University Press, 1990), esp. ch. 3, "Reading Modernism through Postmodernism," as well as Patricia Waugh, *Practicing Postmodernism/Reading Modernism* (New York: Edward Arnold, 1992), Matei Calinescu's *Five Faces of Modernity: Modernism, Avant-Garde, Decadence, Kitsch, Postmodernism* (Durham: Duke University Press, 1987), and ultimately the sections "Prolegomena to Future Contradictions between the Modern and the Postmodern" and "Notes Toward a Theory of the Modern" in Jameson's *Postmodernism*, 297–302 and 302–13, respectively, as well as his numerous remarks on the subject scattered throughout *The Seeds of Time* and elsewhere.

20. On Tertz, see Catharine T. Nepomnyashchy's study *Abram Tertz and the Poetics of Crime* (New Haven: Yale University Press, 1995). For histories of Russian postmodernist writing, see Mikhail Epshtein et al., *Russian Postmodernism* (New York: Berghahn Books, 1999) and Mark Lipovetskii, *Russian Postmodernist Fiction* (Armonk: Sharpe, 1999). For the case of the visual arts, see Margarita Tupitsyn, *Margins of Soviet Art* (Milan: Giancarlo Politi, 1988). The overall thesis about the joint "passing of mass utopia in East and West," illustrated by a number of examples, mostly from the visual arts, is at the center of Buck-Morss's *Dreamworld and Catastrophe*.

21. *Flash Art*, Russian edition, 1 (1990): 157 (in English), 51–52 (in Russian); in the Russian translation, "social theory" is inexplicably substituted by "psychoideology."

22. *Russkaia postmodernistskaia literatura* (Moscow: Flinta/Nauka, 1999), 50. The lack of translations makes it possible for the appearance of Russian books on postmodernism that do not even mention Jameson once, as, for example, Viacheslav Kuritsyn's *Russkii literaturnyi postmodernizm* [Russian literary postmodernism] (Moscow: OGI, 2000), an excellent study that is, however, entirely based on sources available in Russian.

23. Mikhail Epshtein, "Posle budushchego: O novom soznanii v literature," *Znamia* 1 (January 1991): 217–30; it was almost immediately published in an English translation by Gene Kuperman as "After the Future: On the New Consciousness in Literature," *South Atlantic Quarterly* 90 (2) (Spring 1991): 409–44.

24. Epshtein, "Posle budushchego," 229, 230; "After the Future," 440, 443 [translation slightly modified].

25. Epshtein's essays on the topic were collected in his *After the Future: The Paradoxes of Postmodernism and Contemporary Russian Culture* (Amherst: University of Massachusetts Press, 1995) and *Postmodern v Rossii: Literatura i teoriia* [Postmodernity in Russia: literature and theory] (Moscow: R. Elinin, 2000), as well as in the collective tome *Russian Postmodernism*, co-authored with Genis and Vladiv-Glover.

26. Boris Groys, *The Total Art of Stalinism: Avant-Garde, Aesthetic Dictatorship, and Beyond* (Princeton: Princeton University Press, 1992), originally published in German in 1988 as *Gesamtkunstwerk Stalin* (a volume that apparently impressed Jameson considerably, judging by the references to it in *The Seeds of Time*); "A Style and a

Half: Socialist Realism between Modernism and Postmodernism," trans. Julia Trubikhina, *Socialist Realism Without Shores*, ed. Thomas Lahusen and Evgenii Dobrenko (Durham: Duke University Press, 1997), 76–90 (originally published as "Polutornyi stil': Sotsialisticheskii realizm mezhdu modernizmom i postmodernizmom," *Novoe literaturnoe obozrenie* 15 [1995]).

27. Groys, "A Style and a Half," 79.

28. Epshtein, *After the Future*, 210. The English version precedes and differs slightly from the Russian version published in 1996.

29. Mikhail Berg, *Literaturokratiia: Problema prisvoeniia i pereraspredeleniia vlasti v literature* (Moscow: Novoe literaturnoe obozrenie, 2000), 290–91. I will note parenthetically that in my opinion Berg's own theory is not without its own problems, on which I will dwell later in this essay.

30. See the essay "Culture—Culturology—Transculture" in Epshtein, *After the Future*, 280–306.

31. The "periodic table" can be found in the first publication of the "After the Future" essay, 430–31; it is reprinted in the book *After the Future*, 86–87.

32. Jameson, "Foreword," *The Postmodern Condition*, ed. Jean-François Lyotard (Minneapolis: University of Minnesota Press, 1984), xvi; quoted in *After the Future*, 333.

33. Jameson, *Postmodernism*, 17–18; quoted in *After the Future*, 333.

34. Epshtein, *After the Future*, 334.

35. Ibid., 338.

36. Il'ia Il'in, *Poststrukturalizm, dekosntruktivizm, postmodernizm* (Moscow: Intrada, 1996), 196.

37. Il'in, *Postmodernizm ot istokov do kontsa stoletiia: Evoliutsiia nauchnogo mifa* (Moscow: Intrada, 1998), 5–6.

38. See Il'in, *Poststrukturalizm*, 96, 114, 217–18.

39. Ibid., 223.

40. Il'in, *Postmodernizm*, 72 (for Jameson's original statement, see *The Ideologies of Theory*, vol. 1 [Minneapolis: University of Minnesota Press, 1988], 104).

41. Ibid., 86.

42. Ibid., 91–92 (my emphasis—VC). The quote from Jameson is from *The Political Unconscious* (Ithaca: Cornell University Press, 1981), 47.

43. Ibid., 102–03.

44. Ibid., 104–05 (my emphasis—VC).

45. Ibid., 112–24.

46. Jameson, *The Political Unconscious*, 297.

47. Il'in, *Postmodernizm*, 112–13. (I have retranslated Il'in's quote from Jameson back into English to make visible the slight shifts that often occur in his quoting practice.)

48. Nadezhda Man'kovskaia, *Estetika postmodernizma* (St. Petersburg: Aleteiia, 2000), 195–96, 199.

49. Ibid., 196–97.

50. Ibid., 197–98.

51. Jameson, *Postmodernism*, 297–98, 54.

52. Berg, 306–07.

53. Ibid., 22.

54. Jameson, *Postmodernism*, 48.

55. When Berg does turn to the founding figure of the new Russian gay writing, Evgenii Kharitonov (1941–1981), it is to consider his take on homosexuality as compared with another writer's "asocial behavior" as a strategy for "appropriating the discourse of power through fixation of an illegitimate social strategy"; the gay element in the text is presented as a "sophisticated mystification" endowed "with deceptive verisimilitude." Berg generously labels Kharitonov's characters "ignoble and immoral"; Kharitonov, he proclaims, "nurses his homosexuality as a sign of both being second-rate and being chosen" (Berg, 150–56). The insidious homophobia of this entire section of Berg's book is striking.

56. Georges Bataille, *L'Expérience interieure* (Paris, 1954), quoted in Plotnitsky, *Reconfigurations: Critical Theory and General Economy* (Gainesville: University Press of Florida, 1993), 20.

57. Ibid., 4–5 (emphasis added—VC.).

58. Ibid., 257.

59. See Il'in, *Postmodernizm*, 107–08, 125. For an account of the emergence of an indigenous discourse on postcolonialism in the former Soviet Union, see my "Postcolonialism, Russia and Ukraine," *Ulbandus* 7 (2003): 32–62.

60. A.A. Gornykh, "Dzheimison, Fredrik" and "Postmodernizm, ili logika kul'-tury pozdnego kapitalizma," *Postmodernizm: Entsiklopediiia*, ed. A.A. Gritsanov and M.A. Mozheiko (Minsk: Interpresservis/Knizhnyi dom, 2001), 217–22, 605–10.

61. For a detailed and insightful description of this event, see Mark von Hagen, "Teaching and Confronting the Postcolonial in Minsk," *Center for Comparative Literature and Society at Columbia University Newsletter*, Spring 2002, 3, 14–21 (available online at <http://www.columbia.edu/cu/ccls/newsletter/archives/web_version/NewsletterSpring2002.pdf>).

62. Gornykh, "Dzheimison," 222.

63. "Postkolonial'na krytyka i teoriia," *Slovo, znak, dyskurs: Antolohiia svitovoï literaturno-krytychnoï dumky XX st.*, ed. Mariia Zubryts'ka (L'viv: Litopys, 1996), 531–66; introductory essay by Marko Pavlyshyn, translation and comments by Mariia Zubryts'ka and Dariia Horodys'ka.

64. Ibid., 567–79. A translation of "Postmodernism and Consumer Society" (the 1983 version) followed in 2000: "Postmodernizm i suspil'stvo spozhyvannia," trans.

Andrii Pavlyshyn, Ï 19 (2000), (available online at <http://www.ji-magazine.lviv.ua/ n19texts/jameson.htm>).

65. Chas i mistse, abo moia ostannia territoriia," *Andrukhovych, Dezorientatsiia na mistsevosti: Sproby* (Disorientation on Location: Essays) (Ivano-Frankivs'k: Lileia-NV, 1999), 115–17.

66. Ibid., 120–21.

67. Ibid., 121–22.

68. Anderson, *The Origins of Postmodernity* (New York: Verso, 1998), 76.

69. Jameson's latest volume, *A Singular Modernity: Essay on the Ontology of the Present* (New York: Verso, 2002), is fairly generously sprinkled with references to Slavic literary, artistic, and political legacy (mostly Russian and Polish, and dating from the middle of the nineteenth to the middle of the twentieth century), although the argument's primary focus is (understandably in this case) on the intellectual legacy of the West.

Part III

Toward Globalization

8

National Allegory Today

A Return to Jameson

Ian Buchanan

Nationalism has once more appeared on the agenda of world affairs.
—Partha Chatterjee, *The Nation and Its Fragments*

In 1993, Partha Chatterjee was surely right in saying that the spectacular manner in which the concept of nationalism had been brought to the attention of scholars in the humanities guaranteed that any discussion would be "hopelessly prejudiced" from the outset. Then it was the dreadful wars of secession, as we might call them, that sprang up like forest fires in the wake of the complete collapse of the Soviet regime.[1] Now, in the literally still smouldering aftermath of September 11, 2001, that subject has become even more fraught, even more impossible to discuss with clear-headed lucidity. But perhaps for that very reason, its place on the critical agenda ought to be restored, if only to avail ourselves of the opportunity to clarify the sources of our prejudice. One effective way of doing this, I would like to suggest, is to revisit Fredric Jameson's controversial article, "Third-World Literature in the Era of Multinational Capitalism" because the quite heated, but often misdirected, debate it generated turned precisely on the issue of the desirability of nationalism in our time. Indeed, prejudice against nationalism and its alleged evils colored the debate so thoroughly that no one seemed to notice that Jameson's article was in fact about the problem of nation, not nationalism.

National allegory is, to my mind, one of Jameson's most luminous concepts, yet on the evidence of the poor reception of "Third-World Literature in the Era of Multinational Capitalism," it is neither well understood nor well liked.[2] Largely this is because its essential point continues to be missed: to put it bluntly, it is read from the perspective of content when, in reality, it is an essay about form, so most of the critiques of it are entirely misdirected. Complaints about this paper vary in tone from the arch indignation of Aijaz Ahmad to the seemingly more equable and balanced meditations of erstwhile supporters, such as Clint Burnham and Sean Homer, but they all seem to make the same mistakes: for one thing, they all blindly misread 'national allegory' as 'nationalist ideology' and therefore think Jameson is saying something like all Third World writers are ardent nationalists, or at least pundits of this or that type of nationalism. But that is not at all what Jameson is claiming as even the briefest glance at the actual metatext (Ahmad's term) of this paper— namely, *Fables of Aggression*, in which Jameson outlines his theory of 'national allegory'—would make apparent. In what follows, I will attempt to rehabilitate this concept.

This rehabilitation will be a two-step process. First, there is "a labor of the negative" to be performed, whereby Ahmad's critically stifling but influential misreading will be set aside; then, there is an affirmative labor to be performed, whereby something of a return to Jameson (in precisely the Lacanian sense of 'return') will be enacted. Ahmad's critique of Jameson is generally acclaimed as definitive; in fact, I have not been able to find one single rejoinder that is sustained enough to warrant the name. It seems not even those critics who would normally align themselves with Jameson can find it within themselves to defend this paper—not one of the half-dozen monographs on his work offer even a token defense of his position. Worse, a few even add their voice to the chorus of endorsement that has sung out in Ahmad's name since he got angry enough to 'write back', as it were, a decade and a half ago.[3] Jameson was not the only target of this writing back, of course; Edward Said, too, copped a serve, as did the entire field of postcolonial studies for failing to be properly Marxist. This particular critique of Jameson has "several prongs," as Michael Sprinker puts it, of which in my view at least three need to be rejected in a determinate manner if anything like a clear view of Jameson's actual argument is ever to be obtained.[4] These are (1) the already mentioned charge that 'national allegory' is of a piece with 'nationalist ideology'; (2) the claim that there are dozens of examples of texts produced in the Third World that are plainly not national allegories; and finally (3) the claim that the Third World does not exist.

With respect to the first of these charges, it has to be said that nowhere in Jameson's paper does he state that Third World writers are only or can only be nationalists. What he does say is that Third World writers are obsessively concerned with the 'national situation'—nationalism would be but one part of this vastly more complex problem.[5] Therefore, it seems not inappropriate to treat this as a misreading in the 'bad' sense of getting something wrong. Quite simply, he attributes a position to Jameson his textual evidence does not and cannot support—in effect, he moves 'too quickly' (as Žižek puts it in his account of dialectical readings that do not work through all the levels of mediation fully enough) from national allegory to nationalism, which he says is "the necessary, exclusively desirable ideology" underpinning Jameson's paper as a whole.6 In so doing, he skips over the problematic of the national situation and of course much else besides. Yet to even put it like that is already to move too quickly ourselves because, as Jameson theorizes it, national allegory is not a meditation on this problem per se—rather, it uses it as the particular solution to a more general representational problem. I will have more to say about the precise derivation of this notion in a moment; for now, suffice it to say that Jameson's essay is quite explicitly inscribed in the domain of literary history, not political history.

The political problems faced by Third World intellectuals and writers in the great decolonising era immediately following World War II manifest themselves, Jameson says, in formal or literary terms as the problem of "narrative closure."[7] This was a period in which it became clear to the intellectuals that the much-vaunted and hard-won independence would not necessarily spell the end of the violence, poverty, or indeed subalternity associated with colonial rule. As history records, the artificial unities forged in the struggle for independence fell apart and in many instances bloody civil wars ensued. This meant the enemy was no longer the foreign invader, but instead a fellow countryman whose politics were either too radical or too reactionary to be fully shared. "So it is that after the poisoned gift of independence, radical African writers, such as Ousmane, or Ngugi in Kenya, find themselves back in the dilemma of Lu Xun, bearing a passion for change and social regeneration which has not yet found its agents. I hope it is clear that this is also very much an aesthetic dilemma, a cris of representation: it was not difficult to identify an adversary who spoke another language and wore the visible trappings of colonial occupation. When those are replaced by your own people, the connections to external controlling forces are much more difficult to represent."[8] That is, from a literary historical perspective, every political situation is to be understood as a very particular kind of aesthetic problem or crisis for which only a very few solutions will prove either adequate or permissible.

Before I move to the second of my rebuttals, I must add that I find it very telling, indeed, that despite all his caviling about Jameson's overhasty totalization, which, in his opinion, leaves no room for that fabled "thing called socialist and/or communist culture," Ahmad does not himself offer any genuine alternative to nationalism, only some weak category that could at best be called "not-nationalism" since that is all the determination for it he gives (as we'll see in a moment, for Ahmad, the opposite of anticolonialism or nationalism is simply "other things").[9] So, if it were true that Jameson privileges nationalism, Ahmad offers no concrete reason to think he might be wrong to do so. Now, given how little attention Ahmad seems to have paid to "national," it is perhaps not surprising that he seems to have paid even less attention to the other term, namely "allegory."[10] In the very least, it has to be said that Ahmad's conception of allegory is strange: he seems to want the texts Jameson would call allegorical to be more literally about those things they are supposedly allegorizing. Take the following passage, for instance, which he offers as proof that not all Third World texts are national allegories.

> I cannot think of a single novel in Urdu between 1935 and 1947, the crucial year leading up to decolonisation, which is in any direct or exclusive way about 'the experience of colonialism and imperialism'. All the novels I know from that period are predominantly about other things: the barbarity of feudal landowners, the rapes and murders in the houses of religious 'mystics', the stranglehold of moneylenders upon the lives of peasants and the lower petty bourgeoisie, the social and sexual frustrations of school-going girls, and so on. The theme of anti-colonialism is woven into many of these novels but never in an exclusive or even dominant emphasis.[11]

Able dialectician that Ahmad is, he could himself doubtless turn these "other things" into their opposite easily enough—even the phrase "the social and sexual frustrations of school-going girls" is readily enough understood as having broader sociohistorical underpinnings: it is virtually a trope of postcolonial criticism that sexual frustration wells up in a traditional society and flows into its literature at the moment when tradition itself is in crisis due to the secularizing penetrations of capitalism.[12] More to the point, though, it would be a strange allegory indeed that was literally about the thing it was supposed to be allegorizing—following this precept, one could imagine Ahmad complaining that Thomas Mann's *The Magic Mountain* wasn't explicitly enough about Nazism to function as an allegorical critique of it. Thus, it should come as no surprise that none of the examples Jameson gives of national allegories are explicitly about the experience of colonialism and imperialism either; they too are about other things. The first Lu Xun fable Jameson discusses, "Diary of a Madman," concerns cannibalism, or madness, or both; the second, "Medicine," is about the charlatanry rampant amongst traditional healers in turn of the century China; while the third, "Ah Q," is a peripatetic account of the daily life of a coolie. Similarly, Ousmane's novel *Xala* is not explicitly about the experience of colonialism and imperialism, though doubtless it would be impossible to understand the plight of the protagonist if one did not read it against that background.

Of course, the conception of allegory operative here is not the traditional one we might associate with Milton or Bunyan; but, then, Jameson argues, nor is there any reason that it should be. "If allegory has once again become somehow congenial for us today, as over against the massive and monumental unifications of older modernist symbolism or even realism itself, it is because the allegorical spirit is profoundly discontinuous, a matter of breaks and heterogeneities, of the multiple polysemia of the dream rather than the homogeneous representation of the symbol."[13] There is, however, a deeper, more urgent point to be made here. At stake, indeed, is the whole of postcolonial criticism because, whether Ahmad likes it or not, it depends utterly on exactly the same kind of reading strategy Jameson is mobilizing—its force stems from the persuasive way it rereads icons of the Western canon as allegories of racism and the exercise of discrepant power. If one were to uphold Ahmad's blunted conception of allegory, one might very well be justified in saying—contra Edward Said—that Jane Austen's *Mansfield Park* is not about slavery at all, but the social and sexual frustrations of one young girl, Fanny Price. Indeed, it might even be going too far to speak of her sexual frustrations since these are not explicitly mentioned in the text, but have to be read into it.[14] Whatever his difficulties are with Said's project as a whole, the loss of this contrapuntal reading strategy (as Said calls it) would surely amount to a case of losing the baby with the bathwater.[15]

The third of Ahmad's complaints is the one for which he seems to have the most support. This support heralds from two different quarters, in response to the two different ways Ahmad makes his complaint. He begins in a tone of great moral outrage, his complaint stemming from a deep personal wound, as though Jameson had somehow betrayed him. Because "I am a Marxist," Ahmad writes, "I had always thought of us, Jameson and myself, as birds of the same feather even though we never quite flocked together. But, then, when I was on the fifth page of this text (specifically, on the sentence starting with "All third-world texts are necessarily . . ." etc.), I realised that what was being theorized was, among many other things, myself."[16] The upshot of this, for Ahmad, is that "the man whom I had for so long, so affectionately, even though from a physical distance, taken as a comrade was, in his own opinion, my civilisational Other."[17] Leaving all the personal hurt aside, what is interesting about this aspect of the complaint is the way Ahmad goes on to contradict its premise when he takes Jameson to task for, as he sees it, clinging to an empirically untenable three worlds theory. If the notion of the Third World holds no meaning for him, if in fact it doesn't exist, then how come he so readily identifies himself with it? By the same token, if he isn't Jameson's civilizational Other, why take such pains to prove otherwise? My point is that, if the term "Third World" does not somehow claim Ahmad as one of its own, if it doesn't interpellate him, then he could not take it so personally and his objections would have to be of a different, more objective stripe. His attempt to repudiate the existence of the Third World is, in this respect, peculiarly and indeed literally self-defeating: it would deny the very thing he relies on as his authority to speak—his status as an intellectual from a Third World country.

This "identity politics" line is not one I will pursue any further, since, in my view, it is a particularly sterile tack. Instead, I want to focus on Ahmad's claim that the Third World does not exist because, presumably without his being aware of it, this puts Ahmad in a position of agreement with Jameson. The pains Ahmad takes to discredit the very notion of the Third World are empirically in vain in this context because Jameson does not think that the Third World in its original three worlds formulation exists either. And one does not have to be a mind reader to divine this. As Santiago Colás has pointed out, the eradication of the Third World is one of the key indices Jameson draws on as evidence for his claim that we have entered a new phase of capitalism that he refers to as postmodernism.[18] Whether it did once exist is a moot point because patently it no longer does. This is the moment then to explain why I described Ahmad as moving too quickly—since he seems willing to hand out lessons in dialectics, he will not take it as remiss if I offer a corrective or two of my own. When Jameson says he is using the term "Third World" in an essentially descriptive manner, he can be taken literally because having already stipulated that the Third World as such does not exist, he has effectively drained it of its original informing content and turned it into what we might call an empty signifier. In other words, we should take him to mean that the term is not yet to be grasped as a fully formed concept, that it is still somewhere between sheer designation and that more determinate thing we know of as the concept.

Next, I must take issue with Ahmad's concluding remark that even if he "were to accept Jameson's division of the globe into three worlds," he would "still have to insist" that there exists within "the belly of the First World's global postmodernism, a veritable Third World, perhaps two or three of them."[19] First, of all we have to take issue with this inasmuch as it implies that Jameson, by contrast, somehow views the First World as some kind of a 'happy place' where discrepancies of wealth and circumstance do not exist. This is by no means the first time this accusation has been put to Jameson, and indeed I have already had occasion to refute it with respect Mike Davis's egregious commentary on the companion piece to the text at issue here—namely, the program essay on postmodernism. I don't believe I need to add to that here, but it is worth reiterating Colás's reminder that, for Mandel, late capitalism is characterized by its unevenness—as capitalism develops, it constantly produces the Third World as its necessary complement, so the further it develops, the more Third Worlds it produces until eventually the Third World loses all geographic specificity and becomes instead a term designating something like a new class or indeed caste system within the First World itself.[20]

On this point, I must also take issue with Simon During's argument that these dispersed pockets of the Third World are discrete and discontinuous.[21] Jameson doesn't follow this path—as During suggests he should—for very good reasons. Although Jameson declines to offer a general theory of Third World literature on the grounds that the national cultures at stake are too diverse in themselves ever to be properly subsumed by so singular category and might therefore seem superficially sympathetic to During's discrete worlds scenario, he trenchantly refuses this apparently obvious alternate position that we might call pluralism. However different the respective national cultures may be, not one of them, he insists, can claim to be autonomous in Amin's sense of being de-linked, "they are all in various distinct ways locked in a life-and-death struggle with first-world cultural imperialism—a cultural struggle that is itself a reflexion of the economic situation of such areas in their penetration by various stages of capital, or as it is sometimes euphemistically termed, of modernisation."[22] Pluralism is to be refused because not to do so is to pretend that the sad fate of certain Third World nations is not determined by the selfish action of First World nations, or more pointedly still, as Jameson forcibly reminds us here, ourselves.

Now, for the affirmative labor let me begin by returning to the specific paper in question. The first thing that has to be remarked on is its context and I don't just mean the fact that it was initially given as a memorial lecture in honor of the late Robert C. Elliot, although that is by no means irrelevant. I am referring rather to the context of the humanities as a whole as it was in the mid-1980s. Then, as is so often true of the discipline, the humanities were—as ever I'm tempted to say—in the grip of an identity crisis born of the altogether paranoid question of what constitutes its proper object of study, the constant fear being that to admit any old text willy-nilly into the domain of what can 'properly' be studied at university would be to destroy the discipline itself since in some quarters, at least, the discipline is defined by the object. Of course, this 'crisis' was itself intensified by the efforts of poststructuralist critics, Jameson among them, who argued that the humanities were defined not by the things they studied, but rather by the way they studied and that there was therefore no structural limit to what could or indeed should be analyzed. The cyclical affirmations of the canon the humanities knows are basically in reaction to these assaults on its cornerstone, the great book.

Jameson's strategy here is to say if we must have a canon, and if that canon is going to do something besides pretend that it is global in outlook, then it must genuinely seek to incorporate literature from all corners of the globe, not excluding the Third World. My point is that, Jameson was writing back to those conservative critics like William Bennett, whom he names in this text, who would exclude without consideration any and all texts from India, Africa, China, and Latin America simply because they do not form part of the great tradition, all the while pretending to promulgate the study of world literature. What gives Jameson's essay its vitality but is lost to us now, and thank heavens, is the sense that reading, discussing, and thinking about literatures other than our own national productions are in some way novel or—worse—alien. In Australia, of course, the situation was even more fraught because its own national productions were for a long time subject to much the same proscription as so-called other literatures were, so for many years, English texts were studied as its own. Not the least reason for this, I suspect, although one rarely hears it discussed in these terms, was the fact that after the massive expansion of the university sector in the postwar period, the majority of academics in the humanities were in fact English, so for them, English texts were their national productions.

The true Jameson *aficionado* will also notice that something of the precise context, that is, a memorial lecture on the work of Robert C Elliott, informs the essay in subtle but nevertheless important ways. Elliott is best known for his work on satire and utopia as Jameson records, and this is our a cue to look elsewhere in Jameson's work for his influence and sure enough it is to be found in the essays on science fiction. For Jameson, science fiction is the successor to modernism that is not yet postmodernism; what should be underscored is precisely the definition he gives to the Third World literature in its national allegory phase. More interestingly still, First World science fiction is motivated by those very things that Jameson supposes puts most First World readers off Third World fiction in the first place: a combination of a fear of others (demography) and an addiction to our present way of life (anti-utopian politics).[23] These essays, which for the most part were written in the 1970s in the gap between *Marxism and Form* and *Fables of Aggression*, were virtually the only ones Jameson wrote on contemporary or near-contemporary work until he began writing about Third World literature, a fact whose significance we can only speculate about, but doubtless it has something to do with Jameson's conviction expressed here that the political novel died with modernism.

At length then, we arrive at the self-confessed "sweeping hypothesis" that has induced so much hand-wringing and fist-waving—namely, the bold claim that all Third World texts are necessarily national allegories.[24] Before we can evaluate this claim, however, we have to first specify what precisely is at stake and since Jameson doesn't spell out what he means by national allegory, here we have to return to the earlier text, *Fables of Aggression*, for our key. The first thing that has to be said about what Jameson refers to as national allegory in Lewis's work is that it is a specific solution to a more general problem, one that has preoccupied Jameson in several different places throughout his work— namely, the problem of closure. Every writer, according to Jameson, has two basic problems he or she must solve—how to generate their sentences to begin with, and how to impose closure on them once they're in flight. These problems have become especially acute since the breakdown of the realist model because the once rigid rules governing the construction of narratives have all been overturned, leaving writers to create their own parameters practically from scratch. Whereas earlier 'epic' writers such as Scott, for instance, had a secure mold ready-made for them in the form of the epic structure itself, into which they could simply insert a variety of historical material, more or less at will, letting the formula take care of the problems of opening and closing, writers of contemporary epics, such as Joyce, have to resort to more prosaic means. As Jameson reads it, Joyce resorts to an allegorical structure in *Ulysses* for the very reason that his way of generating sentences (namely, the detailed record-ing of what might be called the interiority of daily life in all its mundane glory) implies no specific or logical form of closure. Without the conceit of the epic allegory, any form of closure Joyce imposed would be intolerably arbitrary.[25] The point I want to make here, as a preface to discussing national allegory; is that Joyce's classical allusion occupies the same functional place as Lewis's national allegory, it is a different solution to the same problem.

Let me give another example of this approach from Jameson's work, this time his essay on Wallace Stevens. "In Stevens, the place-name will be at one and the same time the very locus and occasion for a production of images: quasi-Flaubertian *bovarysme*, the daydream about the exotic place, the free association on Java, Tehentepec, Key West, Oklahoma, Tennessee, Yucatan, Carolina, and so forth—and the emergence of another level of systematicity in language itself (the generation of place-names out of each other, their associ-ation now as a prover vocabulary field, behind which a deeper system is con-cealed and active."[26] That deeper system is the exoticism of the Third World. The point, though, is not to accuse him of orientalism (though it shouldn't thereby be seen to excuse him of it either), but to show the degree to which the exoticism of the Third World is in some way structurally required by the work itself. As Jameson reads it, the so-called Third World material in Stevens's work (his casual references to Java and so forth) is not merely the pri-vate fantasy of someone who did not travel all that much but nevertheless longed for alterity, although it is certainly that too.[27] It is rather the means by which the work attains closure. It is perhaps worth noting that Jameson reads Rimbaud's well-nigh hallucinogenic references to Africa and the Far East in much the same way—as that content that is structurally required by the form in order to attain closure.[28] Put simply, the everyday imagery in Stevens that constantly risks falling into a dreary realism is saved from banality by its jux-taposition with otherness, "*Java* tea" being more intriguing to the stifled minds of consumer society than "tea" by itself, something I'm sure a poet so well acquainted with advertising as Stevens could hardly escape noticing. Again, my point is that, for Jameson, the work is to be apprehended as a problem of form rather than content.

We can of course come at this a different way, from the perspective of the critic rather than the writer. And indeed, that is how Jameson approaches it in *Fables of Aggression*. The problem at hand is the discontinuity that no critic can fail to perceive between the stylistic investigation every great writer makes and the narrative object that is eventually constructed—of course, this problem has been formulated in several different ways, by different schools of thought, though perhaps nowhere so precisely as in the phenomenological description of Ingarden who formulated it in terms of the dialectic between the noemic and the noetic; that is, as the movement from sheer sense-data to full-blooded meaning. Jameson says, to "grasp this discontinuity as an objective reality in our culture . . . requires us radically to historicise the gap between style and narrative, which then may be seen as an event in the history of form."[29] His means of doing this may not seem terribly surprising, in that he uses the dialectic, but what is surprising is how he uses Deleuze and Guattari's work to formulate it. He proposes that style be conceived as the equivalent to Deleuze and Guattari's notion of the molecular, while narrative is to be grasped as molar (both terms are to be understood as having been aestheticized, which in this context means emptied of their particular content and deployed in a purely formal fashion).

More precisely, the molecular refers to sentence production conceived "as a symbolic act in its own right, an explosive and window-breaking *praxis* on the level of the words themselves."[30] Jameson's point is that, sentences do not fall ready-made from the sky; they require a type-specific machine to get them going. Usually this takes the form of an obstacle or taboo, (as Deleuze and Guattari say, machines only work by breaking down and continuing to break down), such as Joyce's self-imposed rule in *Ulysses* to deal only with interiority.[31] Once in progress, though, it becomes a kind limitlessness, an inexhaustible energy, an unstoppable productivity, like desire itself in Deleuze and Guattari's terms, that could never be constrained enough for meaning to exist were there not a countervailing force at work, and this is precisely how narrative as a molar force is to be understood. It is a superstructural form that by creating definite, albeit mobile, boundaries, brings the sentence production to some kind of close. The important point to be grasped here is that, sheer sentence production is literally schizophrenic, a private madness no other reader could ever fully participate in. What the molar machine does is devise an instrument—borrowing from Lyotard, Jameson calls it a "libidinal apparatus"—that operates at a collective level to enable other readers to 'invest' in the text; it also means that however 'private' a text may seem, there is always a collective or public level to it, if only we can recognize its pre-objective structure, that is, the model its sentence production appropriates to create a tolerable means of closure for itself.[32]

The Deleuzian purist will note that Jameson ignores Deleuze and Guattari's concept of the line of flight in his use of molar and molecular and therefore misreads—in the strong sense—their tripartite structure as a dualism. This enables him to transform their terms into the coordinates for a new analytical means of thinking the relationship between style and narrative dialectically. "In this use, the molecular level designates the here-and-now of immediate perception or of local desire, the production-time of the individual sentence, the electrifying shock of the individual word or the individual brushstroke, of the regional throb of pain or of pleasure, the sudden obsessive, cathected, fascination or the equally immediate repulsion of Freudian decathexis. To this microscopic, fragmentary life of the psyche in the immediate a counterforce is opposed in the molar (from *moles*, the mass of molecules organized into larger organic unities), which designates all those large, abstract, mediate, and perhaps even empty and imaginary forms by which we seek to recontain the molecular: the mirage of the continuity of personal identity, the organizing unity of the psyche or the personality, the concept of society itself, and, not least, the notion of the organic unity of the work of art."[33] In effect, Jameson's reading of every text poses two integral questions: what is the precise nature of the molecular machine that sets in motion the process of sentence production? What is the precise nature of the molar machine that imbues that sentence production with sufficient closure to enable us to read it? Here we risk moving too quickly ourselves because the molar is not yet the libidinal apparatus: we have to factor in one further step to complete our account of this particular piece of Jamesonian dialectical technology.

The purpose of this dialectical reading is, as I've mentioned already, to grasp the specific nature of the disjunction between style and narrative as an event in the history of form. "The name of Flaubert is a useful marker for this development, in which the two 'levels' of the narrative text begin to drift apart and acquire their own relative autonomy; in which the rhetorical and instrumental subordination of narrative language to narrative representation can no longer be taken for granted."[34] In this sense, Lewis's work continues to grapple with a formal problem regnant in Flaubert, but with one crucial difference, the option of continuing in a Balzacian or Dickensian realist vein was not available to Lewis in Flaubert's wake except at the cost of a profound and deeply unsatisfactory stylistic regression. For this reason, Lewis was compelled to take his stylistic investigations further and further in the direction of what Jameson calls the plotless art novel, risking utter unreadability for the sake of artistic enrichment and innovation. Indeed, the same could be said for all the modernists; one way or another they all courted sheer unreadability in the search for radical novelty. For the same reason, a stronger form of narrative containment than mere character was required; it had to be able to make available for investment a type of sentence production that was never terribly far from a headlong plunge into the abyss of schizophrenic chatter. By stronger I mean independent of the process of sentence production itself and just as importantly impermeable to it as well; so while this structure, the libidinal apparatus, is pressed into service by the inflationary pressures of the style, it remains aloof like the lens of a microscope that enables us to see the squiggling mess of amoeba a simple glass of water contains without being part of any feedback loop. In other words, the libidinal apparatus can be understood as the optic a text draws into itself in order to render itself visible.

In Lewis's work, this is the role nation plays. He doesn't thematize nation, so much as utilize the nation-state system existing in Europe before the First World war as his optic in the sense I have just described. Precisely so as not to get distracted by a content that is in a certain sense irrelevant, or at least only of secondary interest, our best means of getting a fix on what Jameson means by national allegory is always to approach it in terms of function (this, as I have argued elsewhere, is the true nature of the affinity between Jameson and Deleuze—both want to know how it works). In this case, Jameson's own discussion of the term follows this path: nation, he explains, is a pre-objective structure in Lewis's work analogous in function to the notion of topography in Freud's explication of the unconscious: "not only are the Freudian models allegories, they can also be shown to depend for their figural expression on elaborate and preexisting representations of the topography of the city and the dynamics of the political state. This urban and civil 'apparatus'—often loosely referred to as a Freudian 'metaphor'—is the objective precondition for Freud's representation of the psyche, and is thus at one with the very 'discovery' of the unconscious itself, which may now be seen to have presupposed the objective development—the industrialisation, the social stratification and class polarisation, the complex division of labour—of the late Victorian city."[35] The rewarding richness of Freud's analyses depends, at least in part, on our own understanding of the city, our own experiences today fully as much as our grasp of fin-de-siecle Vienna. Deleuze and Guattari go further than this when they say Freud's central fault was his treatment of the city as merely a metaphor, as a map instead of a lived intensity.[36] Wise to this problem, Jameson is careful to specify that Lewis's model is only ever a provisory solution to an ongoing and perhaps even irresolvable aesthetic dilemma.[37]

That aesthetic dilemma is the growing disparity between the rapid evolution of style and the comparatively backward possibilities of narrative structure; but this disparity is not merely aesthetic, it mirrors the fragmentation of the psyche itself under the conditions of modernity, which, in Jameson's view, are to be understood primarily as the manifold, but ultimately progressive, deterioration of traditional ways of life. The first casualty, as it were, at least in the realm of the aesthetics, is the presupposition central to nineteenth-century realism "of the relative intelligibility and self-sufficiency of the national experience from within, a coherence in its social life that the narrative of the destinies of its individual citizens can be expected to achieve formal completeness."[38] One reason for this loss of intelligibility that in light of the larger issue at hand (namely, Jameson's work in the area of postcolonialism) is especially worth mentioning, is imperialism. For Jameson, imperialism and modernism go hand in hand, each one shaping and determining the other in locally specific but still generalizable ways. In particular, imperialism causes a kind of "meaning-loss," as Jameson puts it, for the metropolitan subject inasmuch the flight of capital to the colonies makes it impossible for that subject to grasp the situation as a whole. No enlargement of personal experience or intensification of self-examination can compensate for the mystery of colonial life, locked away as it is in distant and (for most) unreachable lands.[39]

For the metropolitan subject, there will always be a missing piece in the unending puzzle that is everyday life. One might extend Jameson's claim here by turning it around because by power of the very globalizing impulse and tendency of capitalism that drives imperialism itself, the same must also be true of the colonized cities, although their experience of this truth will have an entirely different valency. Nevertheless, whether the subject is in Bombay, Dublin, Singapore, or even Sydney, owing to the time-space distanciation (as Giddens calls it) inherent in imperialism, their experience is similar to the metropolitan subject's in this one respect: they cannot grasp their situation as a whole.[40] Not the least reason for this, of course, is their lack of self-government: ruled by an absentee monarch, the colonized peoples rarely if ever got to glimpse the person in whose hands their lives and livelihood had been forcibly entrusted, except in iconic form. "As artistic content it will now henceforth always have something missing about it, but in the sense of a privation that can never be restored or made whole simply by adding back in the missing component: its lack is rather comparable to another dimension, an outside like the other face of a mirror, which it constitutively lacks, and which can never be made up or made good."[41] This, then, for Jameson is the constitutive problem of modernism itself. Indeed, he will go so far as to say that "it is only that new kind of art which reflexively perceives this problem and lives this formal dilemma that can be called modernism in the first place."[42]

Taking all this into account, national allegory should thus "be understood as a formal attempt to bridge the increasing gap between the existential data of everyday life within a given nation-state and the structural tendency of monopoly capitalism to develop on a worldwide, essentially transnational scale."[43] It would not be going too far to take this statement as Jameson's diagnosis of the situation of all creative writers and intellectuals everywhere in the world today. This situation is, however, complicated by the fact that today—owing to the enormous transformative pressures of globalization—the nation-state, at least in its current formulation, is faced with the prospect of extinction.[44] So the interrogation of the constitution and valency of the nation must be expanded now to include the question of its continued relevance, sociopolitically as well as culturally. Nowadays, all the indications are that the nation is a social institution rapidly being outmoded by a trend toward a more globally conceived concept of the state—Hardt and Negri call it empire, but somehow that does not seem quite the right word, although it is certainly vivid enough. In this respect, it may be appropriate to speak of a (post)national situation, not because nations have vanished since plainly that isn't the case, but because the time of their automatic legitimacy has passed.

If it is true that the nation is receding in political importance in the face of what some are now referring to as achieved globalization, then it might be thought that national allegory would wane with it. Yet the very opposite is proving to be the case, but with a twist. Because the concept of nation has lost its claim to automatic legitimacy, it can neither serve as the horizon nor ground for a debate—it is not what we are working toward or our point of reference. And this is precisely because the constitution of that collective pronoun around which this discussion revolves is itself neither automatic nor immediate. The "multitude," Hardt and Negri's useful, though of course by no means unproblematic, term for this ambiguous and indeed ambivalent collective unit, has become properly transnational, not just geographically, but temporally, or, better, ontologically: their restlessness is that of what Deleuze and Guattari refer to as "a people yet to come."[45] The mobility of the multitude is the cornerstone of Hardt and Negri's political optimism, which would find its final realization in the end of the nation. From this utopian perspective, any attempt to revive interest in concept of the nation must be regarded, strictly speaking, as reactionary; yet given that its replacement, whether we call it empire or not, is at this stage in history an utterly open question, it is perhaps not surprising that it should be so predominant right now. In contemplating the literally abyssal future of life after the end of nation, the mind trembles before such a vast question and falls back on versions of what it already knows. This is not just a matter of addiction, though its affect is certainly akin to that, but a genuine failure of the imagination.[46] In light of this, one might hazard, in conclusion, the following hypothesis: the more tenuous the nation becomes politically, the more determinedly it returns culturally.

NOTES

1. P. Chatterjee, *The Nation and Its Fragments: Colonialism and Postcolonial Histories* (Princeton: Princeton University Press, 1993), 3.

2. For instance, see G. Spivak, *A Critique of Postcolonial Reason: Toward a History of the Vanishing Present* (Cambridge: Harvard University Press, 1999), 71–79.

3. For a more extensive consideration of these monographs, see my forthcoming review in *Historical Materialism.*

4. M. Sprinker, "The national Question: Said, Ahmad, Jameson," *Public Culture* (1993): 8.

5. Fredric Jameson, "Third-World Literature in the Era of Multinational Capitalism," *Social Text* 15 (1986): 65.

6. A. Ahmad, "Jameson's Rhetoric of Otherness and the 'National Allegory,'" *Social Text* 17 (1987): 6.

7. Jameson, 76.

8. Ibid., 81.

9. Ahmad, 8.

10. He is not alone doing this, as Moreiras (2001: 312n7) points out; it is, in fact, a very common error.

11. Ahmad, 21.

12. For instance, in *Provincializing Europe* (2000), Dipesh Chakrabarty offers several compelling demonstrations that the ultramundane is in every case, but especially in the colonial situation, political, which, inasmuch as it refers to the effort to define a distinctly Indian sensibility, is implicitly albeit ambivalently anticolonial. For examples that relate specifically to women, see his discussion of widowhood (117) and domesticity (228).

13. Jameson, 73.

14. Hence the outrage surrounding the recent film adaptation of it, I suppose, that raises the point that not only postcolonial criticism, but also feminist and indeed queer criticism, similarly rely on allegorical reading practices

15. See Ahmad, *In Theory: Classes, Nations, Literature* (London: Verso, 1992). For an evaluation of Ahmad's critique of Said, see Sprinker.

16. Ahmad, "Jameson's Rhetoric of Otherness and the 'National Allegory,'" 65.

17. Ibid., 66.

18. S. Colás, "The Third World in Jameson's Postmodernism, or, the Cultural Logic of Late Capitalism," *Social Text* 31/32 (1992): 258.

19. Ahmad, "Jameson's Rhetoric of Otherness and the 'National Allegory,'" 24–25.

20. Colás, 259.

21. S. During, "Postmodernism or Post-Colonialism Today," *Textual Practice* 1 (1) (1987): 35.

22. Jameson, 68.

23. See especially Jameson, "World-Reduction in Le Guin: The Emergence of Utopian Narrative," *Science Fiction Studies* 2/3 (1975): 221–30.

24. Jameson, "Third-World Literature in the Era of Multinational Capitalism," 69.

25. On Joyce, see Jameson, "Ulysses in History," *James Joyce and Modern Literature*, ed. W. J. McCormack and A. Stead (London: Routledge, 1982); *Modernism and Imperialism* (Derry: Field Day Pamphlet Number 14, 1988).

26. Jameson, "Flaubert and Postmodernism," *Flaubert and Postmodernism*, ed. N. Schor and H. Majewski (Lincoln: University of Nebraska Press, 1984), 14.

27. Ibid., 15.

28. See ibid., 71.

29. Jameson, *Fables of Aggression: Wyndham Lewis, the Modernist as Fascist* (Berkeley: University of California Press, 1979), 7.

30. Jameson, *Fables of Aggression: Wyndham Lewis, the Modernist as Fascist*, 8; *The Political Unconscious: Narrative as a Socially Symbolic Act* (London: Routledge, 1981), 53.

31. "In modern times . . . all creative and original speech flows from privation rather than from plenitude: its redoubled energies, far from tapping archaic or undiscovered sources of energy, are proportionate to the massive and well-nigh impenetrable

obstacles which aesthetic production must overcome in the age of reification." Jameson, *Fables of Aggression: Wyndham Lewis, the Modernist as Fascist*, 81.

32. One could look at all this in Lacanian terms, too, I suppose, whereby the sentence production would be like the death instinct that on Zizek's reading is felt as a kind intolerable immortality, a zombie-like state that longs for symbolic closure; the molar then would be death itself, the only "full" act we can know.

33. Jameson, *Fables of Aggression: Wyndham Lewis, the Modernist as Fascist*, 8.

34. Ibid., 7. For a more developed reading of Flaubert by Jameson, one that, moreover, deploys an historicized version of the libidinal apparatus, which appropriately enough he terms libidinal historicism, see Jameson, "Flaubert and Postmodernism."

35. Jameson, *Fables of Aggression: Wyndham Lewis, the Modernist as Fascist*, 96.

36. See, in particular, their comments on Freud's interpretation of Little Hans's horse phobia, which they say cannot be understood without reference to "Hans's relation to the street." G. Deleuze and I. Guattari, *A Thousand Plateaus*, trans. B. Massumi (Minneapolis: University of Minnesota Press, 1986) 259.

37. Jameson, *Fables of Aggression: Wyndham Lewis, the Modernist as Fascist*, 94. For much the same reason, Jameson abandons the notion of cognitive mapping almost as soon as he conceives of it: the problem, he says, is the very success of the metaphor solidifies what should remain fluid. Cf., Jameson, *Postmodernism, or, the Cultural Logic of Late Capitalism* (Durham: Duke University Press, 1991), 51–53.

38. Jameson, *Fables of Aggression: Wyndham Lewis, the Modernist as Fascist*, 94

39. Jameson, *Modernism and Imperialism*, 11.

40. "In the modern era, the level of time-space distanciation is much higher than in any previous period, and the relations between local and distant social forms and events become correspondingly 'stretched'. Globalisation refers essentially to that stretching process, insofar as the modes of connection between different social contexts or regions become networked across the earth's surface as a whole." A. Giddens, *The Consequences of Modernity* (Cambridge: Polity, 1990), 64.

41. Jameson, *Modernism and Imperialism*, 12.

42. Ibid., 12.

43. Jameson, *Fables of Aggression: Wyndham Lewis, the Modernist as Fascist*, 94.

44. This essay may be read, in part, as an answer to Alberto Moreiras's interesting speculation concerning the persistence of national allegory in the era of globalization. See A. Moreiras, *The Exhaustion of Difference: the Politics of Latin American Cultural Studies* (Durham: Duke University Press, 2001), 306n5.

45. See their book on Kafka; but also see Jameson's uptake of this to theorize late modernism in *A Singular Modernity*.

46. On cultural "addiction" as an anti-utopian force, see Jameson, *Postmodernism, or the Cultural Logic of Late Capitalism*, 335.

9

Who's Afraid of National Allegory?

Jameson, Literary Criticism, Globalization

Imre Szeman

Fredric Jameson's proposal that all third-world texts be read as "national allegories" has been one of the more influential and important attempts to theorize the relationship of literary production to the nation and to politics. Unfortunately, its influence and importance have thus far been primarily *negative*. For many critics, Jameson's essay stands as an example of what *not* to do when studying third-world literature from the vantage point of the first-world academy. His attempt in the now infamous essay, "Third-World Literature in the Era of Multinational Capitalism," to delineate "some general theory of what is often called third-world literature" has been attacked for its very desire for generality.[1] The presumption that it is possible to produce a theory that would explain African, Asian, *and* Latin American literary production, the literature of China *and* Senegal, has been read (inevitably) as nothing more than a patronizing, theoretical orientalism, or as yet another example of a troubling appropriation of Otherness with the real aim of exploring the West rather than the Other. The most well-known criticism of Jameson's essay along these lines remains Aijaz Ahmad's "Jameson's Rhetoric of Otherness and the 'National Allegory.'"[2] More informally and anecdotally, however, within the field of postcolonial literary and cultural studies, Jameson's essay has come to be treated as little more than a cautionary tale about the extent and depth of Eurocentrism in the Western academy, or, even more commonly, as a convenient bibliographic marker of those kinds of theories of third-world literature that everyone now agrees are limiting and reductive.[3]

Looking back on Jameson's essay through the haze of fifteen years of postcolonial studies, as well as the through the equally disorienting smoke thrown up by the explosion of theories and positions on globalization (which have come to both complement and challenge the field of postcolonial studies), one wonders what all the fuss was about. In hindsight, it appears that almost without exception, critics of Jameson's essay have willfully misread it. Of course, such misreadings are to be expected. The reception given to this or that theory has as much to do with timing as with its putative content. As one of the first responses to postcolonial literary studies from a major critic outside the field, the publication of Jameson's essay in the mid-1980s provided postcolonial critics with a flash-point around which to articulate general criticisms of dominant views of North–South relations expressed within even supposedly critical political theories (like Marxism). It also provided a self-definitional opportunity for postcolonial studies: a shift away from even the lingering traces of Marxist interpretations of imperialism (from Marx to Lenin, from Fanon to Anthony Brewer) toward more deconstructive ones exemplified by the work of figures, such as Gayatri Chakravorty Spivak and Homi Bhahba.[4] While criticisms of Jameson's views may have thus been useful or productive in their own way, they have nevertheless tended to obscure and misconstrue a sophisticated attempt to make sense of the relationship of literature to politics in the decolonizing world. I want to argue that Jameson's "general" theory of third-world literary production offers a way of conceptualizing the relationship of literature to politics (and politics to literature) that goes beyond the most common (and commonsense) understanding of the relations between these terms.[5] Indeed, what the concept of "national allegory" introduces is a model for a properly materialist approach to postcolonial texts and contexts, one that resonates with Kalpana Seshadri-Crooks's recent characterization of postcolonial studies as "interested above all in materialist critiques of power and how that power or ideology seems to interpellate subjects within a discourse as subordinate and without agency."[6]

Crooks's description of the aims of postcolonial studies emerges out of her analysis of the malaise or melancholia that has beset postcolonial studies as it enters the twenty-first century. This accords with a general sense by those engaged in the field that while postcolonial studies remains as important as ever in a world of growing material and cultural disparity, its theoretical energies and commitments seem to have hit a barrier as contemporary outpace attempts to make sense of their formative logic. It seems to me that revisiting Jameson's theory of third-world literature—looking at both its problems and its productive potentialities—provides a (perhaps unexpected) way out of this malaise and past this conceptual barrier.

One of the things for which Jameson has been criticized throughout his career is his insistence on totality as a central concept in social and political criticism. In the context of postcolonial studies, it is easy enough to see how this appeal to totality could be mistaken as a Eurocentric, universalist claim par excellence.[7] But this is to conceive of the concept of totality far too rigidly and unimaginatively and, in the process of doing so, to adopt the opposite (untenable) position, falling "back into a view of present history as sheer heterogeneity, random difference, a coexistence of a host of distinct forces whose effectivity is undecidable."[8] It seems to me that what is missing in most theories of postcolonial literary and cultural production (and what thus produces the malaise that Crooks points to) is just such a map of the relative effectivity of those forces that produced imperialism as well as the globalscape of its long aftermath. In the absence of some general theory of the structure of contemporary social and political life and its historical precedents, there is instead a rough assemblage of literary-critical commonplaces (often borrowed from competing theories that cannot be put together in any easy way) concerning power, identity, representation, language, and so on, that originate almost solely from within the hermetically sealed space of academic criticism.[9] In any case, my argument here should also be taken as an implicit argument on behalf of totality—not the "bad" totality that legitimates theories of modernization of development, but the totality constructed, in Michael Hardt and Antonio Negri's words, by an antitranscendental and antiteleological "insurgent science" that "is open, as open as the world of possibility, the world of potential."[10] Here, at least, totality appears as the possibility of metacommentary—not as a secondary step in interpretation but as a condition of interpretation per se; and, as I will argue here, what national allegory itself names is the conditions of possibility of metacommentary at the present time.[11] The question I will pursue, then, is the relationship of allegory (as a mode of interpretation) to the nation (as a specific kind of sociopolitical problematic) and what this relationship entails for a global or transnational literary or cultural criticism.

In an effort to uncover the possibilities and limits of the concept of national allegory, I will first reexamine Jameson's development of the concept of national allegory in "Third-World Literature in the Era of Multinational Capitalism." I will then turn to a consideration of the history of this term in Jameson's own work. While it has been stressed that Jameson's comments concerning third-world literature arise out of meditations on a different matter entirely (i.e., the debates in the American academy in the mid-1980s over the revision of the literary canon), almost no critic has made reference to the fact that the concept of "national allegory" does not originate in this essay.[12] Finally, I will think about the relationship between nation and allegory by looking at Jameson's recent writings on globalization in order to consider its more general significance for contemporary cultural theory and criticism.

One of the first things that has to be made clear about Jameson's account of third-world literature in "Third-World Literature in the Era of Multinational Capitalism" is that the concept of national allegory is exhausted by neither of its component terms. Jameson is aware of the fact that the "nation" and "allegory" are concepts that have both fallen into disrepute: the nation, because of the historical experiences of first- and third-world countries with the virulent nationalisms of the twentieth century, as well the vigorous criticism that has been directed toward the nation over the past several decades; allegory, because of the naive mode of one-to-one mapping that it seems to imply, a presumed passage from text to context that is epistemologically and politically suspect. Attaching these terms to a theory of third-world texts has a tendency to conjure up once again the whole specter of development theory and practice, in which technologies that have become antiquated in the West are passed along to countries where such outmoded technologies (including conceptual technologies such as the "nation" and "allegory") might, in Hegelian fashion, still be of some use. There is no doubt that some of the initial discomfort felt by many critics with the concept of national allegory arises out of a resistance to the political implications of each of its component terms—to the sense, that is, that either of these terms might still have a relevance for the "underdeveloped" third world that they have (as Jameson admits) lost in the "developed" first.

Infamously, Jameson writes that "all third-world texts are necessarily . . . allegorical, and in a very specific way they are to be read as what I will call *national allegories*."[13] Here again, the claim that Jameson makes about third-world texts ("by way of a sweeping hypothesis") cannot help but distract from his broader aim, which is not to pass aesthetic judgment on third-world texts, but to develop a system by which it might be possible to consider these texts *within* the global economic and political system that produces the third world *as* the third world.[14] For Jameson, third-world texts are to be understood as national allegories specifically *in contrast* to the situation of first-world cultural and literary texts. He argues that there is a political dimension to third-world texts that is now (and has perhaps long been) absent in their first-world counterparts. This corresponds to a difference between the social and political culture of the first and third worlds—a difference that must, of course, be understood as broad and conceptual, and which should not be seen as unreflectively rendering homogenous what are two extraordinarily heterogeneous categories.[15] Jameson believes that, in the West, the consequence of the radical separation between the public and the private, "between the poetic and the political," is "the deep cultural conviction that the lived experience of our private existences is somehow incommensurable with the abstractions of economic science and political dynamics."[16] In terms of literary production, this "cultural conviction" has the effect of limiting or even negating entirely the political work of literature: in the first world, literature is a matter of the private rather than the public sphere, a matter of individual tastes and solitary meditations rather than public debate and deliberation. For Jameson, the relations between the public and the private in the third world are entirely different: they have not undergone this separation and division. Literary texts are thus never *simply* about private matters (although, as Michael Sprinker points out in his review of Jameson's essay, they are never *simply* private in the first world either, however difficult it might be to see this now).[17] In the third world, Jameson claims, *"the story of the private individual destiny is always an allegory of the embattled situation of the public third-world culture and society."*[18]

This is a strong and sweeping claim, whose precise meaning in "Third World Literature in the Age of Multinational Capitalism" can be grasped only by careful attention to Jameson's description of allegory, his claims about the relationship of psychology to politics in the first and in the third worlds, and his description of the significance of the term "culture" and the relationship between culture and politics more generally. Of the concept of "allegory," Jameson writes that "our traditional concept of allegory—based, for instance, on stereotypes of Bunyan—is that of an elaborate set of figures and personifications to be read against some one-to-one table of equivalence: this is, so to speak, a one-dimensional view of this signifying process, which might only be set in motion and complexified were we willing to entertain the more alarming notion that such equivalencies are themselves in constant change and transformation at each perpetual present of the text."[19] Read in this more expansive way, the allegorical mode is not limited to the production of morality tales about public, political events—tales that could just as well be described in journalistic terms as in the narrative structure of novels or short stories. On the contrary, "the allegorical spirit is profoundly discontinuous, a matter of breaks and heterogeneities, of the multiple polysemia of the dream rather than the homogenous representation of the symbol."[20] If in the third world, private stories are *always* allegories of public situations, this does not thereby imply that of necessity third-world writing is narratively simplistic or overtly moralistic, or that all such texts are nothing more than exotic versions of Bunyan, as might be supposed in the terms of a more traditional sense of allegory. The claim is rather that the text speaks to its context in a way that is more than simply an example of Western texts' familiar "auto-referentiality": it necessarily and directly speaks to and of the overdetermined situation of the struggles for national independence and cultural autonomy in the context of imperialism and its aftermath.[21]

Why third-world texts speak more directly of and to the national situation has to do with what Jameson sees as the very different "relationship between the libidinal and the political components of individual and social experience" in the first and third worlds.[22] One of the results of the deep division between the public and private spheres in the first world is that "political commitment is recontained and psychologized or subjectivized."[23] Again, for Jameson, the very opposite is the case in the third world. The division between public and private that is characteristic of the West is *not* characteristic of most third-world societies, or perhaps this should be read (in 1986 if not today) as *not yet* or *not yet completely*.[24] This assertion could be taken (again, in a familiar Hegelian fashion) as a claim that socially and aesthetically, the third world lags behind the first in its development.[25] But—and I think that this is how Jameson intends it—it also highlights a genuine, material difference between the first and third worlds that is expressed socially and culturally. The attempt to maintain a different form of social life while accepting the material and technological advantages offered by the West has constituted one of the major challenge faced by non-Western societies for whom modernity *has* been belated; it does not seem to me inconceivable to imagine a different organization of private and public in societies that were the subjects of colonialism as opposed to its agents.[26] In any case, the lack of a corresponding division between public and private in the third world means, for Jameson, that "psychology, or more specifically, libidinal investment, is to be read in primarily political and social terms."[27] If political energies in the first world are psychologically interiorized in a way that divests them of their power, it could be said that in the third world the "sphere" of the psychological does not function as a containment device in which what is dangerous in the public is sublimated and defused. In the first world, these sublimated energies may, of course, return to the public sphere in the mediated form of various cultural products; even so, unlike the situation of the third world, in the first world, such cultural products would nevertheless be taken to be imbued with only *private* significance or with only the most banal form of larger public meaning, that is, as indicators of "styles" or "trends," the Hegelian *Geist* reborn as successive waves of (essentially similar and essentially empty) commodities. Another way of characterizing this division between first and third worlds within Jameson's own vocabulary is to say that, the history that is everywhere actively repressed in the first world is still a possible subject of discourse in the thirdworld.[28] Of course, this characterization of the large-scale societal differences between the first and the third worlds, Jameson adds, must be read as "speculative" and general, and open to "correction by specialists."[29]

Jameson's characterization of the different relationships in the first and the third worlds between private and public, and so also of the psychological or the libidinal, must be read further in terms of his subsequent discussion of the concept of "cultural revolution"; otherwise, it is possible at this point to see his characterization of the vast social, political, and cultural gulf separating the first and the third worlds as a form of Eurocentrism or exoticism in which what is lacking in the civilized West is found at the heart of its "uncivilized" exterior. Jameson links the idea of "cultural revolution," which has most commonly been used to refer to the massive set of social and cultural changes undertaken by communist regimes (and in China in particular), to the work of figures with "seemingly very different preoccupations": Antonio Gramsci, Wilhelm Reich, Frantz Fanon, Herbert Marcuse, Rodolph Bahro, and Paolo Freire. It is in the connection that Jameson makes between cultural revolution and "subalternity" that the significance of national allegory as an interpretive strategy for third-world texts begins to come into focus:

> Overhastily, I will suggest that "cultural revolution" as it is projected in such works [Gramsci, Reich, et al.] turns on the phenomenon of what Gramsci called "subalternity," namely the feelings of mental

inferiority and habits of subservience and obedience which necessarily and structurally develop in situations of domination—most dramatically in the experience of colonized peoples. But here, as so often, the subjectivizing and psychologizing habits of first-world peoples such as ourselves can play us false and lead us into misunderstandings. Subalternity is not in that sense a psychological matter, although it governs psychologies; and I suppose that the strategic choice of the term "cultural" aims precisely at restructuring that view of the problem and projecting it outwards into the realm of objective or collective spirit in some non-psychological, but also non-reductionist or non-economistic, materialist fashion. When a psychic structure is objectively determined by economic and political relationships, it cannot be dealt with by means of purely psychological therapies; yet it equally cannot be dealt with by means of purely objective transformations of the economic and political situation itself, since the habits remain and exercise a baleful and crippling residual effect. This is a more dramatic form of that old mystery, the unity of theory and practice; and it is specifically in the context of this problem of cultural revolution (now so strange and alien to us) that the achievements and failures of third-world intellectuals, writers and artists must be placed if their concrete meaning is to be grasped.[30]

It is *this*, then, that the concept of national allegory points to: the ways in which the psychological points to the political and the trauma of subalternity finds itself "projected outwards" (allegorically) into the "cultural." Very crudely, the cultural is what lies "between" the psychological and the political, unifying "theory and practice" in such a way that it is *only* there that the "baleful and crippling" habits that are the residue of colonialism can be addressed and potentially overcome. A "cultural revolution" aims to do just this: to produce an authentic and sovereign subjectivity and collectivity by undoing the set of habits called subalternity. While these are not habits that can be modified by the transformation of political and economic institutions alone, this does not mean the exclusive attention to the subjective (the psychological) *or* to the cultural is sufficient in and of itself either. The idea of "habit" is for this reason a particularly apt way of understanding the legacy of subalternity, since it draws attention to the ways in which subalternity cannot be reduced simply to "mental" or "psychological" states, but must be seen as residing in the unconscious and inscribed somatically in a whole range of bodily dispositions and social institutions. The problem of cultural revolution accounts for the presence of the political in the psychological by means of a level of mediation composed of cultural objects like literary texts, and provides a framework in which it is possible to assess "the achievements and failures of third world intellectuals" with respect to the task of reclaiming something positive from the colonial experience.[31]

The relationship between the cultural and subalternity may be seen, of course, as almost generically definitive of the intellectual work that has been produced under the sign of "postcolonial" theory and criticism. For example, to point to one of the earliest works that has been claimed for the field of post-colonial criticism, what other than the "habit" of subalternity does Frantz Fanon address in *Black Skin, White Masks?* One of the most important things that postcolonial critics have added to our understanding is the degree to which cultural and discursive domination was (and is) a necessary and essential aspect of colonialism and imperialism. Where Jameson differs from most postcolonial critics, however, is in his insistence that "culture":

> is by no means the final term at which one stops. One must imagine such cultural structures and attitudes as having been themselves, in the beginning, vital responses to infrastructural realities (economic and geographic, for example), as attempts to resolve more fundamental contradictions—attempts which then outlive the situations for which they were devised, and survive, in reified forms, as "cultural patterns." Those patterns themselves then become part of the objective situation confronted by later generations.[32]

He continues:

> Nor can I feel that the concept of cultural "identity" or even national "identity" is adequate. One cannot acknowledge the justice of the general poststructuralist assault on the so-called "centered subject," the old unified ego of bourgeois individualism, and then resuscitate this same ideological mirage of psychic unification on the collective level in the form of a doctrine of collective identity. Appeals to collective identity need to be evaluated from a historical perspective, rather than from the standpoint of some dogmatic and placeless "ideological analysis." When a third-world writer invokes this (to us) ideological value, we need to examine the concrete historical situation closely in order to determine the political consequences of the strategic use of this concept.[33]

There are then (at least) two levels of mediation that must be considered in the movement from the psychological to the political (and back again) through the cultural. Culture mediates; to understand precisely how it does so, it must be understood that the cultural forms and patterns that produce this mediation are themselves the product of an earlier process of mediation, now reified into the forms and patterns of culture that are to be used as the raw materials of cultural production. While few critics now would object to the need for the analysis of any form of cultural production to take into account the circuits of economics and politics that make the text possible in the first place, the significance of this second mode by which culture mediates remains all too often unexplored. In other words, what is often missing is the realization that all mediation in the present takes place through the *reified* cultural forms (and culture in general) of the past; all attempts to resolve the "fundamental contradictions" of the present through cultural production must pass through the concretized history of previous attempts to solve the contradictions of earlier infrastructural realities that have since changed in form and character. This is not to say that culture must be understood as somehow necessarily (and always already) belated, or that it therefore always "misses" the present (a bizarre, if compelling idea), which is to misunderstand in any case what it might mean for cultural forms to attempt to resolve historical contradictions. It is, rather, to point out the need for a more complicated understanding of the process of mediation that considers not simply the site of mediation (say, the text), but also the way in which this site is itself the product of mediation. It is this sense of mediation to which Adorno was trying to draw our attention, too, when he said that "mediation is . . . not between the object and the world, but in the object itself."

Far from reducing the complexity of third-world literary production, the concept of national allegory enables us to consider these texts as the extremely complex objects that they are and *not* just as allegories of one kind or another of the Manichean binaries produced out of the encounter of colonizer and colonized (however ambivalently one might want to understand these). Indeed, while criticizing Jameson's concept of national allegory, much of what passes for postcolonial literary criticism performs a reading of only a first-level mediation, which in turn transforms postcolonial texts into various kinds of political allegories. Where Jameson's concept of national allegory goes beyond this is by foregrounding (metacritically) the cultural/social situation of the reader of postcolonial texts, highlighting the fact that every interpretation or reading is a kind of translation mechanism that it is best to acknowledge rather than to hide the workings of; the critic, too, works out of a cultural situation that is the product of earlier mediations that form the raw material for his or her readings.[34]

Understood through the lens of the idea of "cultural revolution" that Jameson outlines in "Third-World Literature," the concept of national allegory suggests a number of things about how we should think about postcolonial or third-world texts, especially in the period of decolonization and globalization. First, postcolonial literary production needs to be understood as forming a "vital responses to infrastructural realities . . . as attempts to resolve more fundamental contradictions." In other words, it is productive to look at this form of cultural production as a particular kind of cultural strategy, rather than reading it simply and immediately as "literature," in the sense in which this concept is well understood in the first-world academy.[35] Second, careful attention needs to be paid to the deployment of "ideological values" by third-world writers themselves, values that sometimes have a resonance in the Western academy because of the ways in which they politically reempower the project of Western literary criticism. One of the most important of these may that of the "nation" and its strategic use in the literature produced during decolonization; another is to be found in the unquestioned assumption on the part of many critics of the almost necessary social significance of postcolonial literature (or at least, its significance in a straightforward way), when literature may in fact have a relatively marginal role in the postcolony. Another way of putting this last point is that in the examination of postcolonial literature, what needs to be considered is the conditions of possibility for the practice of writing *literature* in these regions, for it is only in this way that we can understand the precise and complicated ways in which this older, imported "technology" participates in the task of cultural revolution that is so important to third-world societies.[36]

Whatever one might think of this formulation of mediation and of its utility for postcolonial literary studies, it might nevertheless seem that in producing it, I have come rather far afield from the initial concept of national allegory. Indeed, my elaboration of national allegory appears to be more or less akin to the general interpretive schema that Jameson has developed with remarkable consistency over the course of his career, specifically in works such as *The Political Unconscious*. And if *this* is what national allegory is finally about, one has to wonder why Jameson would have generated a neologism that could not help inviting confusion. Why, after all, *national* allegory and not something else? In elaborating how this mode of interpretation has specific relevance to the theorization of the role and function of culture and literature in the era of globalization, I want to briefly review the history of national allegory in Jameson's own work. For if there is anything that is troubling about the use of national allegory as a mode of analysis of third-world literary texts, it is to be found in the changes that this concept undergoes throughout Jameson's work, coming to be, finally, nothing less than a substitute term for the kind of dialectical criticism that he would like to apply to *all* cultural texts—whether third world or not.[37] National allegory names a possibility and a limit for texts that Jameson first sees in the fiction of Wyndham Lewis, then in third-world texts, and finally, as a condition of contemporary cultural production as such. What is missing in Jameson's discussion of national allegory is a discussion of the *nation* to match that of allegory. Though it might seem as if the nation has an important role to play in understanding third-world texts, on the question of the nation itself, Jameson has surprisingly little to say in "Third-World Literature": the nation is more or less simply conflated with the "political" and, when it is not, it becomes a term that seems to make reference to a kind of collectivity or community that is idealized when it should be placed into question. It is in this lack of attention to the issue of the nation in the concept of "national allegory" that the strains of the transposition of this concept from an earlier formulation becomes apparent. While there are thus limits to national allegory within "Third-World Literature," it seems to me that looking at some of Jameson's more recent reflections on the nation in the context of globalization can help to locate the nation within his dialectical mode of analysis in a way that brings national allegory forward into the global present even as it clarifies the conceptual work that the nation performs in Jameson's analysis of third-world texts.

The term "national allegory" first appears in *Fables of Aggression* as a description of Wyndham Lewis' novel, *Tarr*. As it is presented in this early work, national allegory originates as a much more straightforward concept than it comes to be in the discussion of third-world texts: it refers to the way in which individual characters with different national origins stand-in for "more abstract national characteristics which are read as their inner essence."[38] When dealing with any one such correspondence between character and national essence, this allegorical mode becomes a form of "cultural critique." For Jameson, the unique characteristic of Lewis's texts is to have assembled numerous national types into one setting, thereby producing "a dialectically new and more complicated allegorical system . . . that specific and uniquely allegorical space between signifier and signified."[39] In *Fables of Aggression*, "national allegory" is thus the name for a specific, formal characteristic of Lewis's novel, rather than a concept that suggests an entire system or mode of reading and interpretation. Indeed, the more general logic that Jameson suggests, as the only way to properly account for the possibility in Lewis's novel of this "now outmoded narrative system," seems to have become transformed with reference to third-world texts into the principle of what is now national allegory itself.[40] In characteristic form, Jameson draws attention to the fact that an explanation for national allegory as a formal principle of *Tarr* can only be found in history—though not in the sense that historical conditions "caused" the formal organization of *Tarr* or that the novel is "a 'reflexion' of the European diplomatic system."[41] Instead, he suggests, our attention should be directed toward

the more sensible procedure of exploring those semantic and structural givens which are logically prior to this text and without which its emergence it inconceivable. This is of course the sense in which national allegory in general, and *Tarr* in particular, presuppose not merely the nation-state itself as the basic functional unit of world politics, but also the objective existence of a system of nation-states, the international diplomatic machinery of pre-World-War-I Europe which, originating in the 16th century, was dislocated in significant ways by the War and the Soviet Revolution.[42]

According to Jameson, all literary and cultural forms provide an "unstable and provisory solution to an aesthetic dilemma which is itself the manifestation of a social and historical contradiction."[43] National allegory can therefore be seen as a once but no longer viable formal attempt "to bridge the increasing gap between the existential data of everyday life within a given nation-state and the structural tendency of monopoly capital to develop on a world-wide, essentially transnational scale."[44] In other words, the formal qualities of *Tarr* point to the fact that life in England can no longer be rendered intelligible with the "raw materials" of English life alone; narrative resources must be sought elsewhere, and what lies "outside" England is for Lewis (objectively and structurally) a system of nation-states (and their attendant national cultures): "the lived experience of the British situation is domestic, while its structural intelligibility is international."[45]

It is striking that the words that Jameson uses to describe the "problem" to which Lewis's national allegory is a solution are almost exactly those that he uses to later describe modernism's characteristic spatiality.[46] Jameson suggests that "space" is a formal symptom of modernist texts *in general*, because they, too, encounter the representational crisis exemplified in Lewis's *Tarr*: the need to make sense of life in a "metropolis" whose immanent logic—that of imperialism—lies beyond its national borders. Just as in his discussion of *Tarr*, the emphasis is on form, even if in his discussion in "Modernism and Imperialism" of the mediated forms of imperial space in E. M. Forster's *Howard's End*, the term "national allegory" is never used. It is significant that the reemergence in the third world of what was described as an "outmoded" category by the time of the Soviet revolution, national allegory in "Third-World Literature" is no longer conceptualized in terms of the work of form on specific "aesthetic dilemmas," nor in terms of a "representational crisis" that involves and invokes the bounded space of the nation. Instead, national allegory names the condition of possibility of narration itself in the third world. It names it, further, as a *positive* condition, one in which there remains a link, however threatened, tenuous, and political, between the production of narrative and the political. It is this connection that in the first world has been shattered so completely that third-world texts appear "alien to us at first approach."[47]

What I think this suggests is that the nation *has* disappeared from third-world national allegories. In "Third-World Literature," what Jameson describes as "national allegory" could just as easily have been called "political allegory": the "nation" seems to serve little purpose here, and can only inhibit analyzes of third-world literary texts insofar as it seems to point to the nation as the (natural) space of the political in the third world. So again, why *national* allegory? It does not have to do with the historical reemergence of the international system of nation-states—or of the emergence of a new form of this system, which we might too hastily identify as globalization—that formed the "structural and semantic givens" for Lewis at the beginning of this century. Nor does it seem to me that third-world literary texts face the representational problems of modernism: in the third world, lived reality is *never* seen as intelligible only in terms of the "national" situation, and so there is correspondingly no aesthetic or formal necessity to grapple with what amounts to the "absent cause" of lived experience. In the third world, it is always clear that the "cause" of the local situation owes as much to experiences beyond it as those that take place in local (sometimes national) space. It is possible that Jameson's use of the 'national' in his exploration of third-world literature is simply a regrettable error. But it seems to me that the "nation" means something else entirely, something different from simply the empirical community or collectivity for which the cultural revolution is undertaken. Jameson's evocation of the nation in his discussion of third-world literature should be taken instead as a reference to a reified "cultural pattern" that "having once been part of the solution to a dilemma, then become[s] part of the new problem."[48]

Instead of seeing nationalist literature as a "vital response to infrastructural realities"—which I would not deny that it also clearly is—the evocation of the nation in the production of third world literature must also, or perhaps even primarily, be read in terms of what Jameson describes in one of the long quotations cited earlier as a reified "cultural pattern" that "having once been part of the solution to a dilemma, then become[s] part of the new problem." The "nation" is the name for a discursive, epistemological problematic as much as it the name for some collectivity; it names the problem of attempting to speak to and on behalf of this collectivity. This is especially the case for literature that is *explicitly* nationalist, literature, in other words, in which one aspect of the allegorical has been rendered literal—-not just "conscious and overt" in comparison to the "unconscious" allegories of first-world cultural texts, but *conscious of this consciousness.* Which means that a new proposition should be placed alongside Jameson's understanding of national allegory: *nationalist literature is always an allegory of the embattled situation of the third-world intellectual with respect to his or her culture and society.*

It is largely because Jameson sees the nation as a reified "cultural pattern" that "having once been part of the solution to a dilemma, then become[s] part of the new problem" that it figures prominently in his recent explorations of globalization. For even though it might now seem as if postcolonial literature circulates within a very different set of sociohistorical coordinates than the one that Jameson outlines in "Third-World Literature," the nation remains an ineliminable structural presence within the contemporary "cultural pattern": the nation is not something that we can get beyond, at least not at the present moment. Far from rendering the concept of national allegory useless with respect to postcolonial texts, globalization makes it an increasingly important interpretive mode or problematic. But here, too, problems arise unless we understand precisely what Jameson means by the nation and how, in turn, he imagines its relationship to globalization.

The nation has been one of the main sites of struggle in the attempt to understand and conceptualize globalization—whether globalization is understood as the name for a set of real, empirical processes that characterize variously the cultural, social, and economic dimensions of contemporary capitalism, or as the name for a number of competing narratives about the evolving shape of the contemporary political landscape and of the character of any future polity.[49] It has been frequently suggested that globalization has rendered the nation-state irrelevant, because (for instance) the nation no longer seems to retain any juridical power or control over capital or labour, both of which cross borders and evade state surveillance with increasing ease (though far more so in the case of capital and its associated modes of credit, finance, etc., than in the case of the physical bodies of individual laborers). Then, there is the (more or less) antithetical position, which holds that the decline of the nation and nation-state has been much exaggerated. Not only are most companies "tethered to their home economies and . . . likely to remain so," but the new forms of sovereignty represented by international regulatory mechanisms such as the General Agreement on Tariffs and Trade and the North American Free Trade Agreement, have been established by nation-states, just as it is supposed powerless nations that have ensured the compliance of national markets with a reconstituted global economy.[50] More recently, commentators have wanted to suggest that neither of these two poles adequately makes sense of the complex, heterogeneous position of the nation-state within globalization. This is, in part, as Jean and John Comaroff point out, because "there is no such thing, save at very high levels of abstraction, as '*the* nation-state'": in many polities, neither the "nation" nor the "state" exists as such, while in other places, there exists a deep fissure between state and government that makes it impossible to speak of anything that approaches typical ideas about what a functioning nation-state looks like.[51] Put differently, "the processes by which millennial capitalism is taking shape do not reduce to a simple narrative according to which the nation-state either lives or dies, ebbs or flourishes. Its impact is much more complicated, more polyphonous and dispersed, and most immediately felt in the everyday contexts of work and labor, of domesticity and consumption, of street life and media-gazing."[52]

Whether it has died or still lives, the nation-state has long been the supreme example of the modern political project of creating citizen-subjects defined through their attachment to specifically national identities. Connected to this project (which is easy to be suspicious of) is a whole history of left political engagement that has made effective use (or so the story goes) of the historical compromise between capital and labor that the nation has also represented, in order to bring about the social gains associated with left activism

over the past one hundred and fifty years or so. Whether or not the powers of
the nation-state have declined over the past several decades, the nation as such
is thus frequently evoked or imagined as the only possible site of progressive
politics and as thus something that should be fought for in order to maintain
or preserve the political project of the left.[53] This desire for the possibilities
(incorrectly) associated with the nation-state cannot help being confused with
more empirical analyses of its function within globalization, which is perhaps
why the defense of the nation continues to be associated with a left that in the
past sought to distance itself from nationalism.[54] Against this position,
Michael Hardt and Antonio Negri have strongly asserted that "it is a grave
mistake to harbor any nostalgia for the powers of the nation-state or to resur-
rect any politics that celebrates the nation."[55] For them, the relative decline of
the sovereignty of the nation-state is the result of an historical, structural
process—the globalization of production and circulation, backed up by those
supraterritorial agreements that have incurred the wrath of antiglobalization
protestors—and is not "simply the result of an ideological position that might
be reversed by an act of political will."[56] They also point out that "even if the
nation were still to be an effective weapon, the nation carries with it a whole
series of repressive structures and ideologies" of which a properly left politics
should be appropriately wary.[57] Too simple an insistence on the political or
conceptual necessity of the nation or of the nation-state needs to be treated
with proper caution, or needs to be seen as a potentially debilitating form of
nostalgia for political possibilities that no longer exist.

If these preliminary comments have of late become somewhat unneces-
sary, it is because the scholarly debate over the fate of the nation-state in globalization "has become something of a cliché."[58] But I make them here anyway
because in the absence of such ground-clearing or stage-setting, it is possible
to mistake Jameson's recent interest in the nation as little more than nostalgia
for a form of modern politics (a politics that believes in the citizen rather than
the consumer) in very much the way that critics have taken his interest in the
third (or, indeed, in the second) world as a search for a genuine Other to a capitalism that in and of itself "has no social goals."[59] A cursory reading of either
of Jameson's most explicit attempts to theorize globalization does little to
dispel this impression. In "Notes on Globalization as a Philosophical Issue," he
laments the "tendential extinction of new national cultural and artistic production" that appear to be the consequence of the domination of the global
cultural industries by the United States and endorses state support of culture
in places like France and Canada.[60] He also makes the claim that in the first
world, the powers of the state "are what must be protected against the right-
wing attempts to dissolve it back into private businesses and operations of all
kinds," a point he reaffirms in "Globalization and Political Strategy," where he
states outright that "the nation-state today remains the only concrete terrain
and framework for political struggle," even though the struggle against

globalization "cannot be successfully prosecuted to a conclusion in completely national or nationalist terms."[61]

While this might seem to be an affirmation of the kind of view of the nation that Hardt and Negri warn against, in the context of Jameson's supple examination of the contradications and antinomies of globalization, a different reason for foregrounding the nation emerges that is of a piece with its presence in his discussion of third-world literature. In both of his recent articles on globalization, Jameson tries to gauge the significance of the global export of American mass culture (through its intersection with the economic, social, and technological) in order to understand what it might mean to try to oppose or to resist its spread around the world. This is, of course, an expression of the cultural imperialist thesis in a nutshell—an understanding of globalization that while still predominant in the cultural imaginary of academics and the general public alike, has been criticized as misunderstanding the contemporary operations of culture and power.[62] But while on the surface Jameson seems merely to express a Western academic's worries about the disappearance of traditional ways of life, the reappearance of the nation as a conceptual concern complicates our desire to see globalization as something to be either lamented or celebrated. For instance, what Jameson finds disturbing about the global triumph of American cinema is that it marks

> the death of the political, and an allegory of the end of the possibility of imagining radically different social alternatives to this one we now live under. For political film in the 60s and 70s still affirmed that possibility (as did modernism in general, in a more complex way), by affirming that the discovery of invention of a radically new form was at one with the discovery or invention of radically new social relations and ways of living in the world. It is those possibilities—filmic, formal, political, and social—that have disappeared as some more definitive hegemony of the United States has seemed to emerge.[63]

This demand for the persistence of other modes of national culture has little to do with the nation as such. It isn't the case, for example, that Jameson lauds French film because it is formally or thematically richer than American film, either due to its relationship to some purer national essence or because it is produced outside of the strict demands of the market as a result of state subsidies. Rather, in our present political and cultural circumstances, the nation names, for Jameson, the possibility of new social relations and forms of collectivity not just "other" to neoliberal globalization, but the possibility of imagining these kinds of relations at all. Such forms of collectivity are not to be found in some actual national space: "today no enclaves—aesthetic or other—are left in which the commodity form does not reign supreme."[64] Rather, the nation is now part of the new problem of contemporary cultural revolution, a part of the problematic of globalization than one cannot avoid even if one shares Hardt and Negri's suspicions about the politics of actually existing nation-states; it once again names a reified "cultural pattern," though with different valences and different connections to other concepts and problems than before.

The nation stands for three things in Jameson's recent reflections on globalization. It identifies, first, the possibility of other modes of social life that are organized in strikingly different ways than the American-led "culture-ideology of consumption." Other "national situations" offer models of different forms of collective and social life—not, it is important to add, in the form of "traditional" or "pre-lapsarian" modes of social being, but in the form of "rather recent and successful accommodations of the old institutions to modern technology."[65] Second, the nation is the name for a frankly utopic space that designates "whatever programmes and representations express, in however distorted or unconscious a fashion, the demands of a collective life to come, and identify social collectivity as the crucial centre of any truly progressive and innovative political response to globalization."[66] These words at the end of "Globalization and Political Strategy" are actually meant to define the word "utopian" rather than the nation. The link between the two terms is made possible in a note that appears a few pages earlier, in which Jameson claims that "the words 'nationalism' and 'nationalist' have always been ambiguous, misleading, perhaps even dangerous. The positive or 'good' nationalism I have in mind involves what Henri Lefebvre liked to call 'the great collective project,' and takes the form of the attempt to construct a nation."[67]

Finally, Jameson discusses the nation not to settle the case either for or against globalization—rejecting, for instance, the false unversality of the "American way of life" in favor of one of so many other (rapidly evaporating) national models, which themselves have never yet yielded positive social alternatives—"but rather to intensify their incompatibility and opposition such that we can live this particular contradiction as our own historic form of Hegel's unhappy consciousness."[68] If "Globalization and Political Strategy" ends with a discussion of utopia, "Notes on Globalization" ends with a discussion of the necessity of the dialectic, and of the Hegelian dialectic in particular. The aim of the dialectic is to understand phenomena in order, finally, to locate the contradictions behind them: in Hegel's *Logic*, the discovery of the Identity of identity and nonidentity reveals Opposition as Contradiction. But this is not the final moment: "Contradiction then passes over into its Ground, into what I would call the situation itself, the aerial view or the map of the totality in which things happen and History takes place."[69] Such a map of the moment when the nation is thought to have been superceded once and for all can only be produced if the nation, the Ground of an earlier moment, is put into play in the dialectic rather than suspended from the outset.

And here we find that we have looped back around to Jameson's discussion of the ineliminable horizon of those objective "cultural patterns" that third-world writers have to confront just as much as first-world critics. Which is a long way of saying that, far from obliterating the Marxian problematic, especially with respect to the contemporary use and abuse of culture, globalization makes it more important than ever.

NOTES

I want to thank Nicholas Brown, Caren Irr, and Susie O'Brien for their helpful comments on an earlier version of this chapter. Portions of this essay were written with the assistance of a postdoctoral fellowship from the Social Sciences and Humanities Research Council of Canada.

1. Fredric Jameson, "Third-World Literature in the Era of Multinational Capitalism," *Social Text* 15 (1986): 69.

2. Aijaz Ahmad, *In Theory: Class, Nations, Literatures* (New York: Verso, 1992), 95–122.

3. Though there has been a good deal of criticism of Jameson's reading of third-world literature, he has also drawn support for his attempt to offer an abstract, general model of literary production in the colonial and postcolonial world. Jean Franco has suggested that Jameson's generalizations are useful because they "provoke us to think of exceptions." With respect to contemporary cultural production in India, Geeta Kapur writes that "Jameson's formulation about the national allegory being the pre-eminent paradigm for Third World literature continues to be valid . . . the allegorical breaks up the paradigmatic notion of the cause . . . it questions the immanent condition of culture taken as some irrepressible truth offering." Michael Sprinker has misgivings about some of Jameson's claims, but finds nevertheless that he puts forward a "provocative hypothesis" that needs to be carefully considered: "Is it not possible, as Jameson here maintains, that certain forms of collective life have until now persisted more powerfully outside the metropolitan countries? And if this be so, of what value are these, perhaps residual but still vital forms of social practice?" Jean Franco, "The Nation as Imagined Community," *Dangerous Liasons: Gender, Nations, and Postcolonial Perspectives*, ed. Anne McClintock, Aamir Mufti, and Ella Shohat (Minneapolis: University of Minnesota Press, 1997), 131; Geeta Kapur, "Globalisation and Culture," *Third Text* 39 (1997): 24–25; and Michael Sprinker, "The National Question: Said, Ahmad, Jameson," *Public Culture* 6 (1993): 7–8.

4. It is important to recognize just how foreshortened the history of postcolonial studies is within academic discourse. For instance, two of the formative essays in the field, Spivak's "Can the Subaltern Speak? Speculations on Widow Sacrifice" and Bhahba's "Signs Taken for Wonders" were published in 1985. Jameson's essay is roughly contemporaneous with these essays and should be taken as an attempt to situate Marxist criticism within the general problematic being developed within postcolonial studies at the time. See Gayatri Chakravorty Spivak, "Can the Subaltern Speak? Speculations on Widow Sacrifice," *Wedge* 7/8 (1985): 120–30; and Homi Bhahba, "Signs Taken for Wonders," *Critical Inquiry* 12, no. 1 (1985): 144–65.

5. All uses of the terms "first world" and "third world" should be understood, following Santiago Colás's suggestion, as being used *sous rature* so as to mark "both the inadequacy and the indispensability of the terms and the system of geo-political designations to which they belong." Santiago Colás, "The Third World in Jameson's Postmodernism or the Cultural Logic of Late Capitalism," *Social Text* 31–32 (1992): 259.

6. Kalpana Seshadri-Crooks, "At the Margins of Postcolonial Studies: Part 1," *The Pre-Occupation of Postcolonial Studies*, ed. Fawzia Afzal-Khan and Kalpana Seshadri-Crooks (Durham, NC: Duke University Press, 2000), 19.

7. This is essentially the critique that Spivak makes of Jameson's theory of the postmodern in her *A Critique of Postcolonial Reason* (Cambridge: Harvard University Press, 1999), 312–37. See also Dipesh Chakrabarty's challenge to the "politics of historicism" in *Provincializing Europe: Postcolonial Thought and Historical Difference* (Princeton: Princeton University Press, 2000).

8. Jameson, *Postmodernism, or, the Cultural Logic of Late Capitalism* (Durham, NC: Duke University Press, 1991), 5.

9. For example, Philip Darby has pointed to the failure of postcolonial theory to engage with international relations theory. Darby, *The Fiction of Imperialism: Reading Between International Relations and Postcolonialism* (London: Cassell, 1998). Chakrabarty's analysis of the politics of historicism, including those historicisms such as Ernst Mandel and Jameson's that remain indebted to Marx's placement of capitalism at the leading edge of historical time, foregrounds the theoretical problems that arise in attempts to think a global totality. While he is right to criticize Eurocentrism of historicism, the difficulty of developing a different model of history that doesn't reduce it to "sheer heterogeneity" can be seen in his unproductive attempt to develop an alternative model of historicity that enables one to "think about the past and the future in a nontotalizing manner" only by passing through the ontological dead zone of Heidegger's thought. Chakrabarty, *Provincializing Europe*, 249.

10. Michael Hardt and Antonio Negri, "Totality," "'Subterranean Passages of Thought': Empire's Inserts," *Cultural Studies* 16, no. 2 (2002): 193–212.

11. "Every individual interpretation must include an interpretation of its own existence, must show its own credentials and justify itself: every commentary must be at the same time a metacommentary." Jameson, "Metacommentary," *PMLA* 86 (1971): 10.

12. Jameson writes that "this whole talk aims implicitly at suggesting a new conception of the humanities in American education today." "Third-World Literature," 75. In his response to Ahmad's criticisms, Jameson states at the outset that "the essay was intended as an intervention into a 'first-world' literary and critical situation, in which it seemed important to me to stress the loss of certain literary functions and intellectual commitments in the contemporary American scene." Jameson, "A Brief Response," *Social Text* 19 (1987), 26.

13. Jameson, "Third-World Literature," 69.

14. Ibid., 69.

15. This is one of Ahmad's major criticisms of Jameson. By utilizing the "Three Worlds Theory" as his primary interpretive matrix, Ahmad suggests that Jameson is unable to see that capitalism, socialism, and colonialism are all present within the third world. Colás also points out that there are "not only many 'Third Worlds' and many 'First Worlds'; but there are also 'Third Worlds' within the 'First World' and vice-versa." Colás, "Third World," 259. It is worth mentioning here Colás examination of the paradoxical function of the third world in Jameson's *Postmodernism: Or, the Logic of Late Capitalism*, which is more or less repeated in his essay on third-world literature: "It is both the space whose final elimination by the inexorable logic of late capitalist development consolidates the social moment—late capitalism—whose cultural dominant is postmodernism, and the space that remains somehow untainted by and oppositional to those repressive social processes which have homogenized te real and imaginative terrain of the 'First World' subject." Jameson, 258.

16. Jameson, "Third-World Literature," 69. This claim, which can be redescribed as the loss of any genuinely historical thinking in the postmodern period, is one of the repeated themes in Jameson's work.

17. Sprinker suggests that:

We may wish to inquire, are First World allegorical forms so utterly unconscious of their potential transcoding into political readings? Leaving aside the whole rich territory of contemporary science fiction, about which Jameson himself has taught us so much, what about so-called film noir? Surely Fritz Lang, Billy Wilder, and the other émigrés who pioneered this form understood perfectly well that they were making sociopolitically coded films. On the contemporary scene, there is the massive presence of Francis Ford Coppola, not to mention David Lynch, filmmakers whose affinities with the supposedly disreputable mode of social allegory Jameson has discussed with great insight.

It is probably possible to cite endless counterexamples in this way; and yet it is important to note that this is to have somehow missed Jameson's fundamental point entirely. Sprinker, "The National Question," 6.

18. Jameson, "Third-World Literature," 69.

19. Ibid., 73.

20. Ibid., 73.

21. Ibid., 85.

22. Ibid., 71.

23. Ibid., 70.

24. Recently Jameson has noted that "it is very easy to break up such traditional cultural systems, which extend to the way people live in their bodies and use language, as well as the way they treat each other and nature. Once destroyed, those fabrics can never be recreated. Some third-world nations are still in a situation in which that fabric is preserved." Jameson, "Notes on Globalization as a Philosophic Issue," *The Cultures of Globalization*, ed. Fredric Jameson and Masao Miyoshi (Durham, NC: Duke University Press, 1998), 63.

25. Johannes Fabian has described this "time lag" as "allochronism"—a denial to the "other" of any possible contemporaneity with the West. See Johannes Fabian, *Time and the Other: How Anthropology Makes Its Object* (New York: Columbia University Press, 1983). See also my discussion of allochronism in the Canadian context. Imre Szeman, "Belated or Isochronic?: Canadian Writing, Time and Globalization," *Essays on Canadian Writing* 71 (2000): 145–53.

26. Dipesh Chakrabarty's work has engaged directly with the need to simultaneously "think" and "unthink" modernity in the conceptualization of third-world histories and third-world politics. See Charabarty, *Provincializing Europe*, 2000, especially Chapter 1.

27. Jameson, "Third-World Literature," 72.

28. Consider, for instance, his discussion of the repressed spaces of empire in British modernism in Jameson, "Modernism and Imperialism," *Nationalism, Colonialism, and Literature*, ed. Terry Eagleton, Fredric Jameson, and Edward W. Said (Minneapolis: University of Minnesota Press, 1990), 43–66.

29. Jameson, "Third-World Literature," 72.

30. Ibid., 76.

31. Ibid., 76.

32. Ibid., 78.

33. Ibid., 78.

34. Julie McGonegal has shown how Jameson's mode of national-allegorical interpretation reveals narratives that reading strategies that focus on "manichean" allegories cannot. Part of her point is that critics of Jameson have confused his elaboration of an interpretative hermeneutic ("third world texts are . . . to be read as national allegories") with the thing itself (third world texts are national allegories, the nation still has significance in the third world, the third world is homogeneous, etc.), and in so doing have missed his metacritical emphasis on the way in which third-world texts necessarily appear to first-world readers as "already read." Julie McGonegal, "Post-Colonial Contradictions in Tsitsi Dangaremba's Nervous Condition: Toward a Reconsideration of Jameson's National Allegory," unpublished manuscript.

35. Raymond Willliams provides an account of the the historical development of the concept of literature in *Marxism and Literature* (Oxford: Oxford University Press, 1977).

36. I elaborate on this rather abstract formulation in *Zones of Instability: Literature, Postcolonialism and the Nation* (Baltimore: Johns Hopkins University Press, 2003).

37. This is intimated in the final footnote of "Third-World Literature": "What is here called 'national allegory' is clearly a form of just such a mapping of the totality, so that the present essay—which sketches a theory of the cognitive aesthetics of third-world literature—forms a pendant to the essay on postmodernism which describes the logic of cultural imperialism of the first world and above all of the United States." Jameson, "Third World Literature," 88n25.

38. Jameson, *Fables of Aggression* (Berkeley: University of California Press, 1979), 90.

39. Ibid., 90–91.

40. Ibid., 93.

41. Ibid., 94.

42. Ibid., 94.

43. Ibid., 94.

44. Ibid., 94.

45. Ibid., 95.

46. See Jameson, "Modernism and Imperialism," 51–64.

47. Jameson, "Third-World Literature," 69.

48. Ibid., 78.

49. For a perceptive taxonomy of the latter, see Michael Hardt, "Globalization and Democracy," McMaster University Institute for Globalization and the Human Condition Working Paper Series, May 13, 2001, <http://www.humanities.mcmaster.ca/~global/tableofcontents.html>.

50. Paul Hirst and Grahame Thompson, *Globalization in Question: The International Economy and the Possibilities of Governance* (Cambridge, UK: Cambridge University Press, 1996), 2.

51. Jean Comaroff and John L. Comaroff, "Millennial Capitalism: First Thoughts on a Second Coming," *Public Culture* 12, no.2 (2000): 325.

52. Ibid., 325. The complexities that exist here can be seen in the way in which globalization itself sometimes provides the basis for the reconstitution or concentration of national energies. Frederick Buell has suggested recently that in the United States globalization seems to be a form of "cultural nationalism for post-national circumstances." Buell, "Nationalist Postnationalism: Globalist Discourse in Contemporary American Culture," *American Quarterly* 50, no. 3 (1998): 550. R. Radhakrishnan makes a similar point when he suggests that "postnational developments are never at the expense of nationalist securities; if anything, they foundationalize nation-based verities and privileges to the point of invisibility." Radhakrishnan, "Postmodernism and the Rest of the World," *The Pre-Occupation of Postcolonial Studies*, ed. Fawzia Afzal-Khan and Kalpana Seshadri-Crooks (Durham: Duke University Press, 2000), 42.

53. See Timothy Brennan's "Cosmo-Theory," *South Atlantic Quarterly* 100, no. 3 (2001): 659–91.

54. See Rosa Luxemburg, *The National Question*, ed. Horace Davis (New York: Monthly Review Press, 1976). In Canada, for example, left nationalism represented by groups such as the Council of Canadians seems to have experienced a revival within the antiglobalization protest movement more generally.

55. Michael Hardt and Antonio Negri, *Empire* (Cambridge: Harvard University Press, 2000), 336.

56. Ibid., 336.

57. Ibid., 336.

58. Comaroff and Comaroff, 318. The same could be said for other attempts to fix the particular spaces in which globalization is played out, although the very best discussions of the function of regionalism in globalization or of the new role played by cities does contribute to our understanding of the "polyphonous and dispersed" impact of globalization. See, for example, Leo Ching, "Globalizing the Regional, Regionalizing the Global: Mass Culture and Asianism in the Age of Capital," *Public Culture* 12, no. 1 (2000): 233–57; Achille Mbembe, "At the Edge of the World: Boundaries, Territoriality, and Sovereignty in Africa," *Public Culture* 12, no. 1 (2000): 259–84; and Saskia Sassen, "Spatialities and Temporalities of the Global: Elements of a Theorization," *Public Culture* 12, no. 1 (2000): 215–32, among others.

59. Jameson, "Globalization and Political Strategy," *New Left Review* 4 (2000): 62.

60. Jameson, "Notes on Globalization," 61.

61. Jameson, "Notes on Globalization," 72; "Globalization and Political Strategy," 65, 66.

62. See especially John Tomlinson, *Cultural Imperialism* (Baltimore: Johns Hopkins University Press, 1991). For an ethnographic consideration of the limits of the cultural imperialist thesis, see James L. Watson, ed., *Golden Arches East: McDonald's in East Asia* (Stanford: Stanford University Press, 1997).

63. Jameson, "Notes on Globalization," 62.

64. Ibid., 70.

65. Ibid., 63.

66. Jameson, "Globalization and Political Strategy," 68.

67. Ibid., 64n11.

68. Jameson, "Notes on Globalization," 64.

69. Ibid., 76.

10

The American Grounds of Globalization

Jameson's Return to Hegel

Caren Irr

We have to understand, in this country, something that is difficult for us to realize: namely, that the United States is not just one country, or one culture, among others.
——"Notes on Globalization as a Philosophical Issue"

Who can produce a convincing theory of globalization? When Americans produce such theories, do they simply project changes in certain sectors of American society to the globe as a whole? If so, do such theories amount to an intellectual form of imperialism, duplicating the effects of American economic domination? Do theories that anticipate a unification or homogenization of global cultures in particular help to create the Americanization they describe? These are some of the questions that have been asked in recent years about efforts by American intellectuals to describe globalization. These questions imply an affirmative answer—suggesting that a necessary blindness to differences in national or cultural situations around the world will accompany any attempt by an American to hypothesize about global conditions. Often that blindness is thought to resemble the philosophical hubris and dialectical rigidity associated by many twentieth-century culture critics with G. W. F. Hegel. The sweeping universal ambition of Hegel's world-spirit has been the target of poststructuralists in particular, so any resemblance between Hegelian idealism and American intellectual or economic imperialism suggests to some that the same poststructuralist assault can and should be made on both targets. A theory of globalization that is American in origin and Hegelian in character, this line of reasoning goes, will celebrate the inevitable absorption of the rest of the world into a single entity and be blind to the paradoxes of its own position.

At least, this is the line of reasoning that has been adopted by some critics of Fredric Jameson's work. Beginning from Jameson's quite evident and consistent use of a Hegelian framework throughout his career, they move toward the assertion that his account of global conditions is unacceptably and too specifically American. These charges often focus on his accounts of postmodernism and Third-World literature, but are made about the emerging theory of globalization one can trace in his work as well.

Readily apparent in anti-Marxist reviews of Jameson's work, this tendency is also and perhaps more surprisingly evident among his more sympathetic critics.[1] For instance, before revising his reading of Jameson's politics of history in his contribution to this volume, in his monograph on Jameson, Sean Homer described Jameson's particular version of the Hegelian dialectic as imprecise and insufficiently attentive to concrete historical circumstances, and he asserts that these effects "can be seen as a consequence of [Jameson's] position as a Marxist within the US and more specifically as an academic Marxist."[2] Further, Homer charged Jameson with generalizing from the American experience of late capitalism to produce the concept of the mode of production at play in *The Political Unconscious* and later in his work on postmodernism and space. Homer read Jameson's work as insufficiently dialectical at the conceptual level and excessively dialectical at the stylistic level, attributing both lack and excess to the pessimism and isolation of American intellectuals.

Although somewhat less pointedly, in *The Jamesonian Unconscious*, Clint Burnham also highlights the Hegelian themes in Jameson's work and reads these against a Deleuzian and Canadian frame of reference that emphasizes dialectical and American elements of Jameson's writing.[3] Similarly, in *The Success and Failure of Fredric Jameson*, Steven Helmling describes a super-Hegelian "full-court press" in some of Jameson's late essays and depicts these as a regression to his earliest themes. This follows Helming's crucial opening assertion that, having written on Sartre, "Jameson was perhaps better positioned than almost anyone in America to respond knowledgeably and critically to the arrival here of that intellectual ferment usually subsumed under the rubric of 'theory.'"[4] Ultimately, it is Jameson's Hegelian reaction to his American situation that determines the shape of his work for Helmling, Burnham, and Homer, as well as host of other reviewers and critics.

Even in the milder, sympathetic forms cited here, however, these criticisms make two critical errors. First, they grant an undeserved universality to the poststructuralist attack on Hegel. The French poststructuralists who have been so influential in recent years were attacking a specific interpretation of Hegel—one made available in Alexandre Kojève's exceptionally influential lectures on the *Phenomenology of Spirit* in the 1930s and often standing in place of a criticism of the French Communist Party. Arguably, their own assault, however, derives from an alternate tradition of interpreting Hegel and is, thus, less absolute than it might sound.[5] Be this as it may, of the several versions of Hegel available in the mid-twentieth century, however, Kojève's is not the interpretation that motivates Jameson's work. As I will demonstrate, Jameson's work draws repeatedly from Hegel's *Logic*. In particular, Jameson has made especially rigorous and interesting use of Hegel's concept of *Grund*. His emphasis on and interpretation of this element of Hegel's system derives more from Theodor Adorno's negative dialectics than from Kojève's anthropological approach. Thus, a criticism on Jameson's Hegelianism that treats it as yet another version of Kojève (and thus of French Stalinism) misses the mark in terms of intellectual genealogy and political implication.

Critics who assume that any use of Hegel produces a necessarily American limit to a theory of global conditions also make a second mistake. By treating national culture almost exclusively as a cause, they grant a permanence and solidity to one of the concepts that needs most investigation in the context of globalization. In Jameson's work, by contrast, we find a recurring treatment of national culture—especially American culture—as a dialectical ground, not as a cause in the Newtonian or simple mechanical fashion. Even in informal interviews, Jameson repeatedly demonstrates how "America" as a concept is, as ground, both a cause and an effect of larger dynamics. He is characteristically ambivalent about his own national situation: "I guess I am anti-american enough, too, to wish for a little more dialectical self-consciousness about the project [of Cultural Studies], a little more positioning of ourselves in the specificities of our situation," he remarked in a 1998 interview.[6] Or, later: "Because I work here, I certainly try to have a pedagogy that addresses the United States. The notion of postmodernity emerges from my experience as an American, and I am an American. But on the other hand, part of my intellectual formation is elsewhere."[7] Recognizing the way in which one's national situation can serve as a concrete limit or frame for the production of concepts, Jameson pairs that recognition with a dialectically apt turn toward the free travel of intellectual life out of that national moment, so that thinking might return in its critical —or here "anti-American"—guise. Once we notice the regularity and centrality of this particular sequence of dialectical reflections in Jameson's work, it seems mistaken at best to treat his Hegelianism as a thoughtless reproduction of American imperial power in the sphere of the concept.

After all, this habit of reflecting on the American conditions of his own thinking is not limited to Jameson's informal remarks. From some of his earliest position statements to some of his recent writing on patriotic feeling in response to the September 11 attacks on New York City's World Trade Center, Jameson reflects on his American situation and its importance for his thinking. In a special sense that we will explore, America is his *Grund*, and we repeatedly find in his work materials for a not-yet-assembled theory of Americanization as an aspect of globalization. On Jameson's account, in a quite properly dialectical spirit, both Americanism and anti-Americanism reveal their Utopian qualities. Critics who charge him with displaying an unreflective American bias have misunderstood his use of the concept of national culture and have failed to read closely and consistently. This results in a missed opportunity for improving our understanding of the controversial role of "America" in globalization.

To correct for these two crucial errors, this essay traces Jameson's use of Hegel together with his scattered remarks on American conditions. In addition to explicating these essential themes of Jameson's career, I also hope to use his work to demonstrate how the problem of theorizing globalization might move past its current stalemate. One important lesson we can learn from Jameson's work is that any account of globalization must and likely will—whether it recognizes itself as doing so or not—include a theory of Americanization. By illustrating, first, how Jameson develops a version of Hegel suitable for an American Marxism and along the way briefly sketching how his concept of a Utopian America develops, this essay will, I hope, contribute to a more supple and internationally useful theory of the present named by the unwieldy concept of globalization.

HEGEL'S GROUND

It is in Hegel's *Logic* that we find his most developed version of the dialectic and consequently his most influential articulation of the concept of the ground (*Grund*).[8] As I will argue, this concept is the key to Jameson's emerging picture of Americanization and globalization, and it has been a primary hallmark of his utopian and materialist interpretation of the Hegelian dialectic throughout his career. Because of its centrality to the dialectic, the concept of the ground has also been addressed in many readings influenced by Heidegger and Derrida, but I will not be addressing those here, preferring to emphasize the vein of interpretation more centrally relevant for Jameson, the Marxist vein.

In the *Logic*, the ground is the location of a utopian negation that reveals freedom at work in the heart of necessity. This freedom is not, as so often in Lockean-influenced American liberalism, a freedom exercised in the subject's choice of perspective on a problem. Rather, this is a freedom evident in a situation of concrete liberation. That is, it is a collective and social freedom embedded immanently in the situation, not a voluntaristic and idealist freedom.

Hegel's account of the ground moves toward these explicitly political themes in part because it is positioned in a crucial place at the core of the second of the three major movements of the *Logic*. While the first book of the *Logic* deals with the objective logic of Being and the last with the subjective logic of the Notion (culminating in the Absolute), the second book—on essence—is the hinge between these two movements. In the second book, the objective logic of Being flowers into the Absolute Subject by moving through a phase of rigorous reflection. The book pairs the thinking subject's entanglement in illusion and subsequent discovery of the essentials of thought with accounts of the object's appearance and ultimate actuality. Within this arrangement, the subject's recognition of the essentials of thought provides the transition to thinking the object. Among the essentials of thought are the principles of identity and difference, resolved in and by the ground.

That is, Hegel's definition of ground is that it is the "unity of identity and difference," where the latter are understood as elements of thinking.[9] Identity meets difference at the site where both identity and difference discover themselves the determinate effects of a particular ground—that is, in the totality. Because this definition sounds so much like an assertion of the identity of identity and difference, Hegel is quick to state it as well in the opposite manner (that taken up, famously, by Adorno): ground is also the difference of identity and difference. The ground does not necessarily (or only?) provide a commonality between identity and difference, however; it also differentiates identity and difference by requiring a turn, a shift away from, say, the observable phenomena to their conditions. Hegel has another way of saying this: the ground is where condition and consequence meet, providing both the possibility of causal explanation in the identitarian sense and complicating causality with the resultant problem of what if anything provides the unity of condition and consequence.

In other words, from the definition of ground as something similar to Marx's concept of production (the invisible abstract relations of production in particular), we move rapidly to a few problems with the concept of the ground—problems akin to determining the relation between production as a base and culture as a superstructure. Especially, Hegel warns his readers in a prophetic paragraph, when the grip of traditional notions of external and hierarchical causality have been broken, the door to sophistry is opened: "the ground, as we have seen, has no essential and objective principle of its own, and it is as easy to discover grounds for what is wrong and immoral as for what is moral and right. . . . Sophistry by this destructive action deservedly brought upon itself the bad name previously mentioned."[10] With sufficient skill in reasoning and an adequate imagination, any condition may come to seem the ground for another. In the absence of all a single cause, of culture may appear holographically conditional for the rest, and thus the concept of the ground loses any utility—certainly any explanatory capacity. For Hegel, however, this situation does not corrupt the concept of the ground; it just reveals its innate potential for drift toward an uninteresting endless immanence. He proposes that a fix is possible not through the subject's voluntaristic choice of another method or concept, but rather in the objects themselves. Even as a drift toward bad infinity is a feature of the endless mutable variety of the world of which we are such a restless part, for Hegel it is also in the structure of that world that we find the resolution to this problem.

When the ground is totally universalized as an endless flux or a bad infinity, we ought not, however, simply turn to weighty judgments, reviving traditional certainties. For Hegel, that return simply defers the problem because it ultimately revives the subject's need to investigate the conditions for his own judgment. An appeal to convention or authority results in a *mise-en-abime* of self-conscious reflection on the impossibility of the isolated human subject serving as ground.

Instead, Hegel moves toward what he calls a good absolute, and his image for this situation is porosity. In section 130, borrowing from physics, he presents the image of a porous substance (say, a stone) as the image for a reconciliation between the condition and its consequence:

> Each of the several matters (coloured matter, odorific matter, and if we believe some people, even sound-matter-not excluding caloric, electric matter, etc.) is also negated: and in this negation of theirs, or as interpenetrating their pores, we find the numerous other independent matters, which, being similarly porous, make room in turn for the existence of the rest. Pores are not empirical facts; they are figments of the understanding, which uses them to represent the element of negation in independent matters. The further working-out of the contradictions is concealed by the nebulous imbroglio in which all matters are independent and all no less negated in each other. If the faculties or activities are similarly hypostatized in the mind, their living unity similarly turns to the imbroglio of an action of the one on the others.
>
> These pores . . . cannot be verified by observation. In the same way matter itself—furthermore form which is separated from matter—whether that be the thing as consisting of matters, or the view that the thing itself subsists and only has proper ties, is all a product of the reflective understanding which, while it observes and professes to record only what it observes, is rather creating a metaphysic, bristling with contradictions of which it is unconscious.[11]

In this complex passage, it is not the image of absence and presence co-existing through sequential or spatial alternation that Hegel is after, but rather the richer sense of difference reconciled with identity that is figured in the simultaneity of qualities available to all the senses. The stone in a sense is the ground for the simultaneous weight and granitey particularity and polished surface and so on. It is the logical co-terminousness of these entirely disparate qualities in a single entity that constitutes what Hegel is calling porosity. It is in this sense that the ground requires both negation and totality within reflection. The polished surface is not the negation of granite particulates in the sense that where there is polish there cannot be particulates. (Quite the opposite, actually.) The polished surface is the negation of the particulates in the sense that consideration of one logically excludes the other within any particular moment, yet both are parts of the same whole and necessarily interdependent and, in fact, deeply identical. This porous ground is, for Hegel, everywhere in the structure of all objects (not just the physical ones). It is because all objects exhibit this necessarily multisensory porosity that the subject experiences a negative freedom, the freedom perhaps most simply conveyed if one continues to imagine the shifts of perception involved in recognizing the various qualities of this porous object. In this sense, then the ground is the hinge concept between necessity and freedom, as well as between the positive and negative work of the concept.

For this reason, it is not surprising that Hegel's ground has been of special interest to Marxists. Shifting terms from the overly personified dialectic of master and slave, the dialectic of the ground finds room for utopian intellectual labor without resorting to a moralistic finger-pointing ("You are the master!" "No, *you* are!"). It is also with the ground, as mentioned earlier, that we find Hegel coming closest to one of the great philosophical paeans to intellectual work—Spinoza's concept of *amor Dei intellectus*. Recognizing that, despite being the source of freedom, necessity seems a hard and cold truth, Hegel describes in his beautiful note to section 158 an inward movement in which freedom appears initially as mere renunciation and loss but later appears in a transfigured form as concrete and positive. Discovering the law of determination within oneself is the precondition for Hegel of freedom: "In short, man is most independent when he knows himself to be determined by the absolute idea throughout."[12] Although this assertion that necessity is the ground of freedom (and thus the ground is identical with a freedom of the negative) could be treated as a resolution to problems in ethics, we can also see here a path by which vulgar materialism transcends itself and moves toward Utopia. It is in this sense that the Hegelian Marxism articulated by Adorno and expanded on by Jameson hovers at the edge between Books Two and Three of the *Logic*. Their treatments are primarily concerned with the contradictory experience of objects in their appearance and actuality, and they make only brief speculative forays into the Utopian terrain of the Absolute.

ADORNO'S HEGEL

Although the Frankfurt school reading of Hegel is itself often narrated as a return to Hegel within the narrative of Marxism, we might also describe their analyses as Marxist or materialist interventions into the idealist tradition, especially the tradition of reading Hegel. Since Adorno in particular sees twentieth-century materialisms as premature or unearned rejections of idealism—so premature that they rapidly restore the errors of idealism—the dominant thread of twentieth-century philosophy would be, on this account, idealist and Hegelian.

At least, this is one of the starting points for the lectures on Hegel that Adorno published shortly before his own masterful and messy reinterpretation of the dialectical tradition in *Negative Dialectics*. In *Hegel: Three Studies*, Adorno rescues a Hegel behind whom most of contemporary thought has regressed.[13] Adorno's is a Hegel of critique and negation, a Hegel whose restlessly mobile dialectic moves out to confront its own consequences, as well as circling back to reflect on its logical and social conditions. Adorno situates contemporaneous ontological and existential readings of Hegel as necessary errors, reproducing components of social development, such as the emptiness of the commodity form and the drive toward total systematization and rationalization. Against these readings, Adorno offers a possible Hegel, one whose truth is recovered from the very heart of untruth; most impressively, Adorno goes directly to the heart of Hegel's untruth—which, for him, is not simply the metaphysical assertion of ultimate reconciliation and unity, but rather the even stronger claim (in *The Philosophy of Right*) that what is real is rational. Seizing a moment of truth from the obviously reactionary drive of Hegel's explicit claim, Adorno dialectically shifts the levels of analysis, taking this untruth as an assertion of the freedom of reason. Precisely by falsely glorying in the rationality of the real, Adorno asserts, Hegel's dialectic demonstrates reason's drive to exceed what is. For Adorno, who reads the moments of unity and reconciliation—the assertions of a whole truth—in the Hegelian dialectic as projections of a utopian condition, the freedom of reason points toward a possible utopian prospect on the other side of necessity.

That is, for Adorno (who seems most compelled by the Hegel of the *Phenomenology*), dialectical process is truth, and it is necessary when reading Hegel to stay with, to hover near, idealism and not leap hastily to a reified position or conclusion. Immanent critique thus requires the labored exertion of the subject-object dialectic; in the process of reflection, the subject of thinking can neither rest too comfortably within the false immediacy of sense-perception or run off too rapidly toward the unreasoned concept. Rather, according to Adorno, the subject learns from Hegel's example as well as from the process of reason itself to transform the dry coldness of bourgeois efficiency into self-divestiture or spontaneous receptivity in the face of the object. The dialectical process has its own temporality of hovering and waiting punctuated by flashes and rapid reversals and shifts of level that reveal the whole in its false/true aspect. For Adorno, it is especially the labor of disciplining the self to tarry with the negative that registers the social ground of Hegel's dialectic; thus, it is this labor that he locates as the spinal cord of the dialectic. Adorno "rescues" Hegel to produce materialist philosophy from its idealist ground without digressing into a reification of method (a la Soviet Dialectical Materialism) or a rejection of method as hostile to the immediate and purportedly subjectless world of facts (a.k.a. American-style empiricism). For Adorno, Hegel is the mark of a kind of utopian discourse of the third way arrived at by means of a negative and socially grounded critique of philosophical extremes.

Although Adorno's most explicit and philosophically ambitious antagonists in this discussion are clearly Heidegger and Sartre, his readings are also in effect positioned against the previous generation's readings, those of Kojève and Hyppolite, the two major French interpreters of Hegel, especially important for their influence on poststructuralist critiques of idealism.[14] In his *Introduction to the Reading of Hegel*, Kojève produced a famous reading of the *Phenomenology* in terms of the master/slave dialectic and the battle to the death for recognition.[15] This account of the dialectic has the virtue of intensifying the social themes of Hegel's philosophy and treating the theme of self-consciousness in its collective form. The openness to a materialist interpretation that is thereby won carries with it as its risk, however, a certain flattening out in the *Darstellung* or writerly presentation of Kojève's text. The transcription of lectures delivered in the mid 1930s, Kojève's *Introduction to the Reading of Hegel* proceeds pedagogically from conclusions—for example, "Man is Self-Consciousness," the work's first sentence—through detailed summary and textual analysis. His fundamental project is to extract and reproduce central themes of the *Phenomenology* and, presumably, to foreground useful interpretations, such as the atheistic and historical Hegel. In contrast to Adorno's *Darstellung*, insistent as it is on the dialectical sentence, we find with Kojève a different kind of labor required—a labor more mathematical in character, having to do with the manipulation of fixed concept-signs rather than, as in Adorno's case, with the more evocatively linguistic or musical conception of the artistic whole. Although consonant with Adorno's reading in terms of its emphasis on the social ground of consciousness, Kojève's *Introduction* differs from it (and from Jameson's development of the dialectic as well) in locating the labor of the concept in its production and resisting a textual presentation of the concept's difficult emergence.

In Jameson's increasingly stylized oeuvre, Adorno's Hegel appears throughout. Particularly Adornian is Jameson's understanding of the dialectic as an immanent and negative project circulating around contradictions that ultimately reveal their social grounds. Also, throughout his career, Jameson has been interested in displacing both moments of present reconciliation and primordial unity. As outlined later, reconciliation or the absolute appears for Jameson, as for Adorno, only on the horizon of a utopian temporality, and the primary unity of the Real is, for Jameson, not only historical but also something only obliquely and temporarily approached.[16] However attractive Kojève's reading of the dialectic in terms of its social subjects, then, for Jameson, it is Adorno's emphasis on the dialectical movement of thought as already social that is most influential.

At the same, time, however, Jameson adapts Adorno's practices to new debates and situations, and these adaptations have their effects on his presentation of Hegelian themes. In comparison to Adorno, Jameson's tone is often considerably more topical and light-hearted, as well as more insistently humane. Where Adorno zooms in on the satanic features of a modern rationality that led to the concentration camps, Jameson focuses instead on continual human immiseration and waste, locating the untruth of the present not in its most horrific instances but rather in its systematic and everyday impoverishment of human life across the board. Approaching not Adorno's mid-century Europe of postwar devastation but rather late twentieth-century American consumer capitalism, awash in sensation and a history-less empiricism, Jameson supplements Adorno's immanent critique with the project of transcoding or metacommentary. Starting positively from one of Adorno's later bugbears, Sartrean existentialism, Jameson retools Adorno's Hegel for late capitalism. In particular, Adorno's emphasis on non-identity and the negative determination of the dialectic becomes, for Jameson, not only a necessary starting point but also a moment beyond which he must pass to move toward the ground of the identity/non-identity contradiction.

In the process, Adorno's preference for the young Hegel of the *Phenomenology* (as against the more explicitly conservative Hegel of *Philosophy of Right*) shifts in Jameson's career to date to an emphasis on the later Hegel of the *Logic*. From his early essays (collected in *Ideologies of Theory*) as well as in *Marxism and Form*, Jameson certainly addresses Adorno's preoccupation with the decay of experience and the necessity for recovering a self-conscious Hegelian subject, but the question of the social ground always supersedes this theme. Similarly, in *The Political Unconscious*, we find that Jameson's complex treatment of the question of causality involves in a considerably broader sublation of the question, especially in the critique of Althusserian and Spinozan tendencies. Then, in *Postmodernism, or the Cultural Logic of Late Capitalism*, the concepts of "logic" and "ground" appear in full flower, precisely where the issue of identity/difference gives way to the dicey issue of what, if anything, constitutes the condition of possibility of a cultural preoccupation with the aesthetics of difference. And, finally, in his shorter recent writings on globalization and *A Singular Modernity*, we find another return to the concept of the ground as Jameson works through various ideologies of modernity as part of his "ontology of the present." In all these instances, Hegelian dialectics are—as Jameson's commentators have noted—associated with the topic of "America," but this association is a deeply reflective one that undergoes several phases of dialectical transformation throughout Jameson's career.

JAMESON'S AMERICAN HEGEL

Although preceded in Jameson's career by several methodologically significant studies of modern literature and philosophy, *Marxism and Form* (1971) is, for our purposes, an especially useful starting point. Deeply marked by the 1960s, this text illustrates, we might say, a fundamental paradox of that decade. "My own intellectual trajectory," Jameson later wrote in a beautiful dialectical sentence in the introduction to the first volume of *Ideologies of Theory*, "is therefore as unrepresentative and uncharacteristic as that of other North American intellectuals of my generation."[17] If American intellectuals of the 1960s were typical in their idiosyncracies, then there is also a national flavor to that situation, in that (as Jameson argues) these idiosyncracies often took the form of a "cultural envy" for European intellectuals' imagined significance in the public sphere. Thus, the attachment to European intellectual trends—in Jameson's case, Sartrean existentialism—is a symptom of a peculiarly American social condition, even as it also expresses a generational resistance to being typical or symptomatic. Placing his own intellectual trajectory within this pattern, Jameson articulates something of what the 1960s have meant for his work, and it is all bound up in this recursive Americanness that finds itself in relation to both European and counter-cultural (within the United States) anti-American positions. Jameson takes the 1960s as a frame and ground for his work, and what that means is expressed in many places, but especially in *Marxism and Form*.

Taking as its task the introduction to an American audience of "twentieth-century dialectical theories of literature," *Marxism and Form* of course now seems deeply idiosyncratic in its turning toward a mainly German tradition at just the moment when French poststructuralism was peaking—an idiosyncracy amplified when one remembers that Jameson is identified on the back cover of this study as "Professor of French."[18] There are further oddities in the selection of figures: Bloch, for instance, might not fit so seamlessly into the Frankfurt school cluster established by the treatment of Adorno, Benjamin, and Marcuse—or, for that matter, does Lukàcs always seem such a natural fit either. But Sartre! Since when does he have anything to do with the others, except in that he is such a major part of the French phenomenological tradition in general terms? With only a little searching, one can develop questionable retrospective hypotheses about the selection of figures treated in *Marxism and Form*; as a transitional text, it sutures Jameson's earliest concerns (Sartre) with dominant themes of his early career (rereading the Marxist literary critical canon) and anticipates a major theme of his mid-career (Blochian utopianism). But surely, overall, it is the centrality of the dialectic itself that is the most idiosyncratic feature of this study, no matter where it begins. After all, Jameson's premise in *Marxism and Form* is that a dialectical approach is especially necessary and appropriate for a critique of the American situation:

it is perfectly consistent with the spirit of Marxism—with the principle that thought reflects its concrete social situation—that there should exist several different Marxisms in the world of today, each answering the specific needs and problems of its own socio-economic system. . . . It is in the context of this last, I am tempted to call it postindustrial, Marxism that the great themes of Hegel's philosophy—the relationship of part to whole, the opposition between concrete and abstract, the concept of totality, the dialectic of appearance and essence, the interaction of subject and object—are once again the order of the day. A literary criticism which wishes to be *diagnostic* as well as descriptive will ignore them only at the price of reinventing them.[19]

The American situation is repeatedly diagnosed throughout the text as the dilemma of capitalism writ large, the dilemma of constituting "a collective totality which fails to have any existential equivalent in individual experience, to determine individual reality while remaining structurally inaccessible to the categories of the latter's understanding or image-making power."[20] And so, anticipating the famous cognitive mapping thesis from the "Postmodernism" essay, Jameson asserts that a Marxism appropriate to the American situation will help to develop categories that bring the collective totality into view for individuals; American Marxism will, as the 1960s slogan says, "name the system" and reveal its effects. The great Hegelian themes previously enumerated thus have as their function for Jameson the overturning of what he sees as the dominant mode of Anglo-American thought (empiricism). Hegelian dialectics set an empirical fixation on facts into flow, into motion, producing a sense of vertiginous shock as "the mind, suddenly drawing back and including itself in its new and widened apprehension, doubly restores and *regrounds* its earlier notions in a new glimpse of reality."[21] This moment is then followed— even more necessarily for Jameson—by the second or Marxist moment of dialectics. Necessary because the risk of a strictly Hegelian approach is a fall into "unconscious egocentrism . . . [or the] optical illusion of our own centrality," the second moment of dialectical criticism produces a "hygienic downgrading of the pretensions of spirit . . . in its regrounding of our beings and our bodies in the physical and socio-historical universe."[22] Although narrated diachronically, for Jameson, these two operations of thought are actually synchronic, because they reflect the inner form of the work of art—indeed the world—itself: "the two dimensions are one, and indeed the propaedeutic value of art lies in the way in which it permits us to grasp the essentially historical and social value of what we had otherwise taken to be a question of individual experience. Yet this is done by shifting levels or points of view, by *moving from the experience to its ground* or concrete situation."[23]

In short, in *Marxism and Form*, Jameson proposes the Hegelian dialectic and the Marxist materialism that, for him, is its necessary completion, as a corrective specially necessary to (1) overturn Anglo-American empiricism, (2) rewrite the handy but conservative nostalgia evident in an "influential and characteristic work of American criticism," such as Wayne Booth's *Rhetoric of Fiction*, (3) begin properly materialist analysis of writers such as Hemingway, and (4) reflect on the situation of American literature and culture as wholes. As this list illustrates, there is a thorough and profoundly self-reflexive Americanist agenda in this study, even though idiosyncratically Jameson proposes that the Marxism appropriate to the American situation is precisely not available in an immanent reworking of the native empirical methods, but rather in a markedly European tradition that moves through the works to reflect on concept production and ultimately the mode of production—or ground—itself.

Turning to one of Jameson's essays from the same period, "Criticism in History" (1976), we find him continuing this emphasis on the Hegelian logic of the ground as a particularly valuable methodological tool, especially for overcoming critical habits of the American academy—here, New Critical formalism:

all apparently formal statements about a work bear within them a concealed historical dimension of which the critic is not often aware; and it follows from this that we ought to be able to transform those statements about form and aesthetic properties and the like into genuinely historical ones, if we could only find the right vantage point for doing so. The picture is then not one of turning away from the formalizing kinds of criticism to something else, but rather of going all the way through them so completely that we come out the other side; and that other side, for Marxists is what is loosely known as history. Only to put it that way is to suggest all the wrong things too, and to convey the idea that it is simply a question of substituting one specialized discipline—that of the historian—for another—that of the literary critic. What I have in mind, however, is the point at which a specialized discipline is transcended toward reality itself, the point at which—and this under its own momentum, under its own inner logic—literary criticism abolishes itself as such and yields a glimpse of *consciousness momentarily at one with its social ground*, of what Hegel calls the "concrete."[24]

In the same essay, Jameson also continues the theme introduced in *Marxism and Form* concerning the dangers of Hegelian dialectics becoming overly subjectivist and sinking into a perhaps culturally magnetic individualism. The aim in the essay as a whole is to recognize and complete the critical psychology of the dialectic, moving through the and past the experience of "dialectical shock" so essential to Hegel's *Phenomenology* and toward the conceptual independence of the *Logic*:

the historical dimension does not come as a merely formal or academic type of completion—it reemerges with a kind of shock for the mind, as a kind of twist or a sudden propulsion of our being onto a different plane of reality. It involves what is properly a transformation process, conversion techniques, a shift in mental perspective that suddenly and powerfully enlarges our field of vision, releasing us from the limits of the various, purely literary methods, and permitting us to experience the profound historicity of their application, as indeed of all mental operations in general.[25]

In this passage, as in so many of his most evocative, Jameson once again describes the feel of dialectics in a visceral vocabulary: shock, twist, shift, propulsion, enlarging, and releasing. Although this subject matter might lend itself to a spaced-out psychedelic account of the sublime, this embodied vocabulary has the effect, I think, not only of concretizing the experience so that one recognizes it when it occurs, but also of pointing the reader toward the need to treat this experience concretely, completing the dialectic by returning to the social ground. The essential character of the several loop-de-loops compressed here in this passage account, one might presume, for the frequent repetition of not only this vocabulary but also this kind of passage in Jameson's work. In its ur-form, the passage itself seems to revolve around certain fetishistic key words—especially "shift" and "shock"—words that—when taken together—are especially evocative of a kind of earthquake experience in which it is the ground that moves. Is it going too far, too quickly, then to suggest that in such a vocabulary of disaster (as perhaps in the strange disaster movies of the same early 1970s moment), one finds a kind of record of the massive reconfiguration of the totality that we have come, in large part under Jameson's own tutelage, to call late capitalism? The massive becoming-self-conscious of capitalism as it shifts the profit margin away from production per se and toward the means of mediation (communications technologies, markets in information) is recorded here as a sharp subterranean realignment forcing some new intellectual language to register on the instruments placed far above and abroad.

    This sense of an imminent disruption leads us next to *The Political Unconscious* (1981), commonly treated as one of Jameson's breakthrough books.[26] Arguing in the introduction that all contemporary theories of literary interpretation are theories of immanence, Jameson famously argues that Marxism and only Marxism—as a method of contradiction and dialectic—can provide the horizon of theory, the horizon that allows literary theory to see beyond itself, to move from the position of "unconscious egocentrism." To put the point very bluntly, we could say that in *The Political Unconscious* consciousness is only possible with Marxism. Of course, here we return to Adorno's theme—specially adapted by Jameson—in which a complete consciousness of truth is a fundamentally utopian and therefore as-yet unavailable form of consciousness. On this logic, something like a complete Marxism is also of the utopian future, like the real—something to be approached fitfully and only momentarily in a sort of herky-jerky modernist dance of the machine-body. But, this is a book all about utopia, and so we should not be surprised that in the dense and rich conclusion, Jameson twists the Adornian dialectic further, moving towards a distinctly utopian (and, it should go without saying, idiosyncratic) defense of the positive dialectic.

In the conclusion to *The Political Unconscious*, Jameson does not give short shrift to the negative or demystifying moment of the dialectic. We still find here an account of the need to puncture the balloon of enraptured individualist self-consciousness with a sense of the concrete that tends toward functionalism, but where this negative moment had been treated as the moment of completion in *Marxism and Form*, here it appears as itself in need of further movement toward the positive, toward the wresting of truth from the darkest and most reactionary moments of untruth. In a controversial argument (that in retrospect greatly clarifies his study of Wyndham Lewis), Jameson figures all ideology as utopian anticipation of collective life. Here, the logic of the social ground is even more self-determining and independent than in previous incarnations. Jameson uses the master/slave dialectic of the *Phenomenology* here not as code for separated social groups or warring factions in a political or psychological drama; rather, to escape the potentially functionalist logic of a negative dialectic taken to its extreme, he moves the ground to the future, treating the utopian moment of the slave's rise to self-consciousness as the figure for concrete and collective future liberation. With this move toward the positive, Jameson not only radically repositions Adorno's argument about negative dialectics, he also further displaces his own earlier emphasis on the critic's psychology, moving the whole apparatus of dialectics further toward the verge of a total and concrete level. In terms clarified below, Jameson moves, in *The Political Unconscious*, even further from *Verstehen* through *Dialectik* toward the Absolute. He moves into the section of Hegel's *Logic* that is the horizon of liberation. Here is his crucial articulation and recognition of this movement:

The preceding analysis entitles us to conclude that all class consciousness of whatever type is Utopian insofar as it expresses the unity of a collectivity; yet it must be added that this proposition is an allegorical one. The achieved collectivity or organic group of whatever kind—oppressors fully as much as oppressed—is Utopian not in itself, but only insofar as all such collectivities are themselves *figures* for the ultimate concrete collective life of an achieved Utopian or classless society.[27]

Here, Jameson is on the verge of proceeding to transcode Durkheim's reactionary sociology of religion; this is his means for rescuing by indirection the Hegelian absolute, with all its religious connotations, at the very moment of its greatest untruth. (We recall at this point Jameson's repeated insistence that the road between Marxism and religion is a two-way street; much as religious eschatology, for instance, might "infect" Marxism, religion itself with its visions of utopian future may be inherently Marxist, if you look at it the right way—that is, concretely.[28]) In this process, the key concept is clearly one of allegory or figure. Standing in the spot that might in another work have been the site of a description of dialectical shock is a considerably more sober assertion of a shift of level, a shift in which ideology is not only recognized as the record of class consciousness and thus of a (usually repressed or unconscious) utopian desire. Ideology also brings forward the unknown classless collectivity through a vocabulary of figures. Here, we are concerned not only with a dialectical criticism that brings the social ground to the individualist literary or artistic experience; we find ourselves as well reading the artful experience embodied by social narratives themselves. Marcuse, some might say, has appeared on the scene to complement Adorno. The "ground" of criticism thus is not merely concrete in the empiricist sense; rather the ground to which one turns lies in the future. The ground is a concrete future utopia.

It may seem that we have strayed far from our initial impulse here, tracing the self-reflexively American character of Jameson's appeals to Hegel, and in particular to the concept of the ground, and perhaps we have. If so, however, it is only to present with that much greater firmness the sense in which the "American" premise of Jameson's turn to Hegel has been vacuumed up into the seams and body of his process of thinking. The transformation evident in the body of work circulating around his *Postmodernism* book—so obviously the site of another dramatic involution of the dialectic—is in part a transformation in the relation of Jameson's Hegelianism to American topics. Taking a noticeably American topic (consumer culture, late capitalism, or "the present"), Jameson does not simply "apply" Hegel to it. Instead, because he sees dialectical criticism as the logic called forth from the conditions of American social life themselves, reflecting more directly on these American conditions necessarily involves his writing in a moment of deep Hegelian self-consciousness if he is not simply to express or record those conditions but also fundamentally expose them in the materialist sense.

As a result, as others have explained,[29] Jameson's postmodernism essay becomes progressively more intricate in its several versions. In the 1990 book chapter discussed here, an earlier version is reprinted, along with Jameson's response to his critics and a lengthy unfolding of related themes in the conclusion.[30] Throughout, the form of dialectics employed in *Postmodernism* is less psychologistic than in some of his earlier work. Even the utopian affect that plays such a strong role in *The Political Unconscious*, while definitely a major theme of *Postmodernism*, has receded to the deep structure of his thinking. We see also in *Postmodernism* a more amply and wildly stylized writing; indeed, this stylistic density has become one of the most famous features of Jameson's account and is often used to situate his concerns as being those of a high modernist aesthete with, again, an unreflective and insufficiently self-conscious approach.

Rather than engaging in some undecidable debate about the status of particular examples or traces of judgments of taste in Jameson's famous essay, however, I simply want to point out that it is as rigorously Hegelian in logic as his earlier work, no matter what the stylistic furbelows, although a further move toward the "object" does seem to have occurred. This latter move is particularly evident if we read at the level of the paragraph (rather than the modernist sentence). The paragraph is here, as so often for Adorno, an essential unit of dialectical motion, perhaps because it is organized around the notion of "the break." As an internally open structure glued together more often by a logical flow than topical consistency, Jameson's dialectical paragraph arrives at a certain moment of completion before lifting a leg up or over to another level; a sequence of paragraphs thus allows a kind of square dance to proceed as the problem in question twists and turns, transferring momentum as it exchanges partners. In this process, the power of thinking turns just as fully on the light break, the gap at the edge of the paragraph, as it does on the shrink-wrapped compression and superficial diversity of clausal "fragments." The paragraph is a unit of transitional totality, we might say. It operates as a ground.

At least, if we approach Jameson's *Postmodernism* with an eye toward the paragraph, we find plenty to work with. The first paragraph of the "Introduction" to the volume begins of course from a deep break, launching into the topic and the concept at hand from the blank space above. Beginning with an oblique but resolutely amoral approach that is vital to the argument as a whole, Jameson rolls into the "Introduction" with a methodological teaser: "It is safest to grasp the concept of the postmodern."[31] Safety, not excellence or truth, is the initial appeal (not "It is best to grasp" or "It is most accurate to grasp"). The problem of tangibly grasping the concept of the postmodern is taken, quite self-consciously, as our initial task, and it is a problem that presents itself not because of inadequacies of the psychologistic subject but rather because of the nature of the postmodern itself. Jameson goes on in this paragraph to move the dialectic first downward, if you will, to the problem of historical versus ahistorical understanding, in which "Postmodernism . . . may then amount to not much more than theorizing its own conditions of possibility."[32] He then moves the problem outward to a modernism/postmodernism opposition, a form of the nature/culture opposition that arrives at its definitive ground when we grasp that "Postmodernism is the consumption of sheer commodification as a process," when culture is the consumption of the production of culture in capitalist terms.[33] That is, from an initial self-consciousness about mentally taking hold of the slippery object called postmodernism, the paragraph moves briskly through two axes of its topic only to bend both of these vectors back toward the question of the concept. Postmodernism as a self-theorizing operation and postmodernism as an ecstatic consumption of its own production are both revealed to be versions of a characteristically dialectical shift toward the self-conscious dialectical thought, however rapidly and densely presented these initial hypotheses might be. It is thus both fitting and methodologically significant that this first paragraph concludes with a sentence devoted topically to the concept and methodologically to a provisional reconciliation through allegory of the logical and historical impulses of the preceding argument:

> The "life-style" of the superstate therefore stands in relationship to Marx's "fetishism" of commodities as the most advanced monotheisms to primitive animisms or the most rudimentary idol worship; indeed, any sophisticated theory of the postmodern out to bear something of the same relationship to Horkheimer and Adorno's old "Culture Industry" concept as MTV or fractal ads bear to fifties television series.[34]

Here, the stylistic opposition of modernism and postmodernism is redrawn as a relationship of development or dialectical unfolding; this move helps as well to begin the process of thinking through postmodernism historically. We find here not only a catalogue of effects, but also an assertion of the objective necessity of a mode of theorizing that is also as dilated and ramified as its object with respect to its predecessor theories. The problems of consciousness and history reveal themselves to be two directions on a two-way street, and the key to the dialectic here is to grasp the historical contradictions of thinking as a single process. While this process is certainly differentiated across its complex terrain (hence the following chapters on a wide range of topics), in *Postmodernism*, this is a differentiation that Jameson is interested in exploring as it turns back in on itself, as it reflexively and dialectically involutes in the first flush of its puberty as a concept.

Jameson's *Postmodernism* dialectic does not treat "America" per se, then. In this "Introduction," he explains and positions his usage of the title concepts of "postmodernism" and "late capitalism" and, in so doing, registers in passing an "Americanocentrism" likely to be visible to others; he justifies this centrism only by qualifying and specifying what is meant by American (a brief reign of international power and a kind of "global style.")[35] Nonetheless, his introduction is not an apology for treating American topics in general terms or for being an American who proposes a totalizing theory. Rather, the "American" scent of the postmodernism theory is allowed—even encouraged—to emanate freely (like the invasive smell of french fries or microwave popcorn?), making its way deep into the crevices of the argument—especially, I would argue, into the concept of "logic" linking "postmodernism" and "late capitalism."

Jameson takes care in his "Introduction" to state specifically what he does not mean by "logic": it is not a concept of "hegemony" or a cultural dominant exactly, nor does it refer to a more Freudian unconscious or "deeper logic" of the base. A positive conception of logic is not, however, offered; it is only exhibited, so reading for it here and in Jameson's subsequent work requires a particular attentiveness. Developing this attentiveness is worthwhile, because it is here—in the movement of the concept, that is, in the logic—that one finds a necessarily unfolded and utopian version of Adorno's concept of intellectual labor. This labor takes shape in the preparation of the ground of a historical thinking, a thinking that works toward a utopian theory of America in the context of globalization.

Turning, then, to Jameson's 1994 essay on globalization, we find the concept of the ground doing much of the work with which we are now familiar, as well as integrating and reconciling these tasks within a utopian approach to the problem of America. Published after a conference on globalization held at Duke University, the essays in *The Cultures of Globalization* mainly take up the project of a large-scale theorizing of globalization.[36] Some begin from the historical *longue durée*, but most are focused on "culture" as a layer of global interaction with its own dynamics and potential for action on the global frontier. In this context, Jameson's essay is significant in its relative disinterest in what is usually taken to be the concrete and its insistence on treating the topic (as the title of the essay indicates) "as a philosophical issue" rather than as an occasion for a new quasi-empirical research program. His essay returns to Hegelian "philosophical issues" in an effort to organize the stalemates and conundrums surrounding globalization.

The essay is organized by sections into different moments of the dialectic, moving through the observable phenomena and toward their conceptual ground. The first section maps out the four logically possible positions on globalization, each of which allows the possibility of a pro- or antiglobalization tone. (This is the same sorting operation undertaken in the response-to-my-critics piece on postmodernism.[37]) These possibilities are then turned into philosophical positions, as they are translated into instances of a relationship between Identity and Difference, and in the same stroke the procedure of the section itself is described:

> But now, having achieved these first twin positions, having in some first moment rotated the concept in such a way that it takes on these distinct kinds of content, its surface now glittering in light, and then obscured again by darkness and shadow—now it is important to add that the transfers can begin. Now, after having secured these initial structural possibilities, you can project their axes upon each other.[38]

Concretizing the "issue" at hand as a sort of chrome-coated Rubik's cube, Jameson describes the first moment of the dialectic as a moment when neutral (or simply "structural") possibilities acquire tonal value—either "baleful" or "joyous" as he later elaborates.[39] The initial moment, thus, is metaphoric in the sense that it asserts a relationship between subjective and objective options. Outlining globalization as a dialectical problem, Jameson draws attention to these metaphoric relationships without preferring among them.

The second or metonymic section addresses the problem of Americanization most explicitly: Is globalization an extension of Americanization? How might be such an extension be blocked, resisted, and so on? At stake here is the introduction of a narrative element. The "structural possibilities" outlined in the first section are placed in relation to a historical dynamic and the underlying logic of preceding stages, as well as possible future effects. Without resolving the question of whether globalization "is" or "is not" equivalent to an extension of Americanization, Jameson asserts the contiguity of these problems. One does not simply replace the other; globalization as an issue requires taking a stance on Americanization.

At this point, in the third section, the essay takes a turn—introducing what Jameson calls "a long parenthesis on the significance of the Gatt and Nafta [sic] agreements."[40] Here, the official efforts to delimit national film industries are offered as allegorical instances of the breakdown of national totalities. Jameson argues that "Hollywood is not merely a name for a business that makes money but also for a fundamental late-capitalist cultural revolution, in which old ways of life are broken up and new ones set in place."[41] In addition to recalling some of the material ground for the question of globalization, this section provides an example of the kind of transcoding we are being encouraged to do here. As this section emphasizes, we are to read the dialectical structure of debates over globalization as well as the phenomenon itself. Where the second section offered us an objectivist reading of subjectively charged issues (is the American culture industry taking over?), the third offers a subjective transcoding of questions often treated, in the American media at least, as distant and "objective" (economy is a vision of human life and a choice about the shape thereof).

After the closing of the parentheses organizing this transitional section on the dynamics of transcoding, we are prepared to move into the fourth synecdochic section. Here, with the spatial and the temporal axes mapped onto one another and with an explicit attention to translations between vocabularies, we are prepared to address global totalities. Rather than address the whole immediately as a unified entity, however, Jameson emphasizes the negative moment and begins with "fundamental dissymmetry."[42] He points to the lack of parity between English and other languages and the scale of various entertainment industries as examples of existing inequities that make any easy equivalence between the United States and other nations a falsehood. American culture thus can neither stand for the whole nor be treated as simply one among others, since it is the export of American-style consumerism itself that is so characteristic of globalization. Pulling again away from pro or con positions on the phenomenon (though perhaps less entirely convincingly here), Jameson asserts that the synecdochic feature is the transformed relationship between culture and economy. From the morass of structural possibilities and tonalities, he again pulls away—considering how this relationship between culture and economy looks from various sides or aspects around the globe (from Europe, from the former socialist countries, from third world utopias, and so on). This is the simple negation, whereby the various sides or aspects are revealed as all dependent on dissymmetry as the logic of the whole. It is not until the next and final section that the complete negation occurs.

In the conclusion to "Notes on Globalization as a Philosophical Issue," the real tarrying with the negative takes place. Seeking out the negations that accrued along the way, Jameson asks, "Suppose, however that what are here identified as so many levels of the same thing were in reality in contradiction with each other; for example, suppose that consumerism were inconsistent with democracy, that the habits and addictions of postmodern consumption block or repress possibilities of political and collective action as such?"[43] Do these negative moments of friction and stalemate turn back into a positive and new totality? Jameson here evaluates Nestor Garcia Canclini and George Yudice's positions as two approaches to the synecdochic moment outlined in the previous section. (Garcia Canclini celebrates some of the aesthetic possibilities of postmodern consumerism, while Yudice sees culture as the forerunner of new movements for freedom.[44]) His point, however, is not to approve or reject these positions, but rather to identify a general logic of reversal: "what holds at the national level is reversed at a distance."[45] The very entity that is the target for Latin American cultural politics (the state) can be a "positive space" in North America and vice versa.[46] The fundamental feature of globalization as an issue is not, for Jameson, the waning of the state or any other surface phenomenon. It is instead the peculiar rapidity of transfers between various scales or levels (the national, the regional, the global, especially) that establishes the new logic of globalization. For this reason, globalization poses basic challenges to what Jameson calls "our categories of thought."[47] Accustomed to treating various nations or identities as totalities, we encounter difficulty reorienting our political vision to the multiscalar operations of globalization. And, here, the appeal to Hegel is made. In this ironic and metalogical moment, Jameson not only identifies reversal as the conceptual problem with which we must grapple; he also reverses one of the left positions on globalization: the claim that globalization as an issue ironically validates a return to Marxist materialism.

Instead of a return to materialism, Jameson instead identifies with globalization a massive crisis of the concept—a problem with the shape of thought to which he offers Hegelian idealism as a certain type of antidote. The Hegelian dialectic gives way to the concept of the ground (and thus ensures materialist transcoding), but what is emphasized in Jameson's essay is the need for a fully dialectical approach that will do much more than list molecular symptoms with no exploration of their molar totality. In its own dialectic, the essay moves from "positions" on globalization, through an account of its phenomena and toward a methodological claim that globalization presents a crisis in the concept of material grounds of thought—a crisis managed only by a fully self-conscious and homeopathic return to the philosophy of the ground.

The recommended "return to Hegel" then serves several functions in Jameson's essay. Globalization is not only being treated here as the material ground for world literature, fusion cuisine, and certain politicotheological extremisms; globalization is also, in this essay, another name for a concrete methodological crisis—the problem of thinking the totality adequately. That is, the return to Hegel signifies here both the need for materialist demystification and a tremendous opportunity to move the wheels of the concept forward. The return to the ground, in particular, required by globalization as a philosophical issue is necessary because the ground is, for Jameson, precisely where these materialist and utopian tendencies meet. Asking what globalization is as a ground for contemporary culture is and must necessarily be a simultaneously empirical and theoretical question. The value of the concept of the ground for Jameson's purposes in a theory of globalization is that it allows us to begin to imagine the globe as porous—as simultaneously an expression of capitalist totalization and utopian transformation.

By emphasizing this concept, Jameson has not only attempted to move through and beyond existing approaches to the topic of globalization—especially strictly empirical or documentary approaches consonant with taking the market as the truth of the process, and simply idealist or ideological ones focused on cultural imperialism. This approach also seeks to overcome identity versus difference issues triggered by third-world approaches, those that begin see globalization as either all about American hegemony or all about anti-American resistance. Reconciling the identity/difference dialectic in the move to the ground, Jameson's approach implies, I think, that one should loosen the fixity of association between certain politics and cultural formations in order to register fully the process under way. The persistence of theses appropriate to imperialism in the context of contemporary globalization is like the persistence of the modern in the postmodern—not a contaminating flaw, but rather an opportunity to convert and transform the grip of necessity.

This all sounds very abstract still, and perhaps this is why in Jameson's own speculative essay he is so insistent on pulling together the moments of negative and "destructive" critique of reified positions with topical pointers— toward NAFTA and other treaties, as well as the problem of Americanization as a whole. Sorting through episodes and themes that are of course the core of emerging theories of globalization means approaching them with a fresh inter-pretive eye—one that will open itself to rescuing the true from the untrue and remain with its objects, revealing, to choose an especially difficult example, the utopian appeal of even the ideologies of American militarism. The video prompter in this process, our high-tech cue card, is the porosity of motion itself. By geometrically rotating the problem of globalization (itself consti-tuted, we are accustomed to thinking, by more thermodynamic flows and transfers), Jameson demonstrates in this essay how an addiction to that special negation associated with porosity might slingshot into another sort of concrete situation. This is most definitely not an excuse for writing American pseudo-universalist accounts (such as Samuel Huntington's) or the reverse anti-Amer-ican resentment narrative; it is a reflexive call for that of which it is a germinating example: a logically self-conscious theory of globalization.

THE AMERICAN GROUNDS FOR GLOBALIZATION

The suggestions for a grounded theory of globalization offered in "Notes on Globalization" thus ultimately cluster around this unlikely proposition: Amer-ica is the utopian ground of globalization. Stated this way, the proposition sounds strangely consonant with other accounts of globalization that rescue "America" for leftists—notably Michael Hardt and Antonio Negri's *Empire*. In their explicitly Spinozan and anti-Hegelian theory of globalization, Hardt and Negri argue for seeing America as a prototype of the "mixed constitution," important among other reasons for its historical responsiveness, to the claims of the democratic multitude.[48] How literally to take this apparently pro-Amer-ican position (especially in the context of a work arguing that there is no longer any third world) is a major question when reading Hardt and Negri as well as Jameson. Do the critiques that both offer of the thesis of cultural imperialism translate into affirmation of the exercises of American hegemonic power, inso-far as this indirectly responds to the demands of the multitude or the struggle toward totality? One would expect so.

In thinking through the appealing and also disorienting concept of "affir-mation"—whatever its source—we might, however, bear in mind Susan Buck-Morss's statements on America. In *Dreamworld and Catastrophe*, her reconsideration of East/West politics well after the Cold War but with a view to retaining what has been known there and then, Buck-Morss makes the important claim that America had long functioned as a counter-Enlighten-ment perspective from the point of view of Europe.[49] Deflating America's ego-centric views of itself by way of a detour elsewhere might thus allow a different grounding for Jameson's Hegelian America.

Referring, that is, not to the actually existing state of America, nor to a hazy ideal, but rather to America as a kind of dialectical by-product and negation of European modernity, we might have a sense of the concept that will help us understand how America can serve as the ground for an affirmative globalization in a Marxist sense. It is as a future but currently false whole that America grounds globalization. "America" thus stands in the position of a utopian synthesis in Jameson's account of globalization, even if the America in question is definitely not the defensively nationalist America of a post-September 11 patriotism. In his short essay on these events, "The Dialectics of Disaster," Jameson takes pains to differentiate what he calls "utterly insincere" media-inspired patriotism from a more properly political collective experience.[50] In this piece, he situates sentimental Americanism as an effect of a media industry that itself arises to capitalize on the evacuation of utopian political projects. Like religious fundamentalism, media frenzies of pseudonationalism fuel the capitalist state's need for war. Observing Americanism, in this sense, then, recalls us to the task of producing "the fundamental theoretical critique of globalization."[51] America as a media phenomenon provides a conceptual ground in this essay for a reminder of the need for a theory of globalization.

We arrive, finally, at a point where *even* America (as a concept, if not as a state or national culture) is utopian. An American narrative is the utopian ground for globalization as it comes to be theorized in scattered elements Jameson's work—or, perhaps, it might be more precise to say it is a ground of "the present." After all, in *A Singular Modernity*, Jameson asserts that more than any particular discourse of modernity what he ultimately wants to insist on is the project of identifying the ontology of the present.[52] Struggling with and within the present is the Hegelian dialectic. If our present is both global and somehow national (here, American), then we turn by necessity to the Hegelian dialectic. For Jameson, here as throughout his career, "the dialectic comes into being as an attempt to hold together these contradictory features...within the framework of a single thought or language."[53] Rather than restricting his own field of vision to a falsely universal American horizon, then, it is, for Jameson, the Hegelian dialectic that allows him to work through the contradictions of an American globalization. By writing in and through these contradictions, he builds up toward an account of the contradictions of a global present. This may well prove an instructive example.

NOTES

1. Reviews of Jameson's scholarship regularly comment on its putatively un-American complexity and politics. Sympathetic or mixed reviews (Culler, Lange, Woodcock, Knapp, Bahr, Farber) tend to praise Jameson for his perceived turn away from a Marxism assumed to be vulgar, while hostile reviews target Marxism itself, rather than his interpretation of the tradition (esp. Wellek). See Ehrhard Bahr, Review of *Marxism and Form. Comparative Literature Studies* 12 (2) (June 1975): 180–82;

Jonathan Culler, Review of *Marxism and Form. Modern Language Review* 69 (3) (July 1974): 599–601; Michael Farber, "Marxism and Art," *Socialist Revolution* 7 (3) (May/June 1977): 99–108. John V. Knapp. Review of *Marxism and Form. Modern Fiction Studies* 21 (4) (Winter 1975–76): 629–31. Bernd Lange, "The Frankfort [sic]School of Critical Theory: New Interest in Marxist Criticism,." *Clio* 2 (2) (February 1973): 174–80. René Wellek, "Marxist Literary Criticism," *Yale Review* 62 (1) (Autumn 1972): 119–26; George Woodcock, "Marxist Critics," *Sewanee Review* 83 (2) (Spring 1975): 324–34.

2. Sean Homer, *Fredric Jameson: Marxism, Hermeneutics, Postmodernism* (New York: Routledge, 1998): 62.

3. Clint Burnham, *The Jamesonian Unconscious* (Durham: Duke University Press, 1995): 81–84.

4. Steven Helmling, *The Success and Failure of Fredric Jameson.* (Albany: State University of New York Press, 2001): 138, 1.

5. For an exciting new account of twentieth-century readings of Hegel, see Bruce Baugh, French Hegel: *From Surrealism to Postmodernism* (New York: Routledge, 2003). Baugh argues against seeing Kojève's "anthropological" interpretation of Hegel as the definitive version, recovering instead the work of Jean Wahl as a precedent for poststructuralist anti-dialectics.

6. Xudong Zhang, "Marxism and the Historicity of Theory: An Interview with Fredric Jameson," *New Literary History* 29 (3) (1998): 376. Further references to this interview appear in the body of the essay.

7. Ibid., 381.

8. Hegel's *Logic.* Trans. William Wallace with foreword by J. N. Findlay. (New York: Oxford, 1975): section 121, page 175. Further references to this work appear in the body of the text.

9. Ibid., section 121.

10. Ibid., section 121.

11. Ibid., section 130.

12. Ibid., section 158n.

13. Theodor W. Adorno, *Hegel: Three Studies*, trans. Shierry Weber Nicholsen. (Cambridge: MIT Press, 1999). Further references to this text appear in the body of the essay.

14. See Judith Butler, *Subjects of Desire: Hegelian Reflections in Twentieth-Century France* (New York: Columbia University Press, 1987).

15. Alexnder Kojève, *Introduction to the Reading of Hegel* (Ithaca: Cornell University Press, 1969).

16. See Fredric Jameson, *The Political Unconscious: Narratives as Socially Symbolic Act* (Ithaca: Cornell University Press, 1981), 284.

17. Jameson, "Introduction," *Ideologies of Theory*, Vol. 1 (Minneapolis: University of Minnesota Press, 1988), xxvi.

18. Jameson, *Marxism and Form: Twentieth-Century Dialectical Theories of Literature* (Princeton: Princeton University Press, 1971).

19. Ibid., 354.

20. Ibid., 354.

21. Ibid., 372, italics in original.

22. Ibid., 368–69.

23. Ibid., 407, emphasis added.

24. Jameson, *Ideologies of Theory*, 120, emphasis added.

25. Ibid., 121.

26. Jameson, *The Political Unconscious*. For an example of the reception of *The Political Unconscious*, Martin Jay and Jane Flax, "On Postmodernism." *History and Theory* 32 (3) (1993): 296–310.

27. Jameson, *The Political Unconscious*, 290–91.

28. "What has sometimes in my own work been thought to be either eclectic or, still worse, synthesizing and 'Hegelian,' will generally be found to involve transcoding of this type, rather than random, but all-inclusionary system building": Jameson, "Introductory Note" to *Ideologies of Theory*, Vol. 2, ix.

29. Jameson, "The Cultural Logic of Late Capitalism" in *Postmodernism or, the Cultural Logic of Late Capitalism* (Durham: Duke University Press, 1991), 1–54.

30. There is much more on this topic, however, in the Conclusion, especially the final section, "How to Map a Totality." This section has the quality of a "methodological program" because it returns to level of concept, having built this up through the book as whole from a range of carefully observed sense-perceptions, through a long sequence of dialectical reflections on phenomena and the theoretical concepts that map them. Rather than reflecting directly, though, on the kind of logic that he uses himself, Jameson seems ultimately to be describing a utopian anticipation of concept-production that takes place through an especially visual correlative for the concept in map production. I do not want to take this visual reference too literally, since he reveals cognitive mapping as another name for class consciousness of new classes, but there does also seem to be an insistence on the visual that exceeds or supplements logic per se.

31. Jameson, *Postmodernism*, ix.

32. Ibid., ix.

33. Ibid., x.

34. Ibid., x.

35. Ibid., xx.

36. Jameson, "Notes on Globalization as a Philosophical Issue" in *The Cultures of Globalization*, eds. Fredric Jameson and Masao Miyoshi. (Durham: Duke University Press, 1994), 54–80.

37. Jameson, "Theories of the Postmodern" in *Postmodernism or, the Cultural Logic of Late Capitalism*, 55–66.

38. Jameson, "Notes on Globalization," 57.

39. Ibid., 57–58.

40. Ibid., 60.

41. Ibid., 63.

42. Ibid., 63.

43. Ibid., 69.

44. Néstor García Canclini, *Hybrid Cultures: Strategies for Entering and Leaving Modernity*, trans. Christopher L. Chiappari and Silvia L. Lopez. (Minneapolis: University of Minnesota Press, 1995); George Yudice, "Civil Society, Cosumption, and Governmentality in an Age of Global Restructuring," *Social Text* 45 (1995): 1–25.

45. Jameson, "Notes on Globalization," 72.

46. Ibid., 72.

47. Ibid., 75.

48. See Michael Hardt and Antonio Negri, *Empire* (Cambridge: Harvard University Press, 2000), xiv.

49. Susan Buck-Morss, *Dreamworld and Catastrophe: The Passing of Mass Utopia in East and West* (Cambridge: MIT Press, 2000).

50. Jameson, "The Dialectics of Disaster," *South Atlantic Quarterly* 101.2 (2002): 297–304.

51. Ibid., 302.

52. Jameson, *A Singular Modernity: Essay on the Ontology of the Present* (New York: Verso, 2002).

53. Ibid., 65.

11

Periodizing Jameson, or, Notes toward a Cultural Logic of Globalization

Phillip E. Wegner

In the opening line of *The Political Unconscious* (1981), Fredric Jameson offers what he describes as the "moral" of the book, and, as many would no doubt concur, of all his work: "Always historicize!"[1] However, to this "one absolute and we may even say 'transhistorical' imperative of all dialectical thought," we need to add another: "Always totalize!" The latter *practice*—not to be confused, as Jameson himself tirelessly points out, with the totality itself—is synthetic; indeed, he later notes that process of totalization "often means little more than the making of connections between various phenomena, a process which . . . tends to be ever more spatial."[2] It is thus this double optic, at once historical and spatial, diachronic and synchronic, subjective and objective, that, as he argues in *Marxism and Form* (1971), marks the originality of Marxism in particular, and of dialectic thought more generally, and which, as he shows in *The Prison-House of Language* (1972), distinguishes this practice from the then-dominant formalisms and structuralisms.

This double perspective moves us in *The Political Unconscious* into an exploration of "cultural periodization" as another fundamental and indispensable dialectical paradox: an attempt to think the open-ended process of history through the synchronic concept of the totality. Discussions of periodization, Jameson goes on to argue, ultimately unfold into larger questions about the nature of the "representation of History itself."[3] These questions in turn can be understood to have a synchronic and diachronic dimension, concerned, respectively, with the specific composition of any particular period, and the unfolding of the "succession" of these variously constituted periods through time.[4] In terms of its composition, one of the fundamental misunderstandings concerning any periodizing representation, Jameson will later argue, is that it "implies some massive homogeneity about a given period."[5] Rather, he maintains that any period logic be thought of as a cultural "*dominant*," a conception "which allows for the presence and coexistence of a range of very different, yet subordinate features," and that in turn stresses the particular class and group interests served by the ideologies of this dominant, as it engages in a continuous struggle with and attempts to assert its hegemony over "other resistant and heterogeneous forces."[6]

This constitutive unevenness of any cultural period is also a key feature of the second dimension of Jameson's conceptualization, the placement of every period within a larger historical or diachronic sequence: the "survivals from older modes of cultural production," the "anticipatory" traces of those that have "not-yet" emerged into the light of historical day, and the diverse articulations of the dominant all jostling up against one another in a particular configuration of relationships, a veritable permanent "cultural revolution," that then defines the complex and continuously shifting identity of any cultural moment.[7] It is this very complexity that thwarts any kind of reductive typologizing operation imagined to accompany a periodizing approach to cultural productions. Jameson goes on to suggest that the best textual manifestation we have of a period, dialectically conceived at once in this temporal and spatial manner, is to be found in what he names the *ideology of form*: "the determinate contradictions of the specific messages emitted by the varied sign systems which coexist in a given artistic process as well as in its general social formation . . . formal processes as sedimented content in their own right, as carrying ideological messages of their own, distinct from the ostensible or manifest content of the works."[8]

While much of the discussion of Jameson's own work has centered on the "ostensible or manifest content" of his texts, far less attention has been paid to the question of their form. Indeed, when the issue of form is raised at all, it is more often than not to decry the "difficulty," "denseness," or even "obscurity" of his prose. The defense in turn, following Jameson's lead in *Marxism and Form*, focuses on the specific form of thinking that occurs in the production or writing of dialectical *sentences*: "For insofar as dialectical thinking is thought about thought, thought to the second power, concrete thought about an object, which at the same time remains aware of its own intellectual operations in the very act of thinking, such self-consciousness must be inscribed in the sentence itself."[9] In a classical dialectical reversal, the demand for clarity and simplicity in prose is unmasked as thoroughly ideological, and difficulty and density posited as "a conduct of intransigence," "the price . . . to pay for genuine thinking," and indeed, even the source of a "purely formal pleasure."[10] Jameson will later maintain that in this way dialectical writing is always to be conceived of as an experiment in representation and thinking, engaging in "a thought-mode of the future."[11]

While such attention to the structure and movement of the individual sentences illuminates central dimensions of Jameson's intellectual project, as well as its place within a larger tradition of dialectical thinking, it may occlude another level of stylistic and formal organization and experimentation to be found in Jameson's project. In his Foreword to Jean-François Lyotard's *The*

Postmodern Condition, Jameson notes that the "insistence on *narrative analysis* in a situation in which the narratives themselves henceforth seem impossible is [a] declaration of intent to remain political and contestatory." Narrative, he stresses, is a fundamental part of any Marxist scholarship and politics because "on the political and social level, indeed, narrative in some sense always meant the negation of capitalism."[12] Such a contestation becomes increasingly significant, he will later suggest, precisely in a cultural situation such as our own, increasingly dominated by the image and the visual, and a retreat to the aesthetic.[13] I will show in the following pages that Jameson's own thoroughgoing commitment to narrative is also manifest in the profound formal unity of his books, as each can be understood to form a coherent narrative in its own right, reading something like a theoretical novel.

However, such a synchronic or totalizing approach to each of Jameson's books, stressing the deep connections between what often appear as the discrete elements (essays and chapters) constituting them, has as its dialectical complement a diachronic perspective, wherein each individual text is understood as one point within a larger sequence. In other words, the reading of Jameson's work that I undertake is also a periodizing one, deploying Jameson's own well-known periodizing sequence of realism, modernism, and postmodernism. Jameson suggests the basis for such an approach in his first book-length film study, *Signatures of the Visible* (1990). A similar dialectic of synchrony and diachrony, of totalization and historicization, is to be found at work in this text. The various essays collected in Part One (all published previously) represent, when considered together, an initial experiment in a new kind of mapping of capitalism's world system (more on this later); whereas the long original essay, "The Existence of Italy," composing Part Two offers what Jameson himself describes as "the most sustained rehearsal of the dialectic of realism, modernism and postmodernism that I have so far attempted, and which I have hitherto misrepresented by staging one or the other in isolation."[14]

In this essay, Jameson deploys the tripartite schema as a tool for thinking about the transformations that occur within the particular and foreshortened history of sound film, "the 'realisms' of the Hollywood period, the high modernisms of the great *auteurs*, the innovations of the 1960s and their sequels."[15] If the historical narrative of sound film can be shown to replicate the tripartite sequence "at a more compressed tempo," then, Jameson argues, a similar proposition "could also be argued for other semi-autonomous sequences of cultural history such as American Black literature . . . or for the history of rock."[16] In order for these "recapitulations" not to seem "paradoxical or willful," we must introduce into our schema the fundamental issue of *scale*: from the most abstract and global economic perspective, each of these three stages corresponds to "structural stages" within the historical development of the capitalist mode of production; on a more local sociohistorical scale, on the other hand, "the moment of realism can be grasped rather differently as the conquest of a kind of cultural, ideological, and narrative literacy by a new class or group; in that case, there will be formal analogies between such moments, even though they are chronologically distant from each other."[17] Moreover, such transformations in the formal practices of any particular social group are to be understood not simply as a matter of individual will, but rather as concrete responses to the particular historical "situations" in which these groups are located. A periodizing narration of these "microchronologies" thus also can serve as a means of bringing into focus the contours of the larger cultural and social histories in which any class or group is situated.

I will explore this proposition on another even more finely tuned scalar level, that of Jameson's intellectual project. I read the "ideology of the form" of his three major texts—*Marxism and Form*, *The Political Unconscious*, and *Postmodernism, or the Cultural Logic of Late Capitalism* (1991)—as embodiments, respectively, of a realist, modernist, and postmodernist critical aesthetic. I will use Jameson's own descriptions of these practices as "instructions" on how to grasp the formal structure and unity of his major texts. Moreover, I also want to suggest that much of Jameson's work in the period between these major statements—interestingly, published precisely at ten-year intervals—takes the form of a working through and trial run of the ideas and strategies they present in their fully elaborated form. Thus, for example, from this perspective we can read the essays collected in the two volumes of *The Ideologies of Theory* (1988) as bringing together some of the most significant preparatory material for both *The Political Unconscious* and *Postmodernism*. By this, I do not mean to offer any neat categorization of every work Jameson has written. Indeed, as Michael Hardt and Kathi Weeks have recently pointed out, there is a "rare combination of continuity and openness to change" in Jameson's intellectual project, such that a number of the concepts and problematics "we associate with a later stage of Jameson's work, such as cognitive mapping, [were] already present in embryo decades earlier."[18] I very much concur with this idea, and, in fact, have suggested as much elsewhere. However, one of the payoffs of such a periodizing narrative of Jameson's intellectual project is that, it enables us to make connections between diverse texts and recognize different manifestations of central concepts in ways that might not have been evident earlier. Moreover, such an approach will ultimately enable me to extend the discussion further, and uncover in Jameson's work since the publication of *Postmodernism* the intimations of a "fourth" period, wherein we see the outline of a formal narrative strategy appropriate to grapple with the cultural logics of *globalization*—a period that, Giovanni Arrighi suggests, represents a new phase in the history of finance capitalism, as well as Hardt and Antonio Negri argue, expresses the transformation of the order of competing imperial nation-states to the unified global sovereignty of "empire."[19]

The reading that I offer here is intended as an experiment in intellectual biography, a strategy of narration through which the history of Jameson's writings "can be clarified, or at least usefully estranged."[20] Finally, however, I also want to return to his insights about the relationship between transformations that occur in the microchronologies of various cultural practices and the histories of the social groups or publics who make up their producers and consumers. It will be my contention here that a reading of Jameson's unique intellectual project, which takes up the twinned dialectical imperatives "always historicize" and "always totalize," can at the same time offer us new ways of representing changes that occur in the intellectual and institutional contexts in which Jameson himself operates. The story I offer is thus also very much that of the adventures of both the new thing called "theory" that emerged during the course of the last three decades, and the intellectual publics for which it stands as a premiere cultural achievement.

It is at the very heart of *Marxism and Form*, in the chapter on Georg Lukács, where the issue of realist representation comes to the fore. The emblematic opposition for Lukács, Jameson reminds us, lies between the work of Honoré de Balzac and Emile Zola, between the full flourishing of European bourgeois realism and the increasingly constricting and fragmented vision of naturalism, and most important, between what Lukács describes as *narration* and description. "Realism itself," Jameson notes, "comes to be distinguished by its movement, its storytelling and dramatization of its content."[21] Thus, while the photographic precision and positivistic attention to detail would seem at first glance to make Zola's work superior to that of his precursor, a closer examination reveals that Zola "has succumbed to the temptation of abstract thought, to the mirage of some static, objective knowledge of society. . . . But from Lukács' point of view, for which narration is the basic category and abstract knowledge a second best only, this means that the novel in Zola's hands has ceased to become the privileged instrument of the analysis of reality and has been degraded to a mere illustration of a thesis." In contrast, "Balzac does not really know what he will find beforehand."[22] This means the very process of the unfolding of narration is in Balzac's hands one of discovery, a means of constructing a fresh and estranging vision of figures both characteristic of a given period and always in the process of change. In such a reading, realist narration becomes something akin to the dialectical process evident in Hegel's *Phenomenology of Spirit*, where the central protagonist of *Geist* can never really know its destination until it has worked through each of the steps of the dialectical ladder.

Moreover, in this very process comes the possibility of a confrontation with a totality unavailable to the schematizing, dissecting social vision of the naturalist writer: for while the totality is never available for depiction or description, an effective figuration of its contours can be called into life through the process of narration. Realist representation then is not a mimetic correspondence of individual characters and "fixed, stable components of the external world . . . but rather, an analogy between the entire plot, as a conflict of forces, and the total moment of history itself considered as a process."[23] If we already see at work here both dimensions of Jameson's version of the dialectic—an awareness of historical process and an emphasis on the relationship between elements of the social totality—it is because the "closed realm of literature, the experimental or laboratory situation which it constitutes . . . offers a microcosm in which to observe dialectical thinking at work."[24]

Of course, the different narrative strategies of these two emblematic figures is not the result of simple choice, but rather are concrete responses to the very different situations in which each is located: "if it is the material substructure, the social situation that takes precedence over mere opinion, ideology, the subjective picture someone has of himself, then we may be forced to conclude that under certain circumstances a conservative, a royalist, a believing Catholic can better seize the genuine forces at work in society than a writer whose sympathies are relatively socialistic."[25] Jameson thus concludes," realism is dependent on the possibility of access to the forces of change in a given moment of history."[26]

Various aspects of this description of the formal strategies of the realist narrative can be applied in some very productive ways to a reading of *Marxism and Form* itself. In the book's Preface, Jameson notes the fundamental differences between what he attempts to do here and more familiar approaches to this kind of material. His chapters "do not present any of the rigor of technical philosophical investigation," and "their status as language remains ambiguous: for they are also far from being simplified introductory sketches, or journalistic surveys of the various positions and key ideas of a writer, anecdotal narratives of his situation and his relationship to the problems of his time." He then argues that while such approaches are of value, "they remain on the level of sheer *opinion* only, which is to say of intellectual attitudes seized from the outside." The dialectical method, he then concludes, "can be acquired only by a concrete working through of detail, by a sympathetic internal experience of the gradual construction of a system according to its inner necessity."[27]

There is a deep kinship between the central emphasis of this passage and the descriptions of the realist narrative offered in the Lukács chapter. The positivistic assumptions at the basis of the "introductory sketch," "journalistic survey," and "anecdotal narrative" make them formal kin to a naturalist representation (and indeed, these approaches to the history of ideas emerge in the very moment of naturalism) as they attempt to grasp the raw material from an "outside" systematizing perspective. A productive comparison might be generated here with the narrative strategies deployed in two of the other most significant surveys of this same material, Perry Anderson's *Considerations on Western Marxism* (1976) and Martin Jay's *Marxism and Totality: The Adventures of a Concept from Lukács to Habermas* (1984). Both of these later works offer more accessible "introductions" than Jameson's text to the work of these thinkers. What distinguishes *Marxism and Form* from these other approaches is "its movement, its storytelling and dramatization of its content," the way it meticulously works through its various objects, constructing its totality according to the logic of the raw material itself. Eschewing both the sweeping survey and abstract conceptual generalizations of Anderson, or the chronological sequence of Jay, the chapters of *Marxism and Form* are ordered like those in a realist novel, with each of its "characters" appearing on stage when and only when necessitated by the development of the work's plot. Crucially, one can say that Jameson, in this book, "does not really know what he will find beforehand," and only discovers his object as its story unfolds.

The plot of *Marxism and Form* is a rich and moving one. We begin our story with the version of the dialectic criticism developed by Theodor Adorno. Jameson focuses here on Adorno's *Philosophy of Modern Music*, a text he will later describe as belonging to the "exceedingly rare" genre of the "dialectical history"—in fact, Jameson argues that he knows of only three examples of it: Adorno's book, Roland Barthes' early *Writing Degree Zero*, and Manfredo Tafuri's *Architecture and Ideology*; all three also crucial books for all of Jameson's thought. The central feature shared by the works making up this genre "is the sense of Necessity, of necessary failure, of closure, of ultimate unresolvable contradictions and the impossibility of the future, which cannot have failed to oppress any reader of these texts."[28] Adorno's vision is thus one of a complete domination of the subject, individual or collective, by the object, the total system of contemporary capitalist society: "the total organization of the economy ends up alienating the very language and thoughts of its human population, and by dispelling the last remnant of the older autonomous subject or ego."[29] The structure of modern musical form, as much as that of Adorno's own dialectical history, mirrors back to the listener or reader the terrible closure of this emergent reality: "the total organizational principle of Schoenberg's system reflects a new systematization of the world itself, of which the so-called totalitarian political regimes are themselves only a symptom."[30] The latter referent should remind us that the situation in which Adorno writes is that of the darkest moments of the Cold War, when a total realization of the human destiny then only recently illuminated in Auschwitz appeared as a real possibility, if not indeed an inevitability.

Such narratives of the "fall" require an earlier idealized moment against which the present can be judged, and, for Adorno, the time of Beethoven serves this figural role, a period when the revolutionary dissolution of the older feudal order was reaching its crescendo. It is also in this situation in which Hegel's landmark formulation of the dialectical method occurs. At this point, Jameson advances a conclusion whose significance in terms of the structure of his own narrative will become evident momentarily: "Historical freedom, indeed, expanding and contracting as it does with the objective conditions themselves, never seems greater than in such transitional periods, where the life-style has not yet taken on the rigidity of a period manner, and when there is sudden release from the old without any corresponding obligation to that which will come to take its place."[31] However, such a moment is no longer his, and so the only options available to the critic, Adorno's work suggests, are to remain "resolutely unsystematic," as in the fragmentary essays and deferred theses of *Notes on Literature*, and to deploy the unrelenting critical stringency of *Negative Dialectics*. In this way, we might keep faith with what remains in the present at least an unimaginable future; or, as Adorno himself had earlier put it, "If there is anyone today to whom we can pass the responsibilities for the message, we bequeath it not to the 'masses,' and not to the individual (who is powerless), but to an imaginary witness—lest it perish with us."[32]

Taking this as its initial starting point, the subsequent narrative of *Marxism and Form* might be understood to give a new content to this "imaginary witness," as it works to occupy what remains for Adorno the impossible exterior perspective on this total system, the objective pole in this dialectical narrative gradually turning over once more to the subjective. The next step takes us through three linked versions of a Marxist hermeneutic recoverable in the work of Walter Benjamin, Herbert Marcuse, and Ernst Bloch. Each offers a powerful dialectical rejoinder to Adorno's vision, as they recover horizons of possibility not made available in Adorno's project.

In Benjamin's work, this takes the form of a fascination with memory and nostalgia, both serving as intimations of a psychic wholeness unavailable in our present. It is in this section as well that we witness Jameson's own initial engagement with the fourfold medieval allegorical schema that will play such an important role in *The Political Unconscious*. Allegory is, Jameson maintains, "the privileged mode of our own life in time, a clumsy deciphering of meaning from moment to moment, the painful attempt to restore a continuity to heterogeneous, disconnected instances."[33] Over and against this stands Benjamin's notion of "aura," a utopian "plenitude of existence in the world of things . . . available to the thinker only in a simpler cultural past," a past embodied in cultural forms such as storytelling.[34] Such forms are "a mode of contact with a vanished form of social and historical existence," a reminder of radically other ways of doing and being in the world; in this way, Benjamin's work recovers, for us, some of the radical political potentiality of nostalgia and memory.[35]

Jameson opens his discussion of Marcuse's work with an important reminder of the political function of hermeneutics, as it "provides the means for contact with the very sources of revolutionary energy during a stagnant time, of preserving the concept of freedom itself, underground, during geological ages of repression."[36] It is exactly this operation that Jameson argues is at work earlier in Friedrich Schiller's *Letters on the Aesthetic Education of Mankind*, with its notion of "nature"; and in Surrealism, with its deployment of the commodity icons of an earlier stage of twentieth-century capitalism. In a prefiguration of his well-known formulation in *Postmodernism*, Jameson also notes that today, "the objects of Surrealism are gone without a trace. Henceforth, in what we may call postindustrial capitalism, the products with which we are furnished are utterly without depth."[37] Marcuse's work then offers us one of the first and most fully elaborated "explorations of the psychological and socio-economic infrastructure" of an entirely new moment in the history of capitalism, and thereby stands as a complement to the project of Adorno.[38] What disappears in such a situation, for both Adorno and Marcuse, is "any effective possibility of negating the system in general." However, here Marcuse takes a new turn, and formulates the fundamental task of the philosopher in such a situation as "the revival, of the very idea of the negation," a revival in short, of "the Utopian impulse" itself.[39] This takes the form of a double hermeneutic, a reading of the "life-style" freedoms of the present as "*figures* of Freedom in general"; and an unveiling of the foundations of such utopian longings in a primeval memory of "a plenitude of psychic gratification . . . a time before all repression . . . prehistoric paradise."[40] If Adorno orients us toward the apparent immobility of the present, and Benjamin toward the otherness of the past, it is in Marcuse's work, as well as in that of his predecessors, that we see a "stubborn rebirth of the idea of freedom" as a potentiality of the future.[41]

The fullest expression of such a hermeneutics of the future is then found, for Jameson, in the thinking of Ernst Bloch. I have dealt elsewhere with the centrality of Bloch's work for Jameson's intellectual project.[42] In terms of the narrative we are tracing out here, I would only stress that Bloch's work fulfills the reorientation toward the future whose intimations we have already seen in Marcuse. While Bloch's hermeneutic engages with an astonishing range of objects, his conceptual content remains at its core quite consistent: "everything in the world becomes a version of some primal figure, a manifestation of that primordial movement toward the future and toward ultimate identity with a transfigured world which is Utopia."[43] For Bloch, this horizon, available in every human cultural creation, takes the form of "the *novum*, the utterly and unexpectedly new, the new which astonished by its absolute and intrinsic unpredictability"; the future then is "always something *other* than what we sought to find there."[44] Moreover, in Bloch's thinking, we see the dialectical sublation not only of the "anxiety" evident in Adorno's work, but of the doctrine of memory central for Benjamin, and whose traces are still present in Marcuse: in Bloch, the "no-longer consciousness," ultimately Freudian at base, is replaced by the "not-yet-consciousness, an ontological pull of the future, of a tidal influence exerted upon us by that which lies out of sight below the horizon, an unconscious of what is yet to come."[45]

The force of the work of all three thinkers, Jameson concludes, lies in the way they restore to any truly Marxist interpretation of cultural texts: "a genuine political dimension . . . reading the very content and the formal impulse of the texts themselves as figures—whether of psychic wholeness, of freedom, or of the drive toward Utopian transfiguration—of the irrepressible revolutionary wish."[46] We have thus come full circle from the indispensable thesis of the negative dialectic of Adorno to the antithesis of the positive utopian dialectic of these three thinkers.

However, the story is not nearly over, for this "revolutionary wish" becomes concrete only in the realm of history. It is here that the next step in Jameson's narrative necessarily brings us, as only now we turn our attention to the work of Lukács. At this point, Jameson suggests a fundamental narrative unity in Lukács's project, one that mirrors the unity of the story he tells throughout this book: "a set of solutions and problems developing out of one another according to their own inner logic and momentum."[47] In addition to the concrete exploration of realist narrative we touched on previously, what also reemerges at this point is a vision of a collective agency, the subject of history, that is absent in the versions of the dialectic we have experienced thus far.

And yet agency also turns out to be fundamentally linked to questions of epistemology, of each group's particular perspective on the world. The elaboration of the differences between bourgeois and working-class epistemologies becomes the project of Lukács's great work of the early 1920s, *History and Class Consciousness*. What defines bourgeois philosophy, for Lukács, is "its incapacity or unwillingness to come to terms with the category of *totality* itself."[48] Most significantly, this means an inability to recognize the sheer and complete historicity of their world and its values. The working class, on the other hand, precisely because of its location within the productive process, understands that any apparently finished "thing," including society itself, is "little more than a moment in the process of production."[49] The fundamental knowledge to be gained from whomever occupies the standpoint of the proletariat—a collective class perspective not necessarily embodied in any particular individual's existential experience—is "a sense of forces at work within the present, a dissolving of the reified surface of the present into a coexistence of various and conflicting historical tendencies, a translation of immobile objects into acts and potential acts and into the consequences of acts."[50] From such a perspective, ontology itself is understood to be thoroughly historical and social in nature. Such a "true" picture of world cannot be rendered in terms of scientific taxonomies as effectively as in the elaboration of plot, and so it is no surprise, Jameson suggests, that Lukács's attention turns to the realist narrative.

At this point in our narrative the social object of Adorno's negative dialectic has been transformed once again as a fluid historical process, the adopted perspective of the object giving way to that of the subject. While the climax of the story is hinted at in the Lukács discussion, it will be in the next chapter, "Sartre and History," where it achieves a full narrative figuration. Of course, this is not Jameson's first extended engagement with the work of the preeminent French intellectual of the middle part of the twentieth century, which was also the subject of his doctoral dissertation and first book, *Sartre: The Origins of Style* (1962). However, it is the publication of Sartre's monumental *Critique of Dialectical Reason* that now leads Jameson to approach his thought anew. The project Sartre engages in this work is akin to that of *Marxism and Form* itself: if "Marxism is a way of understanding the objective dimension of history from the outside," and "existentialism a way of understanding subjective, individual experience," then the goal will be to bring the two together in "a kind of unified field theory in which two wholly different ontological phenomena can share a common set of equations and be expressed in a single linguistic or terminological system."[51] Sartre's fundamental target, Jameson ultimately demonstrates, is the economism of certain forms of "classical or orthodox Marxism": these have the singular "disadvantage of drawing attention to the separation and relatively autonomous development of each class, rather than to their constant interaction in the form of class struggle."[52]

The point here, however, Jameson maintains, is not simply to move from one dialectical pole to the other; to do so would still leave us trapped within the same antinomy of the object and subject, materialism and idealism, synchrony and diachrony, with which we began. Rather, Jameson argues that Sartre reinvents for a new historical moment the fundamental solution of Marx himself as he works to "strike at the very category of the specialized discipline as such, and to restore the unity of knowledge."[53] The genius of Marxism is that it "has at its disposal two alternative languages (or codes, to use the structuralist term) in which any given phenomenon can be described. Thus, history can be written either subjectively, as the history of class struggle, or objectively, as the development of the economic mode of production and their evolution from their own internal contradictions: these two formula are the same, and any statement in one can without loss of meaning be translated into the other."[54] Here, Jameson also implicitly critiques the Althusserian notion of an "epistemological break" (*coupture*) in Marx's intellectual project, dividing his earlier "humanist" work from his "mature" scientific texts. Drawing these two registers together is the notion of class, and it is to this interaction and conflict of these collectives that the narrative of *Marxism and Form* has finally led us.

Jameson's path to this dialectical resolution follows the same narrative structure that it has in the earlier chapters, and in the book as a whole. Thus, for example, while the issue of the "attraction at a distance" that the mass of workers represented for Sartre is raised in the first paragraphs of the chapter,[55] it will not be until its final pages, after the careful and painstaking narrative working through of Sartre's intellectual project that we might begin to "evaluate" this concept.[56] Suddenly, the entire project of Sartre's *Critique* can be cast "in a new light: it is Sartre's own attempt to see *himself*, to see his own class from the outside, to recuperate the external objectivity of both which is granted only through the judgment and look of the other upon them, or in other words through the concrete class antagonisms of history."[57] It is only at this conjuncture that Sartre, and the narrative of *Marxism and Form* itself, "attain the ultimate and determining reality of social being itself" in the social conflict and material praxis of classes and groups.[58]

The question that naturally arises here is what makes such an unveiling of totality possible at this particular historical conjuncture? Jameson answers that "Sartre's *Critique*, at the beginning of the 1960's . . . corresponds to a new period of revolutionary ferment, and in the spirit of Marx himself offers a reworking of the economistic model in that terminology of praxis and of overt class conflict which seem now most consistent with the day-to-day lived experience of this period."[59] With this climax, we are similarly positioned to evaluate the historical conditions of possibility for the writing of *Marxism and Form*. If, as Jameson suggests, "realism is dependent on the possibility of access to the forces of change in a given moment of history," then it is the social, cultural, political, and intellectual ferment of the 1960s that makes his own "realist" narrative possible: "The simplest yet most universal formulation surely remains the widely shared feeling that in the 60s, for a time, everything was possible; that this period, in other words, was a moment of universal liberation, a global unbinding of energies."[60] The realism of *Marxism and Form* is thus both very much a product of this historical conjuncture, its plot rewriteable as a story about the fundamental intellectual transformations *within* the United States that occur as we move from the Cold War 1950s—with its despairing sense of total social closure and historical immobility—to the enthusiasm and utopian optimism characteristic of the 1960s. Indeed, of his own views of Adorno in this early work, Jameson will later write, "In the age of wars of national liberation, Adorno's sense of Apocalypse seemed very retrogressive indeed, focused as it was on the moment of Auschwitz, and obsessed with the doom and baleful enchantment of a 'total system' that few enough—in a 'pre-revolutionary' moment defined notoriously by the sense that *'tout est possible!'*—sensed impending in our own future in the middle distance."[61]

However, as this passage intimates, such a horizon proves to be a short-lived one. In a later reassessment of the 1960s, Jameson offers this very different characterization of this crucial historical moment: "Yet this sense of freedom and possibility—which is for the course of the 60s a momentarily objective reality, as well as (from the hindsight of the 80s) a historical illusion—can perhaps best be explained in terms of the superstructural movement and play enabled by the transition from one infrastructural or systemic stage of capitalism to another."[62] Rather than heralding a fundamental break with capitalism, the 1960s is now to be understood as a moment of the latter's reorganization, culminating in the early 1970s with the emergence of a full-blown postmodern "late capitalism."

A similar institutional restructuration can also be understood to have been under way within the American intellectual academy, a reorganization in which *Marxism and Form* plays a vital role. A few years after the publication of *Marxism and Form*, Jameson explicitly addresses the role of realist narratives in such moments of historical transition. Deploying the conceptual tools made available by Gilles Deleuze and Félix Guattari's *Anti-Oedipus* (1972), Jameson now describes the work of realism not in terms of mapping an open and fluid social totality but rather as a critical "decoding" operation, "a demystification of some preceding ideal or illusion."[63] *Marxism and Form* also engages in an operation of "decoding" of ideals and illusions at work within the American intellectual community. This occurs on two distinct and yet linked levels. The first level at which this decoding is aimed is made explicit in the opening paragraph of the book: "When the American reader thinks of Marxist literary criticism, I imagine that it is still the atmosphere of the 1930s which comes to mind. . . . The criticism practiced then was of a relatively untheoretical, essentially didactic nature, destined more for use in the night school than in the graduate seminar."[64] If recent work by Barbara Foley, Michael Denning, William J. Maxwell, and Caren Irr, among others, enables us today to have more nuanced understanding of the Marxist intellectual labor of the 1930s, Jameson's statement captures the commonplace assumption of its moment of the limitations of Marxist cultural criticism.[65] It is this version to which *Marxism and Form* directs its decoding energies, clearing the space that will soon be inhabited by a much richer variety of species.

Moreover, the very characterization of "criticism" he offers here points toward an even more general target of his text's critical machinery. Literary criticism of a "relatively untheoretical, essentially didactic nature, destined more for use in the night school than in the graduate seminar"—such a description can equally be applied to what has by the late 1960s become the ossified strategies of the then still reigning New Critical formalism.[66] *Marxism and Form* thus participates in a more general assault on these hegemonies: a series of very different interventions that ultimately will be assembled under the common flag of "theory." Jameson suggests such a link late in *Marxism and Form*, arguing that the fundamental operations of "much in modern thought" takes the form of a critical estrangement, "an assault on our conventionalized life patterns, a whole battery of shocks administered to our routine vision of things, an implicit critique and restructuration of our habitual perceptions."[67] Of course, it will be French models—first, briefly, structuralism and phenomenology, and then deconstruction and the various "poststructuralisms"—that will throughout the coming decades play a leading role in this decoding project, and it is no coincidence that Jameson's next book, *The Prison-House of Language*, takes up the project of exploring the potentialities and limitations of these various critical practices. Even here, Jameson suggests that the ultimate advantage of dialectal thought over these other practices lies in its attention to the historical situation that calls forth such strategies in the first place.

In his later essay on realism as a decoding practice, Jameson goes on to argue that ultimately a palpable sense of "fatigue" sets in with these kinds of critical projects, as the very objects of "such semiotic purification" begin to be exhausted: "This is, of course, the moment of modernism, or rather of the various modernisms," the effort to recode, to build a new language.[68] This will be the project of *The Political Unconscious*. If *Marxism and Form* is understood as a work that "unsticks" both U.S. Marxism in particular and contemporary literary criticism more generally, *The Political Unconscious* will offer a highly original method—a recoding, rebuilding, and new language—for both Marxism and literary criticism.

"All modernist works are," Jameson argues, "essentially simply cancelled realistic ones . . . they are, in other words, not apprehended directly, in terms of their own symbolic meanings . . . but rather indirectly only, by way of the relay of an imaginary realistic narrative of which the symbolic and modernistic one is then seen as a kind of stylization."[69] Modernism as a topic is encountered in a similar indirect fashion within the narrative structure of *The Political Unconscious*. In the final paragraph of the climactic chapter of the book (followed by a brief dénouement on "the dialectic of utopia and ideology"), Jameson writes,

> After the peculiar heterogeneity of the moment of Conrad, a high modernism is set in place which it is not the object of this book to consider. The perfected poetic apparatus of high modernism represses History just as successfully as the perfected narrative apparatus of high realism did the random heterogeneity of the as yet uncentered subject. At that point, however, the political, no longer visible in the high modernist texts, any more than in the everyday world of appearance of bourgeois life, and relentlessly driven underground by accumulated reification, has at last become a genuine Unconscious.[70]

Interestingly, this suggests that the very object of the book's narration, embedded as it is in the title itself, likewise remains outside the frame of direct analysis—as with History, in the Lacanian and Althusserian formulation that plays such a central role in this text, the political unconscious is "an absent cause . . . inaccessible to us except in textual form." We can thus only approach it indirectly "through its prior textualization, its narrativization."[71]

Something similar might be said about the place of modernism at this juncture in Jameson's intellectual project: both the central object and the very condition of possibility of his research agenda, it vanishes when we attempt to bring it to the center of our intellectual attention. Thus, we can approach it only in an asymptotic, indirect fashion. This too accounts for the peculiar nature of the "modernist" texts he examines in this book. The work of Conrad, he suggests, represents not yet a true modernism, but rather "a strategic fault line in the emergence of contemporary narrative, a place from which the structure of twentieth-century literary and cultural *institutions* become visible," as the machinery of the older realism breaks down into the two dialectically interrelated phenomenon of "high" modernist literature and a new mass culture.[72]

I would argue that such an indirect approach is also required to map out the modernist form of *The Political Unconscious*. We can begin to do so by first substituting a number of "imaginary realistic narratives" for the plot of *The Political Unconscious*, of which its form is now understood as a kind of "stylization." The book might first be read, for example, as a demonstration of the periodizing hypothesis in relationship to narrative practice. Jameson presents us with four different moments—romance, realism, naturalism, and modernism—each at the center of attention in Chapters 2 through 5. Or we might approach it as a history of the modern novel: the novel emerges from the older romance form, passes through the utopian realism of Balzac and the asphyxiating naturalism of George Gissing, and finally reaches its outermost horizon with the protomodernist narratives of Conrad (thereby, giving new spin to T. S. Eliot's famous dictum that truly modernist texts like James Joyce's *Ulysses* are not novels). Or again, we might recode the text as the story of the modern bourgeois subject, from its consolidation in the moment of Balzac (and to show its historicity, Jameson first demonstrates that there is nothing like it in the classical romance, the earlier form much more concerned with the mapping of space) to its decentering with the rise of a full cultural modernism. Or, we might understand the work as narrating a spatial history of modernity, beginning with the breaking out of the "social and spatial isolation" characteristic of the feudal period.[73] This inaugurates a process of spatial consolidation passing through the moment of the nation-state and on into a truly global imperial spatial network. Finally, there is a purely formal narrative at work, in which Chapters 3, 4, and 5 serve as illustrations of the "three concentric frameworks" of interpretation—political history, or events in time; society, or struggle between classes; and finally the sequence of modes of productions itself—as well as their respective constructions of the text—as symbolic act, ideologemes, and ideology of form—elaborated in Chapter 1.[74] The brilliance and originality of *The Political Unconscious* are that all of these narrative strands unfold simultaneously, making the text available for a wide range of interpretive "realist" decodings.

The very proliferation of these "cancelled realist narratives" also points toward one of central features of the modernist form of *The Political Unconscious*. I pointed out earlier that the realist narrative is best characterized for Jameson as a unity, a figuration on the level of textual form of the larger social totality. In the modernist text, precisely this unity must be reconstituted through the process of interpretation, and thus always remains at a distance from the text itself. And it is this development that tells us something crucial about the historical context within which modernism comes to fruition. In the Conrad chapter of *The Political Unconscious*, Jameson suggests that the "situation" of modernism is one of a dramatic increase in the tempo and extent of what Max Weber calls "rationalization" and Lukács "reification" of every dimension of modern existence. Such a process can "be described as the analytical dismantling of the various traditional or 'natural' [*naturwüchsige*] unities (social groups, institutions, human relationships, forms of authority, activities of a cultural and ideological as well as of a productive nature) into their component parts with a view to their 'Taylorization,' that is their reorganization into more efficient systems which function according to an instrumental, or binary, means/ends logic."[75] Later, Jameson will argue that among the supreme manifestations of such a process is the tendency toward "*autonomy*," at once on the level of "aesthetic experience," of "culture," and finally, "of the work itself."[76] Even more significantly for our concerns, Jameson then turns to the way that these "various kinds of 'autonomy' now inscribe themselves in the very structure of individual works."[77] He argues that this process of "autonomization" "can now be initially observed on two levels of the modernist work in general, or, if you prefer, from two distinct standpoints, two positions unequally distant from the work as a whole. One of these distances—the longer one—discloses the process at work in the becoming autonomous of the episodes; while the more proximate one tracks it down into the very dynamic of the individual sentences themselves (or the equivalent ultimate 'autonomous' unit of formal syntax)."[78]

Crucially, Jameson emphasizes, both here and in *The Political Unconscious*, that these aspects of the modernist work—at once evident in Conrad's fiction, *Ulysses* ("the Joycean chapter is virtually the archetypal emblem of the process of episodization in modernism,"[79]), and in Hitchcock's later "modernist" film—must be understood as "semi-autonomies." Thus, in the case of *Ulysses*, "Autonomy—or, if you like, semi-autonomy—reemerges with a vengeance here, where the chapters run with their pretext, each setting its own rules in a certain independence, which is itself then authorized by the perfunctory allusion of the chapter as a whole to some corresponding section of the *Odyssey*."[80] Such a recognition is indispensable for any periodizing description of the formal structure of the modernist text, "since when these two poles split definitively asunder (when semi-autonomy, in other words, breaks into autonomy *tout court*, and a sheerly random play of heterogeneities), we are in the postmodern."[81]

Such semi-autonomy is, as suggested in my various decodings of the cancelled realist narratives of the text, characteristic of the form of *The Political Unconscious* as well, with each chapter "setting its own rules in a certain independence" from the others. Indeed, this text is marked by what Jameson names "generic discontinuity": "not so much an organic unity as a symbolic act that must reunite or harmonize heterogeneous narrative paradigms."[82] This concept is akin to the description of the dialogism, heteroglossia, and polyphony of the novel offered by Mikhail Bakhtin. Bakhtin's notions themselves also now being understood as most accurately designating the modernist text in the light of which Bakhtin, deploying a "regressive-progressive" dialectic akin to that of Marx's analysis of production, rewrites the entire history of the novel form.[83] This accounts as well for the "tenacious stereotype of the 'plotlessness'" of Jameson's text, "as though there were any non-narrative moments" in it. To further paraphrase Jameson on Joyce's masterpiece, the narrativity of *The Political Unconscious* "is that of the episode and not of the work 'as a whole,' by which we probably mean the *idea* of the work, its 'concept,'" what the title itself is meant to convey.[84] That such a concept cannot be encountered directly, and indeed determines at a mediated distance the contents of any particular text, is indeed suggestive of the book's thoroughgoing modernism as well.

This formal structure is then echoed on the level of the work's content in the centrality for Jameson's thinking at this point of the work of Althusser, whose formulation of the "semi-autonomy" of the various features (culture, ideology, law, the economy, and so forth) of the mode of production;[85] and of the absent presence of the totality of the Real (which Jameson elsewhere describes as another term for "simply History itself"[86]) are crucial to both Jameson's text as a whole and his theorizations of modernism itself. Indeed, within the specific histories of Marxism, Althusser's structuralism might best be grasped as the moment of modernism: it will only be with the full autonomizations of the post-Marxism (though more accurately post-Althusserianism) of Ernesto Laclau and Chantal Mouffe that we enter into a postmodernism proper.

There is another crucial modernist element of this text: the full-blown emergence as some of the sentences previously cited bear out of Jameson's signatory "style." Terry Eagleton acknowledges as much when he entitles his review of *The Political Unconscious*, "Fredric Jameson: The Politics of Style," and opens with a paragraph-long parody of Jameson's prose.[87] Jameson will later suggest that such a practice of parody is itself a particularly modernist phenomenon: "To be sure, parody found a fertile area in the idiosyncrasies of the moderns and their 'inimitable styles.'" All such parodies depend on "a norm which then reasserts itself, in a not necessarily unfriendly way, by a systematic mimicry of their willful eccentricities," the norms here being generated by the individual writer rather than larger institutions (genre, academy, culture) he or she inhabits.[88] Thus, just as such parodies as those found in "Bad Hemingway" or "Bad Faulkner," competitions are simply not available, except by way of a retrospective projection, for writers like Charles Dickens or Balzac, so too the kind of parody offered by Eagleton would not have been conceivable, except retroactively from the fully modernist style of *The Political Unconscious*.

In this way, style becomes a stand-in for the monadic subject of the individual creative genius. However, Jameson argues that such modernist figures themselves need to be understood, "non- and anti-anthropomorphically . . . as *careers*, that is to say as objective situations in which an ambitious young artist around the turn of the century could see the objective possibility of turning himself into the 'greatest painter' (or poet or novelist or composer) 'of the age.'"[89] His description here can be readily transferred from the general situation of high modernism to the academic institutional context out of which *The Political Unconscious* emerges. For this is the moment of "high theory," a movement that both Andreas Huyssen and Jameson will subsequently describe as the final stage in the long history of cultural modernism.[90] And like the earlier moment of "artistic" modernism, this is an "objective situation" in which the possibility is available of becoming the "greatest theorist of the age"—or more precisely, in the appellation awarded to Jameson with the publication of this book, to become "the best Marxist critic writing today, possibly the best social-historically oriented critic of our time" (Hayden White). With the publication of *The Political Unconscious*, Jameson becomes one of the first Americans to join a largely European pantheon of theoretical giants, including Claude Lévi-Strauss, Jacques Lacan, Roland Barthes, Michel Foucault, Jacques Derrida, and Julia Kristeva, as well as the earlier generation of Frankfurt School theorists he had helped make famous with *Marxism and Form*.[91] Jameson's leap in fame is signaled by the special issue of *Diacritics* devoted to *The Political Unconscious*, with the first published interview with him (an event that also marks the emergence of interest in Jameson as an intellectual "personality"), and by the publication of the first systematic guide to any of his works.[92]

Jameson goes on to argue that the emphasis on individual style in the moment of high modernism stands as a protest against the standardization and homogenization of modern life, and thus draws "its power and its possibilities from being a backwater and an archaic holdover within a modernizing economy." Modernism, he maintains, must "be seen as uniquely corresponding to an uneven moment of social development, or to what Ernst Bloch called the 'simultaneity of the nonsimultaneous,' the 'synchronicity of the nonsynchronous' (*Gleichzeitigkeit des Ungleichzeitigen*): the coexistence of realities from radically different moments of history."[93] Thus, the "keen sense of the New in the modern period was only possible because of the mixed, uneven, transitory nature of that period, in which the old coexisted with the new."[94] Within the academic context of *The Political Unconscious*, we see a similar "unevenness," as the then dominant disciplinary structure confronts the new work advanced under the aegis of theory. Indeed, I would argue that it is specifically the interdisciplinarity of theory—the dramatic and dislocating encounter for literary scholars, for example, with work not only from such "foreign" disciplines as philosophy, linguistics, psychology, anthropology, and history, but also from very different national traditions— that strikes its readers in this moment with all the shock of the new, or Bloch's *Novum*. This is the moment both of the monumental figures and the great named avant-gardes: deconstruction, reader-response criticism, feminism, postcolonial criticism, New Historicism, queer theory, to note only a few of the more well-known examples. The expressions of shock, outrage, and even disgust on the part of the defenders of disciplinary practices and standards are also akin to the response of the artistic academies to the work of the high modernists. Indeed, Richard Aldington's dismissal of *Ulysses* as an anarchic work, and, like the Dadaism he claims it most nearly resembled, an "invitation to chaos," is echoed in many of the conservative responses to the new theory. It is in this context then that Jameson's work will come to play an increasingly central and influential role.

However, there is a distinct price to be paid for the proliferation of these movements and unique voices. Jameson argues of earlier modernist enthusiasms,

> One did not simply read D. H. Lawrence or Rilke, see Jean Renoir or Hitchcock, or listen to Stravinsky, as distinct manifestations of what we now term modernism. Rather one read all of the works of a particular writer, learned a style and a phenomenological world. D. H. Lawrence became an absolute, a complete and systematic world view, to which one converted. . . . The crisis of modernism as such came, then, when suddenly it became clear that "D. H. Lawrence" was not an absolute after all, not the final achieved figuration of the truth of the world, but only one art-language among others, only one shelf of works in a whole dizzying library. Hence the shame and guilt of cultural intellectuals, the renewed appeal of the Hegelian goal, the "end of art," and the abandonment of culture altogether for immediate political activity.[95]

Here we arrive at a central contradiction of modernist aesthetics. Each particular practice, style, or movement declares itself to be the new universal; however, the very proliferation of such declarations already signals the ultimate impossibility of any such unification. Such a development, Jameson elsewhere suggests, finds its roots in the "breakdown of a homogenous public, with the social fragmentation and anomie of the bourgeoisie itself, and also its refraction among the various national situations."[96] This would include "not least those relatively homogenous reading publics to whom, in the writer's contract, certain relatively stable signals can be sent."[97] Each modernist practice, style, or movement "demands an organic community which it cannot, however, bring into being by itself but can only express."[98] That *The Political Unconscious* advances similar ambitions is evident in its opening paragraph: "This book will argue the priority of the political interpretation of literary texts. It conceives of the political perspective *not* as some supplementary method, *not* as an optional auxiliary to other interpretive methods current today . . . but rather as the *absolute horizon* of *all* reading and *all* interpretation."[99] Of course, similar claims will be made by all of the great modernist theoretical works and movements of this moment, and the conflicts and incommensurabilties between them echo through the pages of the proliferating journals of the 1970s and 1980s, publications akin to the little magazines of an earlier artistic modernism.

What I am suggesting here is that "theoretical modernism," exemplified for us in Jameson's central achievement of this moment, replays many of the same issues, anxieties, and concerns of high modernism proper—the difference here lying in the fact that theory's modernist period already had the earlier history of the rise and fall of modernism behind it, so that the central positions in the debate had already been set into place.[100] Thus, it should come as no surprise that the response to modernist theory's failure to constitute itself as an absolute, the "shame and guilt of cultural intellectuals" and the call for "the abandonment of culture (read here, Theory) altogether for immediate political activity," should also soon reemerge. Indeed, these are precisely the terms of one of the first important commentaries on Jameson's book, in Edward Said's 1982 synoptic overview of cultural criticism in the "Age of Ronald Reagan."[101] Said finds in Jameson's book "an unadmitted dichotomy between two kinds of 'Politics': (1) the politics defined by political theory from Hegel to Louis Althusser and Ernst Bloch; (2) the politics of struggle and power in the everyday world, which in the United States at least has been won, so to speak, by Reagan."[102] Not only does Jameson privilege the first, Said maintains, but the latter appears at only one place in the entire book, in a long footnote on page 54. The relationship between these two forms of politics is never made clear, and this is because Jameson's "assumed constituency is an audience of cultural-literary critics."[103] In this, he is like many of the major theoretical thinkers and writers of the moment, located "in cloistral seclusion from the inhospitable world of real politics."[104] The "autonomy" of theoretical writing has been secured through a disengagement from the world, an increasingly reified technical specialization and what Said calls an agreement of "*noninterference* in the affairs of the everyday world."[105] In short, the political is "no longer visible" in these theoretical texts, "and relentlessly driven underground by accumulated reification, has at last become a genuine Unconscious."[106] Said's reformed scholarship would instead take up the politically activist stance of "*interference*, crossing of borders and obstacles, a determined attempt to generalize exactly at those points where generalizations seem impossible to make."[107]

As a description of the status of humanist intellectual work among a larger readership in the United States in the early 1980s, Said's characterization is depressingly apt. However, in it, Said elides two of the concerns that are in fact central to all of Jameson's thought: that of genre and what we have been focusing on throughout this essay, periodization. First, Said can be said to be guilty of a generic category error, calling not for another kind of literary scholarship, but rather another kind of public critical engagement; it is as if he were criticizing Marx for taking the time to write *Capital* ("There is no royal road to science") instead of committing himself exclusively to the genre of radical journalism. These are in fact very different tasks, each with its own value in our world, and each a site of real engagement and struggle.

With this kind of generic specification in place, the question then becomes one of what is possible for any particular practice of writing in its historical moment. We return, in other words, to the long-standing debate within Marxism between voluntarism and determinism: is the disengagement from the everyday a matter of free "moral choice" (Said's phrase) on the part of these theoretical writers, or a consequence of the specific "situation" in which they are working?[108] That *The Political Unconscious* has apparently turned from the immediacy of collective praxis glimpsed in the climax of *Marxism and Form*, and toward a more patient examination of the *longue durée* of capitalist modernity tells us a great deal about the very different political situations in which each work appears.

Moreover, Said's discussion can be read as symptomatic of its historical moment in its abandonment of the dialectical view of modernism that Jameson offers in *The Political Unconscious*. Jameson writes, "That modernism is itself an ideological expression of capitalism, and in particular, of the latter's reification of daily life, may be granted a local validity. . . . Viewed in this way, then, modernism can be seen as a late stage in the bourgeois cultural revolution, as a final and extremely specialized phase of that immense process of superstructural transformation whereby the inhabitants of older social formations are culturally and psychologically retrained for life in the market system."[109] The same claim I think can be made of the theoretical modernism that we have been discussing, as it "retrains" us for the very different forms of intellectual and academic life that begin to emerge in the later 1970s. "Yet," Jameson continues, "modernism can at one and the same time be read as a Utopian compensation for everything reification brings with it. . . . the place of quality in an increasingly quantified world, the place of the archaic and of feeling amid the desacralization of the market system, the place of sheer color and intensity within the grayness of measurable extension and geometrical abstraction."[110] Such a characterization fits, to my mind, *The Political Unconscious* and the other theoretical modernisms of its moment. The fact that this insight represents one of the most important lessons of *The Political Unconscious* is borne out in the concluding chapter, wherein this dialectic is then expanded into a fundamental axiom of all cultural criticism.

In his review essay on Tafuri's *Architecture and Utopia*, Jameson advances this analysis one step further, and helps us place Said's intervention even more clearly in its context. Here, Jameson argues that the two positions that result from the fission of this modernist dialectic —a rigorous "pessimism" about the possibilities of cultural work (something we can see in Said's evaluation of contemporary theoretical discourses) and a "complacent free play" that abandons the great modernist projects of cultural and social transformation—are in fact "two intolerable options of a single double-bind."[111] Such a predicament then becomes one of the crucial symptoms of *postmodernism*—and with this, we make the transition to the next period in Jameson's project.

It is in *The Anti-Aesthetic: Essays on Postmodern Culture* (1983), the same landmark collection that reprints Said's essay, that we also find a work that signals a new direction in Jameson's intellectual program. Entitled "Postmodernism and Consumer Society," this short essay, originally a 1982 Whitney Museum Lecture, represents Jameson's first explicit foray into the issues and questions that would come to full fruition the following year, in perhaps his single most influential essay, "Postmodernism, or the Cultural Logic of Late Capitalism."[112] This latter work will serve seven years hence as the first chapter of the book-length study of the same name.

In "Postmodernism and Consumer Society," Jameson investigates two crucial features of an emergent postmodern culture: "pastiche and schizophrenia," characteristic of "the postmodernist experience of space and time respectively."[113] He finds the former exemplified by popular "nostalgia films"—*Chinatown, American Graffiti, Star Wars,* and *Body Heat* (a discussion that has its roots in an essay more than a decade earlier, "On Raymond Chandler"[114])—and the latter in the experimental work "China" by the language poet Bob Perelman. His concluding observation on Perelman's text are especially interesting in that they offer some of the earliest clues as to the formal structure of Jameson's next major work: "In the present case, the represented object is not really China after all: what happened was that Perelman came across a book of photographs in a stationery store in Chinatown. . . . The sentences of the poem are *his* captions to those pictures. Their referents are other images, another text, and the 'unity' of the poem is not *in* the text at all but outside it in the bound unity of an absent book."[115] Similarly, I want to argue that the unity of Jameson's own analysis of postmodernism will not reside in the text, but rather outside it, in the absent totality of our current cultural condition. As a consequence, what disappears in the full *Postmodernism* study are the narrative rhythms that structured the two earlier texts we have already examined. Even the "cancelled realisms" of *The Political Unconscious* are no longer evident in a work that moves from object to object and text to text with no discernable narrative logic. Crucially then, we can read in the pastiche aesthetic of nostalgia films—which Jameson characterizes as "an elaborated symptom of the waning of our historicity, of our lived possibility of experiencing history in some active way"[116]—the schizophrenic form of Perelman's poem—"if we are unable to unify the past present, and future of the sentence, then we are similarly unable to unify the past, present, and future of our own biographical experience or psychic life"[117]— and finally in the formal structure of Jameson's *Postmodernism* book itself, powerful figurations of one of the central dilemmas of the postmodern condition: our inability to tell the *stories* that would enable us to position ourselves within and hence act in our new world.

Moreover, the form of this latest work reflects Jameson's central contention that postmodernism is a cultural situation "increasingly dominated by space and spatial logic."[118] Indeed, while following the lead of the great French theorist Henri Lefebvre, and acknowledging that all social organizations are defined by distinctive productions of space, Jameson argues that "ours has been spatialized in a unique sense, such that space is for us an existential and cultural dominant, a thematized and foregrounded feature or structural principle standing in striking contrast to its relatively subordinate and secondary (though no doubt no less symptomatic) role in earlier modes of production."[119] The central political task of this phase of Jameson's project will thus rest in the search for the forms of narrative, and hence an experience of history, that will aid us in moving beyond such a situation.

As a kind of compensation for the absence of the narrative pleasures of his earlier works, Jameson's *Postmodernism* book examines a breathtaking range of different cultural forms and practices. Jameson discusses the architecture of John Portman's Bonaventure Hotel and Frank Gehry's Santa Monica home; video productions by Nam June Paik; the late *nouvelle roman* of Claude Simon; paintings by Vincent Van Gogh and Andy Warhol (the latter gracing the book's cover); sculpture by Duane Hanson; conceptual and installation art by Hans Haacke and Robert Gober; punk rock and John Cage's avant-garde performances; science fiction by J. G. Ballard and Philip K. Dick; New Historicism and the theoretical nominalism of Paul De Man; market ideology; David Lynch's *Blue Velvet* and Jonathan Demme's *Something Wild*; as well as an equally diverse set of issues and objects in the long concluding chapter, "Secondary Elaborations." Although Jameson's first forays into forms and practices other than those of literature or critical theory had in fact begun in the 1970s,[120] it is with the publication of *Postmodernism* that visual and spatial forms such as film, painting, photography, installation art, and, most significantly, architecture come to occupy a new central place in his thinking.

This proliferation of objects in turn reflects some of Jameson's central claims concerning the nature of postmodernism. First, Jameson contends that within a full-blown postmodernism the semi-autonomy of the aesthetic from other areas of social life—the famous Kantian spheres whose distinct operational logics someone like Jürgen Habermas desires to retain—as well as the hierarchies within culture itself, all begin to dissolve away. "Yet," Jameson notes, "to argue that culture is today no longer endowed with the relative autonomy it once enjoyed as one level among others in earlier moments of capitalism (let alone in precapitalist societies) is not necessarily to imply its disappearance or extinction. Quite the contrary; we must go on to affirm that the dissolution of an autonomous sphere of culture is rather to be imagined in terms of an explosion: a prodigious expansion of culture throughout the social realm, to the point at which everything in our social life—from economic value and state power to practices and to the very structure of the psyche itself—can be said to have become 'cultural' in some original and yet untheorized way."[121] Moreover, Jameson argues that forms and practices such as architecture and "political power" have become in the original situation of the postmodern increasingly "textualized," and hence made more readily available to scholars trained in strategies of literary and philosophical reading.[122] Thus, in a significant way, the disciplinary boundaries that had been blurred in his earlier work now all but vanish without a trace: the entire expanded cultural and textual realm become grist for Jameson's voracious analytical mill. Moreover, this work marks Jameson's own increasing influence in disciplines beyond literary scholarship—something that also occurs in terms of the work of the other great theorists (think, for example, of Derrida's 1980s writings on architecture and his collaborations with Peter Eisenman). And this expansion also means that the stakes in these discussions have been raised, as Jameson argues, "This is surely the most crucial terrain of ideological struggle today, which has migrated from concepts to representations."[123]

However, often overlooked in discussions of Jameson's work on postmodernism is the fact that in both the 1984 essay and the later book he approaches these diverse cultural "texts" through what are in fact two distinct optics. First, his engagement with some of them is aimed at developing what he calls a "symptomology" of various dimensions of the original experience of the postmodern. "Art therefore," he maintains, and which we might expand to cultural and textual production more generally, "yields social information primarily as symptom. Its specialized machinery (itself obviously symptomatic of social specialization more generally) is capable of registering and recording data with a precision unavailable in other modes of modern experience . . . its configurations allow us to take the temperature of the current situation."[124] The "data" that he uncovers in this fashion are the central characteristics of the postmodern, the list of which has now become, in a large part thanks to his investigations, a familiar one: the collapse of critical distance, the waning of affect, the weakening of historicity, the dissolution of the centered subject, the collapse of the referent, and the new centrality of the image and information technologies. The conception of the postmodern that Jameson offers here is thus "a historical rather than a merely stylistic one," as he attempts to grasp the postmodern as "the cultural dominant of the logic of late capitalism."[125] And indeed, in this study, Jameson will draw extensively on the then major work of political economy, Ernest Mandel's *Late Capitalism*, for an explanation of the material transformations that lie at the root of postmodern cultural productions. Each of these two approaches to the postmodern, he goes on to argue, generates very different ways of conceptualizing this material: if the stylistic approach, wherein the postmodern becomes one optional practice among other, results in "moral judgments," the historical offers "a genuinely dialectical attempt to think our present of time in history."[126]

Such a symptomatic approach is made both necessary and more difficult by another crucial mutation that occurs in the postmodern: the shift from the older conceptual category of the "work" to that of the "text." This shift, Jameson contends, "throws the chicken coops of criticism into commotion fully as much as it stirs those of 'creation': the fundamental disparity and incommensurability between *text* and *work* means that to select sample texts and, by analysis, to make them bear the universalizing weight of a representative particular, turns them imperceptibly back into that older thing, the work, which is not supposed to exist in the postmodern. This is, as it were, the Heisenberg principle of postmodernism, and the most difficult representational problem for any commentator to come to terms with save via the endless slide show, 'total flow' prolonged into the infinite."[127] It is precisely this kind of "total flow prolonged into the infinite," or what Hegel calls "bad infinity," that we see in the proliferation of analysis in the 1980s and early 1990s inspired by or imitating Jameson's discussion, as more and more objects and practices are read as symptoms of this new cultural system.

And yet, while he will claim a new global nature for culture within the postmodern, Jameson carefully demarcates the specific horizons of his analysis. First, he points out that his focus remains almost exclusively on the particular cultural productions of the United States, "which is justified only to the degree that it was the brief 'American century' (1945-1973) that constituted the hothouse, or forcing ground of the new system, while the development of the cultural forms of postmodernism may be said to be the first specifically North American global style."[128] Similarly, Jameson points out the particular class content of these forms, practices, and ideologies. They are those of "a new petite bourgeoisie, a professional-managerial class, or more succinctly . . . 'the yuppies'. . . . This identification of the class content of postmodern culture does not at all imply that yuppies have become something like a new ruling class, merely that their cultural practices and values, their local ideologies, have articulated a useful dominant ideological and cultural paradigm for this stage of capitalism."[129] These passing remarks are crucial, for, through them, Jameson leaves open the possibility that the postmodern will in fact be "lived" differently in other locations within a now unified global totality—exactly what, as we will see momentarily, will become the focus of his intellectual work in the years following the publication of this study.

On the basis of this first dimension of his investigation, a number of critics have argued that Jameson's analysis of the postmodern is a despairing one, nostalgic for the critical distances and historicity of the modernist moment, and unable to see any way of challenging the terrible self-replicating stasis of the present.[130] However, this is to confuse only the first part of the story with the whole, as it ignores the fact that Jameson goes on to conclude the 1984 essay with a call for the development of a new "pedagogical political culture"—

the aesthetic practice he names *cognitive mapping*. Jameson opens his earlier essay, entitled simply "Cognitive Mapping," with a confession: cognitive mapping is "a subject about which I know nothing, whatsoever, except for the fact that it does not exist." He goes on to note, echoing a classic Althusserian formulation, that the essay that follows will involve nothing less than an attempt "to produce the concept of something we cannot imagine."[131] The project he begins here thus offers less a fully articulated vision of this political aesthetic practice than an allegory, or a prefiguration, of something only the earliest intimations of which might now be glimpsed. Jameson does, however, go on in this inaugural discussion to outline some of the fundamental coordinates of this type of cultural work: its deeply pedagogical function, as it teaches us something about what would be involved in positioning ourselves in the world; its thoroughly spatial and collective orientation; and finally, its totalizing movement: "The project of cognitive mapping obviously stands or falls with the conception of some (unrepresentable, imaginary) global social totality that was to have been mapped."[132]

Cognitive mapping fills in the absent place of the Symbolic in Althusser's adaptation of the Lacanian tripartite schema of the Imaginary, the Symbolic, and the Real. Cognitive mapping has the effect of coordinating these other two poles, the existential and phenomenological *experience* of people in their daily lives and the abstract and global economic, political, and social realities we always already inhabit. The former is most effectively grasped through literary and aesthetic practices, while the latter is the focus of "theory" or what Althusser himself calls "science."[133] Thus, at once neither what we conventionally think of as art or theory, the cognitive mapping Jameson calls for here,

> will have to hold to the truth of postmodernism, that is to say, to its fundamental object—the world space of multinational capital—at the same time at which it achieves a breakthrough to some as yet unimaginable new mode of representing this last, in which we may again begin to grasp our positioning as individual and collective subjects and regain a capacity to act and struggle which is at present neutralized by our spatial as well as our social confusion. The political form of postmodernism, if there ever is any, will have as its vocation the invention and projection of a global cognitive mapping, on a social as well as a spatial scale.[134]

The rest of the book then moves between the two projects outlined in the inaugural essay, analyzing "symptomatic" texts—the experience of space in the Bonaventure Hotel, the experimental video *AlienNATION*, New Historicism, De Manian nominalism, and market rhetoric—to see what particular aspects of the postmodern condition they might illuminate; *and* exploring other allegories of the cognitive mapping process—the "thinking" of Gehry's house,

Gober's installation projects, and the genre he names "allegorical encounter" films—for further lessons about what such a new political aesthetic might look like. Moreover, this double agenda, a symptomological mapping of postmodern culture and a figuration of new forms of cognitive mapping, will dominate Jameson's intellectual agenda in the next decade.

There is perhaps no more misunderstood concept in Jameson's work than that of cognitive mapping. Often what occurs is an apparently slight but very significant substitution—the concept of "map" for Jameson's "mapping."[135] Jameson himself warns in his original discussion of this practice that "since everyone knows what a map is, it would have been necessary to add that cognitive mapping cannot (at least in our time) involve anything so easy as a map; indeed, once you knew what 'cognitive mapping' was driving at, you were to dismiss all figures of maps and mapping from your mind and try to imagine something else."[136] To slip into the language of the map is then, Jameson argues, to give into the hegemony of the image and the visual (marked too by a resurgence of traditional aesthetics and ethics) that is such a central dimension of postmodern ideology. This confusion of map and mapping is akin to the collapsing together of the concepts of totality and totalization (and ultimately both into totalitarianism) that occurs in many of the criticisms of Jameson's project in particular and Marxism more generally.[137] Cognitive mapping, like totalization, is always already, as the verb form suggests, a *process*, a way of making connections, and situating ourselves as both individual and collective subjects within a particular spatial system. Thus, I would argue that cognitive mapping needs to be understood as way of producing *narratives*, unfolding through time, rather than static images, or maps—and in this affirmation of the power of narrative, we see most clearly Jameson's refusal to accept the apparent closures and ahistoricity of the postmodern that he outlines elsewhere.

Moreover, when Jameson argues early on that cognitive mapping "does not exist" and hence needs to be invented, what he is really calling for is not the development of the aesthetics of cognitive mapping per say, but rather for the production of a *new form of cognitive mapping*, one appropriate to the social, political, and economic realities we inhabit. For as even his earliest discussions of this concept make apparent, cognitive mappings have occurred in the past, and continue to do so on a number of different spatial scales. In Kevin Lynch's original formulation in *The Image of the City*, from which Jameson draws his formulation, cognitive mapping refers to the sense of place and location people construct in spaces such as those of the city: "Disalienation in the traditional city, then, involves the practical reconquest of a sense of place and the construction or reconstruction of an articulated ensemble which can be retained in memory and which the individual subject can map and remap along the moments of mobile, alternative trajectories."[138] Jameson then goes on to suggest that while Lynch's formulation "is limited by the deliberate restriction of his topic" to the spatial scale of the city form, "it becomes extraordinarily suggestive when projected outward" to new scales of the social totality.[139] Such a movement across spatial scales is also, I would argue here, a historical process. For it is the emergence of capitalist modernity that first gives rise to a new scale of cognitive mapping, one that successfully subsumes and supersedes older local ones. This cognitive mapping or narrative practice will subsequently be called *nationalism*, for it is precisely what Benedict Anderson famously calls the "imagined community" of the nation, itself a narrative rather than an image, that unifies and draws together into a coherent ensemble the everyday experience of individuals and the economic and political realities of the newly emerging capitalist states. In the literary realm, the privileged aesthetic expression of this form of cognitive mapping is the novel, especially in the form of what Bakhtin calls its "second stylistic trend."[140]

The achievement of this new scale of cognitive mapping—an achievement that represents a qualitative as much as a quantitative change—creates the ground for the emergence of a whole series of new forms of collective politics and struggle: the industrial union, the party, the national strike, decolonization, and, ultimately, national revolution. Crucially, Jameson's underlying presupposition in calling for a new cognitive mapping is that these older political organizational forms are simply no longer sufficient for acting within the space and social totality we inhabit today. Indeed, Jameson has, scandalously to many, argued that "Politics works only when these two levels [the local and the global] can be coordinated; they otherwise drift apart into a disembodied and easily bureaucratized abstract struggle for and around the state, on the one hand, and a properly interminable series of neighborhood issues on the other, whose 'bad infinity' comes, in postmodernism . . . . it is necessary to add that what is lost in its absence, the global dimension, is very precisely the dimension of economics itself, or of the system, of private enterprise and the profit motive, which cannot be challenged on a local level."[141] In short, the production of new forms of cognitive mapping is imperative for a new and heretofore unimaginable politics to emerge. And it is in this shift in scale—from the national to the global—that also marks what may in fact be a new and the most recent "period" in Jameson's thinking.

Contemporaneous with his first major essays on postmodernism, Jameson publishes what would become one of his most controversial works, "Third World Literature in the Era of Multinational Capitalism." In this essay, Jameson defines third-world literature in the following way: "Third-world texts, even those which are seemingly private and invested with a properly libidinal dynamic—necessarily project a political dimension in the form of national allegory: *the story of the private destiny is always an allegory of the embattled situation of the public third-world culture and society.*"[142] I have argued elsewhere that one of the more underappreciated dimensions of Jameson's argument is the degree to which it unfolds as an exercise in generic thinking; much of the debate surrounding Jameson's essay dissipates if we view it not as offering ontological claims about the nature of all cultural production in the "third world," but rather as a strategic intervention aimed, like all genre criticism, at constituting both a set of interpretive practices, pegged in fact to a particular spatial scale, and an alternative corpus of texts on which these will go to work.[143]

However, the significance of this essay for our concerns lies in the way it marks a new direction in Jameson's intellectual project. In the essay's final footnote, Jameson observes that one of the fundamental philosophical underpinnings of his description of the genre is, along with Hegel's master–slave dialectic, the Lukácsian model of class consciousness or standpoint epistemology we first encountered in our discussion of *Marxism and Form*: here he defines it as a "'mapping' or the grasping of the social totality . . . structurally available to the dominated rather than the dominating classes."[144] Moreover, he goes on to note that his concept of "national allegory" also represents a subgenre of the larger aesthetic of cognitive mapping, with this essay serving as "a pendant" to "Postmodernism, or, the Cultural Logic of Late Capitalism." Thus, when we read the two essays in conjunction in the ways Jameson suggests, we are able to reconfigure the aesthetic category of cognitive mapping to incorporate different kinds of representational acts—acts, moreover, that originate in different locations within the global totality. Such a proliferation of perspectives continues, as I suggested earlier, in the collection of essays that make up the first part of *Signatures of the Visible*: the films that serve as the central objects of analysis here originate in the Hollywood system (*Jaws, The Godfather, Dog Day Afternoon, The Shining*); France (*Diva*); West Germany (Hans-Jürgen Syberberg's 1970s documentary trilogy); Poland (*Fever*); Venezuela (*La Casa de Agua*); and Colombia (*Condores ne entierran todos los dias*).

In *Signatures of the Visible*, as in what he suggests is the diptych of the "Third World Literature" and "Postmodernism" essays, the various perspectives offered on an emerging global reality remain relatively detached from one another. However, in Jameson's next film study, *The Geopolitical Aesthetic: Cinema and Space in the World System* (1994), we see a self-conscious effort to coordinate these various perspectives to produce a more systematic, and hence more totalizing, mapping of the present. Moreover, in the very form of this important and original book we witness the reemergence of the kinds of narrative energies that I suggested were absent in his postmodernism studies. Or to put this another way, *The Geopolitical Aesthetic* itself stands as an allegorical figuration of what a global cognitive mapping might look like. Jameson opens the book with a discussion of U.S. conspiracy films, expanding on an observation in the "Postmodernism" essay that "conspiracy theory (and its garish narrative manifestations) must be seen as a degraded attempt—through the figuration of advanced technology—to think the impossible totality of the contemporary world system."[145] He then reads films from a set of sites all of which might be best characterized as transitional zones: the Soviet Union in its last hours (Alexander Sokurov's *Days of Eclipse*); Taiwan, or the "newly industrialized First-World tier of the Third World or Pacific Rim" (Edward Yang's *Terrorizer*);[146] France, as it faces subsumption into the transnational entity of the European Union (Jean-Luc Godard's *Passion*); and the Philippines, presented as a privileged site for the recognition of a relentless modernization that affects a European First World as well (Kidlat Tahimik's *Perfumed Nightmare*). Not only do these various sites remind us of the insufficiency of the older *national* categories through which we continue to think, or narrate, the present, but their multiple cartographic projections, when brought into coordination by the narrative totality of Jameson's book itself, begin to illuminate the horizon of an emergent "geopolitical unconscious." Each chapter can be said to complete the visions offered in the others, such that none can be fully grasped without taking into account what unfolds in all of them. In this way, Jameson argues, the earlier "national allegory" becomes refashioned "into a conceptual instrument for grasping our new being-in-the-world. It may henceforth be thought to be at least one of the fundamental allegorical referents or levels of all seemingly abstract philosophical thought: so that a fundamental hypothesis would pose the principle that all thinking today is *also*, whatever else it is, an attempt to think the world system as such. All the more true will this be for narrative figurations."[147]

Equally important, the views from each of these locations are dramatically different, and thus offer the possibility of radically transforming and enriching our grasp of our shared global postmodern condition. For example, Jameson argues in his discussion of *Perfumed Nightmare*, "What the First World thinks and dreams about the Third can have nothing whatsoever in common, formally or epistemologically, with what the Third World has to know every day about the First. Subalternity carries the possibility of knowledge with it, domination that of forgetfulness and repression."[148] Moreover, in his conclusion to this chapter, Jameson argues that in both the form and content of this unique film, we see the possibilities of new forms of life coming into being: "Unlike the natural or mythic appearances of traditional agricultural society, but equally unlike the disembodied machinic forces of late capitalist high technology, which seem, at the other end of time, equally innocent of any human agency or individual or collective praxis, the jeepney factory is a space of human labor which does not know the structural oppression of the assembly line or Taylorization, which is permanently provisional, thereby liberating its subjects from the tyrannies of form and of the pre-programmed. In it aesthetics and production are again at one, and painting the product is an integral part of its manufacture."[149] The lessons they hold about radically other ways of human being in the world make such spaces—again not outside, but rather located differently within the global totality—invaluable for all of us, for it is here that we see the reemergence of the sense of historicity, or storytelling, so relentlessly driven out by the hegemonic postmodern. What is history, or storytelling for that matter, but our experience of our capacity to (re)make our world?

The absolute and fundamental necessity of maintaining these multiple perspectives also enables us to make sense of Jameson's interest, in some of his most recent writings, in the political potentialities of Kenneth Frampton's "critical regionalism"—"not a rural place that resists the nation and its power structures but rather a whole culturally coherent zone (which may also correspond to political autonomy) in tension with the standardizing world system as a whole." Such a practice, Jameson goes on the suggest, might contain lessons for any effort at "resisting the standardizations of a henceforth global late capitalism and corporatism."[150] Similarly, Jameson has investigated the struggles to maintain national film industries in the face of the onslaught of Hollywood: "the triumph of Hollywood film (from which I won't here separate out television, which is today just as important or even more so) is not merely an economic triumph, it is a formal and also a political one . . . . it is also the death of the political, and an allegory of the end of the possibility of imagining radically different social alternatives to this one we now live under."[151] The maintenance of such zones of autonomy thus provide exactly the perspectival positions from which aspects of the world order of global capitalism can begin to be glimpsed; however, it is only in their unification and coordination that any cognitive mapping of such a globality can even begin to occur.

It is this emphasis on the multiplication of perspectives, as well as their necessary coordination, in an effort to think the contemporary geopolitical framework that I want to argue, stands as one of the most significant lessons of Jameson's recent work for the collective project of cognitively mapping our emerging global cultural and social reality. However, as Jameson has stressed all along, cognitive mapping must be understood as only a first step; and the issue that I would like to end with is the way Jameson's geopolitical aesthetic might serve as another kind of allegory—an allegory, or perhaps a prefiguration, of the political formations that we will need to produce in order to regain the "possibility of imagining," and in imagining begin to produce "radically different social alternatives to this one we now live under." Eschewing any privileged single perspective and stressing the importance of maintaining the particularity of every local intervention, while also always emphasizing the necessity of linking local struggles and thinking through them the economic horizons of the world system as a whole—whatever collective formations emerge that take up such an "impossible" task will be the global equivalent of the older national parties and political movements. Indeed, it may be exactly these new collective formations whose first stirrings can be seen in such alternative globalization practices as the WTO protests, José Bové and François Dufour's French Farmers Confederation, the Porto Allegre meetings, and even the global antiwar protests—all expressions of what Hardt and Negri have theorized as the creative "singularity of the multitude" in our postmodern global present.

With this, we have come full circle in the narrative of Jameson's work that I have been unfolding in the preceding pages, as the vision of the collective, political agency, and pedagogy that was at the climax of *Marxism and Form* emerges once again at the very center of his ongoing intellectual project. In one final turn, we might reconceive his work throughout the 1970s and 1980s as a keeping faith with the future that may be emerging today, holding open a place for what at the time could only be understood as the impossible project of a collective transformation of our world. His work thus continues the mission that he had claimed early in his career for radical hermeneutics: it "provides the means for contact with the very sources of revolutionary energy during a stagnant time, of preserving the concept of freedom itself, underground, during geological ages of repression."[152] Such an unwavering commitment to the future, and to the reality of freedom, may in fact be the most important lesson of his entire project.

NOTES

1. Fredric Jameson, *The Political Unconscious: Narrative as a Socially Symbolic Act* (Ithaca: Cornell University Press, 1981), 9.

The following essay forms one part of a triptych that also includes my "Horizons, Figures, and Machines: The Dialectic of Utopia in the Work of Fredric Jameson," *Utopian Studies* 9, no. 2 (1998): 58–73; and "Soldierboys for Peace: Cognitive Mapping, Space, and Science Fiction as World Bank Literature," *World Bank Literature*, ed. Amitava Kumar (Minneapolis: University of Minnesota Press, 2002). My deepest thanks go to Susan Hegeman and all the energetic students in my Spring 2000 graduate seminar for helping me work through many of these ideas.

2. Jameson, *Postmodernism, or, the Cultural Logic of Late Capitalism* (Durham: Duke University Press, 1990), 403.

3. Jameson has taken up the question of periodization once again in his most recent book, *A Singular Modernity: Essay on the Ontology of the Present* (New York: Verso, 2002). Here he suggests that in terms of stories of modernity's origins, "periodization is not some optional narrative consideration one adds or subtracts according to one's tastes and inclinations, but rather an essential feature of the narrative process itself" (81).

4. Jameson, *The Political Unconscious*, 28.

5. Jameson, *Signatures of the Visible* (New York: Routledge, 1990), 203.

6. Jameson, *Postmodernism, or, the Cultural Logic of Late Capitalism*, 4 and 159. There is also a resonance here with Raymond Williams's influential reformulation of the classical Marxist base-superstructure model; see Williams, "Base and Superstructure in Marxist Cultural Theory," *Problems in Materialism and Culture* (New York: Verso, 1980), 38; and *Marxism and Literature* (Oxford: Oxford University Press, 1977), 55–141. Interestingly, the year of the original publication of Williams's essay, 1973, also

marks for Jameson the moment of the "crystallization" of the postmodern period (*Postmodernism*, xx).

7. Jameson, *The Political Unconscious*, 99.

8. Ibid., 98–99.

9. Jameson, *Marxism and Form: Twentieth-Century Dialectical Theories of Literature* (Princeton: Princeton University Press), 53. For a brief discussion of the dialectical sentence, see the Introduction by Michael Hardt and Kathi Weeks to Fredric Jameson, *The Jameson Reader* (Oxford: Blackwell, 200), 7–8; and also see Jameson's pointed "On Jargon," reprinted in the same volume, 117–18. The exhaustive bibliography of Jameson's writings printed in *The Jameson Reader* proved invaluable in writing this essay

10. Jameson, *Marxism and Form*, xiii.

11. Jameson, *The Jameson Reader*, 159.

12. Jameson, Foreword to Jean-François Lyotard, *The Postmodern Condition: A Report on Knowledge*, trans. Geoff Bennington and Brian Massumi (Minneapolis: University of Minnesota Press, 1984), xix and xx.

13. For a discussion of this issue, see Jameson, "Transformations of the Image in Postmodernity," *The Cultural Turn: Selected Writings on the Postmodern, 1983–1998* (New York: Verso, 1998), 93–135.

14. Jameson, *Signatures of the Visible*, 6.

15. Ibid., 157.

16. Ibid., 156.

17. Ibid., 156. For a discussion of the issue of scale in spatial geographical analysis that has important lessons for cultural criticism, see Neil Smith, "Homeless/global: Scaling places," *Mapping the Futures: Local Cultures, Global Change*, ed. Jon Bird, et al. (New York: Routledge, 1993), 87–119.

18. Hardt and Weeks, Introduction to *The Jameson Reader*, 20.

19. See Giovanni Arrighi, *The Long Twentieth Century: Money, Power, and the Origins of Our Times* (New York: Verso, 1994); and Michael Hardt and Antonio Negri, *Empire* (Cambridge: Harvard University Press, 2000). Jameson discusses Arrighi's work in "Culture and Finance Capital," reprinted in *The Cultural Turn*, 136–61. For the differences between Arrighi and Hardt and Negri's characterization of the present moment, see Empire, 238–39.

20. Jameson, *Signatures of the Visible*, 155.

21. Jameson, *Marxism and Form*, 196.

22. Ibid., 195. Jameson will return to the question of literary naturalism in each of his next major period texts: see *The Political Unconscious*, Ch. 4; and *Postmodernism*, Ch. 7, Part 1. There is an interesting migration here too from French (Zola) to British (George Gissing) and then U.S. (Theodor Dreiser and Frank Norris) practices of naturalism.

23. Jameson, *Marxism and Form*, 195.

24. Ibid., xi.

25. Ibid., 198. Ironically, it is this insight that Lukács himself seems to have forgotten in his scathing assault on the various practices of modernism. For Jameson's discussion of Lukács's views of modernism, see *Marxism and Form*, 198–201; and "Reflections on the Brecht-Lukács Debate" *The Ideologies of Theory, Essays 1971–1986*. Vol. 2, *Syntax of History* (Minneapolis: University of Minnesota Press, 1988), 133–47.

26. Jameson, *Marxism and Form*, 204.

27. Ibid., xi.

28. Jameson, "Architecture and the Critique of Ideology," *The Ideologies of Theory*, Vol. 2, 40.

29. Jameson, *Marxism and Form*, 36.

30. Ibid., 35.

31. Ibid., 42.

32. Max Horkheimer and Theodor W. Adorno, *Dialectic of Enlightenment*, trans. John Cumming (New York: Continuum, 1987), 256. Jameson treats *Dialectic of Enlightenment*, as well as Adorno's later texts, *Negative Dialectics* and *Aesthetic Theory*, in more detail in *Late Marxism: Adorno, or the Persistence of the Dialectic* (New York: Verso, 1990).

33. Jameson, *Marxism and Form*, 72. For his brief invocation of the four fold schema, see *Marxism and Form*, 60–61.

34. Jameson, *Marxism and Form*, 77.

35. Ibid., 80.

36. Ibid., 84.

37. Ibid., 105.

38. Ibid., 110.

39. Ibid., 110.

40. Ibid., 112 and 113.

41. Ibid., 116.

42. See my " Horizons, Figures, and Machines," 58–62.

43. Jameson, *Marxism and Form*, 120.

44. Ibid., 126 and 137.

45. Ibid., 129.

46. Ibid., 159.

47. Ibid., 161.

48. Ibid., 184.

49. Ibid., 187.

50. Ibid., 189.

51. Ibid., 208.

52. Ibid., 292–93. There is an interesting resonance here with the argument Negri advances in his discussion of the difference between the projects of Marx's *Grundrisse* and *Capital* in *Marx Beyond Marx: Lessons on the Grundrisse*, trans. Harry Cleaver, Michael Ryan, and Maurizio Viano (New York: Autonomedia, 1991).

53. Jameson, *Marxism and Form*, 294.

54. Ibid., 297.

55. Ibid., 207.

56. Ibid., 304.

57. Ibid., 304.

58. Ibid., 305.

59. Ibid., 299.

60. Jameson, "Periodizing the 60s," *The Ideologies of Theory*, Vol. 2, 207.

61. Jameson, *Late Marxism*, 4–5.

62. Jameson, "Periodizing the 60s," 208.

63. Jameson, "Beyond the Cave: Demystifying the Ideologies of Modernism," *The Ideologies of Theory*, Vol. 2, 128. For further development of this idea in terms of a close reading of a passage from Flaubert's "Un coeur simple," see Fredric Jameson, "The Realist Floor-Plan," *On Signs*, ed. Marshall Blonsky (Baltimore: The Johns Hopkins University Press, 1985), 373–83.

64. Jameson, *Marxism and Form*, ix.

65. A view reinforced, for example, in one of the major contemporary anthologies of literary criticism, Hazard Adams' *Critical Theory Since Plato* (1971)—from which I was first introduced to literary theory nearly fifteen years later—whose selections from twentieth-century Marxist cultural criticism are limited to Leon Trotsky's assault on the Russian formalist method (of which Adams writes, "Though Trotsky's interpretations of his opponents' arguments are superficial, his essay is a fair reflection of assumptions that tend to guide materialist theories"), and fellow-traveler Edmund Wilson's critical overview of American Marxist literary criticism of the 1930s. See Hazard Adams, ed., *Critical Theory since Plato* (San Diego: Harcourt Brace Jovanovich Publishers, 1971), 819–27 and 905–13.

66. Jameson deals with the limitations of the New Criticism directly in *Marxism and Form*, 332–33.

67. Jameson, *Marxism and Form*, 374.

68. Jameson, "Beyond the Cave," 129.

69. Ibid.

70. Jameson, *The Political Unconscious*, 280. This concept of the modernist text is already at work in the 1976 essay, "Modernism and its Repressed; or, Robbe-Grillet as Anti-Colonialist," reprinted in *The Ideologies of Theory*, Vol. 1, 167–80.

71. Jameson, *The Political Unconscious*, 35

72. Jameson, *The Political Unconscious*, 207. Also see Jameson's landmark essay, "Reification and Utopia in Mass Culture," reprinted in *Signatures of the Visible*, 9–34; and *The Jameson Reader*, 123–48. A similar indirection is evident in Jameson's previous book, *Fables of Aggression: Wyndham Lewis, the Modernist as Fascist* (Berkeley: University of California Press, 1979).

73. Jameson, *The Political Unconscious*, 118.

74. Ibid., 75–76.

75. Ibid., 227.

76. Jameson, *Signatures of the Visible*, 204.

77. Ibid., 205.

78. Ibid., 205. Also see the discussions of "separation" and "autonomy" in *A Singular Modernity*.

79. Jameson, *Signatures of the Visible*, 207.

80. Ibid., 207–08.

81. Ibid., 208.

82. Jameson, *The Political Unconscious*, 144.

83. For a useful discussion of Marx's "regressive-progressive" dialectic, see Henri Lefebvre, *The Production of Space*, trans. Donald Nicholson-Smith (Oxford: Blackwell, 1991), 65–68. For Jameson's first exploration of the concept of "generic discontinuity," see his "Generic Discontinuities in SF: Brian Aldiss' Starship," *Science Fiction Studies* 1 no. 2 (1973): 57–68. Contemporaneous with this essay is his review of Bakhtin's colleague V.N. Volosinov's *Marxism and the Philosophy of Language* (a text of which Bakhtin claimed himself to be the author): see the review in *Style* 8 no. 3 (Fall, 1974): 535–43.

84. Jameson, *Signatures of the Visible*, 208.

85. Jameson, *The Political Unconscious*, 36–37.

86. Jameson, "Imaginary and Symbolic in Lacan," *The Ideologies of Theory*, vol. 1, 104.

87. See Terry Eagleton, *Against the Grain: Selected Essays, 1975–1985* (London: Verso, 1986), 65. This essay was originally published in the special Fall, 1982 issue of *Diacritics* devoted to *The Political Unconscious*.

88. Jameson, *Postmodernism, or, the Cultural Logic of Late Capitalism*, 16.

89. Ibid., 306.

90. Andreas Huyssen, *After The Great Divide: Modernism, Mass Culture, Postmodernism* (Bloomington: Indiana University Press, 1986), 206–16; and Jameson, "'End of Art' or 'End of History?'" *The Cultural Turn*, 84–85.

91. For example, on Jameson's role in introducing Adorno's work to an English-speaking audience, Martin Jay writes, "If the moment when Adorno's work became more than merely an enticing rumor for the American New Left could be dated, it

would probably be 1967 with the publication of an essay entitled 'Adorno: or, Historical Tropes' by the Marxist literary critics Fredric Jameson in the journal Salmagundi." See "Adorno in America," *Permanent Exiles: Essays on the Intellectual Migration from Germany to America* (New York: Columbia University Press, 1986), 127.

92. See *Diacritics* 12 no. 3 (Fall 1982); and William C. Dowling, *Jameson, Althussser, Marx: An Introduction to The Political Unconscious* (Ithaca: Cornell University Press, 1984).

93. Jameson, *Postmodernism, or, the Cultural Logic of Late Capitalism*, 307.

94. Ibid., 311.

95. Jameson, *Signatures of the Visible*, 75–76.

96. Jameson, "Beyond the Cave," 130. Also see Jameson's recent refinement of this notion in *A Singular Modernity*, 158.

97. Jameson, "Baudelaire as Modernist and Postmodernist: The Dissolution of the Referent and the Artificial 'Sublime,'" *Lyric Poetry Beyond the New Criticism*, eds. Chaviva Hosek and Patricia Parker (Ithaca: Cornell University Press, 1985), 252.

98. Jameson, *Signatures of the Visible*, 77.

99. Jameson, *The Political Unconscious*, 17, emphasis added. This idea of a fidelity to a truth-event is also characteristic of the "modernist" philosophy of Alain Badiou. See, for example, Badiou, *Ethics: An Essay on the Understanding of Evil*, trans. Peter Hallward (New York: Verso, 2001).

100. Also see Jameson's reflections on "late modernism" in *A Singular Modernity*, especially 198–200.

101. Edward Said, "Opponents, Audiences, Constituencies and Community," reprinted in *The Anti-Aesthetic: Essays on Postmodern Culture*, ed. Hal Foster (Port Towsend, WA: Bay Press, 1983), 135. This essay was originally published in *Critical Inquiry* 9 (September, 1982).

102. Ibid., 147.

103. Ibid.

104. Ibid., 149.

105. Ibid., 155.

106. Jameson, *The Political Unconscious*, 280.

107. Said, "Opponents, Audiences, Constituencies and Community," 157.

108. For Jameson's engagements with the voluntarism and determinism question, see *Postmodernism*, 326–29; and "Religion and Ideology: A Political Reading of Paradise Lost," *Literature, Politics and Theory: Papers from the Essex Conference, 1976–84*, eds. Francis Barker et al. (London: Metheun, 1976), 35–56, and especially 41–45. Also see Slavoj Zizek's recent engagement with these issues in "Georg Lukács as the Philosopher of Leninism," *Postface to A Defence of History and Class Consciousness: Tailism and the Dialectic*, ed. Georg Lukács, trans. Esther Leslie (New York: Verso, 2000), 151–82.

109. Jameson, *The Political Unconscious*, 236.

110. Ibid., 237.

111. Jameson, "Architecture and the Critique of Ideology," 68.

112. Jameson, "Postmodernism and Consumer Society," *The Anti-Aesthetic: Essays on Postmodern Culture*, ed. Hal Foster (Port Townsend: Bay Press, 1983), 111–25; now reprinted in *The Cultural Turn*, 1–20. Jameson, "Postmodernism, or the Cultural Logic of Late Capitalism," *New Left Review* 146 (July-August, 1984): 52–92; reprinted in a slightly modified form in *Postmodernism*, 1–54. For an illuminating discussion of the context, origins, and subsequent adventures of Jameson's theorizations of the postmodern, see Perry Anderson, *The Origins of Postmodernity* (New York: Verso, 1998).

113. Jameson, "Postmodernism and Consumer Society," 113.

114. See Jameson, "On Raymond Chandler," *The Southern Review* 6 no. 3 (Summer 1970): 636–39.

115. Jameson, "Postmodernism and Consumer Society," 123.

116. Jameson, *Postmodernism, or, the Cultural Logic of Late Capitalism*, 21.

117. Ibid., 27.

118. Ibid., 25.

119. Lefebvre, *The Production of Space*, 365.

120. See, for example, his essays, "History and the Death Wish: Zardoz as Open Form," *Jump Cut* 3 (1974): 5–8; and "Towards a Libidinal Economy of Three Modern Painters," *Social Text* 1 (1979): 189–99.

121. Jameson, *Postmodernism, or, the Cultural Logic of Late Capitalism*, 48.

122. Ibid., 99, 94, and 186.

123. Ibid., 321.

124. Ibid., 151.

125. Ibid., 45–46.

126. Ibid., 46.

127. Ibid., xvii.

128. Ibid., xx.

129. Ibid., 407.

130. See, for example, the passing comments in Meaghan Morris's *Too Soon Too Late: History in Popular Culture* (Bloomington: Indiana University Press, 1998).

131. Jameson, "Cognitive Mapping," *Marxism and the Interpretation of Culture*, eds. Cary Nelson and Lawrence Grossberg (Urbana: University of Illinois Press, 1988), 347. He uses this formulation again in "Periodizing the 60s," where he notes, "Althusser's proposal seems the wisest in this situation . . . the historian should reformulate her vocation—not any longer to produce some vivid representation of History 'as it really happened,' but rather to produce the concept of history" (180).

132. Ibid., 356.

133. I explore the relationship between Jameson and Lacan's tripartite schemas, as well as that found in Henri Lefebvre's monumental, *The Production of Space*, in my "Horizons, Figures, and Machines."

134. Jameson, *Postmodernism, or, the Cultural Logic of Late Capitalism*, 54.

135. For example, a recent essay on the science fiction film, The Matrix, advances the thesis that in this film "the new cognitive map of multinational capitalism has been drawn." See Chad Barnett, "Reviving Cyberpunk: (Re)Constructing the Subject and Mapping Cyberspace in the Wachowski Brothers' Film The Matrix," *Extrapolation* 41 no. 4 (2000): 359–74. Also, see Jameson's recent discussion of *The Matrix*, "The Iconographies of Cyberspace," *Polygraph* 13 (2001): 121–27.

136. Jameson, *Postmodernism, or, the Cultural Logic of Late Capitalism*, 409.

137. For Jameson's response to these criticisms, see *Postmodernism*, 331–34.

138. Jameson, *Postmodernism, or, the Cultural Logic of Late Capitalism*, 51.

139. Ibid., 51.

140. See Mikhail Bakhtin, *The Dialogic Imagination*, trans. Caryl Emerson and Michael Holquist (Austin: University of Texas Press, 1981), 366–415. And also see Franco Moretti, "The novel, the nation-state," *Atlas of the European Novel, 1800–1900* (New York: Verso, 1998), 11–73.

141. Jameson, *Postmodernism, or, the Cultural Logic of Late Capitalism*, 330.

142. Jameson, "Third World Literature in the Era of Multinational Capitalism," *Social Text* 15 (1986), 69.

143. See my "Soldierboys for Peace."

144. Jameson, "Third World Literature," 88.

145. Jameson, *Postmodernism, or, the Cultural Logic of Late Capitalism*, 38.

146. Jameson, *The Geopolitical Aesthetic: Cinema and Space in the World System* (Bloomington: Indiana University Press, 1992), 155.

147. Ibid., 3–4.

148. Ibid., 199.

149. Ibid., 210. Jameson continues to develop many of the themes announced here in *Brecht and Method* (New York: Verso, 1998).

150. Jameson, *The Seeds of Time* (New York: Columbia University Press, 1994), 191–92 and 202.

151. Jameson, "Globalization as a Philosophical Issue," *Globalization and Culture*, eds. Masao Miyoshi and Fredric Jameson (Durham: Duke University Press, 1998), 62.

152. Jameson, *Marxism and Form*, 84.

Contributors

ROLAND BOER is Research Fellow at Monash University, Melbourne, Australia. He is the author of six books of biblical criticism, including *Jameson and Jeroboam* (Semeia Studies).

IAN BUCHANAN is Professor of Critical and Cultural Theory at Cardiff University, Australia. He is the author of two books, *Deleuzism: A Metacommentary* (Edinburgh and Duke 2000) and *Michel de Certeau: Cultural Theorist* (Sage 2000). He has also edited several other books, including *Deleuze and Feminism* (Edinburgh 2000) and *A Deleuzian Century?* (Duke 1999). He is currently editing a volume of Jameson's interviews.

VITALY CHERNETSKY teaches in the Cinema Studies Program at Northeastern University. His book *Mapping Postcommunist Cultures: Russia and Ukraine in the Context of Globalization* is forthcoming from McGill—Queen's University Press.

SEAN HOMER is the Dissertation Coordinator and a member of the Business Department at City College in Thessaloniki, Greece. He was a Lecturer at the University of Sheffield, UK, and Visiting Lecturer at Brunel University, London. He is author of a monograph titled *Fredric Jameson* (Routledge 1998), and he is currently co-editing (with Professor Douglas Kellner, UCLA) a Jameson critical reader.

CAREN IRR is Associate Professor of English and American Literature at Brandeis University. Her book *The Suburb of Dissent: Cultural Politics in the*

United States and Canada during the 1930s was published in 1998. She is co-editor (with Jeffrey T. Nealon) of *Rethinking the Frankfurt School: Alternative Legacies of Cultural Critique* (SUNY 2002). Her current research concerns gender and intellectual property in the context of globalization.

Carolyn Lesjak is Assistant Professor of English at Swarthmore College. She is currently completing a book on labor and pleasure in the age of Britain's empire. Recent articles include an essay on "Utopia, Use and the Everyday: Oscar Wilde and a New Economy of Pleasure" as well as the entry on Fredric Jameson in the *Edinburgh Guide to Post-War Literary Criticism and Theory*, "Fredric Jameson and Institutional Marxism."

Michael Rothberg is Associate Professor of English at the University of Illinois, Champaign-Urbana. He is the author of *Traumatic Realism: The Demands of Holocaust Representation*, as well as articles in *Contemporary Literature*, *Cultural Critique*, *New German Critique*, and other journals. His essay "W. E. B. Du Bois in Warsaw: Holocaust Memory and the Color Line, 1949–1952" appears in *The Yale Journal of Criticism*. His earlier essay on Fredric Jameson appeared in *Socialist Review*.

Robert Seguin is currently Visiting Assistant Professor of English at SUNY Brockport. His book, *Around Quitting Time: Work and Middle-Class Fantasy in American Fiction*, on the interplay of labor, desire, and middle-classlessness in American ideology, appeared in 2001. He is currently at work on a new project exploring how the social status and conceptualization of intellectuals mediates and informs the narrative representation of social change in the modern United States.

Imre Szeman is Assistant Professor in the Department of English and the Institute for Globalization and the Human Condition at McMaster University (Hamilton, Ontario, Canada). He is co-editor of *Pierre Bourdieu: Fieldwork in Culture* (2000) and author of *Zones of Instability: Literature, Postcolonialism and the Nation* (forthcoming). He is currently working on the second edition of the *Johns Hopkins Guide to Literary Theory and Criticism* and a book entitled *User's Guide to Popular Culture*. He is also a music reviewer for *Pop Matters: The Magazine of Global Culture*.

Evan Watkins is Professor of English at the University of California, Davis. He has published widely in cultural studies and the politics of education. His most recent book is entitled *Everyday Exchanges: Marketwork and Capitalist Common Sense* (1998), and his current project, *Class Degrees*, looks at vocational education and class formation in the United States.

PHILLIP E. WEGNER is Associate Professor of English at the University of Florida, Gainesville, where he teaches modern literatures, critical theory, and cultural studies. His book, *Imaginary Communities: Utopia, the Nation, and the Spatial Histories of Modernity*, was published in 2002. He has begun a second book project, focusing on science fiction, history, and the problems of political agency; chapters have recently appeared in *Rethinking Marxism*, *The Comparatist*, and *World Bank Literature*. His previous essay on Jameson's writing, "Horizons, Figures, and Machines: The Dialectic of Utopia in the Work of Fredric Jameson," was selected as the recipient of the Battisti Award winner for best essay published in *Utopian Studies* (1999).

Index